Justice Holmes

From an etching by Sally Tate

YANKEE FROM OLYMPUS

Justice Holmes and His Family

CATHERINE DRINKER BOWEN

AN ATLANTIC MONTHLY PRESS BOOK

LITTLE, BROWN AND COMPANY · BOSTON

1944

Published April 1944
Reprinted April 1944 (six times)
Reprinted May 1944

ATLANTIC–LITTLE, BROWN BOOKS
ARE PUBLISHED BY
LITTLE, BROWN AND COMPANY
IN ASSOCIATION WITH
THE ATLANTIC MONTHLY PRESS

PRINTED IN THE UNITED STATES OF AMERICA

For my husband
COMMANDER T. McKEAN DOWNS, (M.C.) U.S.N.R.

Here is a Yankee, strayed from Olympus.

— From the essay on Justice Holmes by Elizabeth
Shepley Sergeant, in *Fire under the Andes*

ACKNOWLEDGMENTS

EXPERTS in their field were kind enough to read my manuscript while it was in preparation. For the American scene I want to thank Bernard DeVoto, whose merciless eye at the other end of my work meant more to me than he is ready to acknowledge. For legal matters, Judge Herbert F. Goodrich, former Dean of the Law School at the University of Pennsylvania. For the chapter on Peirce, William James, and Chauncey Wright, Professor Paul Weiss of Bryn Mawr College, co-editor of the *Collected Papers of Charles Sanders Peirce*.

The late Richard Walden Hale of Boston generously answered innumerable questions and acted as guide among the maze of legal documents in Massachusetts courthouses. Dorothy Quincy Upham Vaughan, great-niece of Dr. Holmes, supplied a kind of bold encouragement in my delineation of her ancestors that was urgently needed. I want to thank Charles and Frances Curtis, who began talking to me about Justice Holmes the day I met them many years ago; Mary and Walter Howe, whose hospitality eased the way for me in Washington; Thomas E. Waggaman, Marshal of the United States Supreme Court, a meticulous answerer of detailed and troublesome letters; Professor Frederic T. Lewis of the Harvard Medical School, who was dryly explicit concerning the difference between Dr. Holmes the scientist and Dr. Holmes the poet; Mrs. Frederick Winslow of Boston, Duncan Eaves, and Mary Lawrence; Louis B. Wehle and Allegra Woodworth; Augustin Derby, Dean of the Law School at New York University. I want to thank Harold Ober for counsel and my brother, Henry S. Drinker, whose law office was always ready to answer my questions.

Lastly . . . Every book except those written by the masters needs a blue pencil. But the true editorial gift is rare. I want to thank my friend Barbara Rex for skillful editorial help, for never-failing inspiration and suggestion, and for an amazing sympathy, over a period of three years, with the laments and headaches incident to the preparation of a long manuscript.

C. D. B.

FOREWORD

THE story of Justice Oliver Wendell Holmes is the story of his country. The narrative cannot begin with the flat date of his birth – 1841. This was a man whose presence carried tradition. Everyone who met him felt it, and it was not oppressive but inspiring. Over his shoulder one glimpsed somehow his ancestors. His roots reached deep into American earth; it was the strength of these roots that permitted so splendid a flowering.

Wendells, Olivers, Jacksons, Holmeses: solid people, "sound" people – and adventurous people. They left Oliver Wendell Holmes, Junior, a superb inheritance, one that balanced him as the nine tenths of the iceberg we do not see balances that glittering pinnacle. To know Justice Holmes at eighty – courtly, witty, scholarly, kind – it is well to have acquaintance with his Calvinist grandfather, Abiel Holmes, with his handsome, worldly great-grandfather, Judge Wendell, with his mother from whom he inherited, he said, "a trace of melancholy." Above all it is well to know his father, the sturdy Yankee who wrote bad verse and good books – professor of anatomy, talkative five-foot-five Autocrat of the Breakfast-Table who lived upon applause and said so with engaging frankness.

It is not hard to know these people. They were articulate, given to writing down what they saw and thought. And they were passionately interested in their country. In the books they wrote, in their letters, their diaries, the welfare of the American Union plays a large part. Because of this, the opening page of our story fell naturally into place. Where could it begin except on the autumn day of 1800 when Abiel Holmes, gravely concerned over the approaching election of Jefferson, sat down in his parsonage on Harvard Square to commence the writing of his *American Annals?*

Justice Holmes was the product of Massachusetts, Beacon Hill

Harvard College. How did Harvard, how did Boston feel therefore about Thomas Jefferson, that wild theorist? How did they feel later, about Father Abraham in the White House, about Cleveland, their own Ben Butler, about the Plumed Knight from Maine who attracted to Faneuil Hall the biggest audience since Daniel Webster? To know Holmes it is well to see him not only on the judge's bench but acting out the scenes that shaped him. By his own confession, Holmes was an "internal" man, to whom ideas were more interesting than things. But he was also a man of action. *"Life is action and passion,"* he said. *"I think it is required of a man that he should share the action and passion of his time at peril of being judged not to have lived."*

Holmes shared his country's action and passion on the soldier's field and the judge's bench. The greater part of his story lies in Boston — the nine tenths that balances him. At sixty-one, he left Boston for the larger arena of Washington and national life. By that time, his character and aims were set. The machine was formed and fashioned; it had only to function. Much has been made of Holmes's "escape" from the limitations of Boston. But to one who follows his life from the beginning and back of the beginning, this is no break and no escape. It is a development as inevitable — and as incomplete — as his father's "escape" from the Calvinism of Abiel's day. These Holmes men did not stand still, they grew. This book is concerned with the impetus behind that growth.

If the significance of his life lay wholly in his legal achievements, there would be no place for a biography written by a layman. If its significance lay wholly in his written words, there would be no place for a biography at all. But Holmes's greatness lay most of all in his manner of meeting life. He had a genius for living, a genius for finding himself wholly, using himself wholly. He loved life and believed in it. "If I were dying," he wrote at eighty-odd to a young man, "my last words would be, Have faith and pursue the unknown end." For him the act of learning was always an adventure. Passionately, until the morning of his death, he pursued knowledge. "To know is not less than to feel," he said. *"A valid idea is worth a regiment any day."*

A man who has fought in the ranks, who has shed blood for his country, has a right to say such things. We want to see Holmes fighting, therefore, in order that we may believe his words more fully, experience them more fully. We want to see him fighting and we want to see him living, day by day. We want to hear him talking. His were words of hope and faith. They are part of our heritage as Americans — and so is the story of the man who spoke them.

CATHERINE DRINKER BOWEN

BRYN MAWR, PENNSYLVANIA
July 3rd, 1943

CONTENTS

Contents

PART VI

WASHINGTON. *1902–1935*

ILLUSTRATIONS

PART I

Abiel and His Son Oliver. 1800-1841

CHAPTER ONE

The Reverend Abiel Holmes decides to write a book and marry a Wendell.

ON an autumn morning of the year 1800, the Reverend Abiel Holmes, aged thirty-six, handsome, widowed and lonely, sat down in his study near Harvard Square in Cambridge, Massachusetts, to begin the writing of his new book. It was his fourth book; it was to be called *American Annals,* and the very contemplation of it caused its author's blood to run faster.

Since that day when, a boy of fifteen, as poor as he was eager, he had traveled down from Woodstock to enter Yale College, there had run in the veins of Abiel Holmes this unremitting sense of adventure where things of the mind were concerned. So would it run, and so would this excitement mount in the veins of his son Oliver Wendell Holmes and his son's son of that same name. Minister of the First Parish in Cambridge, Autocrat of the Breakfast-Table, Justice of the Supreme Court — none made literature his calling. But all three lived hard and wrote what they lived, and for all three, the utterance was as important as the living.

Abiel Holmes, lifting his eyes from the piles of scribbled, carefully documented notes on his desk, looked out the window across the parsonage yard to where bare maple branches swept low over a board fence, hiding the red bricks of the college beyond. In the middle of the yard the free end of the long pump arm slanted skyward. Old Liza had left it up again, Abiel noted. Why didn't she wait and let him carry in the water as he had told her to so often? Liza was getting too old to keep this big ramshackle house. Even Mary

Holmes had hated it. The image of his young wife, dead five years, rose dimly before Abiel — Mary Stiles. Mary had been too gentle, too meek to hate anything. Strange, when her father, President Ezra Stiles of Yale College, had been such a vigorous, aggressive kind of man. But Mary — when chimneys would not draw, when wells went dry or roofs leaked gapingly in winter; when life, in short, became too difficult — Mary had sighed and had taken to her bed. Without complaint, smiling gently, she had left chimneys and fires and house and a hard world forever.

What this parsonage needed, Mary's widower reflected now, was a wife. Frowning, Abiel turned back to his desk. This was no time to be thinking of wives. There was a task at hand. He would begin these *Annals* at the beginning, with Columbus, and he would keep on with them, God willing, until his hand was too palsied to hold a pen.

Abiel Holmes loved challenge and looked as if he loved it. Under the clerical gown and bib his shoulders were broad; his thick dark hair hung to his shoulders, curling crisply at the ends; his level deep eyes sparkled with health, his color was high. He wore the dark robe of Calvinism with an air and loved the religion it symbolized. Abiel was a passionate antiquarian and scholar; already he had written a *History of the Mohegan Indians*, a biography of his late father-in-law, President Stiles of Yale College, and was all but finished with a history of Cambridge. He had even written a book of bad poetry. The histories were dull books, correct and dry. But in writing them Abiel had prepared himself, all unconsciously, for something bigger. He had read histories of states and histories of towns, clerical accounts and military accounts and the records of travelers who wrote in Spanish and French and Latin and English. And as he read, there had formed in Abiel's mind a picture into which these several parts fell into place, so that it seemed to him extraordinary that no one, among all these makers of particular histories, had taken the broad view and written of the country as a whole.

Abiel had a warm pride in his country — and a Calvinist conscience that translated pride quickly into a sense of debt. When you were proud of something, you got out and worked for it. . . .

Abiel came honestly by his patriotism. His father, Captain David Holmes, had fought in two American wars and, worn-out, had died at fifty-seven, leaving seven sons and two daughters to help build the country he had fought for. Abiel had been fifteen when his father died; he remembered well those stories of the Canadian Wilderness. Captain Holmes, fighting Indians in the Old French War of 1758, had walked single-file through the forests with his men, dressed in a soldier's hat and fringed leggings, carrying his flintlock on his hip. Once, leading forty men to the attack, Captain Holmes had met his Major's forces stumbling out of the woods after battle, wounded, carrying their dead. One of them had been scalped; "chopped with a tomahawk," Captain Holmes had written in his Orderly Book.

Was it history, Abiel wondered now, sitting at his desk by a quiet Cambridge window — was that history which had happened to one's own father? Was it history that his father's friend, Major Putnam, was captured outside Fort Ann and tied to a tree by the Indians, faggots piled around him? Was it history how he escaped and how, seventeen years later, the Major and Captain Holmes, on hearing the first news of Lexington, joined the Continental Army and served four long years? Captain Holmes was over fifty when he offered his services as regimental physician; no scalpings came his way this time, but he had told tales of hardship and heroism to be forgotten by no man's son.

Surely, these things were at least the footnote to history! Surely, thought Abiel Holmes, his quill gone dry above his paper with thinking — surely a man could put these things into footnotes without being charged with immodesty? . . . Well, he had his father's Orderly Books, four large volumes written in the Captain's own hand during the wilderness campaigns of '58; if he worked from them rather than from word of mouth, it should be as authoritative as any other source.

There was so much of history that Abiel knew by word of mouth! How could he pass it by? It was in his blood. His mother and his mother's mother had told him stories. If the men of the family were adventurers and soldiers, the women had been remarkably articulate for their day, even learned. Great-grandmother Holmes, wife of John, who had settled in Woodstock in 1686 — Great-grandmother had been known to the neighbors as a learned woman "who could write short-hand." On Sundays she took her tablet to church and "wrote after" the minister, bringing home his sermons to discuss later in the week with family and friends. Great-grandfather John, a bluff man, very handy with axe and

HOLMES DESCENT*

David Holmes   m. 1658   Jane ——
b. about 1635 in England   d. in Dedham, Mass.
d. 1666 in Milton, Mass.   after 1691

John
b. 1664 in Milton, Mass.   m. 1690   Hannah Newell
d. 1713 in Woodstock, Conn.   b. 1671
   d. 1743

David (Deacon)   m. —— Bathsheba ——
b. 1692 in Woodstock
d. 1745

David (Captain)   m. (1)   Mehitable Mayhew
b. Aug. 11, 1721, in Woodstock   7 children
d. March 19, 1779   (2) 1761 Mrs. Temperance Bishop
   d. Aug. 3, 1803

David (General)   Abiel   Sanford   Lathrop (Doctor)   Leonard   Hartwell   Temperance   Liberty
b. Aug. 17, 1762   b. Dec. 24, 1763   b. May 7, 1768   b. Apr. 17, 1770   b. Mar. 17, 1772   b. June 14, 1774   b. Apr. 3, 1776
d. June 30, 1832   d. June 4, 1837   d. 1801
m. (1) 1790 Mary Stiles
   d. Aug. 29, 1795
   (2) 1801 Sarah Wendell
   d. Aug. 19, 1862

Abiel   Ann Susan   Sarah Lathrop   Oliver Wendell   John
   b. May 15, 1804   b. Nov. 27, 1805   b. Aug. 29, 1809   b. March 29, 1812
Mary Jackson   d. Apr. 5, 1877   d. Nov. 6, 1812   d. Oct. 7, 1894   d. Jan. 27, 1899
b. Jan. 17, 1802   m. March 29, 1826   m. June 15, 1840, Amelia Lee Jackson   unmarried
d. June 14, 1825   Rev. Charles Wentworth Upham   d. Feb. 1888
m. Sept. 23, 1822
Dr. Usher Parsons

Oliver Wendell   Amelia Jackson   Edward Jackson
b. March 8, 1841   b. Oct. 20, 1843   b. Oct. 17, 1846
d. March 6, 1935   d. Apr. 3, 1889   d. July 18, 1884
m. June 17, 1872   m. May 25, 1871   m. Oct. 24, 1871
Fanny Bowditch Dixwell   John Turner Welles Sargent   Henrietta Wigglesworth
d. Apr. 30, 1929

Edward Jackson
b. Jan. 3, 1873
m. July 8, 1897
Mary Stacy Beaman

*This table omits the full genealogy of the first four generations, showing only the direct line of descent.

saw, was proud of his learned wife. He was a little afraid of her, too. Mr. Dwight was minister in Woodstock then; he was a singular man, with a wild way of talking that sometimes got the better of him even in the pulpit. But his sermons were proportionately vivid, drawing a congregation from miles around. One season he gave a series of sermons describing the plight of the Israelites in Egypt. From Sabbath to Sabbath his literary sense grew until it quite ran away with him. Tears were in his eyes, his voice shook as he described these ancient sufferings.

Down in her pew Mistress Holmes, tablet on knee, raised her bonneted head suspiciously. How could Mr. Dwight know these things? The Scriptures made no mention of such sights. Mr. Dwight's voice, that had been thundering, sank to a thrilling whisper. He leaned out from the pulpit. The streets of Egypt, he said hoarsely, *were paved with the skulls of martyred Israelites!*

Mistress Holmes, closing her tablet with a snap, sat bolt upright. The sound she made was loud, and remarkably like a sniff. Her husband looked at her and looked away quickly. If she got up and walked out of meeting it would be a most awful scandal. John Holmes knew well she was capable of it. Mrs. Holmes did not walk out of meeting — but she never again could be induced to write after Mr. Dwight, and said so to anyone who cared to listen.

It was a story to give any historian pause, or any minister. Abiel thought of it often, preparing his sermons and writing history. A man must not sacrifice truth on the altar of vividness. And yet — of what use truth if people went to sleep listening to it? Mr. Dwight's very recklessness had made him one of the most famous preachers of his day; he had garnered many souls for the harvest.

How the Holmes women had loved learning! Women, who John Calvin — if not Scripture — taught were the mouthpiece of the Devil, women had been the instrument, in the Holmes family at least, of keeping the flame of culture alive in those rude pioneer settlements. Grandmother Hewet, for instance. Abiel remembered her, at eighty-five, pink and pretty, with gentle manners and a spicy way of talking. She had taught herself to read Latin back in the times when you might wake any black night to find a tomahawk quivering in your cabin door. "When I was a girl," she had told Abiel, "I begged to go to school with the boys. But the elders were angry, and said Latin was not for woman's head. Go home, Tempy, they said, and learn to spin and weave . . . So I taught myself to read Vergil. . . ."

"*Forsan et haec olim meminisse juvabit . . .*" said Grandmother Hewet softly, in her light old voice. "Abiel, I still find it beautiful."

No wonder, thought Abiel, that his mother had grown up loving learning, with Grandmother Hewet behind her. Mrs. Holmes still lived in Woodstock, a two days' journey. She had raised her seven sons; Abiel, the second, had gone off to Yale when his father died. His mother had insisted he go; she had managed somehow to supply him with money and with what Abiel called seasonable clothes. When Abiel said his mother "never ate the bread of idleness," he was probably understating it. But she loved learning, and of all her sons Abiel seemed the only one inclined toward learning. Mrs. Holmes delighted in poetry, Watts and Young and Milton. She could quote *Paradise Lost* by the page. Abiel grew up with its long rhythms in his bones, rhythms that mated well with Genesis, Isaiah.

Abiel found it hard to leave Milton out of the pages of his *Annals*. How apt the verses were!

> . . . such, of late,
> Columbus found the American, so girt
> With feather'd cincture, naked else and wild,
> Among the trees in isles and woody shores.[1]

How could he leave that out of his *Annals?* Abiel did not leave it out; as with his father's stories, he compromised by putting it in a footnote.

It was fortunate for the *Annals* that their author was a traveled man. He had been three times to Georgia and back, traveling by stagecoach and saddle horse. Indeed, he had not only been to Georgia but he had lived there seven years as a minister in the old New England colony. Right after his graduation from Yale College he had gone South. People were just returning from the Revolutionary wars; they were pleased to find a Connecticut man so far from civilization, even though the man was a youth of twenty-one. When, returning North, he had settled in Cambridge as minister, Abiel brought with him a view of his country that went far beyond the First Parish. Almost immediately, he had begun writing to his friends in faraway places, begging historical facts. To friends in Georgia and in Virginia, in the Carolinas and westward in Tennessee.

Military facts, economic facts, facts of American church history, jumbled together, set down any old way: —

1791 . . . Samuel Slater sets up his cotton gin.
1792 . . . Connecticut raises mulberry trees and silkworms and the Rev. Jason Atwater at Branford has a silk gown from his own worms.

Jason Atwater was a friend of Abiel's. That Sabbath when Jason had rustled into his pulpit in the new silk gown, Yankee farmers nodded to each other across the pews. Perhaps silkworms would pay. . . .

Abiel Holmes lived history day by day, writing it on the run, setting it down as it happened.

And now the facts were gathered, they lay on Abiel's desk, over-flowing the shelves of his study, neat in their folders, ready to be "written." The memory of Mary Holmes was no longer a hurt; to a vigorous man the past fades quickly. Abiel's concern was his parish and his country, present and past. And the Union, this autumn of 1800, was most certainly threatened — but this time by no foreign foe. With the rest of Cambridge — the rest of Massachusetts almost — Abiel Holmes was a Federalist by conviction. Not so passionate a Federalist as, for instance, Judge Wendell, whom Abiel met often at the Historical Society and the Society for Propagating the Gospel among the Indians. Men like Judge Wendell, Stephen Higginson, George Cabot, were such furious Federalists you could not say the name of Thomas Jefferson without their changing color and pounding their fists on the table or their canes on the floor. Abiel's interest was more remote; he was the historian, the observer. Four years ago he had seen John Adams elected against Hamilton, he had watched the first Massachusetts President through four stormy, bitter years, had felt the sharp waters of Republicanism rise. With the recent elections, Boston's worst fears had come to pass: an over-whelming victory put Thomas Jefferson in a place held hitherto — as Judge Wendell had said the other night — by men of common sense, gentlemen whose moves a citizen could predict.

Boston had not really loved John Adams, first of the great clan. These Adamses were not easy to love. Austere, stubborn men — but at least they were not democrats. Adams had stood for the principles of Washington, of those disciplined men who harnessed the wild forces of revolution into law, order, federalization.

And now into the new White House at Washington would enter this other Virginian, who had written the Declaration of Independence it was true, but who stood for something far from what John Adams and most of respectable Boston considered law and order. *The common man:* the phrase was always on Jefferson's lips. The common man was what Jefferson actually believed in. Strange, perverse disloyalty, from one whom all New England knew to be a gentleman and a scholar! Any educated man, any man of property, was aware the common man was not to be trusted with governmental affairs. *Liberty, equality, fraternity:* these were words to be used by men of discretion, men of property who understood the meaning of stewardship. Men, thought Abiel Holmes, like Judge Wendell and John Lowell, Fellows of the Harvard Corporation, members of good sound churches. . . .

All this dissension was not only bad for the country but it might be exceedingly bad for the old religion. Men said Thomas Jefferson was an atheist. Abiel Holmes was an American but he was also a Connecticut Calvinist; religion came before patriotism. Abiel would have liked religion and patriotism to be one, merged as they had been in the days of his forefathers. A century ago the split had come and for a century the crack had been widening. Now in November, 1800, the thousands who had voted for Jefferson laughed aloud at John Calvin's doctrine of total depravity. How could free men believe such things? Even in Boston one heard the bold question . . . "Eliza," said one of the Eliots to her kinswoman, "do you kneel down in church and call yourself a miserable sinner? Neither I nor any of my family will ever do that."

It was a wholly deplorable pride that the times seemed to foster. But he could not, Abiel realized, put off any longer the shaping of his first page.

He dipped his quill.

AMERICAN ANNALS;

OR

A CHRONOLOGICAL

HISTORY OF AMERICA

he wrote on the title page.

From Its Discovery in MCCCCXCII to ——

Abiel left a blank for the second date. How long would he survive? It was a clan of octogenarians . . .

By Abiel Holmes, D.D.

he continued, and paused.

" —*suum quaeque in annum referre* . . . TACITUS," he wrote, and put his pen down and looked with satisfaction at the page. "Refer everything back to its own year": The Latin looked well, under his name. Abiel put the sheet aside and took a fresh one. This was, now, the true beginning. Should he say a prayer, ask the guidance of Him without Whose inspiration no man could write a book about anything? But the first sentence was already formed; the words burned in their author's mind. Abiel Holmes did not wait to pray. The blood came up in his face, and moved by the panorama of his country's history, his prose that had been so dry, so correct, swung out with a bold cadence that was new to him: —

A NEW WORLD has been discovered, which has been receiving inhabitants from the old, more than three hundred years. A new empire has arisen, which has been a theatre of great actions and stupendous events. . . .

Abiel's quill went on and on. The wind rose, the old house creaked; windows rattled. Squinting down at his manuscript, Abiel was conscious suddenly that it was dusk. He stood up, his head light with fatigue. . . . There was no sound in the house; outside was a great clamor of November wind; the woodshed roof was wet. It must have been snowing, Abiel thought.

Downstairs his dinner, cold hours ago, lay on the table: stewed rabbit in cold yellow gravy, cold boiled potatoes. The fires had gone out, the house was like a tomb. . . . Tonight was Monday, there was no prayer meeting. He would not stay alone in this cold house, Abiel decided suddenly. He would go over to Boston and call on Judge Wendell and tell him the *Annals* was actually begun. As an active member of the Historical Society, the Judge was enormously interested and had been urging the *Annals* for years. The Wendells had tea at six; Abiel was always welcome. It was a three-mile walk down Main Street, across the bridge and past Beacon Hill, but Abiel had made it often in less than an hour.

Suddenly refreshed, Abiel went into the hall for his wide black hat and greatcoat and, coming back to the dining room, seized an apple from the table. He hurried out the parsonage door and closed it behind him. On the steps he paused. It would not do for the Reverend Dr. Holmes to be seen crossing West Boston Bridge eating an apple. There were over two thousand inhabitants in Cambridge and five churches; among them the First Parish and its pastor held a high position. Everything he did was remarked.

Throwing away his apple, Abiel walked out the wooden parsonage gate and turned left down Main Street to the bridge, bending his head against a sharp November wind. In the road the muddy ruts were frozen, the steeple of the Meeting-house rose to a low sky, heavy with snow. As he crossed the bridge, the full force of the wind caught Abiel; he held his hat with both hands. It was good to lean against the wind, good to feel it buffet him, after all those hours of sitting still. With every step Abiel's spirits rose.

Accustomed, like his Puritan forebears, to intense and uncomfortable self-analysis, Abiel Holmes, stepping off the bridge to the cobblestones of Boston, wondered suddenly why he felt so elated. Sally Wendell would be at home. She was always at home on Monday nights. Perhaps she would open the door to him, dressed in the blue India silk he thought so pretty. Sally Wendell . . . Suddenly, and with the force of something long felt and never confessed, Abiel knew it was not the Judge he had walked three miles to see. It was Sally. But Sally was not a girl at all, she was thirty-one; Boston thought of her as a spinster, long past marriageable age. Sally was a tiny little thing, and so slim with her quick movements like a bird, her bright brown[2] eyes, she did not seem any age at all. When a man was with Sally he did not think about age and suitability.

Abiel smiled to himself in the darkness. How good it was to be so gay! There were persons who seemed born with cheerfulness in them. The Judge was cheerful too; he had the formal manners of a man of position, but his manners were not solemn, they were easy; his speech flowed quickly and so did his wife's. Mrs. Wendell said Sally got her laughter and quick chatter from the Jacksons; they were all talkers and delegates and politicians. . . .

Abiel had smiled but he had not believed it. Sally's gayety came from something quite different. Observing his parishioners, Abiel had noted long ago that this gay, careless grace went with riches. Inherited riches, like the Wendells', gave to the owner a delightful assurance, as though the person knew he would be welcome every-

Abiel Holmes

From a portrait by Edward Savage probably painted in 1795

where. Captain David Holmes, for instance, had not been gay. Abiel remembered his father as a tired man; his old wounds troubled him; he worried about the sawmill or the rents. Of Abiel's brothers only one, Liberty, had had this careless grace. And Liberty had gone off with the gypsies and turned finally into a rather disreputable itinerant Methodist preacher. Abiel's mother and grandmother had been wonderful company for young and old. But their speech, though colorful, was grave, and had purpose behind it. The things they desired, the things they strove for mightily, did not result in either money or gayety. Their sons desired to learn Latin, or the surgeon's art. As soldiers they fought doggedly, conscientiously, with their country's welfare in mind, as Captain Holmes had fought. There was time for self-improvement, but not time for grace.

Passing the dark bulk that was the West Church and skirting the hill with his long stride, Abiel Holmes thought on these things — and knew it was not of these things he was really thinking. The Holmeses, Abiel's mother had told him once, were slow at courting. Deacon Holmes, his grandfather, would never have married at all if the young lady had not suddenly, one evening, suggested it herself. . . . Abiel did not stop to ask what had awakened him tonight. It may have been the stimulus of his book, unrolling at last on the page after years of planning. It may have been simply that the time was ripe and Abiel knew his suit would be well received. . . . Turning east toward Oliver Stret, Abiel was aware only of his exhilaration, aware that in a moment he would be with Sally Wendell.

Against a narrow, dark street the tall windows of the Wendell mansion shone with candlelight between drawn curtains. Behind the house the long garden was a dark blur; elm branches creaked in the wind. Walking up the brick path to the door, Abiel heard the pleasant tinkle of a piano. Sally must be playing the new Broadwood; only last week it had arrived from London. Her voice rose, high and sweet: —

> Behold, my love, how green the groves,
> The primrose banks, how fair.

Abiel Holmes, taking three steps in a highly unministerial bound, reached for the brass knocker that shone under the lantern, and felt his heart pound pleasantly in his breast.

CHAPTER TWO

Mr. and Mrs. Abiel Holmes.
A son is born.

JUST after New Year's Day, 1801, a young Boston girl named Louisa Storrow[1] wrote a chatty little note to an absent mother: —

> Now, Mamma, I am going to surprise you. Mr. Abiel Holmes, of Cambridge, whom we so kindly chalked out for Miss N. W., is going to be married, and, of all folks in the world, guess who to. Miss Sally Wendell. I am sure you will not believe it; however, it is an absolute fact, for Harriot and M. Jackson told Miss P. Russell so, who told us; it had been kept secret for six weeks, nobody knows for what. I could not believe it for some time, and scarcely can now; however, it is a fact they say.

Sally Wendell did not wait till June for her wedding. At our age, she told Abiel, there is no time to lose. We will be married at the end of March in your Meeting-house, and we will invite everybody in Cambridge and Boston.

Abiel smiled. He did not like the practical details of life. How good it was to have, suddenly, this brisk tiny creature arranging everything! The Wendells knew everyone on both sides of the river. It seemed to Abiel they were related to everyone. Wendells, Jacksons, Olivers, Dudleys, Cabots, Eliots, Quincys, Bradstreets, Phillipses — these were Sally's cousins and forebears. They had had their portraits painted by Copley and Stuart; they had gone to London and dined with titled cousins of the great world and had brought home silver plate and furniture by Chippendale. But they had not been Tories; they had been patriots — Governors of Massachusetts and delegates to the Congress in Philadelphia. Judge Wendell himself had sat in the Senate and in the Council of the Commonwealth. Like his forebears, he was a godly man. The Judge's father, Colonel Jacob Wendell, had been interested in Abiel's parish long before Abiel had come from Woodstock to be pastor; there was a big handsome Bible still in use in the Meeting-house that bore the Colonel's name and the date 1740.

It seemed to Abiel Holmes extraordinary, when he stopped to think of it, that he, the son of Captain David and Temperance Holmes, was marrying the granddaughter of Colonel Wendell, who had lost forty buildings in the great Boston fire of 1762. To lose forty buildings? It implied a kingdom! Abiel could live contentedly on a few hundred dollars a year and had done it (with "findings" from the parish). But this fact of the buildings stuck in his imagination as it would stick also in the imagination of his son Oliver fifty years later. Abiel occupied, most certainly, a position of leadership in his community. But intellectual and spiritual leadership carries honors altogether different from the prestige that comes from being a Wendell, a Quincy, a Jackson, with silver plate by Lamerie and a table set with Sèvres porcelain.

In March, 1801, Thomas Jefferson was inaugurated third President of the United States, bringing with him a new era and a new philosophy. He strode through the Capitol, fiery-eyed, tense with purpose. And John Adams, staunch and stubborn, representative of a century that was past, rose to his feet and, turning his back on the White House and a world that had treated him unkindly, went home to his farm at Quincy, Massachusetts. In his barnyard he found a hundred loads of seaweed. A fine load of manure, said Mr. Adams, paraphrasing Horace, was fair exchange for the honors and virtues of the world.

And in that same month of March, in the First Parish Church of Cambridge, Sarah Wendell became Mrs. Abiel Holmes and, without benefit of wedding journey, walked down the Meeting-house steps and across to take charge of the parsonage. Already the old house wore a different aspect. Its new mistress had had it swept and garnished from top to toe and had brought roomfuls of handsome furniture — cabinets and tables and lowboys and highboys of dark satiny wood. Every cockroach had been banished and the long pump arm no more slanted crazily. It had been replaced with a new-fangled thing one pumped up and down; even the cracked old bucket was gone.

Abiel Holmes found life suddenly extraordinarily pleasant. He was deeply in love with his wife. In his study, writing the *Annals*, preparing his sermons, he thought of Sally, listened for her high clear voice down the steep stairway. It troubled him, this passionate connubiality. Was it quite in keeping with God's representative — and a man of nearly forty at that? In his diary Abiel recorded a story his mother had told him; it came very close to home, bothering Abiel with a little feeling of shame concerning himself. . . . After his father died, his mother, a handsome woman, had offers of marriage which she rejected, apparently, with scorn. When Abiel had been nearly twenty, a very respectable man had begun visiting her, with obvious intent. Mrs. Holmes desired to put a stop to this before it reached an open declaration. One evening, leading her suitor into the parlor, she prayed him to listen while she read some favorite lines from Young's *Night Thoughts*.

The suitor was all smiles and ears. Was not poetry, after all, the prelude to love?

"Though gray our heads,"

read Temperance Holmes serenely, her face bland,

> "our thoughts and aims are green,
> Like damaged clocks, whose hand and bell dissent,
> Folly sings six, while Nature points at twelve."

Her success was complete; the disheartened suitor disappeared without further importuning.

That, said Abiel's conscience, was the way to treat love in middle age. But the story bothered him. One night he told it to Sally on the way home from prayer meeting. It was summer and the maple leaves beside their door were heavy, the air sweet with honeysuckle. Abiel's voice and laugh were elaborately casual. But Sally did not laugh at his story. "Abiel," she said, "why are you afraid to be happy? Surely the Lord loves a cheerful heart! And besides, didn't the Reverend Dr. Mather himself have three wives before he was done, and fifteen children? People" — her voice quickened, there was a matter-of-factness in it that never failed to reach Abiel, cutting straight through the tortured labyrinth of his introspection — "people don't have to be dreary to be good."

With Sally in the parsonage, Abiel Holmes found little time for introspection. The house seemed filled with people, coming and going. Sally knew the private troubles of everyone in the parish, worried over them, sympathized, shed tears. She was always buying presents for somebody's baby or somebody's grandmother. Within a year after they were married, Sally presented her husband with a daughter. Mary Jackson Holmes, they named her, after Sally's mother.

Abiel was filled with a deep happiness. Around him life moved and flowed, quietly, but with a sense of accomplishment, fruition. Before sunrise one August morning of 1803, a messenger from Woodstock rode in to say that Abiel's mother was dead. She was seventy; she had gone suddenly, leaving no message for her sons. Abiel made no complaint. Long ago those sons had received what this woman had so abundantly to give. Now she was gone. It was time for her to go; she was with the Lord. The family was scattered; Abiel seldom saw his brothers or his sister Tempy. There was no generation behind him now; for a moment, realizing this, a man knows panic. Abiel got out his diary and wrote in praise of Mrs. Temperance Holmes, stilted pages from which their author's feeling struggles outward: "Were I to attempt a delineation of her character I should probably betray the son. My mother never *ate the bread of idleness*. She always commenced the Sabbath at sunset on Saturday, as did my father in his lifetime."

Stilted pages, as became a minister of the Gospel; stilted but not devoid of love.

A year later, another daughter was born to Sally Holmes. Ann Susan, they called her — again a Wendell-Oliver name. Sally's mother was pleased with these namings. She was getting old; it would be easier to leave this world, she said, with namesakes behind her.

In the autumn of 1804, Mrs. Wendell died. In his big house in Boston the Judge was lonely without his wife. At seventy-one he had retired from his more active posts. He spent more and more time with his daughter and son-in-law in the Cambridge parsonage, enjoying his grandchildren but enjoying even more the part he took in the preparation of Abiel's *Annals* which were nearly ready for their first edition. It was pleasant to see his daughter large again with child. Himself one of twelve children, the Judge admired prolificity in women. When a third daughter was born in 1805, they named her Sarah Lathrop Holmes — after her mother and a brother of Abiel's who had been lost in a shipwreck off the coast.

1805 . . . The *American Annals* appeared, two stout volumes published in England and the United States, received everywhere with acclaim. Edinburgh University gave Abiel an honorary degree *in absentia*, and in London the *Quarterly Review* gave praise most unusual for an American book. Abiel had risen above 1776 as it were. He had spoken not as partisan or revolutionary or as a belligerent, victorious colonial. He had spoken as an American who needed no defense and no apologia, citizen of a nation that could stand alone, looking upon its English cousins with the affection of an old relationship. Moreover Abiel had brought heaven into his book, and God — brought them in comfortably, as one brings in a Father who looks down upon His world and finds it one family.

Gratified by this new friendliness from across the water, the London reviewer enlarged upon it: —

> There is a sacred bond between us of blood and of language which no circumstances can break. Our literature must always continue to be theirs; and though their laws are no longer the same as ours, we have the same Bible, and we address our common Father in the same prayer. Nations are too ready to admit that they have natural enemies; why should they be less willing to believe that they have natural friends?

Judge Wendell was delighted. "We must put that paragraph in our next edition of the *Annals*, Abiel," he said and Abiel agreed thoughtfully. . . .

There was no dearth of material certainly, for a new edition. On a clean sheet Abiel wrote the date 1805, and under it: —

Thomas Jefferson was chosen President, and George Clinton Vice President, of the United States. . . . A Professorship of Natural History, with a botanic garden, was founded in Cambridge. . . . Andrew Craigie, esquire, generously added another adjoining tract, making the whole site for the garden upwards of seven acres.

Andrew Craigie, esquire, was certainly spreading himself out handsomely in Cambridge, Judge Wendell remarked. Craigie was getting up a company to develop the Port, he talked of building a second bridge to Boston. He even wanted to move the courthouse bodily from Harvard Square and set it down somewhere else. Craigie was making money hand over fist. He had bought the old Vassall mansion and now, said Judge Wendell, he was getting the Craigie name into history as a benefactor of learning.

As a fellow of the Harvard Corporation, Judge Wendell was only too glad to welcome the Craigie money. But with Jefferson elected again, speculators like Craigie had better look out, the Judge added. Jefferson, with his wild Republican ideas, his sympathy with French Jacobinism, and his outspoken distrust of what his followers dubbed "privilege and aristocracy" — Jefferson would have the whole of respectable Boston reduced to pauperism. It was amazing, said Judge Wendell gloomily, that the country had weathered these four Republican years as well as it had. There would be internal uprisings yet, if Stephen Higginson over on Mount Vernon Street was any judge. Even among the Federalists there were many with the Democratic taint about them. Bringing states like Ohio into the Union was a dangerous business; it meant more wild men in coonskin sending representatives to Congress. Before we knew it, Jefferson would let in Louisiana. Tennessee was in — why, these log-cabin rascals would vote down New England commercial interests till there was nothing left in Boston but the old religion! "And not much of that," Judge Wendell added gloomily.

Abiel smiled. How vehement the Judge became, and his friends with him, when the name of Jefferson was mentioned! As for the old religion, Abiel did not really fear for it. He was not even frightened by the recent appointment, at Harvard, of a Unitarian as professor of Theology, although the appointment had caused as much talk around town as the Presidential election. Henry Ware was a brilliant man, certainly, and a very dangerous influence to youth; several parents had already withdrawn their sons from the University because of him. This new doctrine of Unitarianism was insidious. Expose your son to it and before the month was out he was talking about "free will" and gibing openly at the notion — stamped plainly in the New England Primer — that *In Adam's fall, We sinned all.*

Deliberately, Abiel omitted Ware's appointment from the *Annals* for 1805, although he saw fit to include the new professorship of Natural History and the erection of a college rooming house. The best way to silence these new creeds was to ignore them; in the end the true faith survived.

Abiel Holmes had as yet no conception of the fires that smouldered beneath his very pulpit, nor that these embers, bursting at last into flame, would be a conflagration to drive him from his own Meeting-house door. He thought of himself as a liberal-minded man. Was not one of his best friends a Unitarian? Young William Ellery Channing, who had come from Newport three years ago as proctor at the University, had promptly joined Abiel's church. The following year, when Channing was ordained minister in the Federal Street Church, Abiel himself had delivered the prayer. It was too soon for Abiel Holmes to see that the real significance of the Unitarian movement was social not theological, that it had far more to do with the Rights of Man than with the denial of the Trinity. A dissenter himself, Abiel had not as yet the dissenter's fierce opposition to all who disagreed with him. He was forty-two; he was still growing, he looked forward, not back.

1806 . . . *The President*, wrote Abiel in his *Annals, sent captains Lewis and Clarke to explore the river Missouri, and the best communication from that river to the Pacific ocean.*

The Lehigh coal, obtained at the Mauch-Chunk mountain in Pennsylvania, which had for some time been only used by the blacksmiths and people in the immediate vicinity, was brought into notice. William Turnbull had an ark constructed, which brought down 300 bushels to Philadelphia.

The pages for 1807 were very full. Aaron Burr, arrested on a conspiracy, was released after a long trial. At Weston, in Connecticut, a very large meteor fell right into the orchard of Mr. Elijah Seeley. Eliphalet Pearson retired that year, professor of Hebrew at the University. Pearson lived in an old mansion house just north of the college, a rambling, delightful clapboard affair known to Cambridge as the Gambrel-roofed House. For a long time Judge Wendell had had his eye on it; his own house in Boston had become too big for him, he said. And besides, since Jefferson planned this absurd, this wicked Embargo on New England shipping, a gentleman must retrench and put by a little for the hard times that were undoubtedly coming. Judge Wendell proposed to his daughter and son-in-law that they leave the musty old parsonage and share the Gambrel-roofed House, provided he could obtain it at a fair price.

Abiel and Sally Holmes accepted. Promptly, Judge Wendell sold his mansion on Oliver Street — garden, pear trees, marble fountain, and all — and for seven thousand dollars bought the Gambrel-roofed House and moved in with his daughter, his son-in-law, and their three small children.

The move suited everyone. Sally Holmes exchanged one old house for another old house it was true. But the Gambrel-roofed House was newer by seventy years than the parsonage and many times more attractive. Westward its windows looked out over the highroad to Lexington and Concord. To the east, through tall elm trees pastures stretched, pleasant with clover and sweet grasses. Far beyond one glimpsed sunlit sails gliding down the river. Across a field within stone's throw stood the red brick buildings that Cambridge still called "the colleges." Sally had her flower garden instead of the square bleak parsonage yard. Moreover, this house belonged to the family; when Sally desired to renew a doorsill or tear down an old woodshed she did not need to consult the parish.

For Abiel the house was perfection. How good it was to sit upstairs in one's study writing about America, and to feel history within one's very walls! Downstairs in the east room General Ward had laid out his plans for fortifying Bunker Hill; those dents in the wide floor planking had been made, so Cambridge said, by soldiers' muskets. Abiel had his suspicions about this, but most certainly General Warren had slept here the night before Bunker Hill battle. General Washington himself must have been often in the house. To one entering the wide front hall, the curving staircase was beautiful. Abiel Holmes knew little of beauty. But he knew that this staircase, pointing upward, invited the scholar.

It amused Abiel that his father-in-law, who was entirely delighted with the whole arrangement, should continue to grumble concerning his purchase and pretend it was all the fault of Thomas Jefferson. What, the Judge asked moodily, was the country coming to? England's Orders in Council were bad of course; England was treating us outrageously on the high seas. But was there no way to stop her except retaliatory measures that would ruin all the merchants of New England? Nothing Great Britain did could be as bad anyway as what Napoleon Bonaparte was doing. Bonaparte had conquered Italy, Austria, Egypt; he had made himself Emperor. It was Bonaparte we should be quarreling with, not England.

So thought Judge Oliver Wendell and so thought his Federalist friends on Court Street, Chauncy Street, and Bedford Square. A Presidential election was due next autumn, fortunately enough. There was talk of Jefferson's desiring a third term, but even Judge Wendell did not think that could happen. The likely thing was that Jefferson would succeed in getting his henchman, James Madison, elected. Nevertheless, with Madison in the White House, affairs might improve. At any rate, no one could be so dangerous as Jefferson with his Republicanism and his Embargo that caused good Boston ships to rot at the Long Wharf.

Abiel had heard the Judge actually follow the word *Jefferson* with the word *tyrant*. How distorted men's judgment became when their pockets were touched! The temper of Boston, Abiel thought sometimes — and did not say it — was changing. She cared less for outrages to the Rights of Man, and more for outrages to her shipping interests. Touch a Massachusetts man in his pocket and the thrust went through to the heart and was immediately defended in terms of great principles. Jefferson's Embargo was not spoken of as a nuisance. It was, said Boston, a threat to our Federation, a threat to freedom, to the principles of Washington and the Founding Fathers.

In March, 1809, the day arrived that Judge Wendell and his friends had longed for. Jefferson went out and Madison came in.

But Madison arrived in times too sick for any administration to cure. Washington Irving saw him at the Inaugural Ball. "Ah, poor Jemmy!" said Irving. "He is but a withered little apple-john." Poor Jemmy began auspiciously by lifting the Embargo — and in Boston, Salem, Providence, flags flew, bells pealed. Shipwrights and corders were at a premium; in Boston yards the hulls could not be raised fast enough. The Federalists in Washington who felt themselves responsible for this repeal, good Massachusetts men like Pickering and Judge Wendell's cousin, Josiah Quincy, came home in a burst of glory and were feasted. On a bright summer morning, they all got on a boat and sailed down to Gloucester Point to keep the day in celebration. But it was all a mistake. Back went another embargo, just as bad, and back flooded Boston hatred for Madison and the administration that was ruining trade.

All this, Abiel Holmes recorded in his *Annals*, but without comment, adding for the year 1809: —

  1) the establishment of the Miami University in Ohio.
  2) an act of the Massachusetts legislature to amend the Constitution of the Board of Overseers of Harvard College.
  3) the organization of a Bible Society in Boston.

That was all. What was the use of entering into this everlasting faction? And besides, since Jefferson had returned to Monticello he had read the first edition of the *Annals* and had actually begun sending historical material from his own library. The most valuable things that nobody else could possibly lay their hands on: the *Mémoires de L'Amérique* in particular was an invaluable collection of what Abiel, recording its receipt, called in capital letters *"official Papers and Documents."*

How could any historian resist such blandishment, so honestly delivered? Judge Wendell, seeing the packets arrive with the Monticello stamp upon them, watched them carried upstairs and was silent for once. As an active member of the Historical Society he could hardly pretend not to be interested; he was in fact enthralled. Well, a rascal could be a scholar. A rascal could even be a gentleman born.

1809 . . . June, July . . . Leaving his study with reluctance and walking downstairs and across the Yard to his Meeting-house, Abiel Holmes told himself he must beware of neglecting his spiritual, pastoral duties for the fascination of compiling these *Annals*. He had not neglected the parish and he knew it; the Sunday School needed attention perhaps, but the new library was receiving books too fast to house them. A man's sermons could be used twice and thrice. Abiel exchanged pulpits with many churches in and around Boston; in particular his sermon on the death of George Washington was often asked for. Abiel kept the church records in his own hand. He liked keeping records and would not have trusted them to another. Lately, for instance, there had been the deplorable matter of a young woman whom Abiel had been forced to excommunicate from the church, for "contumacious behavior." It had been one of the most distressing events of his ministry and Abiel's wife had made it no easier by taking the woman's side from the very beginning. Weak spirits, Sally maintained, needed divine guidance even more than those of stouter heart, less liable to temptation.

Abiel had become very stiff-necked — and very unhappy. On a Sabbath afternoon in full service he had given sentence: *"I pronounce this woman to be a person from whom the followers of Christ are to withdraw as from one who walketh disorderly. The sentence now passed is but a representation of a sentence inconceivably more awful to be passed on the transgressor at the judgment seat of Christ."*

The transgressor herself, seated just below the pulpit in face of the whole congregation, covered her face with her hands and looked about to fall from the chair. Abiel, catching sight of her, had paused. "Unless," he added suddenly, rather to his own surprise, "punishment be prevented by seasonable repentance."

Afterward Sally had waited for him at the Meeting-house door. She had taken his arm, looking up at him, and for the first time in weeks, Abiel's heart was warm once more within him. At home he locked himself in his study, and going down on his knees, prayed for humility and strength. The episode had affected him deeply. What an awful thing, to be banished from God's house! Of the modest house of God that was his own particular care, Abiel loved every foot. The slim spire with its graceful belfry, topped by the big gilt weathercock; the rows of square white pews, the tall windows that let in the morning sun. Of course, there were things that could be improved. The pew seats, for instance, raised on hinges to give standing room during prayer. After the Long Prayer they were released, and came down with a bang that was not conducive to worship. Sally did not like the choir and the music. She wanted an organ. There was nothing sinful in a church organ, she said, and besides, the bass viol was always out of tune and the strings broke regularly on Sabbath evening as if by design of Satan. Bass viol and flute, Abiel had replied firmly, were music enough in God's house.

But afterwards, he visited half the churches in Boston to examine the organs and inquire as to the cost of installation.

From the doorsill of his parsonage Abiel Holmes looked out on Cambridge Common where a seventeen-starred flag hung now from the staff and the revolutionary cannon sat fat and cocky, not yet rusted through. It was good to see the Common green with summer, good to take one's spade back of the house and dig in the vegetable garden. The months passed, and in his almanac Abiel made occasional notes of meetings and appointments, adding little that was personal.

But on August 29, 1809, Abiel broke his rule. Alongside the date and the printed prediction that the day would be "pleasant," he added a little mark: —

> = August 29 Pleasant
> August 30 Commencement, Cambridge College
> = *son b.*

Then he threw black sand on the ink to blot it.

" = *son b.*" Thus modestly was announced the advent of Oliver Wendell Holmes, doctor, professor, Autocrat of the Breakfast-Table — and poet laureate to Boston for half a century.

CHAPTER THREE

*Mr. Madison's war and the Hartford
Convention. Oliver Wendell Holmes
is a boy in Cambridge. Abiel Holmes
sees a threat to the old religion.*

AUGUST, 1809, a boy born into a quiet college town. Not
even a town — a village of tree-lined lanes, of open fields where
raspberries grew wild, of salt marshes where the tide rose and fell
and where the heron built his nest. A courthouse on the square, a
market house near by with the big hay scales outside. The red brick
buildings of the college and the Washington elm whose branches
swept the sky. Five churches, well filled on Sundays. Mr. Brattle's
fine mansion with the big gardens behind trimmed hedges that
looked, said the elders, like English hedges. On the road to Watertown were some elegant new country seats, and Mr. Craigie had
built a second bridge to Boston, splendidly lighted by two rows
of lamps.

The states were seventeen when Oliver Wendell Holmes was
born. Abraham Lincoln was born that year too, far westward in
Kentucky, one among thousands of sons born to the new settlers
beyond the western ridge of mountains. Josiah Quincy, down in
Washington representing Massachusetts in Congress, heard with
alarm about these potential voters appearing in log huts. What would
become of New England's commercial interests if these Western

farmer-woodsmen brought votes to Washington? When Oliver
Holmes was two years old, it was proposed to bring Louisiana in
as a state. Josiah Quincy rose to his feet and thundered. The bonds
of the Union, said he, must be dissolved rather than admit these
Westerners! . . . "as it will be the right of all, so it will be the duty
of some, to prepare definitely for a separation; amicably if they
can, violently if they must."

Keep the West out! roared New England — and Abiel Holmes
wrote quietly in his *Annals:* —

1812 . . . *An act of congress was passed for the admission of
Louisiana into the Union . . .*

Federalist New England, jealous New England, clung angrily to
its original pre-eminence in the thirteen states. Rich, powerful New
England, hating the Embargo, prepared to secede if Congress declared war on England — a war that would ruin coastal shipping immediately, perhaps forever.

Treacherous New England, Madison called her — and Congress
declared war on England. The coastal trade stopped and New England reeled from the blow, then raised her shrewd head, deciding if
she could not launch ships she could build factories. Just outside of
Boston, Judge Wendell's friends — Francis Lowell, Amos Lawrence
— laid the foundation of great fortunes in their cotton mills. There
was, actually, a boom in New England. "Wheels roll, spindles fly,"
said a newspaper. If the Lowells and the Lawrences could not ship
their cotton cloth by water they could ship it, they said, by land.
The roads south out of Boston were dusty with ox teams drawing
canvas-covered wagons named like ships. Country people, watching
the wagons pass, read these names and laughed: *Mud-clipper, Commerce Renewed, Jefferson's Pride.*

Abiel Holmes, pursuing his quiet path from parsonage to Meeting-
house, felt the war in ways remote from commerce, but to him vital
none the less. One Sunday during service he had just stood up to
begin the Long Prayer when the congregation stirred, looking
toward the western windows. Abiel heard the sound of drums. A
fife squealed against the Sabbath quiet; there was the tramp of
marching feet. Just outside the Meeting-house the feet stopped. An
order was shouted, the drums rolled again. In the family pew

Oliver * Holmes, aged five, raised his head delightedly. Incredibly, a whole company of Cambridge militia was marching into church! Drum and fife going full tilt they continued up the steps to the visitors' gallery. Not until they sat down did the music cease. Abiel kept on with his prayer, making no rebuke. Better for soldiers, returning from the wars, to come to church noisily than not to come at all.

But in what strange ways, he thought later, walking across the Yard toward home — in what perverse ways was God invoked in time of war. What twisting of the Word to earthly purpose! Judge Wendell's friends, for instance, were growing richer by the day, and the richer they grew the surer they were that God was on their side. They said so, by letter and public speech, using language that was actually scriptural. If Mr. Madison insisted on continuing this war it would be New England's *duty* to secede, the Federalists said. As Paul among the apostles, they would labor to this end.

Judge Wendell, observing his friends, was increasingly doubtful about God's being so definitely on their side. Mr. Madison's war was going very badly indeed, but it seemed to the Judge that disunion was a sorry price to pay for peace and a renewal of one's shipping interests. Down to their Disunion Convention at Hartford went the brains and breeding of Boston. Judge Wendell watched them go. Men he had known all his life: George Cabot, Harrison Gray Otis, Prescotts, Bigelows, Putnams, eager to draft a Nullification Resolution and hand it to Mr. Madison. Judge Wendell was an old man now, eighty-one. Too old, he said, for faction. What a little time ago, he told Abiel, since that spring of '76 when the British Fleet lay off Nantasket Road and General Greene had bidden him hire men to watch the streets for British spies! . . . Well, times changed and the hearts of men changed with them. What, Judge

* All the evidence shows that Oliver Wendell Holmes was called Wendell by his family and friends. But curiously, he was also referred to, in New England and farther abroad, as Oliver. (See my Chapter 25, page 1, Sir Frederick Pollock's remark, and William Roscoe Thayer's edition of the *Letters of John Holmes to James Russell Lowell and Others*.) [1] In order that the reader may not confuse the two Oliver Wendell Holmeses, father and son, I have referred to the father, in his boyhood, as Oliver — seldom, however, permitting him to be addressed directly as Oliver.

This purely literary device is necessary only in a few early chapters. By the time Oliver Wendell Holmes, Junior, is born (1841), the father already is established in the reader's mind as Dr. Holmes, the poet.

Wendell asked his son-in-law, did President Madison think of this Hartford affair?

Madison was sick at heart, Abiel replied. Men said he looked shattered and old. Even the burning of the White House last summer by the British had not affected him so bitterly as this Hartford Convention. How could Massachusetts, how could Boston, Cambridge, Harvard College, look out upon Bunker Hill in the hour of their country's need — and plot disunion? . . . "No foreign foe has broken my heart," said Madison. "To see the Capitol wrecked by the British does not hurt so deeply as to know sedition in New England."

Judge Wendell, shaking his head, sighed an old man's tremulous sigh. John Adams out in Quincy even declared that George Cabot, President of the Hartford Convention, wanted to be President of New England. That was nonsense of course; nobody who knew Cabot could think that of him. Cabot was a patriot, but he had got off on the wrong foot, somehow. When you reached eighty, said Judge Wendell, you knew that people were not always villains. Often enough they were just mistaken. . . .

But whatever George Cabot's ambitions, he was fated not to attain them. The Hartford delegates had scarcely time to get down to Washington with their Resolutions in their pockets when a frigate from Belgium, dropping anchor in New York Harbor, brought news of peace with England. Couriers galloped to Boston in record time; the town had the news on Monday morning. Up went the flags, out rang the bells. Shops and schools were closed. In Cambridge Dame Prentiss let her scholars go. Young Oliver Holmes, almost six now, ran all the way home in the February cold, tossed up his cap — he called it a "jockey" — and shouted with the other boys, "Hurrah for America!"

1815 . . . Cambridge, Massachusetts, was quiet, but for an intelligent boy it was no backwater. If Cambridge did not grow as the West grew, Cambridge still felt itself an important part of America. Was it not the very cradle of history? Oliver Wendell Holmes was nurtured on this conviction. Within doors the world belonged to his sisters; Mary and Ann were older, their activities female and sedate. It was outside the Gambrel-roofed House that Oliver claimed a boy's world. His brother John, born in 1812, a fat, fair-haired little creature, tagged after him. On the grassy slopes of Winter Hill the two played soldiers among the ruins of Revolutionary forts. Roaming the old burying ground beyond the Common they gazed in awe at the flat stones where lead had been picked from the coats of arms to make bullets for Revolutionary muskets.

And when the hurricane came that September of 1815, blowing fiercely in from the sea, leaving salt crystals on Cambridge windows, Oliver's grandfather, driving out from Boston next day, said the beautiful English elms that Mr. Paddock had planted near the Common were all lying in the street, blown down. The American elms stood up because they were more slender and yielding.[2] It was like the willows and oaks in the fable . . . Well, it was always good when something American stood up and something English fell down.

Oliver's father insisted the British were no longer our enemies and it was a Christian's business to foster peace, not strife. But in the attic hung an old flintlock musket that had belonged to Oliver's grandfather, Captain Holmes. Abiel told his son that when he was ten he could have it for his own. Against such hopes, against such testimonies of battle, the words of peace spoken by his father were to Oliver entirely unconvincing. And on Sabbath evenings when the countryside was hushed, Oliver heard from far off the rumble of waves breaking on beaches ten miles to the eastward, heard also on other nights the voices of the great guns in Boston Navy Yard. He thought they roared from astonishment because some sloop of war had come suddenly into the harbor. The *Wasp*, perhaps, that every Cambridge boy knew had captured two British ships, then disappeared mysteriously over the face of the waters.

Every country superstition that presented itself, Oliver absorbed. Hired men, drinking tea in the kitchen, told stories of the Evil One who wandered about at night. If a boy wrote his name in his own blood and left it handy, Satan would pocket it and henceforth the boy would belong to the powers of darkness. Hell was very close to a boy raised in Congregational New England. In a field near the house were bare spots known as the Devil's Footsteps, and there was a breach in one of the college buildings through which the Evil One had gone out from a circle of wicked youths who had summoned him to their unhallowed orgies. Oliver examined the hole, put his foot into it, and one afternoon crawled halfway through it before he retreated backwards in terror.

Sometimes Oliver's grandfather took the boys to Boston and down to the wharves where Oliver saw the earringed sailors, smelled strange sea smells. John loved the ships with their tall crossed yards, but Oliver, looking upward, thought of the steeple on his father's Meeting-house and was assailed by a nameless and unreasoning fear. He was ashamed to tell it. When the terror visited him, it was not to his father that Oliver went for comfort; talks on right behavior as a bulwark against Satan were neither comforting nor convincing. It was Grandfather Wendell who understood. Grandfather's hand, so dry and old, lay over a boy's fingers with a light, kind comfort. Grandfather, white-haired, bent, sleeping half the day away, was obviously very near to leaving this world. Yet he did not seem to fear his departure at all, nor the terrible things that might await him. In itself that was more reassuring than any talk on virtue. When his time came, Grandfather said, looking straight into Oliver's blue eyes — when his time came he would go gladly.

Just after Christmas, when Oliver was eight, his Grandfather began eating his meals upstairs in the big four-poster bed, instead of coming down to the table with the rest of them. One snowy day he did not come down at all. When Oliver's father motioned the children to follow him upstairs, Oliver knew what to expect. Death and the panoply of death were not hidden from children in those days. Oliver and John, Mary and Ann, went to the funeral.[3] The Meeting-house was filled with people from Boston; their carriages lined the Square outside. Josiah Quincy, small, bewigged, looking like a portrait by Copley, made an oration: "Full of years," he said, "our friend has descended to the grave, regretted and beloved by all who knew him; happy in the consciousness of a life well spent, and rejoicing in the prospect of felicity in a future state, of which a firm faith in his Redeemer gave him the assurance."

Oliver missed his grandfather. Abiel Holmes, observing his son, whose customary chatter was stilled, wondered if he had been seeing too little of the boy. He began inviting Oliver to drive with him to Dorchester or Lexington to hear him preach; the two would jog off together in the two-wheeled chaise behind a quiet horse, and the boy loved it. They would leave on Saturday and come home on Monday. Abiel, on these trips, talked religion to his son. Oliver listened vaguely. By the time he was ten the Westminster Catechism had lost its bite not only for Oliver Holmes but for most of New England. Oliver was still afraid of the Devil, but the doctrine of transmitted sinfulness, justification, sanctification, meant no more to him than the mystic syllables by which his friends counted each other out in their games.

But to Abiel Holmes the old doctrines had become more important than ever. It seemed to him that New England was rushing toward Unitarianism like the Gadarene swine to destruction. Theologically, Unitarianism meant God as One, rather than God as Three in One. As long as the movement had been confined to theology, Abiel had paid little heed. Any good historian knew such quarrels were forgotten in a generation and the true doctrine prevailed. But Unitarianism had obviously gone far beyond doctrinal matters. The old morality was disappearing with the old religion. Abiel, who had cautioned his congregation against singing Watts's hymns with levity, saw crowds go to church gayly, in their best bonnets, as if they were going to a show. Pipe organs and mummery took the place of solemnity and the Long Prayer; if men still loved God they most certainly did not fear Him. And fear of the Lord, Abiel told himself passionately, was the beginning of wisdom.

The truth was that the Unitarian movement was a natural concomitant to events that were not churchly but sociological, not local but nation-wide. The Jeffersonian ideal of individualism, opportunity for all, refused to jibe with the notion that man was born wicked, doomed forever. Federal or Democratic-Republican — no matter what one's politics, the ideas of Jefferson and of Rousseau before him had penetrated too far to be revoked. The Rights of Man — was this consistent with a doctrine of total depravity and everlasting damnation? If you could get ahead on earth, said Yankee common sense, you could get ahead in heaven. And to this notion the new applied science was a potent ally. A man who had seen his mother die of the smallpox and who now saw his son saved by vaccination could no longer believe that prayer was the only salvation against present danger. Lavoisier had said that matter was indestructible; even smoke was but another form of the wood it rose from. John Dalton advanced his atomic theory. Down in Monticello, Thomas Jefferson was experimenting with the rotation of crops, using calculus as well as common sense on his farm, and at the same time planning a university that was to embrace all creeds.

With every step that science took, Abiel was in keen accord, setting it down in the *Annals* whether it was a mere tally of the number of spindles in Baltimore's cotton factories or the founding, in 1818, of the Massachusetts General Hospital in Boston. But to the new spirit that went along with science, the new agnosticism, Unitarianism — whatever name man called it by — Abiel was deeply opposed. When a man invented a cotton loom, a water-driven spindle, let him dedicate it to the glory of God! Let him go down on his knees and thank the Father who had put this invention into the mind of His humble servant. Life was becoming easy, conditions of daily living much softer. And man, Abiel Holmes observed, no longer feared his Maker. His house warmed by stoves, man looked out at the raging blizzard and smiled, forgetting to propitiate his God.

Abiel ceased exchanging pulpits with such men as William Ellery Channing. On Sundays the Meeting-house saw no more Unitarians. It was good, thought Abiel, that he had long ago entered his son Oliver in Phillips Academy up at Andover; the Academy was a very bulwark of Orthodoxy. Perhaps Oliver would go to Andover Theological Seminary and be a minister. It was too soon to tell, the boy was still in dame school. As for Harvard University, Oliver would go there of course; his mother would hear of no other plan for her son. Sally's father had been graduated from Harvard and so had her grandfathers on both sides. Channing was on the Corporation now, and that was dangerous. But John Kirkland was president, and Kirkland, an intimate friend of Abiel Holmes, was a clergyman and the son of a clergyman, and a godly man.

Kirkland lived just around the corner from the Gambrel-roofed House. Everyone knew him and loved him. He was an easygoing, scholarly gentleman who, when he was done examining his students, was apt to regale them with a dish of pears. He was often in Abiel's study; Oliver, opening the front door to let him in, thought how good it was to see a clergyman smile like that. The Congregationalist ministers who came to stay over Sunday at the Gambrel-roofed House, the boy had observed, did not know how to smile. Their faces were long, their voices nasal; the sight of them around the house made the Sabbath even drearier. There was a sourness about them, something Oliver Holmes did not trust and that struck deep in him, nullifying, had his father but known it, every sermon he gave his son upon the benefits of the orthodox religion.

When Monday came and these visitors departed, Oliver's

mother shared the children's unspoken relief. Cambridge itself, the houses around the Common and the Square, offered far more attractive company. The Channings and the Wares lived near by. The Lowells had bought the old Oliver house on Tory Row; they called it Elmwood. The Stephen Higginsons had come over from Boston too, and lived almost next door. Mr. Higginson had been a merchant, one of the richest men in Boston — ruined like many others by the sudden peace with England. British ships, arriving with cotton goods, woolen goods, had put the Higginson mills out of business in surprisingly short order. Mr. Higginson had sold his great mansion near Boston Common; his friends had bought land in Cambridge, built him a house, and given him the position of Bursar of the University. Stephen Higginson appeared entirely uncrushed by misfortune. All the energy he had put into his mills he put now into the college. He was forever making improvements — planting trees in the College Yard, hanging lamps over the gates. President Kirkland approved the elms but he ordered the lamps put out. Times were hard since the war, the scholars had walked in the dark for a hundred years and they could walk in the dark now.

Higginson laughed. So did his wife, pretty young Louisa Higginson in whose company Sally Holmes delighted. (It was Louisa who had long ago written her mother the news of Abiel's engagement to Sally Wendell.) Louisa had been sorry to leave Boston where she had had much success — the Honorable George Cabot himself having remarked that nobody received company better than she. Stephen Higginson came often to Abiel for advice in matters pertaining to scholarship. The Holmes children loved to see him come. He had been greatly puzzled over a load of Hebrew Bibles that had recently been delivered to the Divinity School with the title pages all printed at the wrong end of the book. He had gone to Kirkland about it and Kirkland had explained that Hebrew was always written that way. Grinning jovially, Higginson brought the story to Abiel. He had been wrong about Bibles, he said, and over-lavish in the use of whale oil. What unscholarly, extravagant gesture would he make next? And what — he demanded — would he do without the good advices of his neighbor Abiel Holmes?

The College Yard remained unlighted. Oliver and John Holmes, returning home late on winter afternoons, their skates over their shoulders after an hour on Craigie's Pond, met Dr. Kirkland swinging his lantern. As for Mr. Craigie, he too had been ruined by the peace, but unlike Mr. Higginson, Craigie had gone hopelessly into debt. He could not leave his house for fear of bailiffs except on Sundays, which were blessedly bailiff-free. Then only he emerged, dressed in his black breeches and buckled shoes, and leaning on his cane walked slowly down to Christ Church to attend service. He had become a legend, a figure of mystery. Oliver and his friends, skirting cautiously round the Craigie mansion, peered in a shuttered window, knocked upon it and fled.

1819 . . . *The Alabama territory*, wrote Abiel Holmes in his *Annals, was admitted, as a state, into the Union.*

The crisis that New England feared had arrived at last. And what a turmoil it occasioned, this admission of Alabama to statehood! On the floor of Congress, Josiah Quincy raged. "You have no authority," he shouted, "to throw the rights and property of this people into the 'hotch-potch' with the wild men on the Missouri, nor with the mixed, though more responsible race of Anglo-Hispan-Gallo-Americans who bask on the sands in the mouth of the Mississippi. . . . Do you suppose the people of the Northern and Atlantic States will, or ought to, look with patience and see Representatives and Senators from the Red River and Missouri, pouring themselves upon this and the other floor, managing the concerns of a seaboard fifteen hundred miles, at least, from their residence?"

Abiel Holmes made no comment upon this. If people were pouring westward out of Boston and out of Massachusetts, he left it to the merchants to deplore. Merchants and mill owners knew well that as the West went up, Massachusetts went down. Tabulating statistics for his *Annals*, Abiel was aware that the nation was shifting from the Atlantic seaboard. Massachusetts tollkeepers, counting the wagons that passed on the turnpikes, the horns of their oxen pointing westward, wondered if anyone would be left in New England. Abiel Holmes's concern was not with merchandise, with the problem of turnpikes to carry Boston goods to Pittsburgh, with the building of canals, waterways, docks, dams, with the finishing of the great Cumberland Road, begun so long ago. This was all the talk around him — but it was talk that did not greatly concern a Calvinist minister. In Abiel's parish the population remained about the same from year to year. Everyone in Cambridge continued to know everyone else. The new barber was the only foreigner in town. Of the two thousand Irish who had landed in Boston during the past year only one, a day laborer, had found his way to Cambridge.

Abiel Holmes the annalist made no attempt at prophecy or economic interpretation. Every river that was opened, every newspaper that was founded, every great cause that was argued in the courts, he recorded with a little flourish of pride that had to do not with financial shiftings but with a simple pride in the growth of his country.

The steam boat Comet *arrived at the village of Arkansas, in 8 days from New Orleans; the first steam boat that ascended the Arkansas river.*

1819 . . . The first steam ship sailed for Europe in May.

The case of Dartmouth College was decided in the Supreme Court of the United States. It was considered as a case of great importance to the literary and charitable institutions of our country. . . .

Daniel Webster had won this case, and Webster was a Boston man now. Black Daniel, they called him — Daniel of the beetling brows, the magic voice, not yet forty. Abiel Holmes admired him extravagantly, took his sons to hear the great man speak whenever the occasion was near home and recorded the rolling periods afterward in his *Annals*.

Oliver and John Holmes cared little for oratory. But Oliver loved the crowd. The more people there were around, the better he was pleased. He was ten, growing too old for the dame school, his father said.

In September of 1819, Sally Wendell put a new slate in Oliver's bag, a pair of new breeches on his short legs, and, standing in the doorway of the Gambrel-roofed House, kissed her son and sent him off alone down the long road to Mr. Biglow's school in Cambridgeport, one mile away.

CHAPTER FOUR

Oliver Holmes goes to school and college.
His father finishes the Annals of America.

OLIVER HOLMES liked the Port School. It made him
feel very much the man to be taught by Mr. Biglow instead of
Dame Prentiss, who rustled to her desk in stiff skirts and required
every lesson to be thoroughly prepared. Mr. Biglow was large and
red-faced and good-natured. He smelled of cigars, sometimes of something stronger, and he required very little of his students. Often
he did not appear until nearly noon. On these occasions it was understood that Mr. Biglow was having one of his headaches, which
to Oliver seemed quite reasonable and rather pleasant. To Oliver's
father it did not seem nearly so reasonable. When Abiel heard of it
he frowned and said a man like Will Biglow who had been master
at the Boston Latin School should know better how to conduct
himself.

The citizens of Cambridge had been at some pains to open this
school to save their children the long trip into Boston. Observing
his eldest son, who came home day after day with a satchel empty
of books, Abiel was uneasy, but decided to let matters slide. After
all, the boy was acquiring a pretty good education at home, hearing
his elders talk and tumbling about the library, which numbered,
by now, nearly two thousand books. There were many volumes
of sermons, which Oliver never opened, and there were the great
English classics, historians and poets over which the boy pored by
the hour. There were odd volumes of periodicals — the *Annual
Register*, the *Christian Observer*. Above all there was the new Amer-

ican edition of Rees's *Encyclopedia*. Oliver read Rees like a novel,
searched the illustrations from A to Z. He read poetry too, but only
for the story; Dryden in particular had a tale to tell. One day, taking up the blue calf-bound Dryden, Oliver found a dozen pages
torn out; the lyrics from "All for Love" were gone entirely and in
their place lay a sheet on which was written plainly, in his father's
handwriting: *Hiatus haud deflendus.*

The omission is by no means to be mourned . . . Sighing, Oliver
slipped the book back in its place and turned to *The Life of David*,
which had to do not only with adventure but with love. The Bible
itself presented some green patches among the deserts. But of all
the books in his father's library, Oliver's favorite was Pope's
Homer. . . .

> Aurora now, fair daughter of the dawn,
> Sprinkled with rosy light the dewy lawn . . .

On summer mornings very early, when he went into the back
yard to bring in wood for the kitchen stove, the grass, all wet and
shiny, looked just like that, Oliver thought with satisfaction. . . .

Hiatus haud deflendus . . . It was not easy, Abiel Holmes noted,
to forestall a growing boy, to look ahead and guide him from danger. Oliver could recite the Westminster Catechism, both Longer
and Shorter, without slip, but the blank expression of his face during
this performance left little doubt the feat belonged to memory
rather than to natural piety. As a little boy, Oliver had been much
affected by the last words of John Rogers the Martyr, as printed
in the *New England Primer*. Just before he was led to the stake,
said the *Primer*, Rogers had despatched his portrait to his children,

> That you may see your father's face,
> When he is dead and gone.

When he recited this, Oliver's eyes had invariably filled, his lip
had trembled. But his father well remembered that the very next
moment the boy had run off, whistling and singing. Oliver was
always singing. He had managed to whittle himself an octave flute
and played it upstairs in his room, everything from Mr. Moore's
Irish melodies, which his mother taught him, to Watts's Hymns,
which Abiel, after much wrestling with the spirit, had finally con-
sented to substitute in church for the old Tate and Brady. Issuing

the new hymnals that first Sunday, Abiel had cautioned his flock. "Let none regard these sacred songs as mere entertainment. Above all, let none perform with levity."

There was small doubt that Oliver, up in his attic room, performed with levity — or certainly with gusto. To Abiel, nearing sixty, the younger generation, both male and female, seemed appallingly frivolous. But he loved children, and his rebuke left no scar. Moreover, Oliver was so like his mother it was hard to rebuke him. He was small, and if he had had his way he would never have stopped talking. At the table he was forever being shushed and forever breaking out again. And how busy he was! — Always deep in some project, making wooden skates to use on Craigie's Pond, or out with his gun looking for squirrels around the fields of Cambridge. Abiel had given him the gun over his mother's protest. It was Captain Holmes's old flintlock. Abiel had kept his promise, but Sally Holmes said the gun was too big; it would explode and blow the boy to pieces.

Everything seemed too big for Oliver, his father remarked, although the boy managed the clumsy flints well. His small hands were surprisingly dexterous. But would the boy never grow? He was small and slight and homely, with a long upper lip, blue eyes, and heavy straight brown hair that fell down continually over his forehead. Sally Holmes said the Irish lip came from the Dublin Tracys, on her side of the family. As to Oliver's remaining so small — what, Sally asked sturdily, did it matter? Smallness was *part* of Oliver; it made him quick. Abiel and his brothers were tall and long. She had not raised a very *beautiful* family, Sally added. The girls had big noses and straight hair, but it had not stopped them from acquiring husbands. Mary Jackson, the eldest, had just got herself engaged to Dr. Parsons of Providence, a very good match indeed. Ann, at fifteen, was vivacious enough to make the young men forget her lack of beauty. Would Abiel desire any *more* young men visiting this house than came already? As for little John, at seven, he grew homelier by the year. But after all, Sally added, who would want a lot of pretty sons around the dinner table? They would not seem like boys at all.

The year John left Dame Prentiss for the Port School he was already taller than his older brother. John was more silent than Oliver, and slower moving, but the things he said surprised the family and made them laugh. "I have only had one compliment in my life," John remarked moodily one day at tea, watching Nellie, in her white apron, bring in the plum cake. "It was when I was six, and Nellie was brushing my hair. She turned me round and said to Mother, 'I don't think John's so *awful* crosseyed, Ma'am.'"

Down at the Port, Oliver's schoolmates were of more importance to him than his books. Dick Dana was there (afterward to write *Two Years before the Mast*). In Oliver's class there was a girl who was very good at writing compositions; on the first page of one of them she used the word *trite*. Oliver was impressed. He had never heard the word; in the Gambrel-roofed House, home truths were not trite, they were part of morality, to be respected, not sneered at. The girl's name was Margaret Fuller. She had a long neck that arched and undulated like a swan's. Oliver, who did not like her very much, compared it to something less flattering. She was the most self-conscious human being Oliver had ever seen. He had heard her tell Dick Dana that she often stopped on the stairs to ask herself questions: *How came I here? How is it that I seem to be this Margaret Fuller?*

To Oliver Holmes this was just plain silly; he could not know it was a trait that would some day mark a place called Brook Farm and a group called New England Transcendentalists.

There was nothing even remotely self-conscious about Oliver Holmes. He was voluble and mischievous. By the time he was fourteen he had been caught twice smoking cigars behind the barn and had been punished for taking John to the public hanging over north by Jones Hill. Abiel Holmes was troubled; neither punishment nor prayer made this boy look sternly on solemn things. His most frequent sin seemed to be laughing at the wrong time. The long faces of visiting Calvinist ministers in particular sent him, for no sound reason, into gales of mirth. Once when he was a very little boy he had even laughed aloud in the Meeting-house at the grimaces of one of these from the pulpit.

Oliver spent quite a lot of time in church. On Sunday there were three services; the long one was held in the afternoon. Until Oliver was six, Harvard College held all its services, including morning chapel, in the Meeting-house; the students sat upstairs in the east gallery. When the University Hall was built the students stopped coming to the Meeting-house except for Commencement exercises. And Commencement, as every Cambridge boy knew, transformed the Meeting-house and the whole town into a place of carnival and delight. The Common was covered with tents made, in thrifty Yankee fashion, of old sails. Candy booths, Punch and Judy shows, lined the sidewalks round the Square. On Monday morning the men began putting up the tents and kept at it all night; you could hear their hammers plainly from your bed. Every August, Oliver counted the tents, telling his brother triumphantly there were many more this year than last. . . .

And on Tuesday morning early, standing by the Meeting-house you heard first of all the Lighthorse coming with their trumpets. That was the Governor, arriving to take his seat in the Meeting-house. By nine o'clock every pew was filled. The Harvard Washington Corps was gorgeous in cockaded hats, tall polished boots, and clanking swords. And how grand the Honorable George Cabot looked, descending from his carriage in black breeches and silk stockings, wig and buckled shoes!

When the procession had disappeared into the Meeting-house, if you were quick you escaped your elders and went down to the Market where the ginger-beer carts rang their bells and popped their bottles and you could buy musk melons, coco-nut milk, or the new confection from Boston called *ice cream*, so delicious and so dear to buy. All day the festivities continued. People picnicked in the church yard, sitting on the stones. By nighttime the Common was littered with watermelon rinds, peach stones, straw, and the delightful Commencement aroma of rum and tobacco smoke. Inside the College Yard there was plum cake to be had. The Faculty did not approve of this extravagance. Once they ordered it suppressed, and the order caused a minor rebellion.

The scholars themselves were almost eclipsed in all this festivity. About fifty were graduated each year; they dashed about among the crowd in the August sun, their gowns floating behind them, their tall beaver hats looking hot and magnificent. Oliver Holmes knew each of them by name. With every Cambridge boy it was a point of pride to know the list of every class alphabetically from *Amory* to *Wentworth*, and not only the names but the nicknames, their owner's haunts and favorite games. Oliver looked forward to that day when he himself would thus be listed and could tell his brother John, grandly, that he and his cronies had been over to Porter's last night, for beer and oysters.

In the summer of 1824, when Oliver was almost fifteen, there was a ceremony at Commencement that eclipsed every Commencement, Oliver was sure, both past and future. General Lafayette was in Boston, come over from France at the invitation of Congress to visit the Republic he had helped to save. On Commencement morning Lafayette sat on the Meeting-house platform with the Governor and President Kirkland, and the next day at the Phi Beta Kappa celebration he sat there again. Professor Edward Everett, a member of Abiel's church, made the Oration, hurling impassioned periods first at the audience and then at the General. The Meeting-house was in tears, there was not a dry eye. Oliver's mother, sitting close to him, sobbed audibly and Oliver, who had not heard a word but had kept his eye fixed on General Lafayette — so remote, so distinguished in his long black coat, so breath-taking somehow — felt tears rise hot in his eyes and when his mother squeezed his hand squeezed back mightily.

Abiel Holmes, his heart bursting with pride, saw the procession and the General leave his Meeting-house. When the church was empty he entered the last pew and went down on his knees. Thanking the Father who had permitted him to be pastor in this place and on this day, Abiel, his hands before his face, prayed once more for humility and strength.

Then he went home and, sharpening his quill, took a fresh sheet and wrote the whole ceremony for the *Annals*. Primly, with careful understatement, Abiel strove to bring before his readers the cheering, weeping throng that had left his Meeting-house not three hours since. The result was elegant, accurate, and somehow very typical of its author: —

1824 . . . *professor Everett, in an oration, addressed the general with pertinency and pathos, the auditory testifying their concurrence by their tears and applauses.*

That autumn of 1824, after five years at the Port School, Oliver Holmes was taken up to Andover for a winter at Phillips Academy. His father drove the boy twenty miles and left him there. It was Abiel's last chance to make an orthodox Congregationalist out of his son; the Academy was a very factory for the stamping of good orthodox brains. But Oliver, at fifteen, withstood the virus and sailed pleasantly through the winter without being marked even slightly by moral or religious suasion. Copybook maxims in particular irri-

tated him; Oliver preferred to doubt what he was told until investigation confirmed it. In the study hall there was a big clock; on
its dial was written in large letters: —

YOUTH IS THE SEED–TIME OF LIFE.

The more Oliver read this handy motto the more he resented it; he
was far too alive to accept any dreary Calvinist notion that the
present was a mere time of preparation for the future. Now was
now, and Oliver was prepared to enjoy it as such. He had a delightful
friend name Phineas Barnes who came from the State of Maine, a
big plump boy with fine red cheeks. The two laughed over everything that happened, whether grave or comic. Oliver's only real
difficulty was his smallness; he grew to five feet five and there
he stopped. Everyone was taller, everyone was heavier — and everyone let Oliver Holmes know it. In particular his desk mate, a great
oaf of a boy, used to kick him persistently under the desk. "You
are a bully," Oliver told him shrilly, his blue eyes blazing defiance.
"When you are a man you will be a murderer." (Years afterward,
the prophecy came true and Oliver Holmes, learning that the man
was to finish his days in the madhouse, expressed himself as gratified.) One of the teachers had a dream that said he would drop
dead sometime. Oliver and his tall desk mate used to sit fascinated,
watching the man lead prayers, hoping the moment would arrive
NOW, before the bell rang for dismissal.

Once Oliver was feruled severely. But none of these episodes left
a scar; the boy was too busy to cherish yesterday's malice. He liked
the Latin versifying he was required to do. Translating the *Æneid*
into couplets he made a phrase one morning that pleased him: —

The boiling ocean trembled into calm.

When his Latin master praised it Oliver was thrilled, and put the
line away to show his father when he went home. Here at Andover
he read Gray's *Elegy* and *The spacious firmament on high*, finding
them more to his taste than the poems his mother had read him which
had tinkled overmuch, like Cowper's "The rose had been washed,
just washed in a shower." . . . But he missed his mother's music
and when he went home was glad to stand around the piano in the
evening with Ann and John, singing Irish melodies while his mother
played.

One night while they were singing, Abiel came into the room and walked to the window. The panes were frosted thick; Oliver saw his father take out his pocketknife and draw something on the glass, then turn and leave the room. When the song was finished Oliver walked to the window. Outside, the branches of the big maple, thick with ice, clashed in the wind. It was blowing hard from the northwest, a night of stars and clear, biting air. Without touching the window, you could feel the cold come at you. On the white pane Abiel had drawn a tangle of branches with the stars above them.

Per aspera ad astra, he had written above.

"What does it mean?" the others asked. "Tell us, what did Father write?"

" 'Through roughness . . . tangles . . . adversity,' " Oliver began. "It's poetry . . . '*Through adversity to the stars*,' " he finished, pleased with his translation.

But the phrase surprised him. His father's face as he walked through the room had not been gay. It had been grave, troubled. Surely his father, so quiet, so pious, so gently spoken, so certain of what was right and what was wrong — surely, his father's life had progressed through no adversity?

Turning back to the group around the piano, Oliver forgot the phrase. It came back to him a month later at Andover, reading a letter from his father. It was a typical letter and Oliver, having read it, sat looking down at it rather sourly: —

CAMBRIDGE, 5 *January,* 1825

My DEAR SON, —

We received your letter of 30th Dec. and thank you for the wish of a happy New Year. We cordially reciprocate the wish, and our desire is, that you may improve your time and talents, and be attaining those virtues and graces, which will make *all* time pleasant and profitable to you. . . .

Your opportunities for such improvement are very much greater than those of most others, and we shall expect the more accordingly. Be diligent in your studies; punctual in your attendance at the Academy; and strictly observant of its rules. Avoid bad company, and choose the virtuous only for your companions.

I need not enlarge. . . .

He need not indeed, Oliver reflected. Two dollars had been enclosed. "Be prudent," his father had written after mentioning the money.

Be prudent. Be diligent. Be punctual. Avoid bad company . . . How, wondered Oliver Holmes, did fathers think sons could grow up at all, with ten hundred admonitions weighing them down? Had Grandfather — had Captain David Holmes — talked this way to his son? Oliver did not believe it: soldiers were different; they had not such words as "prudence, diligence," always at their tongue's end. Looking at his letter, Oliver was minded to tear it up. But a scene came suddenly and for no reason to his mind . . . His father, tall, a little stooped, standing against a frosted window while music flowed around him. *Per aspera ad astra* . . .

Oliver got up and put his father's letter away carefully. Then he took his pencil and in a round boy's hand wrote in his *Æneid*, on the flyleaf, *Per aspera ad astra.* . . .

Next autumn he would be a schoolboy no longer. He would be at Harvard University. When you entered college you were already a man. It was splendid to think of, but it was solemn, too. It would be pleasant if Phineas Barnes were coming to Harvard instead of to the new college at Amherst. Perhaps, Oliver thought vaguely, he himself would be permitted to board at the college hall. Or was that privilege reserved for seniors? He would ask his father as soon as he got home.

October, 1825 . . . Oliver Holmes was a Harvard scholar and proud of it. He was sixteen — quite sure he was a man. But he did not live at the hall, he lived at home in his old room facing west under the eaves. Every morning he rose in the dark at the clanging of the college bell and ran across a brown, grassy field to chapel. John Kirkland was still president of Harvard, Josiah Quincy was Mayor of Boston, John Quincy Adams was President of the United States. Missouri was a state, come in after Maine. One free state and one slave to match as usual — but Missouri lay north of the slavery line and Adams said that her inclusion marked the "title-page to a great, tragic volume."

January, February . . . April . . . On the Charles River the ice was thawed. Time to get out the wherry and row round to Boston. Oliver Holmes stepped into his skiff, whistling the song the class of '29 had sung last night at the oyster supper. . . . And three hundred miles to the westward, Clinton's Big Ditch was finished. Along its banks the drivers walked, their lines slackening across narrow water: "*I got a mule and her name is Sal, Fifteen miles on the Erie Canal.*"

> 1825 . . . *The ceremony of breaking ground for the continuation of the great national road westward of the Ohio was performed at St. Clairsville on the 4th of July.—On the same day the ceremony of breaking ground for the great canal of the Ohio was performed on the Hicking Summit by governor Clinton, of New York, who had been invited for the special purpose.*

Writing his *Annals*, Abiel Holmes recorded the nation moving westward and was careful, as always, to write "governor" with a small *g*—"governor" Clinton, "professor" Everett. One must be watchful never to make titles that might lead men of the New World back to the vanities of the Old.

> 1825 . . . *and Eli Whitney [died] at New Haven, aged 57 years.*

"By his invention of the cotton gin," Abiel wrote in a footnote, "he 'was the means of changing the whole course of industry in the southern section of the Union.'. . . Mr. Whitney, at the instance of the government of the United States, next directed his mechanical ingenuity to the manufacture of fire arms, in which he was eminently successful; . . . and his death . . . was regarded as a public calamity."

How the face of America was changing! thought Abiel Holmes. In Cambridge lanes the college boys teetered about on huge, high-wheeled velocipedes. There was soon to be gaslight on the streets of Boston. Abiel loved material progress so long as it did not interfere with things of the spirit. That same year he recorded proudly the opening of the New Faneuil Hall Market: "'one of the boldest, most useful, and splendid public improvements, that have lately taken place in the eastern states.'" "The Quincy Rail road" was opened too, with appropriate ceremonies. Over its rails three wagons loaded with twenty-one tons of stone were moved with ease by a single horse, a distance of three miles.

1826 . . . The first volume of Commentaries on American Law,
by James Kent, was published at New York.

On the 4th of July, John Adams died at Quincy, in the 91st year
of his age; and Thomas Jefferson at Monticello, in Virginia, in
his 83d. year.

It was the last entry; except for a concluding paragraph, the
Annals of America were finished. Abiel had accomplished his design;
he had recorded the events of one hundred and seventy years of
colonial history and fifty years of the history of the United States.
For twenty-six years he had been writing this book; it had been his
constant companion. He would write his last paragraph on the same
desk, looking out on almost the same Cambridge landscape he had
looked out on a quarter century ago when the *Annals* were begun.
Preparing to compose his peroration, Abiel turned back to the old
edition of 1805 and opened the book at the first page!

A NEW WORLD has been discovered, which has been receiv-
ing inhabitants from the old, more than three hundred years. A
new empire has arisen. . . .

Once more Abiel Holmes felt a stirring of his blood. When he wrote
those words, America embraced sixteen states, five million people.
Now America reached across the Western mountains, mile on mile
through forest, over prairie, across great rivers to the Pacific Ocean.
Twenty-four states, ten million inhabitants. . . .

Searching his original Preface, searching also his first pages of
actual history, Abiel was startled to find no mention of God, no
credit given duly to the Heavenly Father of all these Americans,
the Good Shepherd without whose help no flock could cross the
western mountains, no ship arrive in harbors west or east. He was
young when he wrote those pages. He had forgotten, in his country, his God.

He would revise for this second edition, which would have a new
title, *The Annals of America*, the peroration of the first. There, at
least, he had not excluded the counsels of heaven. He read again the
sentence by General Washington which he quoted then and would
quote now—a sentence he had often used in sermons: —

No people can be bound to acknowledge and adore the invisible
hand, which conducts the affairs of men, more than the people

*of the United States. Every step, by which they have advanced
to the character of an independent nation, seems to have been
distinguished by some token of providential agency.*

Then, with a rolling phrase, a succession of capital letters, Abiel
wrote the last words of his book: —

*Following this valedictory counsel, and favoured with the bene-
diction of Heaven, may the Republic be preserved through all
the revolving years of future Time.*

CHAPTER FIVE

Oliver Holmes is graduated from
Harvard. Abiel loses his parish.

OLIVER HOLMES, a sophomore at Harvard, continued to have a splendid time. Lessons were not hard. The professor assigned a task and you did it; no more was required than the mere doing. Classes were surprisingly like Andover and no whit more taxing to the intellect. Oliver played cricket, rowed on the river, skated on the Fresh Pond with his friends and regaled himself afterwards with beer at Porter's. A splendid time, he was sure, was what one came to the University to find.

The Corporation and Overseers had lately been trying to remedy this pleasing misapprehension, which was all too prevalent among the students. They held a meeting that was by no means inspired by President Kirkland or Abiel Holmes. Kirkland was as easygoing as ever; he liked things to stay as they had been. Moreover, as a former teacher at Andover, Kirkland, like Abiel Holmes, was more interested in moral philosophy, Hebrew, and the evidences of religion than in these new subjects the Corporation was pushing: Natural history, modern languages. German especially seemed beyond the point; Latin, Greek, and Hebrew were sufficient tools surely.

It was George Ticknor of Boston who was largely responsible for the revolutionary meeting held by the Overseers. Ticknor had been one of the first Harvard graduates to go abroad for study. And what Ticknor found at the German universities had made him profoundly dissatisfied with conditions at home. Repeatedly, from abroad, he had written long reports to Stephen Higginson, suggest-- ing drastic changes at Harvard — changes in the library, in the sys-- tem of compulsory attendance at classes, in the general curriculum. Higginson, impressed, had persuaded the Overseers to appoint Ticknor professor of French and Spanish Languages.

And now Ticknor urged upon the Overseers an immediate in- stitution of the German system of elective studies. Jefferson had adopted it years ago, at the University of Virginia. Harvard was nothing but a grammar school, Ticknor said passionately. The stu- dents were treated like babies, led by the nose, supervised within an inch of their lives. How could a boy become a man under such a system? It was time, said Ticknor, that Harvard University looked eastward to Göttingen, to Bonn and Berlin, centers of the world's learning, where such men as Schelling, Hegel, and Humboldt led in philosophy and science.

Ticknor prevailed. The elective system was put in over the pro- test of Kirkland. Oliver Holmes, had he desired, could have studied the new philosophy, could have learned German, read Kant in the original.

But Oliver Holmes had no slightest desire to learn German. He would, however, have liked to learn something about the heavenly bodies. Ever since he had paid a silver piece to look through a tele- scope on the Common and had seen the transit of Venus, he had been intensely curious about the stars. There was talk of erecting an observatory at Harvard, but as yet it was only rumor. Chemistry and mineralogy were attractive, but what Oliver liked chiefly was to write and talk. He did both whenever he could find an audience. He wrote poems for the college *Annual* and long letters to his school friend, Phineas Barnes.

When there was a college debate, Oliver took part and found on the platform opponents worthy of his powers. Ben Curtis and George Bigelow — already, the two of them knew they were going to be lawyers and nothing but lawyers; they could talk a black sub- ject white and vice versa. Charles Sumner was not so facile. Arrogant, opinionated, he was ready to fight for his principles. Cousin Wendell Phillips seemed to have politics in his blood; perhaps because his father had been Mayor of Boston. Politics, but not causes. No one would have dreamed that Phillips, so handsome and urbane, would one day be the maddest of Abolitionists. When a college temperance society was proposed, Phillips, at a public debate, argued it eloquently out of existence. He was president of the Hasty Pudding Club, to which Oliver Holmes belonged. James Freeman Clarke was the one who loved causes. Temperance, prison reform, abolition of debtors' prisons — when he spoke of these things, Jamey's blue eyes burned with a steady fire. As for Ben Peirce, black-eyed, black-haired, and fiery, he had a speaking voice that reached into one's very backbone.

There was plenty to debate, in the winter of '28. A Presidential election was due in the autumn. John Quincy Adams would run for a second term. Almost everyone at Harvard was for him. Against him would run a wild man, an Indian fighter, an out-an-outer from Tennessee — a kind of man never before seen in Presidential politics. A man of the people, redolent of coonskin and the frontier — General Andrew Jackson, whose only virtue was that he had beaten the British at New Orleans. How, asked Cambridge, Harvard College, and the people Oliver Holmes knew, how was it possible that America could so forget its traditions as to consider this wild man as the creature of its choice?

As the weeks passed, excitement mounted. On street corner and platform the candidates were matched; men talked of little else. From pulpit and forum the preachers rebuked their flocks. "To our shame be it, for the last eight years every interest of the nation is postponed to the comparatively inferior concern of choosing a President." [1]

It was not a mere matter of politics, this election, and men knew it. The thing went far deeper. Thoughtful observers saw a change coming over the face of America. "Our age," said Channing, "has been marked by the suddenness, variety and stupendousness of its revolutions. The events of centuries have been crowded into a single life. Overwhelming changes have rushed upon one too rapidly to give us time to comprehend them."

Steam, said the news weeklies, the illustrated papers, was annihilating distance. They loved the phrase: *Steam is annihilating distance.* In Oliver's class at Harvard, Sam Smith said he had been talking to a sea captain who said a ship could be made that would actually carry coal enough to get it across the ocean without sails — though not, of course, able to carry passengers. Even far inland, steam was potent. All these canals, turnpikes, bridges, newly dredged harbors were bringing the states closer together. Before one knew it the country would be settled as far west as the Pacific Ocean! Harvard College, pondering these things, had a debate: *How can one man be President of the United States when it is eventually settled from Atlantic to Pacific?*

Oliver Holmes hurled himself into it; he cared not on which side. The debate was long and heated; in the end the noes had it. The country could *not* be governed by one President. It would have to be cut up into republics, each with its separate president. Andrew Jackson would be president of Tennessee, John Quincy Adams would be president of New England. The answer satisfied everyone.

But the country did not agree with Harvard College. As spring progressed into summer it became alarmingly plain that the country was going to vote for Jackson. "We are almost all Adams men here," wrote Oliver to Phineas Barnes, "and consequently rather down in the mouth." It was pleasanter to write more localized news: President Kirkland was resigning, Harvard would have to elect a new president. It might be Mr. Josiah Quincy, late mayor of Boston, a distant cousin of the Holmeses. There would be great times at his inauguration, with illuminations, balls, and a dinner. No doubt the *Recorder*, Oliver added, thinking of his father, would gibbet the college afterward for the immorality and impiety of a public dinner. He himself had changed little since Andover days: —

> I wear my gills erect, and do not talk sentiment. I court my hair a little more carefully, and button my coat a little tighter; my treble has broken down into a bass, but still I have very little of the look of manhood. I smoke most devoutly, and sing most unmusically, have written poetry for an Annual, and seen my literary bantlings swathed in green silk and reposing in the drawing-room. I am totally undecided what to study; it will be law or physick, for I cannot say that I think the trade of authorship quite adapted to this meridian.

Oliver was nineteen that summer. "I am," he wrote Barnes, "a plumeless biped of the height of exactly five feet three inches [2] when standing in a pair of substantial boots made by Mr. Russell of this town, having eyes which I call blue, and hair which I do not know what to call. . . . I am not dissipated and I am not sedate, and when I last ascertained my college rank I stood in the humble situation of seventeenth scholar."

Seventeenth in a class of fifty-nine was neither good nor bad. Oliver was a senior, he had been elected to Phi Beta Kappa. His brother John was a freshman. Oliver need live at home no longer, his father said; he could take a room in Stoughton Hall. Delighted, Oliver wrote his address as *Stoughton 31.* At night the watchman cried his rounds, and in Commons Oliver ate with a three-pronged iron fork and complained with his mates about the cold puddings.

But he was particularly glad not to be living at home this winter of '28–'29. Something distressing was happening to his father. There was a controversy in the First Parish, a very serious controversy. The matter concerned his father's refusal to accept the new Unitarian doctrines. To Oliver, his father was wholly in the wrong.

The First Church of Cambridge often exchanged ministers, on Sundays, with other churches. Abiel preached in Boston and surrounding towns, and in the old days the preachers he had invited to his Meeting-house had been very pleasing to his congregation. Channing had come there and other liberal thinkers. But for the past few years, Abiel had not invited preachers with the Unitarian point of view; he had exchanged only with the strictest Congregationalists, men with the old-fashioned Calvinist hell-fire in their sermons. His congregation, very definitely, did not like it. They said so and when Abiel would not listen they held meetings, made impassioned speeches, and finally, after months of wrangling, dispatched a letter to Abiel, signed by many — but not all — the leading men of the parish. The letter was long and polite, oiled with the very unction of piety. But it said in effect that if the pastor refused to comply with the wishes of his flock, his flock desired another shepherd.

Abiel read the letter and did not yield an inch. Thirty-seven years ago he had been called to this parish to teach certain doctrines. The doctrines had not changed. This parish, Abiel said firmly, had no authority to change them.

Sally Holmes stood staunchly by her husband. Liberal-minded herself, reared in more worldly surroundings than her husband, she had never, during all the years of her marriage, been able to espouse the old religion. She was both too practical and too cheerful to accept a doctrine that sent her children to hell before they had learned to speak. She had never said so; there had been no occasion to say so. Her husband was the kindest of men; never once had she seen him strike fear to his children's hearts by any doctrine whatever. But as he grew older, Sally had watched him sadly. Whether right or wrong, Abiel, plainly, was going to lose his church. How easy it would be for him to escape this bitter cup! A little tact, a little twisting of words, and they could go on happily as before, with the Meeting-house and the parish sustaining them.

But Abiel would not twist his words. The battle, he said, was not his but the Lord's. Yet his voice, when he rebuked his flock, was neither bitter nor denunciatory. It was firm, but as always it was gentle. Strife was not fitting in God's house.

The congregation, glancing at each other, stirred restlessly. Their pastor was out of line with the times. Did he not understand what was going on around him? The older church members supported him staunchly, but to the younger, Abiel's gentleness was more irritating than if he had screamed back. Leaning a little forward, his long, fine hands resting on the arms of the pulpit, he spoke quietly, his face benign. "If I seem to disregard the wishes or the taste of my hearers, it is because I am more desirous to *save* than to *please* them."

The congregation, angry, desired to be saved in its own way. More meetings were held and on June 8, 1829, it was voted that "the Rev. Dr. Abiel Holmes be, and he hereby is, dismissed from his office of minister of the gospel and teacher of piety, religion and morality in said parish, and that all connexion between said Holmes, as such minister or teacher, and said parish, do and shall henceforth cease."

Abiel read this ultimatum — and refused to accept it. The parish had no ecclesiastical authority for such a step, he said. Sally Holmes, observing her husband's thin face, the stoop of his shoulders, wondered if he could survive this battle. It would be different, she thought, if he loved a fight. Even in his own house he had, except for herself, no support. There were no daughters left to sympathize; Ann, the younger sister, had married and gone to her own house. The boys were silent entirely; Sally knew well what was behind their silence. For all his gentleness, Abiel had been fanatically stubborn about this whole affair. Even the dismissal could not budge him; next Sunday he would mount his pulpit as always, he said.

But on Sabbath evening Abiel heard that another preacher would be there before him. It was the end; Abiel left the First Church. He did not go out alone. Sixty of the members went with him; it was the parish at large, the non-communicants, who had opposed him.

Abiel and his flock held service in the old courthouse on the Square. They had hopes, some day, of building a new Meeting-house. But no new church, Sally Holmes knew, could take the place in her husband's heart of the old wooden Meeting-house where he had worshiped for so long.

Oliver was sorry for his father. But he was young, he was about to be graduated from college, and he was extremely occupied with his own affairs. He was Class Poet; he was vaguely in love with a different girl each week; graduation was only two months away and he had not the slightest idea what he was going to do after he had received his diploma. Everyone else in the class of '29, it seemed to Oliver, had settled upon a career. Sam Smith was going to Andover Theological Seminary; Ben Peirce was going to teach mathematics, Curtis and George Bigelow were going to the Law School under Judge Story.

The last thing Oliver desired was to be a minister and the next last thing, a mathematician. There was not, in truth, much choice of careers. He would like to be an author, but how could a man keep alive on a few poems and stories? It was too bad he was not to inherit a fortune so he could settle down and be a gentleman of letters. There were no gentlemen of letters in New England it was true, but there were gentlemen painters like Mr. Washington Allston who lived in the big mansion in Cambridgeport. Why could not he, Oliver Wendell Holmes, be the first New England gentleman of letters?

Judge Story was a gentleman to admire, certainly. The Judge lived the kind of life a man of parts would like to look forward to — presiding handsomely in court in the mornings and driving to Cambridge to teach in the afternoons. The law was a good starting point for a career. Oliver Holmes, for want of better advices, went over and enrolled as a law student under Judge Story and Mr. Ashmun. They were brilliant men, the Law School was new, and the acquisition of Judge Story as professor had occasioned much congratulation among the Corporation and Fellows. A student could master almost any subject if he had an inspiring teacher. It was rather a pity, thought Oliver, that Judge Story, so colorful, so vigorous, did not happen to teach something else. *Belles-lettres*, say, or one of the sciences such as Dr. Jackson taught over at the Medical School. In his junior year, Oliver had worked quite hard at chemistry and mineralogy; he had been sorry when the courses were ended.

His father was pleased with the idea of his son becoming a lawyer and, besides, circumstance made it a convenient career. At home, Grandfather Wendell's big law books lined the upper shelves, thick brown volumes bound in calf. The tools were at hand. Lightheartedly and a little vaguely, Oliver Holmes, in the autumn of 1829, embarked on a study of the law.

Opening his grandfather's books, Oliver felt a slight uneasiness. The books seemed quite impossible to understand. The suspicion assailed him that if he ever did understand them, they would still be dull. But this, he told himself, would wear off; ignorance always makes a man timid.

It did not wear off. For four months, Oliver pursued the law, becoming each month more dismayed. What awful stuff it was! Sawdust and more sawdust. In its pages one caught no glimpse of that subject which was the only thing worth studying in the world: *man.* How could Judge Story, how could Daniel Webster, have pursued this horrid phantom to the end? In January, sitting at his table, his books open before him, Oliver gazed out on a world white with snow, a world on which the low afternoon sun threw long purple shadows. No darker, no purpler, thought Oliver morosely, than the shadows in his own heart. A panoply of shadows! . . . The figure pleased him; he raised his head, his eyes bright once more with pleasure.

Reaching for his notebook to record the phrase, he found its pages choked with a quite different idiom: *equity, agency, carrier, procedure.* Flinging notebook and Blackstone's *Commentaries* to the floor, Oliver took a fresh pad and commenced a letter to Phineas Barnes. "I am sick at heart of this place and almost everything connected with it. I know not what the temple of the law may be to those who have entered it, but to me it seems very cold and cheerless about the threshold."

Spring came, and instead of writing law Oliver sat by the window looking out on a green world, and wrote poetry. How easily the verses came, pouring out upon the paper, quips and puns, conceits and figures! He spent his time, he wrote Barnes, "writing poetry like a madman, and talking sentiment like a turtle dove." Cambridge had the most delightful girls, and lately Oliver had made excursions into

Boston, too. There was one girl in particular who seemed quite perfect, Miss Amelia Jackson of Bedford Place. She was almost as small as he—a prerequisite for any man of five feet five—and she said she loved to listen to him talk. Her father was Judge Jackson and her uncle was Dr. James Jackson who taught physic in the Medical School. Not that it mattered who one's father and uncle were, but the Jacksons were such wonderful people, brilliant, active in large affairs.

Dr. Jackson's talk in particular fascinated Oliver. His stories of the patients in the Insane Asylum, his stories of the hospital on Fruit Street where he had been the very first physician. Dr. Jackson was a writer, too; he had published a textbook from his lectures. "Some day," Oliver told him, "Sir, you must write your experiences as a physician." Dr. Jackson laughed and said perhaps he would when he got too old to practise medicine. With his thick hair, high color, long nose, and strong Yankee chin, the doctor did not look as if he could ever be old. The nose and chin looked very familiar to Oliver Holmes. The Jacksons were, of course, his cousins on his mother's side. And his mother, Oliver observed, seemed to like Miss Jackson almost as much as he did.

Miss Jackson liked poetry, Oliver soon discovered. Especially the poetry of O. W. Holmes. Oliver wrote more verses than ever, covering the backs of his old law papers with lines evenly matched. In September of 1830 he conceived a poem that had nothing to do with love, purple shadows, or Miss Amelia Jackson. It had to do with an old, worn-out ship, but it came from the heart all the same and was written furiously, in anger and indignation.

The frigate *Constitution*—*Old Ironsides*—whose victorious return to harbor Boston had once greeted with such wild joy, lay now rotting at the wharf. The government announced suddenly, tersely, that the vessel was taking up too much room and must be scrapped. Boston protested, the whole country protested, but with no result. Abiel Holmes was almost ill over it; Oliver, bursting in the door one afternoon, found him sitting moodily at his desk, trying to compose a letter to the *Boston Daily Advertiser*. Now that the second edition of the *Annals* was in print, what weapon, said Abiel Holmes, had he against such outrage?

Oliver went upstairs and, sitting down by the western window, got out pen and paper. The lines poured from him, swept from him in a tide. It was as though he were writing someone else's poem, dictated carefully by its author and transcribed by Oliver Holmes.

> "Ay! pull her tattered ensign down,
>   Long has it waved on high,
> And many a heart has danced to see
>   That banner in the sky;
>
> . . . .
>
> "Oh better that her shattered hulk
>   Should sink beneath the wave;
> Her thunders shook the mighty deep
>   And there should be her grave;
> Nail to the mast her holy flag.
>   Set every threadbare sail,
> And give her to the God of storms—
>   The lightning and the gale!"

There were three stanzas. Oliver copied them, finding very little to change. It was late when he took the poem downstairs. His father was still at his desk; Saurin's *Sermons* lay open before him. Silently, Oliver laid his poem on the desk and left the room.

A moment later his father called him. When Oliver came in, Abiel Holmes was standing by the desk, the poem in his hand. He began to speak, and his voice choked. With enormous surprise and a great lift of the heart, Oliver, looking up, saw tears in his father's eyes, saw that the hand holding his verses was trembling.

The poem, published next day in the *Advertiser*, swept Boston like wildfire, then reached beyond Boston all over the country. Printed in broadsides, the verses were sold on the streets of Washington. The government, overwhelmed, gave orders that the frigate *Constitution* be preserved.

In Boston a shout of triumph went up. And in Boston, Cambridge, and far beyond the river Charles, Oliver Wendell Holmes, son of the Reverend Dr. Abiel Holmes of Holmes Place, was famous.

CHAPTER SIX

*Oliver changes his profession. He goes
abroad to study. Abiel Holmes sees his
son receive a prize.*

SUDDEN FAME did not determine Oliver Holmes to be a poet
by profession. The conditions of being the first American gentleman
of letters were as baffling as ever; "Old Ironsides" brought fame but
not money. Moreover the whole episode, it seemed to Oliver, was
fantastic. On Wednesday nobody had heard of him, on Thursday
night he was celebrated. By Friday week, Oliver told himself, he
would be forgotten. For all his frivolity there was a practical, Yankee
streak in this young man.

What success did for Oliver Holmes was to give him courage
to abandon the law. There had been no doubt in his mind that he
hated the law, from Blackstone to Kent. But with no alternative in
mind it would have been impossible to go to his father and announce
he was dropping the law because the law was disagreeable. His talks
with Dr. Jackson, Oliver found increasingly fascinating; lately he
had been looking into medical books and seeking out his brother-
in-law, Dr. Parsons, to answer his questions. Here, in medicine, was
a profession that concerned MAN. Here was a way to earn money
and study mankind at the same time. To Oliver, Dr. Jackson was
the wisest man he knew. He would ask Dr. Jackson now — tomorrow
— if he could attend his lectures in Boston, and if Dr. Jackson said
yes, he would go to his father that night and be done with the law
forever.

The moment was propitious in more ways than one. Only a month before, Abiel's faithful parishioners, the ones who had "gone out" with him from the First Church, had raised money enough to begin building a new church; Abiel himself had been a heavy contributor. Ground had been broken; before Abiel's eyes the church was rising day by day, a fine clapboard edifice just south of Harvard Square. Washington Allston had designed it and was very proud of it. He used to walk up from Cambridgeport sometimes on a moonlight night, call for Abiel, and take him across the Square to look at his handiwork. Abiel was filled with hope concerning the future. His son's decision did not come as a great surprise; Abiel was aware the boy had been wasting his time at the law. If Oliver wished to study medicine, then let him begin immediately, and let him apply himself with more diligence than heretofore. "You are twenty-one," Abiel told his son gravely. "You have had many advantages of education and background. At your age I had my own parish in Georgia; I was earning my living."

There was more of the same. Oliver, standing on one foot and then the other, listened automatically. How often during his lifetime he had heard about these "advantages"! But this time, his father was justified and Oliver knew it. "It's all true," Oliver said slowly. "It's true too about the difficulties ahead in my chosen profession." His face brightened, his voice resumed its customary cheerfulness. "*Per aspera ad astra*, Father," he said.

Abiel laughed. He could not help it. But when Oliver had left the room he sighed, shaking his head. How incurably frivolous the boy was! Would he ever settle down and amount to something?

Oliver found a boardinghouse in Boston — it was at 2, Central Court — and flung himself into medicine, certain that it would prove delightful from start to finish. Dr. Jackson's lectures fulfilled his every expectation. Jackson never spoke of *curing* a patient, only of *taking care* of him. Nature — the doctor quoted Hippocrates — would do the curing. But when Oliver went down to the hospital and saw the white faces of the sick, row upon row in the long corridors, he was horrified. That night gray faces, wasted limbs, pursued his dreams. It was worse a few days later when he walked into the operating theater for the first time, notebook in hand. Dr. Bigelow stood there, a saw in his hand. His old black suit was splashed with the blood of a score of operations; beneath him on the table a man, made mercifully half-drunk with whiskey, screamed while Oliver's friends of the medical class held him down.

Even the skeleton that hung over the table in the students' room made Oliver wince. All day and for many days when he should have been memorizing the names of bones, he found himself moralizing upon the mortality of man.

At home he was quiet, disposed to seek out his father and start conversations on the brevity of life and the dangers that beset us. Abiel was astonished. He did not know that his son had witnessed, that morning at the lying-in ward, a young mother die in the agonies of childbed fever. "I knew Oliver was clever," Abiel told his wife that night in their room. "I knew he was talented, too. But he never gave evidence, before, that he could think on spiritual subjects."

Oliver worked too hard that winter to find time to write his impressions. But early in the spring he sat down one night and wrote to Phineas Barnes, facetiously as always, but with an undercurrent of seriousness and conviction: —

March, 1831

I must announce to you the startling position that I have been a medical student for more than six months, and am sitting with Wistar's Anatomy beneath my quiescent arm, with a stethoscope on my desk, and the blood-stained implements of my ungracious profession around me. I do not know what you will say, — but I cannot help it. . . . I know I might have made an indifferent lawyer, — and I think I may make a tolerable physician, — I did not like the one, and I do like the other. And so you must know that for the last several months I have been quietly occupying a room in Boston, attending medical lectures, going to the Massachusetts Hospital, and slicing and slivering the carcasses of better men and women than I ever was myself or am like to be. It is a sin for a puny little fellow like me to mutilate one of your six-foot men as if he was a sheep, — but *vive la science!*

I must write a piece and call it records of the dissecting room, so let me save all my pretty things, as plums for my pudding. If you would die fagged to death like a crow with the king birds after him, — be a school-master; if you would wax thin and savage, like a half-fed spider, — be a lawyer; if you would go off like an opium-eater in love with your starving delusions, — be a doctor.

"I must write a piece. . . . *Let me save all my pretty things, as plums for my pudding.*"

Oliver Holmes was finding himself. Action was important; one's blood called for action, whether it was the slicing of carcasses or the shove that sent a wherry from boat-slip to river. But what really mattered was to *remember* the slicing, remember the glint on the river beyond the bridge's shadow. Not to remember dimly, as a vague, completed pleasure. The act of memory must be one with the experience itself. While the thing was happening, Oliver experienced it with a joyful, painful vividness, phrase by phrase as it were, dimly conscious that later when, pen in hand, he called upon these phrases, they would come back to him.

It was a kind of double living, the success of which could be proved only by Oliver's readers. Strangers, reading what he wrote, must feel as Oliver had felt. If they did not so feel, then Oliver knew that he had failed, and his own experience turned to ashes within him. There was in this no shred of altruism; Oliver Holmes had no desire to give boat trips to the poor of Boston or to the rich. He was an artist and acted from the artist's necessity to record and thus fix forever — shake off forever — the impressions that crowded so mercilessly, demanding release.

Around the supper table at 2, Central Court, Oliver observed his fellow boarders with acutest interest, trying to place them, each in his proper niche. He ended by putting them all into an essay and calling it "The Autocrat of the Breakfast-Table." This was not the real Autocrat that we know today; it would be twenty-six years before Oliver wrote for the *Atlantic Monthly* the series that made him famous. This was only the germ, the first beginning of the Autocrat. Imagining himself at the head of the table at 2, Central Court, Oliver conversed with his fellow boarders: —

"Madam," said I, "society is the same in all large places. I divide it thus:

"1. People of cultivation, who live in large houses.
"2. People of cultivation, who live in small houses.
"3. People without cultivation, who live in large houses.
"4. People without cultivation, who live in small houses.
"5. Scrubs."

An individual at the upper end of the table, turned pale and left the room, as I finished with the monosyllable.

Reading over what he had written, it occurred to Oliver it sounded smug. He added a sentence: —

"I have heard you spoken of, as a respectable young man," said a fellow creature.

"I am not a respectable young man — if I were nothing better, I would take an anodyne that should make me sleep until the funeral flame of the universe had split the stone above me."

Signing the essay with his initials, Oliver sent it to the *New England Magazine*. It was published in November. Nobody noticed it. Oliver followed it with one more paper on the same subject and then turned again to medicine.

Recovering from the shock of the operating theater and the dissecting room, he began to love medicine. His brother John was graduated from Harvard that summer of 1832 and thought of going to the Law School. "If I do," John said, "I shall stay there until I have my degree. For the honor of the family," John added. "To prove there is one Holmes, anyhow, that can get through law school."

Oliver laughed. "Does President Quincy know your name yet, John?" The new president of Harvard was notoriously forgetful of names. When a student entered his study, Quincy's greeting never varied: "Good day. What's your name?"

John grinned. "Cousin Josiah Quincy has changed his greeting. When I walked into his study just before Commencement he looked up as brisk as you please and said, '*Good* morning, Holmes — What's your name?'"

Josiah Quincy's vagueness on small matters did not extend to his principles. There he was as firm as Abiel Holmes. Quincy had lately come out against slavery, denouncing the plantation interests as a "dangerous and rising tyranny." For a president of Harvard this was surprising radicalism. Slaves were property, and a due esteem for property, Boston well knew, was the cornerstone of civic virtue. There was a graduate of Harvard, however, who agreed with Quincy. Down in Congress, John Quincy Adams had presented an abolition petition from the Philadelphia Society of Friends. In Boston William Garrison published the first issue of his wild, inflammatory newspaper, with its engraved heading of a slave in chains. The *Liberator*, the paper was called.

New names were appearing on the Harvard faculty. "I have met Professor Longfellow," Oliver wrote to Phineas Barnes; "one of your 'down East' folks, and a very nice sort of body he seems to be."

Oliver's classmates were coming into prominence in various fields. Sam Smith, recently graduated from the Andover Theological Seminary, had just written a hymn which, while it did not at once attain the popularity of "Old Ironsides," was popular enough to cause slight twinges to the official class poet of '29. The hymn began "My country, 'tis of thee." Oliver read it and found obscurity in the lines. One phrase especially rankled; Oliver took it to its author . . . "Like *that* above," Oliver quoted. "What does 'that' refer to, Sam?"

"That rapture," Smith replied serenely. Oliver's lip curled. If *he* had been responsible for the line, he told himself indignantly, *his* heart would not with rapture swell, "like that above." . . .

In the autumn of 1832 there was a Presidential election. Andrew Jackson was running for a second term. The Whigs fought hard against him — as bitterly opposed to the man they called King Andrew as the English Whigs had been to King George IV. Jackson was elected. . . . If the President should tour New England, said Josiah Quincy, Harvard must give him a degree. The University had given honorary degrees to Washington, Monroe, and both Adamses; if they withheld one from Jackson, it would be a slur to the office of President of the United States.

John Quincy Adams was disgusted with his Alma Mater. "A degree?" he said. "To that barbarian, that brawler from Tennessee?"

Abiel Holmes, lacking but a year of seventy, watched the controversy mildly. He missed writing the *Annals;* there was so much he could record! Daniel Webster was a Senator; his speeches against Calhoun and nullification were magnificent and there was talk that he would be the next Whig candidate for President. Abiel's new church grew in strength and influence, but to Abiel's distress his elders plunged into a lawsuit with the old parish over possession of the church moneys. Abiel's church was only one of dozens that split in the great Unitarian schism; there were so many lawsuits over church properties that the Supreme Court made a final decision: church moneys belonged always to the church that remained; the "go-outers" could take nothing with them.

Abiel lost the communion plate, the library he had so painstakingly gathered volume by volume, the poor fund, and Jacob Wendell's big Bible with the date 1740 on the flyleaf. Loss of his possessions did not disturb Abiel. What shocked him was the ferocity of the lawsuit; his faithful parishioners fought tooth for tooth with their one-time brethren, savagely ignoring their pastor's preaching of peace.

Oliver Holmes, observing these skirmishes, decided that the parishioners were enjoying themselves. Where meekness of spirit was concerned, Oliver told his father, there seemed little to choose between the followers of orthodoxy and heterodoxy. . . . In January, 1833, Oliver completed his studies under Dr. Jackson. The next step was a foregone conclusion — he must go abroad and become familiar with the great European hospitals. Fortunately, the Wendell inheritance made it possible. When Dr. Jackson had been young the place to go was London; Jackson himself had worked as a "dresser" at St. Thomas's. Now he recommended Paris. The best physicians in the world, he said, were to be found at La Pitié and at the Hôtel Dieu.

Dr. Jackson's son was a medical student in Paris; his father wrote that Oliver Holmes would join him soon; "Holmes knows more about my courses this winter than any one — he spent three or four months in the hospital as apothecary. . . . He can tell you much that is interesting. Do not mind his apparent frivolity and you will soon find that he is intelligent and well informed. He has the true zeal."

In March, 1833, Oliver went down to New York to sail for France. It was his first sight of any city larger than Boston, and he was not impressed. Half of Boston, he found, was sailing with him on the packet: Dr. Bigelow, the Curtises, the Whitwells, Bob Hooper, and Tom Appleton. In Paris more of Boston awaited him; besides young Jackson there were Warren and Bowditch. The latter, son of the great author of the *Practical Navigator*, bore a name, Holmes found, that was a powerful introduction in Europe. "The students from all lands are gathered together," Oliver wrote home, "and the great harvest of the year is open to all of us. . . . The young men here are more feared and perhaps more respected than with us. I can say more particularly in scientific matters that there is nothing at all resembling the patriarchal authority which so often has held the place of sound reason."

At La Pitié, at the Hôtel Dieu, Oliver sat at the feet of great men in medicine. For each he had a description, and his pictures did not lack for vividness: Andral the eloquent, Broussais the old volcano. The master surgeon, Baron Dupuytren. Lisfranc, in his big white apron — drawer of blood and hewer of members, who regretted the passing of Napoleon's guardsmen because "they had such magnificent thighs to amputate." The lively Ricord, whom Oliver called the Voltaire of pelvic literature — a skeptic as to the morality of the race in general, who believed that every woman had taken her pleasure where she could find it and that even the vestal virgins would be the better for a treatment with his mineral specifics or a course of his blue pills.

Of all these doctors, it was Louis whom Oliver admired most, the great Dr. Louis who told his students: —

> *Formez toujours les idées nettes.*
> *Fuyez les à peu près.*

Oliver repeated the words often, and strove to act upon them. But it was hard to be precise when the instruments for precision were not yet available. Chevalier's microscope was used only by the initiated. On the stone floor of the autopsy room at La Pitié, Oliver stood for hours working over points which later the microscope would settle easily.

By the summer of 1834 Oliver began getting letters from home, suggesting his return. But he longed to travel; months ago he had written eloquently to his father, beseeching funds. "A boy is worth his manure as much as a potato patch."

It was a telling phrase; Abiel had put out many dollars on his garden behind the Gambrel-roofed House. He sent the money. Oliver went to London. On a summer evening he went to the opera and watched the Royal Family enter its box. "The king," Oliver wrote, "blew his nose twice, and wiped the royal perspiration repeatedly from a face which is probably the largest uncivilized spot in England."

Oliver traveled, before he was through, to Scotland, Holland, and Italy. "Have you got any news?" he wrote gaily to his parents. "Any scandal — any fun, from the ancient seat of learning? How come on the *bourgeoisie* of the community? How flourish the red and white roses of orthodoxy and heterodoxy?"

Oliver Holmes had grown up. He was a man; he no longer feared his father but spoke his mind as he saw fit. He went to every theater in Paris and wrote home enthusiastically to a parent who would never dream of entering these palaces of sin, adding at the end, "There is no need of cutting or tearing off this last page about theatres; where society is far advanced they must exist and are a blessing . . . but as generations change if they do not degenerate, you must excuse these little remarks, and not waste your next letter in refuting them."

Early in November of 1835, Oliver sailed for home. He had been abroad thirty months; the Parisian medical world had taught him three principles of the profession. Oliver listed them: "*Not to take authority when I can have facts; not to guess when I can know; not to think a man must take physic because he is sick.*" Before he left Paris, Oliver had been able to procure one of Chevalier's microscopes. Dr. Jackson would be enthralled; Jackson kept up with the times. In his stateroom Oliver unwrapped the instrument, fingering it lovingly. If he could manage to slant the pipe a trifle, the eye would not water looking down; when he got home he would rig up an arrangement so a candle could be fastened to the platform, throwing light onto the slide.

Oliver returned bearing gifts — a shawl for his mother, Italian lace for his sisters. But the objects he really valued were not half so conventional: four skulls and two human skeletons. One skeleton was for himself, but the big one — Oliver called it the "showier one" — was for his brother-in-law, Dr. Parsons. His sister Mary would scream when she saw it and so would the children. Oliver felt its long bones through the wrapping: was every man, dead or alive, so much taller than he?

The trip from Le Havre to New York took forty-three days; it was December when Oliver reached Cambridge. Snow had fallen. How white and deep it was, and how quiet the lanes of Cambridge after the noisy cobblestones of Paris! His mother looked well and as brisk as ever, but when he saw his father, Oliver was shocked. Why, his father was an old man, white-haired, frail. His hickory cane stood always by the door; walking down the icy path to the gate, he leaned heavily on it. Oliver, watching, saw him stop to speak to a child, reach a mittened hand in the pocket of his greatcoat and give the child something. Since Oliver could remember, his father had carried candy to give to children. But this time it was an old man's gesture. Tears scalded Oliver's eyes.

John was at home, working away at the law and not too communicative about it. It was their father who did the talking, retailing news both local and nation-wide. The air was full of faction, Abiel said. Full of terrible strife. Only four months ago William Garrison, whose anti-slavery paper, the *Liberator*, became with every number more inflammatory, had been dragged about the streets of Boston by a mob — a rope around his neck. The anti-Catholic faction had been busy with mischief. Of course Oliver had heard about the burning of the Ursuline Convent in the summer of '34, but did he realize the fire could be seen from their own Cambridge doorstep? The flames had been terrible against the night sky. *Hell to the Pope!* the rioters had chalked on what remained of plaster. The better element of the community was shocked of course.

Oliver's mother, breaking in, said she was not so sure of this last. What about Mr. Houghton the butcher, a respectable character certainly? When Louisa Higginson had expressed her horror, Mr. Houghton had only said, "Well I dunno, Mis' Higginson, I guess them bishops are pretty dissipated characters."

Oliver roared with laughter, then, catching sight of his father's face, was suddenly sobered. In his father's smile was more of benediction than of mirth. It was as though Abiel had passed beyond mirth to something more merciful, something that left the mark of kindness on his face. How beautiful the old were, when they were *good!* Two years ago, Oliver could not have thought of his father in such terms, but he thought in them now.

Abiel the annalist was eager with his news. Extraordinary mechanical inventions had appeared in the factories and on the farms; news of them tempted men into wild financial speculation. Had Oliver heard of McCormick's new machine, drawn by horses, that reaped a field in a third the time it used to take? The sewing machine, the steel plough board, iron used to build ships — had Oliver heard of these in Europe? One of the strangest things of all had been the sending of a shipload of ice to Calcutta. Ice! Loaded from the Long Wharf in the heat of August, Abiel said wonderingly. Sam Eliot's new house on Beacon Street actually had a box constructed to hold ice; it kept the meat in warm weather. The house had a bathtub too, fastened to the floor upstairs. Everyone in town went calling on the Eliots, pretending they came to see the fine English furniture and

European paintings. But it was the icebox and bathtub they really talked about.

His own church, Abiel said, was prospering. But the country at large seemed in the grip of a feverish excitement; it was like a body that had grown too fast for its heart. Men blamed it on Andrew Jackson. Jackson had been too long in the White House. Power was dangerous; there was rumor he might accept a third term and the Whigs were busy organizing for the 1836 election. It was a pity Oliver had missed Jackson's visit to Cambridge in June of '33. The University had given him a degree over the protest of half the Corporation. Abiel had gone to the ceremony; in spite of himself he must confess the man had something about him that inspired respect. He was lean as a greyhound and held himself like a soldier; his long white hair streamed in the breeze like a flag of battle. He had answered President Quincy's oration briefly; Cambridge had been surprised there was no backwoods accent. The cheering afterward had been tremendous. Abiel had caught himself shouting with the rest although he approved none of Jackson's politics, domestic or foreign.

People sought stimulation as drunkards seek liquor; Abiel suspected they even came to church to hear theatrical preaching rather than to attain calm and humility before the Lord. Crazy sects were arising. Had Oliver heard of the Groaners, the Campbellites, the Perfectionists? Out West they had huge camp meetings, orgies of excitement, and dared to call it religion.

Oliver had not heard these things, nor was he abashed by the recital. All his life, humility had been preached to him; since his return home his brother-in-law, the Reverend Charles Wentworth Upham, had joined his voice to the chorus. But to Oliver, his father's news meant merely that the world was moving. Oliver desired not to censure or impede, but to move with it.

What he immediately sought was a medical degree from Harvard. With six months in which to win it, he prepared his dissertation on Acute Pericarditis, received his M.D. and was made a member of the Massachusetts Medical Society. Then he wrote another dissertation, choosing a local subject this time: "Intermittent Fever in New England." Page by page he examined the works of old colonial writers and recorded their every mention of fever, omitting only the moralistic treatises of the Reverend Cotton Mather which, Oliver observed, were more likely to cause a fever than to cure one.

He handed in his essay to the proper committee, and some weeks later announced the result to the brother-in-law who had cautioned against the sin of pride: —

To Charles W. Upham

BOSTON, *August* 4, 1836

MY VERY DEAR SIR, — The lesson of humility which you were anxious I should receive has found some other customers. The Boylston prize was almost unanimously awarded to my dissertation. . . . It is somewhat pleasant to have cut out a fifty-dollar prize under the guns of two old blazers [the doctors Haxall and Bell] who have each of them swamped their competitors in preceding trials.

Oliver had a wonderful time that Commencement season. It was Harvard's two hundredth anniversary and the festivities were memorable. At the alumni dinner Oliver, standing on a chair, was immensely surprised to find himself singing a solo. And at the Phi Beta Kappa celebration, Oliver recited a poem he had written for the occasion. It was no mean feat; the recital took an hour and ten minutes. Oliver declaimed the whole from memory, standing on the platform, stretched to his full height of five feet five. The audience loved it. When Oliver mentioned a local name — Dr. Jackson's for instance — they clapped loudly, and when he said something funny they cheered.

Abiel Holmes, hearing of all this, was disturbed. Oliver's Boylston Prize had not won for him half the applause these foolish performances were receiving. To be known as a wit could be of no possible advantage to a physician; it might even militate against him. This frivolity of Oliver's seemed not to decrease with age but rather to flaunt itself. Moreover, people seemed unable to resist it.

Abiel determined to speak to his son, caution him against being too free with his quips and his puns. But when he told his wife, she shook her head doubtfully, reminding Abiel that his son was no longer a boy, to be advised, scolded, protected. Oliver was twenty-seven. He was a grown man, and must follow his nature.

CHAPTER SEVEN

Oliver Holmes is a physician. Death of Abiel
Holmes. Oliver marries a Jackson and names
his first-born Oliver Wendell Holmes.

OLIVER moved across the river to Boston, rented a room, and set himself up as a physician. A lamp burned behind his office door, plainly to be seen through the glass, signifying that night and day the smallest favors — or fevers, said young Dr. Holmes — were welcome. A drunken young man put his fist through the door one night and broke the light, but beyond this nobody noticed either light or doctor's sign.

Dr. Holmes was not humbled by this neglect of the public. Attendance on the sick distressed him; he felt sorry for them. He busied himself writing medical essays; as if one Boylston Prize were not enough he decided to try for another. He wrote on "Neuralgia" and "Direct Exploration in Medical Practice." It seemed to him the profession was too wrapped in theory and the dusty prestige of learning. Why could not the doctors recount what they *saw* in the hospitals, what they felt with their hands and smelled with their noses, rather than what some long-dead medico had thought about?

Before the New Year (1837) Oliver had the satisfaction of seeing his poems in print, published in Boston in a small volume. His verses had been printed before, in college *Annuals* and various modest collections, but unsigned, "in order that," Oliver wrote a classmate, "nobody might suppose I was ambitious of being considered a regular scribbler." Now, with a Boylston Prize to his credit and a physician's sign on his door, he risked recognition and the obloquy of being called a wit. "Old Ironsides" was in the little volume; there was a poem on the Cambridge Churchyard, there was one on the September Gale of 1815, when Oliver's Sunday breeches had been torn from the line in the parsonage yard.

And there was a poem about an old man Oliver had often seen in the street, a venerable relic of the Revolution, who had helped throw the tea overboard in Boston Harbor. Major Melville, his name was, and the poem was called "The Last Leaf." It described the old man, tottering about —

> . . . a crook is in his back,
> And a melancholy crack
>   In his laugh.
>
> I know it is a sin
> For me to sit and grin
>   At him here;
> But the old three-cornered hat,
> And the breeches, and all that,
>   Are so queer!
>
> And if I should live to be
> The last leaf upon the tree
>   In the spring, —
> Let them smile, as I do now,
> At the old forsaken bough
>   Where I cling.

Of the whole volume, Abiel Holmes preferred this poem. It was like himself, he said, smiling. A relic of the past, of times and ways that were vanishing. "Nonsense!" his sons replied stoutly. "Father, you will live to be a hundred."

Abiel shook his head. He continued in his pastoral duties, preaching occasionally on Sundays from his pulpit. But except for his immediate family he kept to himself; he was too tired, he said, to visit all these new people in Cambridge. Professor Longfellow was boarding at Craigie House now, with Dr. Worcester, who was revising his American Dictionary. New generations of Lowells, Danas, Higginsons, Channings, Wares, were coming up. Young Dick Dana who had shipped as a common sailor and traveled half around the world in two years, trying to cure weak eyes, had come home and was studying for a Boylston Prize in elocution. Life was moving fast, Abiel said. He would not try to move with it.

In January, 1837, Abiel preached a sermon that touched his congregation deeply. Its subject was "The vanity of life, a reason for seeking a portion in Heaven." Abiel did not say it was his farewell. Perhaps he did not himself realize it. But all who heard it sensed a prophetic note.

They were not mistaken. It was Abiel's last sermon. That very week he was taken ill. It was not an illness Abiel's son could diagnose or cure. It was more a weakness, a fading away. Abiel Holmes, at seventy-three, was preparing for his departure. He was not bedridden; he walked slowly about the house, sitting in the evenings before the fire while his wife or sons read aloud from the Bible, from Saurin's *Sermons*, or sometimes, to Abiel's great pleasure, from the *Annals of America*. There was a new President in the White House. Andrew Jackson had named his successor and had gone back to his Hermitage in Tennessee. The successor did not interest Abiel, but the state of the nation interested him deeply.

Abiel had said that the country, under Jackson, was growing too fast for its heart. He had been terribly right. The inventions Abiel had catalogued for his son — the steam locomotive, the steel plough board, the sewing machine and the reaper — Jackson had not brought these to the nation, but they had come while he was President and they had brought mad speculation with them. Jackson's eight years had weathered it somehow — the speculation and the wildcat schemes, the too quick westward expansion, unsoundness of the state banks and floods of paper money loosed upon the country. Now Jackson was gone, and punishment fell. Panic broke in a fury north, west, and south, the worst financial panic the Union had ever experienced. The country, looking as usual to the White House, blamed it on Martin Van Buren.

Abiel Holmes was not greatly surprised; it was by no means the first time he had seen the mighty humbled and the rich made poor. Men put too much store upon earthly things, upon corruptible possessions and the piling up of riches. The vanity of life, Abiel had lately told his congregation, was reason for seeking a portion in heaven.

Late in May of 1837, Abiel had a stroke. It left him helpless, he could speak only with difficulty. Sally Holmes, strong, competent, tended him, her sons helping when a man's arm was needed. Sally was sixty-eight; she seemed not a day over fifty. Her gray hair curled

crisply at the edges, her brown eyes were bright as ever, her skin
pink. When Nellie, carrying basins and trays up from the kitchen,
wept audibly at the sickroom door, her mistress rebuked her. "Have
you forgotten that Dr. Holmes loves a cheerful face?"

Sitting by her husband's side, Sally waited through the long hours.
When Abiel roused, she seemed to know by a touch of the hand
what he wanted. Once Oliver, coming in the door, stood while
she finished singing, softly, Abiel's own hymn that he had written
long ago about his Meeting-house . . .

> Thy flock, Immanuel, here was fed,
> In pastures green and fair,
> Beside still waters gently led,
> And thine the shepherd's care.
> ....
>
> Here may the church thy cause maintain,
> Thy truth with peace and love,
> Till her last earth-born live again
> With the first-born above.

On Sunday morning, June 4, the watchers round the bedside
noticed a change. Abiel was restless, his lips moved. Oliver, leaning
over the bed, caught the words his father was trying to articulate.
"If any have injured me, let the injuries . . . let the injuries . . ."

Oliver repeated the words aloud, looking at his mother with a
puzzled face. Sally Holmes did not hesitate. She stood up and spoke
clearly to her husband. *"If any have injured me, let their injuries
be written in sand."*

Abiel's eyes opened, his lips moved in acquiescence. On the dark
plank floor the sun made a pattern by the window; outside, maple
leaves stirred in the breeze. A church bell sounded, then another.
Sally Holmes, her eyes on her husband's face, waited for the bell
from his own Meeting-house. Among many voices she would know
it and so, she was aware, would her husband.

The bell spoke. Abiel turned his face toward the sound, and died.

After his father's funeral, Oliver Holmes returned to Boston.
John stayed on in the old house with his mother. Oliver worked on
his medical essays for the Boylston Prize — and a few weeks later was
able to write his moralistic brother-in-law, the Reverend Upham

(of whom he was in reality very fond), a second brief note of victory: —

BOSTON, *August* 3, 1837

DEAR MR. U————. Both prizes unanimously.

Oliver had received not only the first but the second prize, one for each essay. Sally Holmes was proud of her son, sad that his father could not have lived to see his triumph. John, studying away at the law, and none too enthusiastic about it, expressed himself as surprised but gratified. At twenty-five, John knew himself for a man without ambition either for riches or for fame. What he desired was the love of his friends and this he achieved in abundance. People adored John Holmes. He was as quiet as his brother was talkative, yet the things John said delighted Cambridge and were repeated from mouth to mouth as they had once been repeated in the Holmes family. John was content, and his contentment was not the least part of his charm. Looking upon his brother, John marveled. It seemed to him that Oliver lived on a hot griddle, forever jumping and dancing, forever eager for what was to come next. The law — poems for banquets — odes for class dinners. Boylston Prizes by the half dozen — skeletons from Paris — microscopes — plans for a medical school — plans to found a family. And always, Oliver talked about it.

Listening, John wondered why his brother was not worn out long ago and ready for the grave. On the contrary, Oliver's incessant chatter seemed to renew him; he generated his own heat as he talked. Once only, goaded by an evening of steady soliloquy from Oliver — soliloquy that by no means excluded some carefully contrived boasting — John burst out suddenly before the whole family, "If you ever find a girl that can shut you up, Oliver — marry her! And marry her quick."

To Oliver, this was a highly unreasonable remark, lacking sense completely. Talking was one of the things he did best. Why should he want anyone — least of all a girl — to shut him up? But he remembered what John said; the words remained and would not leave him.

Some four weeks after Oliver won his Boylston Prizes — August 31, the date was — Ralph Waldo Emerson spoke at the annual Phi Beta Kappa celebration at Harvard. Oliver went of course. Emerson was six years his senior and, like Oliver, had been Class Poet. But Emerson had been a student of Channing's at the Harvard Divinity School, and had become a Unitarian Minister. He seemed now on the way to repudiate not only Unitarianism but Christianity. He had already lectured around Boston, but orthodox theologians refused to take him seriously; even Abiel Holmes had merely remarked that William Emerson's youngest boy seemed to be slow in settling down.

Today Emerson spoke on "The American Scholar." He had scarcely opened his mouth when half the audience — the older half — closed up tight with disapproval.* They could not know the speech marked an epoch. The very title was a paradox — The *American* Scholar. Scholarship belonged to the Old World, to England, to ancient Greece, Rome, Palestine. Where had Emerson got these impudent ideas? From Dr. Channing no doubt; Channing was always preaching an American kingdom of letters. But Channing at least spoke like an orator, with periods that were rounded and flowery. Whereas Emerson's address was a series of sharp, short statements, hurled from his mouth like charges from a musket. . . .

"Our day of dependence, our long apprenticeship to the learning of other lands, draws to a close. We have listened too long to the courtly muses of Europe! . . . We will walk on our own feet; we will work with our hands; we will speak our own minds. . . ."

In the audience, Oliver Holmes felt the hackles rise on the back of his neck. He sat bolt upright, his eyes fixed on the speaker's face. But this was marvelous, what Emerson was saying! It was a revelation; it was what he, Oliver Holmes, had longed to hear. It was what he had felt when he wrote "Old Ironsides," "The Last Leaf," and those essays describing the breakfast table at 2, Central Court. Homely essays whose characters spoke plainly, as one's neighbors speak. As . . . as *Americans* speak!

That was what Emerson was advocating. That was what he was urging these frowning scholars to do — to write like Americans, to think for themselves. "Meek young men grow up in libraries," Emerson went on, "believing it their duty to accept the views which

---

* One undergraduate, Edward Everett Hale, wrote in his diary afterward that Mr. Emerson was half crazy, his speech "not very good, and very transcendental." Another, James Russell Lowell, said the speech was our Yankee version of a lecture by Abélard.

Cicero, which Locke, which Bacon have given; forgetful that Cicero, Locke and Bacon were only young men in libraries when they wrote these books. . . ."

Two hours later, Oliver Holmes, walking across Harvard Square, tingling still from head to foot, told himself he knew what he had heard, today. He had heard the American *Declaration of Intellectual Independence*. And some day, somehow, he was going to act upon it.

All that winter of 1837–1838, Dr. Oliver Wendell Holmes waited for patients in his Boston office with the plate-glass door. When patients did not come he wrote poetry and more medical essays and spent long hours at the Massachusetts General Hospital, following his beloved Dr. Jackson on his rounds, asking questions and refusing to be satisfied with the answers. . . . Why did so many women die of childbed fever? Dr. Bigelow, a splendid surgeon, went from bed to bed in his workmanlike, bloodstained frock coat, using his instruments skillfully, then wiping them on an old towel and returning them to his bag. Why, out of a dozen strong young women, did six die? Oliver made himself a nuisance with his questions. He filled whole notebooks with details of these deaths and still his questions haunted him, unanswered.

In the evenings when he was not working, Oliver was restless. He supped out whenever he was invited. Boston had supper at six and called it "tea." It was natural that Oliver should go often to the Jacksons', both to the doctor's and to his brother the Judge's on Bedford Place. Amelia Jackson was as charming as ever. Phineas Barnes married and Oliver wrote him a long letter: "I wish I were [married] too. I have flirted and written poetry long enough. I have several very nice young women in my eye."

In 1839, Holmes accepted a part-time teaching position at Dartmouth College. He was required to be there only in August, September, and October, but the position had a salary and, what was more important, it carried the title *Professor of Anatomy*. Holmes was emboldened, when autumn came, to proceed with a long-cherished plan. With three other young physicians, he set up a small private medical school on Tremont Street. The school was moderately successful. Holmes began to feel himself established in his profession.

Walking to Bedford Place in the evenings to call on Amelia

Jackson, Oliver eyed the smaller houses along the side streets. Here would be a pleasant, economical place to live. Among the "several very nice young women" in Oliver's eye, there was no longer any doubt who held first place — Amelia Jackson of the warm heart, the quick tongue and bright brown eye. Oliver had known her, on and off, all his life; she called his mother "Cousin Sally." And how like his mother she was, Oliver thought often, watching Amelia's slight figure, her quick, impulsive ways. Amelia laughed easily and cried easily too; Oliver had been charmed by tears that dried as soon as they were shed, leaving their owner looking prettier than ever, refreshed, as it were, by her own spring rain.

The figure pleased him. He would tell it to Amelia if she should happen to cry again. But what if she didn't cry? Of course she would. He was going to marry Amelia; they were to live together forever and a day, and forever held opportunity for rivers of pretty tears. Oliver could not remember exactly when he had first known he wanted to marry Amelia Jackson. It may have been a week; to him it seemed an eternity. He had not asked her to marry him; he had not even hinted of love. Amelia had given him no chance to hint; she was always talking or asking questions so that he would talk. He was at his best with Amelia; with her in the room he could be unfailingly brilliant no matter who was present. To know her there, warm, attentive, eager for his success, gave him a blissful confidence.

Walking across Chauncy Street, Oliver came in sight of the Jackson house. Judge Jackson, long since retired from the Supreme Court of the Commonwealth, lived in one of the most beautiful houses in town, with a long garden behind it that looked, people said, like Judge Wendell's garden long ago on Oliver Street. Miss Amelia was in the library, the maid said. Oliver loved the Judge's library. It numbered no more books than the library at home and it was true there were far too many by Blackstone and Story and Chancellor Kent. But in all the long shelves there was not a volume of sermons. And there were so many new books! Carlyle's *French Revolution*, the poems of Wordsworth. American books too: Bryant's poems, the stories of Washington Irving in the *Knickerbocker* magazine. . . . Judge Jackson sent for everything as soon as it was published. On the library table there stayed a small blue volume called *Poems* by Oliver Wendell Holmes. Amelia had put it there;

she had not changed her opinion as to who was her favorite poet.

She was standing by the table when he came in, her long full skirts swept the floor. She picked up his poems. "This," she said, "is a very small book, and I know it by heart. Soon I shall be tired of it. When are you going to write more poetry?"

Oliver laughed. With all these poets on the shelves — Milton and Cowper, Horace and Coleridge — she surely did not need more volumes by O.W.H.?

"But I like my poets better alive than dead," Amelia said.

She moved a little forward, his book in her hand, her bright brown eyes looking sidewise at him. Oliver was entranced. For once, his tongue failed and he could think of no reply. He stood there, silent, and his brother's voice rang in his ears . . . *"If you can find a girl who can shut you up, marry her, Oliver, and marry her quick."*

He knew now, very suddenly, what John had meant. Amelia Jackson could shut him up. She could make him stop talking and *feel*, make him conscious of life itself, warm, urgent, to be sensed wholly, received wholly, not merely for reproduction on paper. . . .

It was a sensation delicious, exhilarating, and irresistibly impelling. Oliver took a step forward.

"Amelia," he began. "My *dear* Amelia . . ."

On the fifteenth of June, 1840, Boston enjoyed a delightful wedding. Miss Amelia Jackson married Dr. Oliver Wendell Holmes. The guests, leaving their carriages up the hill on Beacon Street, walked down a narrow, cobbled street to the pillared portico of King's Chapel.[1] Everybody was cousin to someone in the next pew, or if they were not related their grandparents had been intimately acquainted. The Jackson connection was enormous; the church could barely hold the Wendells, Olivers, Quincys.

At Judge Jackson's after the ceremony, the collation was magnificent. Jellies and sillabubs, iced cream in molds, fruits and meats of every description — and wine of course in abundance. Replete with food, wine, love, and the good will of their friends and relations, Oliver and his bride drove gayly off in the Judge's carriage.

It was autumn when they returned to Boston; on the Common the trees were bare of leaves, the cobbles glistened with a hard No-

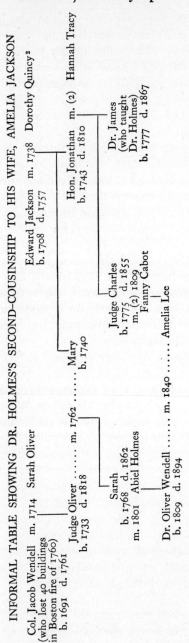

INFORMAL TABLE SHOWING DR. HOLMES'S SECOND-COUSINSHIP TO HIS WIFE, AMELIA JACKSON

Col. Jacob Wendell   m. 1714   Sarah Oliver
(who lost 40 buildings
in Boston fire of 1760)
b. 1691   d. 1761

Edward Jackson   m. 1738   Dorothy Quincy[2]
b. 1708   d. 1757

Judge Oliver ..... m. 1762 .... Mary
b. 1733   d. 1818   b. 1740

Hon. Jonathan   m. (2)   Hannah Tracy
b. 1743   d. 1810

Sarah
b. 1768   d. 1862
m. 1801   Abiel Holmes

Judge Charles
b. 1775   d. 1855
m. (2) 1809
Fanny Cabot

Dr. James
(who taught
Dr. Holmes)
b. 1777   d. 1867

Dr. Oliver Wendell ...... m. 1840 ...... Amelia Lee
b. 1809   d. 1894

vember rain. They went straight to their own house on Montgomery Place. Amelia had discovered it months ago; her father had bought it and given it to her, a three-story brick house just off the Common to the east, with ample room to raise a family. It had gaslight, running water in the kitchen sink, and it was set in a pleasant, quiet spot, a sort of dead-end court with a brick wall around it, a gate in front that gave down three steps into the street. Number 8, Montgomery Place, the address was.

Amelia plunged happily into housekeeping. She had a talent for domesticity, for making a man comfortable. Watching his wife bustle about the house, keys at her belt, Oliver was reminded again of his mother. Amelia had the same merry eye, the same unassailable practicality, and beneath it the same warm generous heart. And if there was not yet in Amelia that touch of poetry which raised his mother above practicality and the importance of jangling cupboard keys — well, that would come with age and a knowledge of the ways of mankind, Oliver sensed dimly.

In all her duties, Amelia Holmes displayed exemplary promptness. Eight months and twenty-eight days after her marriage — the date was March 8, 1841 — she gave birth to a son. Dr. Holmes sat down and wrote to everyone he knew, varying his announcement with a skill that pleased him quite as much as it pleased the recipients of the letters.

MY DEAR ANN [this to his younger sister, Ann Upham], Last evening between eight and nine there appeared at No. 8 Montgomery Place a little individual who may hereafter be addressed as

— HOLMES, Esq.

or

The Hon. — HOLMES, M. C.

or

His Excellency — Holmes, President, etc., etc., but who for the present is content with scratching his face and sucking his right forefinger.

There was no hesitancy over the name; what could it be but Oliver Wendell Holmes? They would call him Wendell, his father decided; he himself had always preferred it to Oliver. Looking into the cradle upon the son that bore his name, young Dr. Holmes was content.

The months passed; as Christmas approached, Holmes remembered his friend Phineas Barnes. "I believe you learned, when you were here," he wrote Barnes, "that there was a second edition of your old acquaintance, an o.w.h."

He was developing a virtuosity in these announcements, Holmes told himself with satisfaction. Much neater than his own father's announcement of his — Oliver Holmes's — birth in the old almanac . . . "*Aug. 29 . . . son b.*" — with nothing but a little mark to emphasize the importance of the event.

o.w.h. Small print and no capital letters. In his cradle o.w.h. lay quiet and noisy by turns, as a healthy baby should. *o.w.h., a second edition.* There was none to prophesy that the letters might grow large and larger until the whole country might see them, and countries beyond the water: —

OLIVER WENDELL HOLMES, Chief Justice of Massachusetts, author of *The Common Law*, Associate Justice of the United States Supreme Court.

PART II

Oliver Wendell Holmes, Junior. 1841-1861

CHAPTER EIGHT

State of the Union when o.w.h. was born. Boston.
Dr. Holmes becomes Professor of Anatomy
at the Harvard Medical School.

o.w.h. was born into a Union of twenty-seven states, presided over by the Whig, General William Henry Harrison, who had got into the White House by way of the most ridiculous Presidential campaign ever staged before or since. Tippecanoe and Tyler too, the log cabin never lived in, the hard cider never drunk. In a month old Tippecanoe was dead of pneumonia; his Democratic Vice President took his place and pleased nobody. Henry Clay was in the Senate, battling Tyler with all the fire and fury that still burned at sixty-odd. John Quincy Adams was in Congress fighting the gag rule. Plymouth County, Massachusetts, had sent him there and it had made the old man very happy. But it had not made his friends in Boston happy. An undignified move, they called it on Bedford Square. The idea of a man once President of the United States and ambassador to three countries, getting out and running for election like any twopenny politician! "My election as President of the United States was not half so gratifying to my inmost soul," wrote Adams in his diary. "I say this to record my sentiments; but no stranger intermeddleth with my joys, and the dearest of my friends have no sympathy with my sensations."

Daniel Webster was Secretary of State. Settled outside of town in his country place, Marshfield, he was Boston's hero more than ever. Shipowners and millowners could count on his shrewd, eloquent support. The China trade flourished; clippers, slim and beautiful, raced from Minot's Light eastward to Liverpool. The panic of 1837 was almost forgotten. If the eighteenth century had died in '37 — as some economists say it did — Boston was happily unaware of it. Boston aristocracy, substituting the ledgers of the countinghouse for the heraldic marks of a past century, lived comfortably, worked hard, and prospered. In the Cabots' spacious yard on Winthrop Place just round the corner from the Holmeses, pear trees bloomed, the garden nymph looked down from her fountain, and from the stable in the alley old Samuel drove the pair round to the door, harness gleaming, livery spotless.

In Lawrence and Lowell, spindles whirled. Every sound businessman knew the twelve-hour day was an excellent thing for workers. "The morals of the operatives," one of them told the Massachusetts Legislature, "will necessarily suffer if longer absent from the wholesome discipline of factory life." In the middle states the working day had been reduced to ten hours — a dangerous move. Had not man long ago been commanded to eat bread by the sweat of his brow? The five Lawrence brothers, all rich, all philanthropic, were sure of it. They themselves had never shirked hard work. Hard work was a Puritan principle, a Calvinistic inheritance. *In Adam's fall, We sinned all* . . . Adam's fall could be expiated not alone by prayer and churchgoing but by hard, continuous labor. If the labor resulted in money, so much the better.

Money, work, and God. A reasonable trinity, one that America could worship with enthusiasm. Laziness, thriftlessness, reckless spending — these were sins against the Holy Ghost. A man of fortune must work unceasingly to increase his money. Only in Europe did men live without working. It had resulted in tyranny.

Work, money, God: a new religion took hold of the American Union, to rule a hundred years and more.

And yet — voices rose in protest. In New England, in Boston, the very hold and center of the arcana, voices cried Nay. Combat this new materialism not with prayer but with good works! Reform the prisons, the insane asylums. Give rights to women. Abolish debtors' prisons — drunkenness — pauperism. Be merciful to the deaf and dumb, teach the blind to live. Samuel Gridley Howe, the mantle of his Greek adventures still upon him, exiled himself to South Boston and, with his spirited young wife, Julia Ward, taught the blind until the whole country talked of sightless, deaf, speechless Laura Bridgman.

Reform, reform! And if reform move too slowly for the winged spirit, withdraw from wickedness to Brook Farm and dig the soil, to Fruitlands and read Goethe, enjoying the perfect life. "Not a reading man but has a draft of a new community in his waistcoat pocket," Emerson wrote to Carlyle. "I am gently mad myself, and am resolved to live cleanly." Dr. Holmes's schoolmate of the sinuous neck, Margaret Fuller, translated the *Conversations with Goethe*, wrote midnight letters to Beethoven, and held her own Conversations in West Street. It was her mission to GROW, she said, and she hastened to fulfill it.

It was all mad, foolish, inspired — and to Dr. Holmes it held no appeal whatever. Of all the literary group about to burst into flower — Emerson, Lowell, Longfellow, Motley, and the rest — Dr. Holmes was the only one with a scientific training. It removed him from these others, leaving him neither time nor faith for fancy new remedies, spiritual or social. It seemed to Holmes that the great men were not in the reformer's pulpit — they were at Harvard. Dr. Bigelow in medicine, Dr. Warren in anatomy, Asa Gray in natural history. All over the East, scientists were organizing into groups for closer intercourse and the exchange of ideas; in Boston the American Society of Geologists held its first meeting, the Lowell Institute was attracting crowds to its forums. In the hospital, the sight of people dying left Dr. Holmes no heart to reform the living; first of all a way must be found to make men stay alive. Every autumn, scores of people died in Boston from typhoid fever. Charles Sumner had it. When he recovered, people were surprised to see him looking quite plump. "Almost human," Julia Howe said. In summer Asiatic cholera came to town. The deaths from puerperal fever continued to distress Holmes. These mothers were young and strong. Why should they die?

People said homeopathy would cure puerperal fever. Holmes loathed homeopathy. He gave two lectures against it, angry, witty lectures, called it a pseudo-science, and all the while continued his studies of puerperal fever. In England, Scotland, Vienna, doctors had already suspected the fever was contagious. But American doctors did not read German and there was little scientific exchange with England. Lister was a boy in his teens, the germ theory was unknown, contagiousness was proved only by the observations of common sense and the deductions of what was called medical logic.

Common sense happened to be the quality Dr. Holmes possessed perhaps beyond all other qualities. Slowly, painstakingly, he collected his evidence. Puerperal fever was carried from bed to bed by doctors, nurses, midwives. No one knew whether the physician carried infection in the atmosphere about him, or by direct application of hand to surface. The fact remained that the physician who came to a delivery direct from the autopsy room brought death to his patient. Even a change of clothes was not sufficient safeguard. Physicians whose maternity patients showed a high mortality rate confessed that even though they left their coats in the autopsy room, the mother died after they had attended her.

Only the courage of a few physicians had brought this to light. Dr. Gordon of Scotland had confessed the disease was as communicable as smallpox, and that he had himself been the disagreeable means of carrying it to a great number of women. One midwife lost sixteen mothers in a month; others in the same district had none infected with the fever. A certain doctor in England, after seven patients died from the fever, changed his clothes, underwent "a thorough purification." Yet his next patient died. Could the contagion be carried in his gloves? The doctor discarded them. Could it be in the instruments with which he had given enemas to the women, using the same instruments from bed to bed?

But behind those physicians who dared make public their failures lay a dark regiment of unpublished deaths. A doctor whose patients die by the half dozen soon loses his practice. Better for the doctor to say the deaths were unavoidable.

It was a terrible body of evidence. Case by case, citing name, date, place, circumstance, Dr. Holmes put it all down. He called his paper "The Contagiousness of Puerperal Fever," and read it in Boston before the Society for Medical Improvement. In April, 1843, he published it in the *New England Quarterly Journal of Medicine and Surgery*.

The profession rose up in arms, hurling angry refutation. Dr. Holmes had trod on too many toes. Reputations were at stake; the controversy would rage for years. Now and again Holmes answered his critics. "I am too much in earnest for either humility or vanity, but I do entreat those who hold the keys of life and death to listen to me also for this once. I ask no personal favor; but I beg to be

Dr. Holmes

heard in behalf of those women whose lives are at stake, until some stronger voice shall plead for them."

Holmes's own wife was safely delivered that autumn. They named the baby after her mother: Amelia Jackson Holmes, born October 20, 1843. The household on Montgomery Place was very busy. Holmes lectured, wrote medical essays, wrote verses and more verses. The dinner for Charles Dickens, nearly two years ago, had established the doctor forever as Boston's premier *poète d'occasion*. The town had gone quite wild over Dickens; at this particular dinner, given by the Young Men of Boston, Dr. Holmes had stood on a chair to lead his song. Richard Dana had been disgusted at this adulation; his two years before the mast had not made him tolerant. "I shan't go to see Dickens unless sent for," he wrote in his diary. "I can't submit to sink the equality of a gentleman by crowding after a man of note."

Tom Appleton went, though, and said the great man looked like a thousand London shopkeepers — if you took the genius out of his face. Appleton was perhaps the only man of birth in Boston who did not work for his living. He wrote a little, traveled in Europe, imbibed culture. "I have the temperament of a genius without the genius," he said. Surprisingly, Boston forgave him. Besides being handsome and invariably entertaining, Appleton was rich.

Dr. Holmes went right on with his poems: a poem for the dinner after Edward Everett's inauguration as president of Harvard, a poem for the Berkshire Jubilee. He wrote one about the steam boats, too, that came up to the wharves every hour. One could hear their whistles from Montgomery Place. They were frail-looking, paddle-wheel affairs with a thin, straight funnel; the clippers could beat them down the harbor if the wind was favorable. But to Holmes they were all-glorious: —

> See how yon flaming herald treads
> The ridged and rolling waves,
> As, crashing o'er their crested heads,
> She bows her surly slaves!
> With foam before and fire behind,
> She rends the clinging sea,
> That flies before the roaring wind,
> Beneath her hissing lea.

As a poet, Dr. Holmes was nothing if not direct. He knew well enough it was dangerous for him to make fun of doctors, but he could not resist it. His beloved Dr. Jackson was compiling a book, *Advice to the Young Physician.* "Enter the sick room with grave demeanor," wrote Jackson. "Then your patient will know you feel for him. But leave with a cheerful countenance, so the sick man will think his case is not too serious."

Holmes thought it over; how wise Dr. Jackson was! Would he himself ever reach this point of experience? He got out his pen to write some advice to young physicians himself. The result was so far from serious that it would have made Abiel Holmes turn in his grave: —

> If the poor victim needs must be percussed,
> Don't make an anvil of his aching bust;
> (Doctors exist within a hundred miles
> Who thump a thorax as they'd hammer piles;)
> So of your questions: don't in mercy try
> To pump your patient absolutely dry;
> He's not a mollusk squirming on a dish,
> You're not Agassiz, and he's not a fish.

Boston read the verses and rocked with mirth. Was it any wonder Dr. Holmes was not sent for by the solvent sick? The insolvent he treated daily in the wards on Fruit Street; they did not read books. But the ladies of Chauncy Street and Bedford Place, enjoying the vapors or something more serious, did not relish the advent into their sickroom of a small, sprightly man who might at any moment break out with a pun. Even anatomy, in which Holmes was deeply, seriously interested, tempted him to farce: —

> I was sitting with my microscope, upon my parlor rug,
> With a very heavy quarto and a very lively bug.

With it all, no one could possibly have said Dr. Holmes lacked seriousness of purpose. No one did say it. Wit bubbled from him; he could no more stop it than he could stop the blood flowing in his veins. He hated solemnity; he had seen too much of it in his youth and the reaction was lasting. Sanctimonious people made him sneeze, he said, and go home with a violent cold.

Amelia Holmes forgave her husband's puns. What good wife does not? She was too busy to hear them, half the time. Small Amelia was two now. Wendell was five, old enough to walk out the front door and sit on the steps of Montgomery Place under the iron trellis with its hanging lamp. At night the lamplighter came by, and by day sometimes the town crier.

That June of 1846, Wendell heard new sounds along the streets. Drums, and the high whistle of a fife. They were drumming for recruits to the Mexican War. All that month the sound recurred, echoing down from the Common. Boston anti-slavery men said New England should leave the Union rather than agree to the annexation of Texas. On the front page of Garrison's *Liberator* the ugly word *secession* was flaunted. Dr. Holmes shook his head; he was too much the scientist to have faith in extreme measures. Moreover the emotionalism of the Abolitionists made him suspect their sincerity — Burleigh with his long hair, Wright with his wild gesticulations. When Holmes did not come out openly for anti-slavery and temperance reform, James Russell Lowell, ten years his junior and as yet only an acquaintance, wrote him a long, severe letter, charging him with light-mindedness, with making frivolous poems in a time of national stress.

> I listen to your suggestions with great respect [Holmes replied]. I mean to reflect upon them, and I hope to gain something from them. . . . It is a mistake of yours to suppose me a thorough-going conservative. I am an out-and-out republican in politics. In a little club of ten physicians I rather think I occupy the extreme left of the liberal side of the house. The idea of my belonging to the party that resists all change is an entire misconception. . . . But I must say, with regard to art and the management of my own powers, I think I shall in the main follow my own judgment and taste rather than mould myself upon those of others. . . . As years creep over me . . . I shall not be afraid of gayety more than of old, but I shall have more courage to be serious. Let me try to improve and please my fellow-men after my own fashion at present.

Holmes did not lack the capacity for indignation. But at the present time he was occupied with men's physical rather than their moral ills. The sufferings of the sick, both men and animals, had always affected him strongly. When he needed a freshly killed rabbit for dissection he ran out of the room, asked Dr. Cheever to kill it, and begged him not to let the rabbit squeak. The operating room, the surgeon's knife, still filled him with horror. It was natural he should become intensely interested in experiments being carried on in Boston by a dentist, Dr. Morton, to produce insensibility by inhaling ether. Dr. Morton had tried ether on himself, sealing himself in a room and falling unconscious. In September of 1846 Morton used ether while pulling a patient's tooth. Shortly afterward, Dr. Warren of the Harvard Medical School asked Morton to give ether to a patient in the hospital about to undergo an operation.

The experiment was successful. Dr. Holmes was as happy as though it had been made on himself. After the drunken screams of former patients, what heavenly mercy was this! If only he could have helped! He could not — but he could suggest words for the men who made the discovery. He sat down and wrote to Dr. Morton: —

BOSTON, *Nov.* 21, 1846

MY DEAR SIR: Everybody wants to have a hand in a great discovery. All I will do is to give you a hint or two as to names — or the name — to be applied to the state produced, and the agent.

The state should, I think, be called "Anaesthesia." This signifies insensibility — more particularly (as used by Linnaeus and Cullen) to objects of touch.

The adjective will be Anaesthetic. . . . The words anti-neuric, aneuric, neuro-leptic, neurolepsia, neuro-stasis, etc., seem too anatomical; whereas the change is a physiological one. I throw them out for consideration.

I would have a name pretty soon, and consult some accomplished scholar, such as President Everett or Dr. Bigelow, senior, before fixing upon the terms, which *will be repeated by the tongues of every civilized race of mankind.* You could mention these words which I suggest, for their consideration; but there may be others more appropriate and agreeable.

Yours respectfully,
O. W. HOLMES

"Consult the president of Harvard." It was the sovereign remedy. How many of Dr. Holmes's family belonged to Harvard University! Before he was born, his great-uncle, Jonathan Jackson, had been treasurer of Harvard — a position much honored in Boston. Judge

Wendell had been a Fellow and Judge Jackson — Holmes's father-in-law — had been an Overseer. President Josiah Quincy had been a Holmes cousin.

In the spring of 1847, President Everett and the Corporation named Dr. Holmes Professor of Anatomy and Physiology in the Medical School. It was an enormous satisfaction. The doctors Jackson and Bigelow had thrown out hints that he might expect the appointment. Now it was accomplished. His life was laid out as he would have chosen. The path stretched ahead, broad and brisk, filled with honorable business that a man must bestir himself daily, hourly, to fulfill.

Looking at his family, Dr. Holmes felt a fervent satisfaction. He had two boys now, to enroll as future sons of Harvard. Wendell had a brother: Edward Jackson Holmes, born October 17, 1846.

Two boys and a girl; the family was complete. The household grew and prospered. Around the corner on Tremont Street, newsboys cried their wares. Newsboys had been invented with the telegraph, Dr. Holmes said — and the telegraph was several years old. Boston had opened a line with Springfield in January. The Mexican War was in full swing. James Lowell said it was all wrong. But Zachary Taylor had taken Monterrey and already Kearny's Dragoons moved on toward California. Along the Oregon Trail, prairie schooners crawled westward, a dusty, never-ending line. Fifteen thousand of the people calling themselves Mormons crossed Iowa.

And on the steps of Montgomery Place a small boy sat under an iron trellis and watched the world go by. One afternoon the butcher's boy stopped to talk. This was complimentary; the butcher's boy was big, and occupied with great businesses. Preparing at last to move on to regions of his own the butcher's boy made his salute. "Good-bye!" he said genially. "See you when your mother is hung."

Wendell Holmes sat frozen, glued to the steps. Why had they not told him? *When* would she be hanged? At sunrise? He had heard they did it at sunrise. Going inside, Wendell sought his mother, looked at her mutely. . . . At supper nobody talked of hanging. Wendell went up to bed; his mother came and kissed him good-night, heard his prayers. When she was gone he lay trembling. Downstairs on his mother's desk lay the new album she had given him for stamps. She had promised to help label the rarest ones. They were going to do it the first thing in the morning.

See you when your mother is hung . . . when your mother is hung. . . .

Wendell fell asleep. In the morning when he woke, the sun was shining; downstairs he heard his mother's voice.

Why, the butcher boy lied! The butcher boy was joking! Sitting on the side of his bed, hearing from below the blessed, familiar sounds of morning, Wendell's breath came deep with relief.

Springing to his feet, he threw on his clothes and clattered joyfully down the stairs to breakfast.

CHAPTER NINE

Wendell Holmes is a boy in Boston.
He meets Mr. Dixwell, his
future father-in-law.

WENDELL HOLMES was six years old — a sturdy boy with clear, alert, blue-gray eyes, a high color, and dark shiny hair that never kept its part but fell over his high forehead. Every morning, he walked up Montgomery Street and round the corner to the dame school. Montgomery Place was convenient for purposes of education. Looking uphill across the Granary Burying Ground, Wendell Holmes could see the new building going up that was to be the Boston Athenaeum library. Park Street Church was on the right as you turned the corner. Brimstone Corner, Boston called it, recalling the old days when Calvinist hell-fire had been preached from its pulpit.

There were half a dozen dame schools around the Common; the Cabot boys, Eliot boys, Bigelows, Wadsworths, Lees, attended them. Charles Eliot, older than Wendell, was taught by Mrs. Cushing on Bowdoin Street. Cabot Lodge later went to Mrs. Parkman; she was one of those New England women, indomitable and kind, who can teach a boy anything. Once, irritated beyond endurance, she cried out to Cabot Lodge: "Use your mind! I do not care what you answer if you only use your mind."

There was a Presidential election in the fall of '48. Wendell saw the Common draped with flags and knew there would be fireworks that night. Zachary Taylor won. Daniel Webster was angry. Clay sulked in his tent — once again right rather than President. Polk died, buried in his own dooryard fifteen weeks after he left the White House. The issue was land and more land. Two by two the states came in: Arkansas and Michigan, Iowa and Florida, slave and free, free and slave, always one to balance the other.

And as the country expanded the towns raised their standards of living, contrived ways to be comfortable, ways to be clean, and were proud of their handiwork. For months Boston had dug trenches to bring water from Cochituate, fifteen miles away. On an autumn day of 1848, the aqueduct was finished and the town held a grand celebration. Bells pealed, a hundred guns roared salute. School was not kept that day. Wendell Holmes, holding his small fat sister Amelia by the hand, stood on Tremont Street to watch his father pass in the long parade with the president of Harvard and all the professors. Biblical texts decorated the streets, inscriptions telling the history of the great water enterprise. There was a palanquin with men in Oriental costumes from the Salem East India Society; there were brass bands, and there was the entire Handel and Haydn Society riding on floats. There was a full-rigged sloop from the Seamen's Bethel. Mayor Josiah Quincy gave an oration; on Boston Common the crowd stood silent to hear him. Then he ordered the water turned on. It shot eighty feet in air. Wendell Holmes gasped; around him, people cheered. "A great country we live in!" they shouted, hugging each other, whacking each other on the back. "What other country in the world brings lake water fifteen miles to town? Has the Old Country got steam rail roads, bath tubs, ice boxes, towns that grow every year not by the hundred inhabitants but by the thousand?"

John Quincy Adams died, fallen at his post on the floor of Congress — the old oak, struck down at last. Boston, that had sneered when Adams went to Congress, claimed now its hero, went to the funeral [1] in crowds, and when they came home told stories about Adams. Wendell heard them. How the old man always rose at five, sponged in ice-cold water and, sitting by the fire with his candle, read aloud from the Bible. Dr. Ellis had been down to New York City not long ago with Mr. Adams. When they got into bed in their hotel room on the Battery, Adams told stories until Ellis roared with laughter. Then Adams said, "It is time to go to sleep and I am going to say my prayers. I shall say also the verse my mother

taught me when a child. I have never failed to repeat it every night
of my life. I have said it in Holland, Prussia, Russia, England, Washington, and Quincy. I say it out loud always and I don't mumble
it either."

Then in a loud, clear voice the old Puritan began his "Now I lay
me . . ."

And when he was dying: "This is the last of earth," said Adams.
"I am content" — and did not speak again. Boston was proud of him;
Wendell Holmes was proud of him. The Adamses, Daniel Webster
— what heroes the Commonwealth could claim! . . . Someone else
died that year of '48, someone far away and fabulous. John Jacob
Astor, the immigrant, leaving twenty million dollars. A fortune such
as America had never heard of, one that made Stephen Girard's nine
millions seem a pittance. In what other country could a poor immigrant rise to be a millionaire?

When Wendell was eight he was taken from the dame school and
sent to Mr. Sullivan in the basement of Park Street Church. Cabot
Lodge went there too. Wendell liked Mr. Sullivan — a pleasant, sad-
faced gentleman whose grandfather had been Governor of Massachusetts and whose great-uncle had been a general in the Revolutionary War. The boys he taught were too young for the Boston
Latin School — but not too young for the ferule. When a boy was
caned, his friends stood outside the door, counted the blows, listened
to hear whether the victim cried. Wendell Holmes was a sturdy boy,
full of life. But he was not especially mischievous and never looked
for trouble. If he was caned he did not tell about it; his father had
tasted the rod at Andover and strongly disapproved of schoolmasters
who used it.

After school hours, emerging on Park Street, Wendell faced the
South End boys who waited, ready with hard snowballs or mud,
thirsting to attack the private-school boys. You called these South
Boston boys "muckers" or you called them "toughs"; they were
mostly Irish and they gloried in their toughness. The potato famine
had sent thousands of Irish families to America; Boston had developed
a caste system toward them almost like the Southern feeling for the
Negro.

Around the tea table on Montgomery Place the family discussed
these matters, great and small. Dr. Holmes was unfailingly interested
in local news. They had paved the bottom of the Frog Pond with

stones, taken the American flag off the big elm on the Common and run it up a flagstaff. The lower part of Beacon Street was hideous with excavations and wagonloads of dirt; there was talk of filling in the marshes as far down as the Mill Dam.

Jenny Lind was coming to town to sing at Tremont Temple. She was a nightingale and an angel and a specimen of sweet womanhood, and Mr. Dodge the hatter had paid six hundred dollars for his choice of seats to her concert. Boston shook its head; such extravagance sounded more like New York City. A local guidebook described Boston's merchant princes as "cautious, systematic in their business transactions, ready to advance in their proper time, and distinguished from that recklessness which marks the New Yorker." In a Washington Street window Wendell saw a lump of California gold, said to weigh fifteen pounds. Higginson[2] told Dr. Holmes he had been down to Watertown to help fit out Jonas Thaxter for California, and Dr. Holmes said California was a nice place for disposing of old sticks.

But if New England was cautious with money, she was prodigal with emotion. The Abolitionists became more and more vocal. The Free-Soilers held a meeting in Faneuil Hall; it was broken up; windows were smashed, heads battered. In April of 1851 Wendell Holmes, from his window, heard more rioting. Thomas Sims, the fugitive slave, was captured and imprisoned in the courthouse, not seven blocks from Montgomery Place. For nine days Boston talked of nothing else. Opinion was fiercely divided. Whether or no slavery was morally wrong, slaves were property and property must be safeguarded. On the ninth day, the judge decided in favor of Sims's owner and at dawn next morning the Negro, under heavy escort, was led to the wharf and put on a brig for Savannah. Conservative Boston sighed with relief: law and order had prevailed, the agitators were defeated.

But not all Boston was pleased. That day, funeral bells tolled. Sims could not hear them, manacled to his berth on the brig *Acorn.* But Wendell Holmes heard them, calling angrily, sorrowfully, above the roofs, the treetops of Boston. He had no doubts as to which side he was on. The boys at school talked about it; one of them had had a brother wounded in the crowd that tried to free Sims. Rioters, the newspapers called this crowd. Lawless mob, troublemakers. . . .

Wendell Holmes was ten, that spring of 1851. In the natural order of things, the next step was the big public Latin School over on Bedford Street. But Dr. Holmes was not at all sure he liked the Latin School. Gardner was good enough at Latin and Greek, but he was a rough-and-tumble sort of schoolmaster, very free with the ferule and the strap. Dr. Holmes, talking with the young sons of his friends, heard too much of football and too little of learning. Epes Sargent Dixwell was a different breed altogether. He was leaving the Latin School to start a school of his own on Boylston Place, just west of the Common. Dr. Holmes, hearing of it, did not hesitate. Wendell should go to school under Epes Dixwell.

Everyone knew the Dixwells. They lived in Cambridge in a big house on Garden Street. Mrs. Dixwell was a Bowditch, daughter of that great navigator whose name Dr. Holmes had long ago said was such a powerful introduction on the continent of Europe. Epes Dixwell himself, a brilliant student, had been two classes ahead of Dr. Holmes at Harvard. He had practised law for a few years before he went to schoolteaching. He would have stayed at the Latin School forever if the city fathers had not passed an ordinance requiring its teachers to live within city limits. Epes Dixwell had no intention of leaving his pleasant house and garden and moving his wife and daughters over to Boston. But as master of his own private school he could live where he pleased. He built a small schoolhouse, limited his enrollment to fifty, and charged each pupil $250.

Wendell Holmes was a member of the first class to enter the school. He had not far to walk. Up to the Granary Burying Ground, past the Paddock elms, turning left past Park Street Church, then down along the Common to Boylston Street. Beyond that were farm land, marsh and slum. Every morning, Wendell waited in the yard with the other boys till Mr. Dixwell appeared, a tall spare man, walking briskly, dressed in a costume that caused the boys to marvel. One's own father put on a black swallowtail coat and dark trousers every morning for business.

But Mr. Dixwell flaunted a costume worthy of a circus impresario. His light overcoat was thrown back to reveal a dark purple frock coat, a green velvet waistcoat, and black and white checked trousers. Every boy desires his hero to look like other people. But aside from his clothes, Mr. Dixwell had an appearance any boy could be proud of. Once when he was in Paris with his brother-in-law, Dr. Bowditch, the concierge at their hotel had remarked that

Bowditch had the grand air, "*tout à fait comme Christophe Colomb.*"
A Boston man, telling the story, said he wondered if, had the
concierge known Americus Vespucius, she would have said Mr.
Dixwell looked like *him*.

Perhaps, the boys told each other, this mad costume of Dicky's
could be explained on the grounds that he was descended from a
regicide? His ancestor, John Dixwell, had helped to behead Charles I.
The descendants of regicides must have a wild streak somewhere.
More likely his color blindness accounted for it; perhaps Dicky
thought he was dressed in gray? When he sat down to read the Bible
aloud in the mornings, Mr. Dixwell always took off his square, steel-
rimmed spectacles and laid them on the desk. His large, handsome
nose looked bleak without them, his dark side whiskers almost rakish.

Epes Dixwell loved Latin and Greek as he loved life itself. The
fact that education must include mathematics he accepted grudgingly,
showing distinct annoyance on days when algebra took the place
of Latin. He liked to have the boys read Cicero aloud and illustrate
the lesson with prints of the Roman Forum and surroundings. Each
print was colored to show its district. Cautiously, from the floor, new
boys tested Dicky's sense of color, found it always lacking.

A smattering of French was included in the curriculum. Modern
history was disregarded entirely; so was the history of America.
In Boston, Horace Mann and Samuel Howe preached educational
reform; the country heard them and leaped ahead under their direction. Epes Dixwell saw no reason to follow. To the education of
Wendell Holmes this was not a serious drawback. The boy liked
books, and there was in Epes Dixwell more than a touch of the
teacher's genius. Under such a master a boy cannot help but learn.
He drinks in learning like mother's milk, no matter how outmoded
a system the master may profess to follow.

Wendell made no particular record as a scholar. He was healthy,
red-cheeked, strong, and while he cared little for football and
cricket, he loved outdoors and the things a boy could do outdoors.
In winter he skated with his friends. Just over the fence at the
western end of the Public Garden was a muddy beach; beyond it
the Back Bay invited — black deep ice from the Mill Dam to Boston
Neck. Farther up the Bay the skating was dangerous; tide water,
rushing in and out the Mill Dam gates, made the ice thin.

On days when the snow was good Wendell dragged his sled to

The Holmes Children

*Left to right: Edward Jackson Holmes, Oliver Wendell Holmes, Jr.,
Amelia Jackson Holmes*

The Gambrel-roofed House in Cambridge

school, left it in the yard, and when school was out hurried with his friends to the Long Coast. This ran from the corner of Park and Beacon Streets, right through Boston Common to the West Street entrance, then down Tremont Street Mall until your sled stopped. Or you could start at the crest of Beacon Hill and fly straight down to Washington Street.

But whichever route Wendell Holmes preferred, it was exciting business. Nobody merely coasted — they raced, and the technique of racing was not easy to acquire. On Saturday afternoons people lined the Long Coast to watch. The fastest sleds had names: spectators bet on them as they would on a horse. Wendell's sled was long, it curved upward in front and was painted yellow, adorned with a bright red flying horse. At the top of the hill, dragging his sled by its rope, Wendell took a fast running start, threw the sled ahead with the rope along its middle, then launched his body through the air, lighting chest first so softly the sled was not retarded by a second.

In spring when the weather opened, things happened on Boston Common. Tukey was City Marshal then, and Chief of Police. A large, handsome, sportive man, graduate of Harvard, he was addressed as Esquire. Boston loved him because he gave it plenty of shows. The Light Guard paraded the Common, Flagg's Boston Brass Band blew their shining horns. When the line was opened connecting Boston with railroads to Canada and the West, Tukey put on a Railroad Jubilee that lasted three whole days. Boston had never seen such an affair; it put the Water Festival in the shade entirely. Why, said Boston citizens, the Great Exhibition over in London, Queen Victoria's Glass Palace itself, could not compete with the Railroad Jubilee! Whole books were written about it. The parades were endless; floats illustrated every means of transportation from oxcart and prairie schooner to the newest, shiniest steam engine. On the Common there was a huge dinner tent where speech followed speech. How Dr. Holmes missed writing a poem for the occasion was a simple mystery. England, said the citizens of Boston, would hear of this Festival. "We shall soon see," local news sheets said proudly, "in English journals, the speeches delivered at our State House."

Just west of the Common was the Public Garden. Here the visiting circuses camped; the big tent could be entered at the corner of Beacon and Charles Streets. The great drawing card was the announcement that the elephants would bathe in the Frog Pond. It was a delirious business to stand and watch the huge beasts wade in to the end of their chains, fill their trunks with water, and then solemnly spray themselves down the backbone.

The Common was a forum for cranks and that was fun too. One afternoon a woman appeared in the most extraordinary costume — not skirts at all but trousers, full and stiff, reaching to her ankles and tied there. Her name was Amelia Bloomer; she was actually crusading for this indecorous costume. Wendell Holmes, peering over the heads of his neighbors, thought the woman looked queer but handsome.

One March night there was a tremendous fire near the Holmes house. Wendell's father took his son's hand and ran after the engines. Tremont Temple, a theater that had been converted to a Baptist Church, was blazing from cellar to roof. All the volunteer companies in the city could not save it. It fell into the street with a crash.

Dr. Holmes had not outgrown the tastes he had formed in Paris. He loved the theater and often took his children to the matinee. Pentland's Circus came to the Howard Atheneum with Mrs. Sherwood, the daring bareback rider. Booth played *Julius Caesar* there, and Mr. Hackett was an uproarious Falstaff. The Boston Museum had an excellent stock company; Wendell saw *Dominique the Deserter* and *Ingomar the Barbarian*, thrillers with black-haired villains and lovely, innocent heroines. A seat in the gallery cost only twelve and a half cents. Ninepence, Wendell called it. Saturday matinee left time afterward to run upstairs and see the "curiosities" from Polynesia and Africa. Once Wendell's father took him at night. Four rows of white gas globes along the front made the Museum a place of splendor and enchantment.[3]

And in March, when the ice broke in the harbor, it was fun to walk with your friends down to Commercial Wharf and watch the clippers come in. As each merchant ship approached the city, its flag was run up on the flagstaff of the Old State House. Wendell's friends recognized the flags instantly. It might be Mr. Lodge's *Don Quixote* coming down the harbor, or his *Sancho Panza.* When she docked, the boys swarmed aboard, begging Chinese fireworks from the captain, ginger, sweetmeats, lychee nuts. Over on Lewis Wharf boys crowded to beg postage stamps from the sailors, rare issues from Hawaii, triangular stamps from the Cape of Good Hope. The *Flying Cloud* was launched one fine summer day at East Boston; Wendell saw her slide down the ways to water lined with paddle-wheel steamers, with great square-rigged ships maneuvering slowly down to free water.

Two months of the summer the Holmes family spent in the Berkshire Hills, near Pittsfield. Grandmother Holmes had inherited two hundred and eighty acres from her father, Judge Wendell, who had bought thousands of acres from the Province of Massachusetts. Dr. Holmes built a house there; his mother and John came up sometimes from Cambridge to spend a month. Longfellow lived near by. "Drove over in the afternoon to Dr. Holmes' place on the old Wendell farm," he wrote in his diary. "A snug little place, with a view of the river and the mountains."

Mr. Nathaniel Hawthorne lived just down the way. He was a quiet gentleman, not very interesting from Wendell's point of view. Much more exciting was Mr. Herman Melville who had been to sea in the Pacific, had actually been captured by cannibals and held prisoner for months. Wendell had read Melville's books: *Typee*, *Omoo*, and the story of the great White Whale. Wendell was powerfully affected by the stories he read; his family teased him when they caught him emerging red-eyed from his room with a book in his hand. He was twelve when his father sent for the new book by Charlotte Yonge that was making such a stir: *The Heir of Redclyffe*. Wendell seized upon it, buried himself in it. The last half he read in his own secret place high in the branches of the big pine tree, crying safely and unseen while beautiful young Amy knelt by her husband's bedside and, "taking no heed of time, no heed of aught that was earthly," saw him close the "dark fringed eyelids" forever.

The house was called Canoe Meadow and the Holmes children loved it. From the wide front porch you could see Greylock Mountain and the Housatonic River. The hillsides were wild with scrub and pine, high pastures where the granite rocks showed rough and gray, warm under a boy's bare foot at noontide. Before the house a great single pine tree spread its branches. Wendell, starting off for an afternoon's fishing or going out with his pail to gather blueberries, met his mother and Amelia trundling the red wheelbarrow with soil for their little garden. "Great A and Little A" his father called the two. Dr. Holmes was always busy somewhere about the place, fixing and mending, making small contraptions for his private use. The latest was the stereoscope, a pipe you looked through at pictures and saw everything in the round. Standing on one foot and then the other, Wendell watched his father's hands among the tools — neat, deft, never dropping anything, never hitting a nail sideways. . . .

Mountain and swift-tumbling upland river, ice-cold in the pools below the dam. Granite rocks and ragged pine trees, blueberries rattling cheerfully into the pail. The smell of clover in the south meadow, cows coming slowly through the pasture gate at sundown. And at night the stars looking down on a wide, quiet countryside.

Amelia Holmes, saying good-night to her children in their rooms, carried the lamp to the hall bracket above the stairs. How good it was here, she thought, a little sigh of thankfulness escaping her. How safe and how accustomed everything, by night and by day! God grant the children's lives would stay this way always — peaceful and content, free from harm and those dark evil winds that blow across the world.

CHAPTER TEN

The nation grows restless. Wendell Holmes gets ready for Harvard.

IN May of 1854, when Wendell Holmes was thirteen, another fugitive slave — Anthony Burns by name — was captured and placed in Boston Court House. This time, emotion rose to even higher pitch. Richard Dana, slim, aristocratic, offered himself as Burns's lawyer.

It was a great personal risk and Dana knew it. Whether Burns went free or not, the lawyer who pleaded for him would lose every rich and respectable client he had. Few business firms desire, as legal counsel, a fanatic radical who champions the cause of "freedom" against the cause of property.

Dana pleaded well; all Boston looked for his words in the newspaper, discussed them round the supper table. But the Vigilance Committee, sure that Burns would lose, decided to try a rescue. Wendell Phillips, Theodore Parker, T. W. Higginson, Samuel Howe, led a mass meeting in Faneuil Hall. Afterward an angry, excited crowd poured out of the hall, moved up to the courthouse and surrounded it.

Higginson and his men drove a joist against the door, battered it down. . . . Three blocks away, in his room on Montgomery Place, Wendell Holmes heard the noise. Shots were fired, feet ran on Tremont Street. . . . Late that night, Higginson came to the Holmeses, his head bandaged. Burns was still a prisoner. "It was one of the very best plots that ever — failed," Higginson said. Three days later, Judge Loring decided the case in favor of Burns's owner. Down to the Long Wharf marched the Negro under heavy escort. Boston streets were draped in black.

The Free-Soilers gathered themselves for greater effort. Dana was one of their leaders; another was John Quincy Adams's son, Charles Francis of the keen eye, the bulldog jaw. Daniel Webster was dead. Even if he had lived, the Free-Soilers could not have counted on him. Webster had shocked the radicals by sliding off the issue in his Seventh of March speech on the annexation of Texas. But he had saved the Union for ten more years; he was New England's hero, and when he died he was mourned as no American since Washington had been mourned. Thousands went down to Marshfield to bid him farewell, filing past his coffin in front of the big old house where, under a tree that he had planted himself, Webster lay, dressed in his blue coat with the gilt buttons and white neckcloth, his massive forehead fronting the New England sky.

But the Abolitionists said that Webster had failed them. When the Bar Association met to honor him with an oration that said Webster's great voice had "never failed to rescue the oppressed," Dana argued until the committee put a pen through the words *"never failed,"* and substituted *"so often* rescued."

And now, in May of '54, men talked of Kansas and Nebraska. Would Stephen Douglas persuade the Senate to repeal the Missouri Compromise? Would Kansas actually permit the slave trade? Douglas prevailed. The Compromise was repealed, and in country towns from Maine to Nebraska fires went up where men burned Stephen Douglas in effigy. Out in Michigan the *Antis* met to form a new party in preparation for the next Presidential election. *Republican,* the party called itself.

It was becoming impossible for Boston to maintain the middle course. Property versus freedom: both were sacred. A hard choice for New England to make. Dr. Holmes brought a book home from the Athenaeum: *Uncle Tom's Cabin.* Wendell was old enough, his father thought, to read something besides Fenimore Cooper. *The Pathfinder, The Deerslayer, The Prairie, The Last of the Mohicans, The Ways of the Hour* — week by week these titles appeared on the doctor's library card.

The Holmes children read *Uncle Tom's Cabin,* wept over little Eva, thrilled when Eliza crossed the ice. But to Dr. Holmes as to his children, these things were far off, would never touch their lives. The doctor's friend Ticknor, the publisher, remarked of Mrs. Stowe's book that it deepened the horror of slavery, but did not change a single vote. It occurred to few that war was coming. Howe had a letter from Theodore Parker, written from Italy. "What a pity," wrote Parker, "that the map of our magnificent country should be destined to be so soon torn in two on account of the negro, that poorest of human creatures, satisfied, even in slavery, with sugar cane and a banjo."

Julia Howe read the letter over her husband's shoulder. "This is poor, dear Parker's foible," she said. "He always thinks he knows what will come to pass. How absurd is this forecast of his!"

(*He is trampling out the vintage where the grapes of wrath are stored* . . . In Julia Howe's mind the words were not yet formed.)

Not all the Southern arguments could be answered easily. "What about your own wage slaves, New England?" asked South Carolina. "What about the thousands of women workers in the cotton mill of Lawrence?"

This was the largest mill in the world. Its streets were tree-shaded, its women workers — until lately — New England born, intelligent young persons of self-respect. But since the influx of foreigners in the late forties and fifties, things had changed, and not for the better. There were five thousand women workers in Lawrence, nearly all under twenty-four. The towns of Lawrence and Lowell were fast becoming horrors. Boston knew it — and tried not to know it. There were plenty of troubles to occupy one's time besides slavery either in a mill or in a cotton field. Yellow fever arrived in town. Dr. Holmes sent his family up to Pittsfield; Higginson took his to Vermont for the water cure. People accepted these epidemics philosophically. Man was born to die, and when typhoid and diphtheria arrived with the late autumn months, it was pleasanter to talk about Mr. Forrest's splendid performance of *Hamlet* at the Boston Theatre. At home in the evenings Boston played bezique or whist or listened while the young lady of the house rippled off, at the pianoforte, Mendelssohn's "Songs without Words," or "spirit waltzes" or — as Higginson wrote from Waterboro — "other things tender and terrible."

Dr. Holmes still worked in the hospital wards on Fruit Street, still fought his battle against puerperal fever. From Philadelphia, the doctors Meigs and Hodge continued their diatribes against him. Holmes did not reply. He was a professor in the Harvard Medical School; his main business was to lecture to his students — and he did it more than well. Harvard had two chairs of anatomy; the second, in Cambridge, was held by Jeffries Wyman, the brilliant microscopist and research man. Holmes admired Wyman enormously, and said so. The university had duplicated the chair so that there existed almost side by side, as the *Anatomical Record* has it, "Wyman, the scientific anatomist with but few students, and Oliver Wendell Holmes, the poet anatomist, with many of them."

Holmes, a born talker, could have lectured successfully on anything. In the early fifties he had gone on the Lyceum Circuit all over New England, but he had given it up as a waste of time and strength. He had been appointed lecturer one winter at the Lowell Institute. An old trouper, Dr. Holmes knew all the tricks and loved his trade. In the Medical School the students called him Uncle Oliver and flocked to his one-o'clock lecture — the worst hour of the day. Other professors avoided it. By then the students had already listened to successive lectures on materia medica, chemistry, practice, and obstetrics — an hour to a lecture. They were weary to the bone. But they climbed the steep steps to Holmes's classroom door, pounded on it till the janitor unlocked it. Shouting and shoving they stumbled down the steep steps to get the best seats in front.

On a table lay the cadaver, carried in on a board, often the worse for wear. Eliot's house on Beacon Street may have boasted an icebox, but the Medical School did not. Holmes stood by the table — tiny, sometimes gasping with asthma. He spoke without notes and believed in speaking simply. "We don't *ligate* arteries," he said. "We *tie* them." He was deeply in earnest; he loved anatomy. Moreover, the students knew that sooner or later, if they stayed awake, Uncle Oliver would be funny. One day, pointing to that part of the corpse which, if it had sat up, would undoubtedly have cushioned its owner against the table, "These, gentlemen," said Holmes, "are the tuberosities of the ischia, on which man was designed to sit and survey the works of Creation."

When men are old, and their teeth fall out, their faces seem to shorten. "No doubt," Holmes told his students, "you have noticed the extraordinary way in which elderly people will suddenly shut up their faces like an accordion." Holmes was much interested in the marvels of dentistry. "Had the art been thus perfected in the last century," he said, "we should not now see the Father of his Country, in Stuart's portrait, his attention divided between the cares of the State and the sustaining of his uppers in position." Pathological anatomy and dissection seemed to the doctor "like inspecting what remains of the fireworks on the fifth of July."

Holmes made his pictures and comparisons purposely, to fix the objects in the student's mind. But there was about his figures and metaphors a kind of enchantment, a gentle surprise that woke the student, did not make him laugh aloud but made him smile and remember the words forever. The microscopical coiled tube of a sweat gland was like an elf's intestine. The mesentery reminded Holmes of his Grandfather Wendell's shirt ruffles.

When he said something good, Dr. Holmes was as pleased as his students. He took it home, repeated it at the evening tea table. He still loved to quote Dr. Louis: —

> *Formez toujours les idées nettes.*
> *Fuyez les à peu près.*

Wendell, sitting halfway down the table, knew the words by heart. He tried to ignore them — but he could not; they became part of him. "The difference between green and seasoned knowledge," the doctor propounded, his cup halfway to his lips, "is great. Our American atmosphere is vocal with the flippant loquacity of half knowledge."

That was good, and Dr. Holmes knew it. He set his cup down. "The difference — " he began again . . . Wendell, closing his mind automatically, retreated to a world of his own. When his father stopped talking, he would tell what had happened this morning when Mr. Dixwell asked Henry Bowditch to scan six lines of Vergil — that is, he would tell it if Amelia did not start talking first. Wendell talked fluently, once he got started, but shyness held him back, sometimes, from starting. Not so Amelia. Nothing held her back. Neddy was just as bad, but Neddy had inherited his father's asthma and wheezed when he began to speak. During the wheezing it was possible sometimes to step in. One thing was certain: whoever got the floor, held it through the meal — and usually this person was Dr. Holmes. Mrs. Holmes listened, smiling, trying to stem the flood and give place to the children. No one knew who it was that started the custom of giving an extra helping of marmalade to the person who made the cleverest remark. But Wendell, watching his mother's face as she heaped jam on his plate, knew somehow that it was she who had split the conversation open, had given him his chance.

At thirteen, Wendell was already as tall as his father. His face was too thin for beauty, his chin too long. The doctor himself was homely; his upper lip was long, his features unbeautiful. He said grimly that he regarded his face as a convenience rather than an asset. Wendell was convinced that he himself was really ugly — long afterward he said it was his father who convinced him. He was growing like a weed; his hands and feet were hard to manage. But there was something in his face that arrested. His color was high, his eyes, blue-gray under straight dark brows, were startlingly clear and intelligent.

He was an entirely normal boy; healthy, strong, active. But he was not like the rest of the family. And already, the beholder felt it. The doctor, Amelia, Neddy — even Mrs. Holmes — were chatterers, quick, voluble, always moving about the room, jumping up, sitting down, interrupting each other. They were like a nest of wrens, a visitor said, leaving the house one afternoon. Among them Wendell stood apart. He could be noisy; his laugh was a great shout, coming from deep within. But there was about him a quality of reserve, something romantic, something that beckoned, giving promise of depths to be explored.

Life remained, for Wendell, largely a family affair. All around him lived the friends of his parents and of their parents before them. Within a stone's throw were the doorsills of Bowditches, Jacksons, Lees, Higginsons, Choates, Everetts, Grays, Gardiners, Cushings, Wendells, Hunnewells, Cabots, Lodges, Bancrofts. Everyone knew his neighbor. It would still have been possible to rally Boston against a foreign foe by the cry, heard one March evening long ago — *"Town born, turn out!"*

The horse railroad was open now for travel to Cambridge. Old Boston had objected strenuously to the laying of these rails; they said it was a desecration to tear up the cobbles of the old historic squares. Dr. Holmes did not care; he liked material progress. Often on Saturday afternoons he took Wendell down to the river to row. In a boathouse the family kept its little fleet — skiff, dory, and shell. Late in June the baths opened, at the foot of Chestnut Street.

Wendell and his friends watched eagerly for the day. Braman's Baths was a row of low wooden buildings on piles, sharp with the smell of salt water. Long gangplanks and passageways led to the swimming basin, anchored in the river. On shore the district bustled with pile drivers, derricks, half-built houses. The marshes were disappearing; month by month the city crawled westward.

On fine Sunday afternoons the family went over to Cambridge to see their grandmother and Uncle John. Sometimes they rode in the horsecars, sometimes they walked up to the corner of Beacon and Charles Streets and took a bus. The buses were flat-topped, each with its name painted just under the roof. *Jenny Lind, Daniel Webster.* There was one weatherbeaten driver of whom Amelia always asked the time of departure. "Quarter a'ter, half a'ter, quarter to, and *at!*" the driver would reply. Amelia would laugh uproariously and repeat the whole thing to her mother.

Debarking on Harvard Square, the family walked across to the Gambrel-roofed House. Grandmother Holmes was wonderful. She was beautiful to look at, tiny, with a pink face and white hair smooth under her cap. Her eyes, deep in her face, were a sparkling chestnut brown. She seemed to have lived forever. Wendell never tired of her stories. She could tell you what it felt like before the battle of Bunker Hill, when people had shouted down Wendell Street, down Oliver Street — "*The red coats are coming and killing as they come!*" She said *her* mother could remember the hurled tomahawk quivering in the cabin door. She treated Dr. Holmes as if he were a boy, ordering him about, telling him to fetch her footstool. Wendell was entertained. "Grandmother," he said, "if you come to tea at our house you will win the extra marmalade by three lengths."

Amelia and Neddy followed their uncle about the place, begging for a story as puppies beg a biscuit. Wendell scorned to beg for stories but he listened nonetheless; grown men had been known to beg for John Holmes's stories. Uncle John, settled finally in his chair under the big cherry tree, looked at the group on the grass before him . . . " 'Melia, would you like to hear about Caesar Augustus?"

Amelia had heard about Caesar Augustus a score of times. "Yes!" she said breathlessly. "Go on — " Uncle John always told the story differently. Wendell, a little apart from the group, standing with his back against a tree, pretended boredom but listened, fascinated.

"*My story has a moral*," Uncle John began, watching the faces before him fall, then brighten as he continued. "Caesar Augustus came home victorious from the wars, and Rome gave him a triumph. A big one, the biggest since Pompey. Everyone in town turned out."

Here Uncle John paused for elaborate, always different descriptions of just who turned out. . . . "The people cheered and cheered. The streets were deep in flower petals. Over by the Colosseum the lions roared, starving for the fights tomorrow. Everything was going beautifully. Suddenly, from the crowd along the Appian Way a little boy stepped out. A dirty, ragged little boy without any shoes on.

"He was close enough to touch the Emperor's chariot, to touch his robe. But he did not look awed, this little round-faced boy. He put back his head and laughed. Then he looked again at the Emperor's crown of laurel and laughed louder than ever. Before anyone could catch him, he darted back in the crowd and was lost.

"That night in the palace, getting into bed, Caesar's wife talked about the triumph. How splendid it had been! No Caesar before had had such a triumph. She was *sure* Pompey had not had half so many captives, so many people to cheer. But the Emperor, lying in the dark, saw nothing but a round, dirty boy's face, laughing.

" 'My dear,' Caesar said to his wife — and his voice sounded small and tired. 'My dear, was anything wrong with my appearance today? Was my crown on quite, quite straight?' "

Uncle John, leaning forward in his chair, looked around for Wendell lounging against his tree, a blade of grass between his lips. "Do you want the moral, Wendy?"

Wendell smiled, shaking his head. Uncle John was more fun than Father, more fun than three fathers . . . So there was always someone in every triumph to tell you your crown was on crooked? "If Father had been emperor, he wouldn't have seen that little boy," Wendell said softly.

Nobody heard him. Amelia was already clamoring for another story. Wendell wondered if there would be time before supper to run over to the Dixwells' on Garden Street. Fanny Dixwell had a book for him. She had refused to tell him the name, but he felt sure it was a Cooper; the last time they were all at Grandmother's she had come in with *The Sea Lions* in her hand; Wendell had tried to wheedle it from her.

October, 1856 . . . Only a winter remained before Wendell Holmes would be ready for Harvard. In November, walking home from Dixwell's School he saw along Tremont Street Mall the rows of stands and pushcarts that always appeared at election time. If Buchanan won it would be a calamity; Buchanan supported the Fugitive Slave Law. Everybody knew that. But whoever won, whoever lost, you could buy doughnuts on the Mall, hot brown bread and seedcakes, ginger beer, spruce beer in jugs. Lobsters and oysters, too, if you had the price.

Buchanan won. In January, 1857, the Abolitionists, defiant, held a Disunion meeting in Worcester. Higginson and his friends had sent out the call. It was an act of real despair; it seemed to the Abolitionists they had worked in vain for twenty years; the planting interests could not be beaten. A few years later, Higginson would be leading his troops on the Union side — but now he wrote home to his mother: —

> The Disunion Convention was very successful and commanded general respect, whatever the newspapers may say. I am sorry, dearest mother, you differ from me about it, but I never was more sure of being right. It is written in the laws of nature that two antagonistic nations cannot remain together; every year is dividing us more and more, and the sooner we see it, the better we can prepare for a peaceful and dignified policy.

Two months later, Buchanan was inaugurated — Buchanan the conciliator who tried to please both sides and ended by pleasing neither. He was possessed of what Channing said had ruined the old Federalist Party in 1817 — too much the wisdom of experience, too little the wisdom of hope. The inauguration was scarcely over when Chief Justice Taney delivered the decision that was to mark Buchanan's administration for all time. Dred Scott the black man was declared by the Supreme Court to be neither person nor citizen but a chattel or thing, and as such was delivered back to slavery. Out in Springfield, Illinois, Abraham Lincoln said flatly but carefully, "We think the decision is erroneous. We know the court that made it has often overruled its own decisions, and we shall do what we can to have it overrule this."

1857 . . . The few who whisper *War!* are called fanatics, foolish prophets of disaster. In Boston the Saturday Club — brand-new and exceedingly spry — meets at the Parker House: Agassiz, Motley, Longfellow, Emerson, Dana, Lowell, Professor Benjamin Peirce the mathematician, Dr. Holmes. They eat mutton and goose, drink wine, and talk of Charles Sumner's continued illness following the Brooks assault in the Senate. And the next moment the talk turns local. Sam Eliot has lost all his money in the financial panic. Worse than '37, all over the country. Eliot may have to put up his Beacon Street house for sale; icebox, bathtubs, and his entire library. Can nothing be done to save the books? A subscription gotten up? Eliot's boy is a tutor at Harvard . . . Charlie — the one with the birthmark on his face. They're going to make him a professor. . . . Underwood wants to start a new magazine; Lowell says he'll edit it if Holmes and Longfellow will write for the first number. The *Atlantic Monthly*, Holmes calls it. Underwood has been in England snaring British writers . . . Can't we have a magazine without England? Plenty of good writers here in Boston.

Summer came and went. Neddy Holmes was ten and at Dixwell's; Amelia was thirteen and went to school around the corner. Wendell at sixteen had outgrown every garment he possessed. Mrs. Holmes looked up at her elder son and sent him, with a piece of woolen homespun under his arm, down to the tailor on Washington Street.

CHAPTER ELEVEN

*Harvard College. Autocrat of the
Breakfast-Table. Uncle John gives
his autograph.*

THE transition from Dixwell's Latin School to Harvard College was for Wendell Holmes no revolution. He crossed the Charles River it was true; also, he lived no longer at home, being a boarder in Cambridge at the house of a Mr. Danforth. But he was doing what his father had done, what his uncles and cousins had done and were doing. Not to go to Harvard would have been eccentric; to go at sixteen was the rule. Wendell Phillips wrote a credo, called "Five Points of Massachusetts Decency." Cousin Phillips's Abolitionism made him almost an outlaw from the conventional world; yet in his credo, Point Number Two was expressed with simple comprehensiveness: —

To be a Harvard man.

The Cambridge scene was little changed since Dr. Holmes's day. The horsecars rolled along Cambridge Street now, and there were three or four new college buildings. But Harvard Square was still unpaved; you walked on the hard mud under the trees. Across a field the Gambrel-roofed House still stood, benign and weathered under its elms; in the old paneled library Uncle John and Grandmother Holmes were there to give tea to a freshman and his friends. In Holworthy Hall lived old Professor Sophocles, cooking his own meals and keeping his hens in a yard near by. Persons favored with the present of an egg found on it in purple ink the name of the hen that laid it.

It was all very rural and neighborly. The University numbered about four hundred students, presided over by the Reverend Mr. Walker — a kindly, easygoing divine, reminiscent of President Kirkland, loving religion and his Sunday pulpit, loving Greek and Latin. To President Walker, education meant what it meant to Epes Dixwell; in the Harvard curriculum the classics maintained very definitely the place of honor. Young Professor Child tried desperately to interest the boys in Chaucer. But Cambridge, while recognizing vaguely that Child was a great scholar, considered his passion for Anglo-Saxon poets and old English ballads not only unnecessary but a little queer.

There was no choice of subjects; the elective system so laboriously inaugurated by Ticknor had been swept away during the administration of the Reverend Jared Sparks. President Walker followed Sparks, and where the curriculum was concerned, Walker desired above all to maintain a safe *status quo ante* — not difficult now that the elective system had been dispensed with. There were dangerous new men on the teaching staff it was true; on Thursday mornings, Louis Agassiz strolled through the College Yard, smoking his cigar in sublime disregard of law and order. Covered with the honors of European scholarship, Agassiz had arrived ten years ago from Switzerland, every hair on his magnificent head bristling with energy, charm, genius. He talked with a strong foreign accent; he did not care two straws for courses on Christian morals and he saw no reason why the new science should be at war with the old religion. He was trying to find a place to house his zoological specimens, and had even opened a girls' school in Cambridge to raise money for the project.

Agassiz, however, spent little time at the college, being far more interested in scientific research than in his lectures. It was the same with Professor Asa Gray, the natural-history man. Gray talked much of a botanist he had met in England named Charles Darwin, who had a theory concerning the origin and development of plant life. The two were in correspondence; Gray said Darwin's book would be out before long. Neither Gray's nor Agassiz's lectures were compulsory; students received no academic credits for attending. From

President Walker's point of view this was a definite safeguard; the younger students were not exposed to dangerous ideas and the older ones got no credits for the lectures and stayed away in droves.

People said Professor Peirce, the mathematician and astronomer, had a kind of spiritual affinity with Agassiz. Benjamin Peirce was bearded like a lion; his dark eyes were fiery and within him one felt the same fury, the same exuberance that was Agassiz's. In the classroom Peirce was brief and impatient. Stupid students were terrified of him, the brilliant greeted him with joy. Two years before Wendell had entered college, Peirce had published his great volume on *Analytic Mechanics;* Europe and America acclaimed him. The Peirces had always lived in Cambridge, up on Quincy Street; the neighbors said mathematics was as natural to the professor as eating. Everything he saw he computed into some kind of horrid analytic solution — his children's tops as they spun, the probabilities of the three-ball game in billiards. His grown-up son, James Mills Peirce, was as brilliant as the father. Cambridge said that when the two sat down to cards, James looked at his hand, made a rapid calculation on the law of chances, and remarked grimly, "Hand over your money, old man."

President Walker sometimes wondered how these three men — Agassiz, Gray, and Peirce — had drifted into professorships in a college that was designed to turn out ministers of the gospel or educated gentlemen. None of the three men were atheists—yet everything they said and the way they said it was upsetting to boys reared in good orthodox surroundings.

For Wendell Holmes, impact with these men of science was inspiring, but it was by no means a revelation. Two of them were members of the Saturday Club that dined each month at Parker's. Meeting Wendell on Cambridge lanes they greeted him genially in the name of his father. So did Professor Lowell and Mr. Longfellow. Longfellow had resigned his professorship; it gave him no time to write, he said. He had married Tom Appleton's sister and had bought Craigie House; it was Longfellow House now. Wendell Holmes could have gone there — could have gone indeed to all these Cambridge houses and been welcomed in his father's name. But he did not go. Except for the Dixwells on Garden Street, he avoided his father's friends, preferring to think of himself as a college man, pleasantly divorced from the family fold.

As a matter of fact his time was no more his own than when he lived on the third floor at Montgomery Place. From six[1] in the morning, when Mr. Danforth's servant pounded on his door with firewood and a can of water, until evening curfew at nine, Wendell's days were regulated, nearly every hour accounted for. The students were treated like boys at boarding school — forbidden to shout from the windows of their dormitory, forbidden to "collect in groups." In the College Yard the penalty for swearing was high; you could not throw snowballs or get into a good fist fight with your friends.

On Sundays if Wendell desired to go to King's Chapel across the river with his family, he had to bring back with him a signed certificate saying he had really been to church — and to what church. If a boy carved his name on a bench in the classroom, if he went to sleep in chapel, if he raised his voice outdoors in song, he was called up before the faculty and "privately admonished." Parents were forever being notified that their sons were "not fulfilling the purpose for which they came to college" — and the whole report solemnly copied into the Faculty Books.

In Wendell's freshman year, John Quincy Adams's grandson, Henry Adams, was a senior. Henry took this honor lightly. The Faculty Books are filled with grave, exasperated notes about Adams. It was voted that he be "privately admonished for calling up to a college window under aggravating circumstances," and for smoking in the Yard. Once, in dining hall, Adams got into what young Benjamin Crowninshield, in his diary, called "a little spate with Joe Bradlee. Joe threw some bread at Henry, who was late at dinner. Henry threw a rice croquette at Joe and it bid fair to be a fight."

Small wonder that Longfellow wearied of a professorship which entailed all the duties of a nursery governess; small wonder the Messrs. Agassiz and Gray were careful not to tie themselves to the college with any tie stronger than a weekly lecture. . . .

It was an extraordinary situation. A more brilliant group of scientists, scholars, and creative writers had never congregated about a university — yet Harvard clung to her ancient rules, doing all she could, apparently, to prevent these professors from functioning fully. Teaching was the same old system of grammar-school recitation. You got through college by memorizing the textbooks. Even philosophy was committed to memory. A student was not expected to question either textbook or lecturer. He learned a principle, a definition; from it he made certain deductions. If they agreed with the deductions in the book, he got a good mark; if they differed he got a bad one. Term after term, professors gave the same lectures; the story goes that one professor's notes dropped apart before he wrote a new lecture. Dr. Holmes himself, although a brilliant lecturer, used, in one of his anatomy classes, the same identical notes for thirty-five years. Why not, when man's anatomy did not change?

There were exceptions of course. Jeffries Wyman scorned the system and made his anatomy students find out the nature of a bone by looking at a bone. Josiah Cooke the new chemistry professor used "laboratory" in his course. The leaven was beginning to work. But in Wendell Holmes's college years it was only just beginning. The new spirit of science was abroad — but so far, there was no real tie-up with education. On the Harvard faculty only one man really sensed the affinity, a man trained as a chemist, but an organizer and educator at heart: Charles Eliot, son of Dr. Holmes's friend Samuel Eliot who had lost his money in the panic of '57 — Charles Eliot with the stiff manner, the purple birthmark that covered his right cheek. Long ago, the South End boys had run Eliot off Boston Common because of this scar; the experience had not encouraged him to be openhearted. His students wrote home that the new chemistry professor was "cold as an icicle."

Looking on his Alma Mater, Eliot chafed angrily at a system that refused to let a student think for himself, that treated college men like schoolboys and yet dared to call itself a "university." The classes were too big; even President Walker recognized it. How could any professor teach eighty freshmen, all sitting there wriggling and making spitballs like so many infants from the Latin School? By mathematical tables Eliot worked out a system to divide the classes into sections, giving the professors smaller groups to work with. It would raise the whole standard of scholarship, he told the president.

Walker was only too glad to turn over to this young zealot as many administrative duties as the zealot would undertake. Tall, stiff, with his scarred young face, Eliot knocked at the president's door on evenings before the Corporation met, and the two worked out a plan. Faculty meeting became used to an interruption from the chair: "I think," President Walker would remark in his mild voice, "we had better pause for a few minutes and ask Mr. Eliot to draft a resolution."

The leaven was working. But Wendell Holmes, pursuing his well-charted way, could not know it. He was too young to know it. Recognizing no new spirit, no new genius abroad, at sixteen he was content to study what was laid before him. Most certainly he did not overtax himself. At the end of his freshman year he stood twenty-second in a class of ninety-nine. He was having a good time and a good time was important. He was getting to know the world about him. He did not pick his friends for their intellectual brilliance. Well down in the second half of the class stood a boy from Philadelphia named Norwood Penrose Hallowell — a tall, brown-haired, good-natured boy whom Wendell liked at sight. Wendell's cousin, John Morse, was a year ahead but the two saw much of each other. Then there was Henry Bowditch who had gone to school at Dixwell's. Henry worked hard, he was headed for Medical School. Dehon, Lee, Curtis, Phillips, Scollay Parker, Ed Wigglesworth — all from Boston. Wendell looked with suspicion upon Wigglesworth, who seemed to him a trifle pompous — looked with suspicion also upon Wendell Phillips Garrison, son of the Abolitionist. At seventeen, Bill Garrison was annoyingly sure he was right about the universe.

Lodging at Mr. Danforth's, Wendell was not subject to quite as strict rules as the boys in the dormitory — but he was subject to almost the same discomforts. His room, bleak and uncarpeted, was nearly filled with a large featherbed and warmed only by the open fire. The dormitory boys heated a cannon ball on extra cold days and placed it over the fire in a skillet. It gave out a pleasant round red glow. As soon as the weather got warm, it was highly rewarding to roll the cannon ball downstairs; it made the proctors mad and the noise was superb. A large part of every student's time was spent trying to keep warm. Ben Crowninshield used to stuff a lampwick in his keyhole to keep out the draft, and pour water round his window frames. Ice makes excellent insulation. When he caught cold and the cold hung on, Crowninshield sent for the leech woman. "Awful hard time," the boy wrote afterward in his diary. "Fainted — bled like a pig."

It upset Dr. Holmes that the boys at college did not show more interest in athletics. As usual when he felt strongly about something

he said so in the public prints. At the moment he had a superb ve-
hicle in the *Autocrat of the Breakfast-Table*. "Such a set of black-
coated, stiff-jointed, soft-muscled, paste-complexioned youth," he
wrote, "as we can boast in our Atlantic cities never before sprang
from loins of Anglo-Saxon lineage. . . . We have a few good boatmen, — no good horsemen that I hear of, — I cannot speak for crick-
eting — but as for any great athletic feat performed by a gentleman
in these latitudes, society would drop a man who should run round
the Common in five minutes."

A few good boatmen? Wendell Holmes was challenged furiously
in his father's name. Yet what the doctor wrote was essentially true.
Collegiate sport was an individual matter. You went out and ran
to "get up a good swett." If you were interested in developing your
physique you "dumb-belled" in between classes. Or you went over
to the Tremont Gymnasium in Boston and lifted weights or worked
on the horizontal bar under the "professor's" direction — often
straining yourself for life in the process.

Wendell Holmes would have none of it. What he liked in the
way of exercise was an hour's skating on the Fresh Pond with plenty
of beer and oysters afterward with his friends. Sometimes on Saturdays he started out with Henry Bowditch, Hallowell, and John
Morse, and walked to Boston along frozen rutted roads or through
the snow, around by Mount Auburn, Watertown, Newton, Brighton,
and Cambridge Crossing. Some of the more sportive spirits went
down to the pit on Federal Street to watch Grip John's dogs kill
rats, thence to Parker's for an evening of drinking, thence to Cambridge in a hired sleigh, hurling snowballs at the new gas globes
on the way.

If Wendell Holmes was with these uproarious spirits, on the Faculty Books his name does not appear for "private admonishing." He
was by nature convivial, a member of the Hasty Pudding Club and of
the Porcellian like his father before him. But Wendell was essentially
independent. He did as he pleased, exercised when he pleased, or
went without exercise if he happened to prefer a stroll up to Garden Street for tea with the Dixwells or across the Square to talk to
Uncle John. Most certainly he did not embrace exercise because the
Autocrat recommended it. The *Autocrat* was out in book form now;
Mr. Lowell stopped Wendell on Kirkland Street to tell him in high
glee that the Germans were going to publish it under the grandiose

and humorless title of *Der Tisch-Despot*. In France, where the family breakfast table was a thing unknown, the whole affair was a mystery. *"L'Autocrate à la table du déjeuner?"* exclaimed a French reviewer. *"Titre bizarre!"*

And the more famous the *Autocrat* became, the more Wendell distrusted his father in this new guise of town prophet and interpreter. There was no telling what he would expose next. Wendell was afraid to talk at home, to tell about the class dinner, the club elections. Were all writers so conscienceless? Everything, everything was grist to the Autocrat's mill. Wendell suffered agonies concerning this indecent lack of privacy. He went gloomily to Uncle John. "Father loves it," he said. "At home last Sunday he showed me a whole desk full of letters from admirers. Mr. Lowell says Father not only *named* the *Atlantic* but he *made* it with this Autocrat. Father says the Autocrat is unburdening him of what he was born to say."

Uncle John grinned. His private opinion was that it would take more than one *Autocrat* to do that. "Don't take it so hard, Wendell," he said. "You will get used to your father. I did, long ago."

Wendell was grateful. How well Uncle John understood the feelings of a college man! . . . And no sooner was the *Autocrat* in print than Dr. Holmes commenced a novel for serialization in the *Atlantic*. At home on Sundays Wendell heard of nothing else. It was about a girl named Elsie Venner whose mother had been bitten by a snake just before Elsie's birthday. Elsie was born with the mark of the beast upon her. Studying the habits of reptiles so as to make Elsie more deadly as well as more beautiful, Dr. Holmes procured a long, very active garter snake and kept it in a cage in the Medical School. He got a stuffed rattlesnake too, and hung it over his books. The parlous worm, he called it. The pizen sarpent. . . .

"Father is nothing if not thorough," Wendell told his Uncle John one evening in Cambridge, staring grimly into the fire.

Uncle John laughed. "I was asked for my autograph the other night, Wendell," he said. "It was at a party in Cambridge. A little boy was collecting the signatures of celebrities. He pushed a piece of paper into my hand. . . . Would it interest you to know how I signed it?"

Uncle John paused, pulling at his cigar. It was a large cigar and smelled awful. Uncle John always smoked five-cent cigars so his taste would not become too refined. He said he hated people whose taste was refined.

Wendell waited. Uncle John's pauses were enough to kill a person from curiosity. Signed the paper — what could he possibly have signed it but "John Holmes"?

"Well?" Wendell said.

"I signed it," Uncle John said slowly — "I signed it, 'John Holmes, *frère de mon frère.*'"

CHAPTER TWELVE

*Harvard College, continued. Father
and son. Fanny Dixwell.*

DECEMBER, 1858 . . . Wendell Holmes was a sophomore
at Harvard. The panic of '57 was almost forgotten; at evening parties, people served wine and meat again instead of hot chocolate and crackers. But at Pittsfield the Holmes house was gone – sold in the hard times when the Wendell stocks yielded no profit.

Around Montgomery Place, houses were going up; shops were creeping onto Tremont Street. Dr. Holmes decided to take his family across the Common to the new part of town that had lately been filled in from the Back Bay swamp. He found a house on the river side of Charles Street. The back rooms had a beautiful view across the water to the northern hills. Wendell's room was on the third floor. As a sophomore, Wendell was no longer permitted every week end at home, but he came for the six weeks' vacation after Christmas.

Climbing the stairs late one January afternoon, Wendell wished the house were even higher. His father was practising the violin downstairs in the little room to the left of the front door. Last summer at Nahant the doctor had been suddenly seized with a desire to play the fiddle. Learning the violin was a mere matter of application, he said cheerfully. Application and persistence. He had persisted – and the result was dreadful.

Wendell flung his hat on the rack by the door. Cigar smoke drifted down from the upstairs sitting room. Wendell took the stairs two at a time. Uncle John was sitting in the big leather chair by the fire, his head in his hands, his whole attitude one of extreme dejection. Wendell roared with laughter. "Uncle John," he said, groping in his pockets for his tobacco pouch, "do people often burst into musicality at fifty?"

John Holmes shook his head. "It's not music. It's manual dexterity. Don't you remember the stereoscope, at Pittsfield? Before that it was the microscope and before that it was whittling with a pen knife."

"But the stereoscope didn't make a noise," Wendell said.

Uncle John sighed. "At Agassiz's the other night they asked me if it was true, about your father playing the violin. I said unfortunately yes, that my brother has often fiddled me out of the house. Like Orpheus, harping Eurydice out of the infernal regions."

Wendell grinned and was silent. Once he had asked Uncle John whether his father did all these things for fun or for self-improvement and Uncle John had replied with a whole lecture on the New England mind. Grandfather Abiel Holmes, it seems, had raised his boys to believe in the Devil. Then things changed around New England and the Devil sort of disappeared. People were lost without the Devil to fight. So they stood on platforms like Cousin Wendell Phillips, and denounced slavery. Or they frequented hospitals and fought puerperal fever. . . .

From downstairs the fiddle screeched like a thing in pain. It was a battle, plainly, between Dr. Holmes and the violin. Plainly, also, the doctor was losing. Wendell took a long pull on his pipe. "But you, Uncle John," he said. "You aren't always striving and sweating after something you can't have."

John Holmes leaned toward the fire, rubbing his bad knee. "Striving?" he said. "Me? Why no, Wendy. I gave up the law twenty years ago. I just stay round and look after your grandmother over in the Gambrel-roofed House. I like it that way."

He smiled up at the long figure slouching by the fire. "You have to know the answers to things, don't you, Wendell?"

By the end of his sophomore year at Harvard, Wendell Holmes had fallen from twenty-second in his class to thirtieth. The indefatigable James Kent Stone, grandson of the great New York Chancellor, was first. Henry Bowditch was eighth. Dr. Holmes grumbled to his wife. "Thirtieth! What kind of position in the class is that?"

Amelia Holmes shook her head. "The boy is just eighteen. He's thin as a fence rail. I measured him yesterday on the pantry wall. Six feet three and a little over. I don't believe he has his growth even yet. It takes *energy* to grow."

Dr. Holmes, observing his own five feet five in the mirror over the bureau, remarked that that was something he didn't know much about. But the boy seemed so lazy. Spent hours mooning on the window seat in the library, with a book in his hand. It wasn't as if he hadn't a good brain, either, and a kind of natural aptitude for books. He wanted application, that was all.

Amelia, sitting in the bedroom rocker darning a sock, remarked to herself that her husband was growing more like his father every day. The things he expected from the boys! Neddy was half dead trying to be first in his class at Dixwell's. It was a good thing, perhaps, that Wendell didn't seem to hear half of what his father said to him. One night long ago, when she and Oliver Holmes were engaged, Oliver's father had given him a long lecture about something, she had forgotten what. Oliver, furious, had burst into the house on Bedford Place complaining that fathers ought not to let themselves become too steeped in virtue. . . .

Amelia reminded her husband of it, now. Dr. Holmes laughed. "Did I say that, 'Melia?" He looked pleased. "*Too steeped in virtue!* Graphic kind of phrase. I must have said it. Not at all the phrase a woman would invent."

Amelia Holmes went on with her darning. A sigh escaped her. Were all men so in love with the word and the sound of the word? One quoted phrase of his own, and already her husband had forgotten everything she had said about her sons. Things she had been planning to say for months and had waited for the right moment. On the landing outside, the big clock struck six. Tea time. Amelia rose. It would be useless to pursue the subject. Something was wrong between father and son, and nothing she said could right it.

Wendell Holmes, pursuing his pleasant undergraduate path, was not disturbed about what his father thought. He was used to it. What did surprise him was the attitude of his classmates toward the whole business of scholarship. They looked upon books as something to avoid or, if you forced yourself to read, something to brag about if the book was signed Plato or Aristotle. At home, or at Uncle John's, the library was open to everyone. You read what you desired to read. The men who came to the Holmes house to tea, to dinner — Emerson, Dr. James Freeman Clarke, Mr. Lowell, Mr. Appleton — never read a book because it was the thing to do. They read with passionate interest and with passionate interest discussed what they had read.

In his sophomore year, Wendell wrote an essay called "Books," and the *Harvard Magazine* published it. "Read for ideas, not for authors," Wendell wrote. "I cannot get beyond the belief that it is best to read what we like." It was a boyish essay, long-winded and stiff, smacking of the sophomore. "Those who have somewhat higher aspirations than the mass of their companions and who in the ranks of boyish insipidity find none who meet or satisfy their desires, must as an alternative turn to books." Find your knowledge first-hand, the essay urged. Not from commentators but from the great minds of all the ages. Plato, Confucius, Buddha, Zoroaster. Read the way Emerson reads.

Dr. Holmes was astonished by this outburst. "The way Emerson reads!" he repeated to his wife. "What about the way the rest of us read? Zoroaster! 'Melia, where do you suppose Wendell got hold of Zoroaster, or did he just make it up?"

That Christmas, Wendell had books for presents. Plato's *Works*, translated into English by Burgess, published in London. "O. W. Holmes, Jr.," was written on the flyleaf. "From his father and mother. Christmas, 1859". . . . Homer's *Iliad* — "From A. J. H. and E. J. H." Amelia and Neddy had done themselves proud by him, Wendell said, smiling. He had asked for the Plato. Professor Lane had recommended the translation grudgingly. Plato should be read in Greek, he said. But even Lane conceded that the content, the philosophy, might best be mastered first in English.

There were more teachers of Greek and Latin than of any subject at Harvard — and every one of them but Lane taught the classics as mere grammatical discipline, a matter for the memory, not the mind. But to Lane, who had studied philology at Göttingen and Berlin, Greek culture was something living, something of which he was a passionate champion. When he finally recommended Plato to Wendell Holmes, Lane did it with fire in his eye. Holding the book in his hand, thrusting it toward the boy, "This was written yesterday," he said. "It will be your exciting privilege to discover a new writer."

All the six weeks' winter vacation, Wendell read the *Republic*, searching its pages with curiosity. Why, this man thought like a Boston Transcendentalist! Truth was truth, goodness existed in itself. Downstairs on winter evenings Wendell had heard much talk about Platonic Idealism. Attacking the source, he found it not wholly to his taste. After a month's study he wrote out his conclusions; they covered fifteen pages. It might be a good idea to offer this piece to the University *Quarterly* next fall; there was a yearly prize for the best undergraduate essay. Someone not professionally connected with Harvard should read it first — someone familiar not only with the classics but with comparative philosophy from Buddha to Christ . . . Emerson! Emerson knew everything, had read everything. Moreover, when you asked Emerson a question he looked you straight in the eye with neither amusement nor condescension, and answered you as man to man.

Wendell gave his essay to Emerson, and Emerson sat down in the big leather rocker by the fire and read it while its author fidgeted on the sofa. When he was done Emerson arranged the sheets neatly, held them out to Wendell and shook his head. "When you shoot at a king you must kill him."

That was all. Wendell took his fifteen pages upstairs and flung them in the wastebasket. A month later Emerson came again. "Have you given Plato another chance?" he asked, his deep eyes kind under the bushy gray brows. "Hold Plato at arm's length as you've been doing, Wendell. That's good. But say to yourself, 'Plato — you have pleased the world for two thousand years. Now let's see if you can please *me*.'"

For the first time in his life, Wendell Holmes began to work his mind. He studied deeply, painstakingly, hour after hour under the white globe in his room, forgetful of time, surprised when the gong rang for supper or when, on the landing below, the clock struck a deep, slow midnight. At college, Professor Lane was delighted. But he did not let his pupil know it. "If you keep on, Holmes, you may learn something. When will you be ready to read Plato in Greek? Failing that you should read him in German. The Germans know how to talk metaphysics."

That winter, Cornelius Felton was appointed President of Harvard to succeed Walker, who had resigned, having had more than his fill of administration. Dr. Holmes had been in college with Felton; in July the whole family came over to Cambridge for the inauguration. Wendell sat with the juniors in the audience. On the platform, well back among the assistant professors, Charles Eliot looked gloomily at his shoes. Felton would be no more responsive to change, newness, the elective system, than Walker had been. Felton was pleasant enough to work with. But Harvard was exchanging one old classical scholar for another old classical scholar.

When the yearly marks were computed, Wendell Holmes stood number thirteen in his class. That should get him into Phi Beta Kappa. His father was Phi Beta; it was wholly necessary that Wendell should be also. He was nineteen. Next fall he would be a senior. In the language of the initiated, he spoke of himself as "a Cambridge man."

Plato . . . violin playing . . . their son's standing in the junior class. These were the things the Holmes family occupied themselves with in the winter of 1859–1860 while their country rushed precipitously down the slope that led to civil war.

If the Holmes family felt that war was coming, if they feared it as the country feared it, there was little they could do. In January, Ben Butler, speaking in Tremont Temple, had said with greatest confidence and a shake of his thick bullet head that there was no possible danger of disunion. In April, 1860, the *Boston Post* reiterated that slaves were property, to be protected as such. John Brown, "that bold and fearless lunatic," was mouldering in his grave. *Garrisonianism, John Brownism*, were disquieting manifestations, but not really dangerous. A Presidential election was coming. Seward was Boston's favorite and the Republicans would surely nominate Seward at Chicago. Abraham Lincoln was a "mere local politician, adroit in stirring up the hatred of one section of his country against the South." The man had, the *Post* admitted, a talent for demagogical appeal that was perhaps worth fifty or a hundred dollars to those who hired him to speak — but "those who heard him in New England were surprised that he should anywhere be considered a great man."

Stephen Douglas, out stumping the West, did not agree. "If I beat Lincoln," he said, "my victory will be won. He is a strong man of his party — full of wit, facts, dates — and the best stump-speaker, with his droll ways, in the west."

It was all politics, and politics was the business of politicians. If Seward should lose the nomination it would be because he talked too much. Slavery was a ruinous subject for a Presidential candidate to approach with anything like frankness. Lincoln had come out flat against slavery in the new territories — but he said nothing about tampering with it in the slave states themselves. Whereas Seward stood up and prophesied that "an irrepressible conflict" was at hand. "Did any property class ever reform itself?" he demanded. "Did the patricians in old Rome, the noblesse or clergy in France? The landholders in Ireland? The landed aristocracy in England? Does the slaveholding class even seek to beguile you with such a hope? Has it not become rapacious, arrogant, defiant?"

Sheer madness, such oratory. Nothing Seward said afterward could talk him out of that speech. He lost the nomination. Boston was disgusted. So the choice was to be between Douglas and this Black Republican? (The other candidates did not count.) The *Boston Post* burst into fury one day, ridicule the next. "Tell us about Abe Lincoln!" they said bitterly. "Tell us about Honest Abe!"

> Tell us of the fight with Douglas,
> How his spirit never quails;
> Tell us of his manly bearing,
> Of his skill in splitting rails;
>
> Tell again about the cordwood,
> Seven cords or more per day;
> How each night he seeks his closet,
> There alone to kneel and pray.
>
> Any lie you'll tell we'll swallow, —
> Swallow any kind of mixture;
> But Oh! don't, we beg and pray you, —
> Don't, for God's sake, show his picture!

The Holmes family was Republican, but the Holmes family saw no reason for indignation when Abe Lincoln was ridiculed. It was all politics, and this was definitely a mud-slinging campaign. Respectable people were already more than a little tired of it. October brought welcome diversion in the form of a visit from Edward, Prince of Wales. Harvard gave him an elegant evening reception. Reporting the affair next day, the *Post* remarked on how very pleased the Prince seemed to be when he was introduced to Dr. Holmes.

Election day was drawing near — the most significant Presidential election the Union had ever faced. But in Boston, life pursued its ordinary course. The clippers sailed as usual from the Long Wharf and as usual were advertised in the morning papers: "The A 1 fast-sailing Packet Ship *Clarissa Currier*, for Melbourne, Australia." . . . "The magnificent Clipper Ship *Derby* — The extreme Clipper Ship *Derby*, for San Francisco."

And Wendell Holmes was a senior at Harvard. He was very busy and important. Besides being a member of Porcellian and Hasty Pudding and Phi Beta Kappa, he was editor of the *Harvard Magazine* and it was his business to produce an article on art. For a long time, Wendell had been a passionate admirer of Albrecht Dürer; in his last year at Dixwell's he had even bought an etching set and taught himself the process. Now he had a chance to talk about it and did, with an enthusiasm that was almost belligerent. "Dürer's works," he wrote, "are dearer to me, and more valued instructors than any book and than any other art."

That same month of October, the *University Quarterly* published an essay on Plato, signed "O. W. Holmes, Jr." To kill a king takes much ammunition — all summer, Wendell had worked on it. But this time there was no trace of cocksureness in what he wrote. The article was long; its sentences were stilted, uncertain. But the final paragraph had in it a young seriousness that was somehow touching: —

In quitting this subject, on which free criticism as well as praise has been used, I should wish my last words to be those of the reverence and love with which this great man and his master always fill me; it seems to me that on the subjects that are the highest, and also the most difficult, few final *results* are yet attained; I do not feel sure that each man's own experience is not always to be that which must ultimately settle his belief, but to see a really great and humane spirit fighting the same fights with ourselves, and always preserving an ideal faith and a manly and heroic conduct; doubly recommended, moreover, to our hearts by the fact of his having only himself to rely on . . . fills my heart with love and reverence at one of the grandest sights the world can boast.

The essay won the undergraduate prize.

Over on Garden Street, Mr. Dixwell heard about it and about the Dürer article, too. When Wendell dropped in one day after class, Fanny Dixwell asked him to bring the articles and read them to her. Wendell looked at her suspiciously. "Are you going to laugh at me, Fanny?" Fanny was twenty now. Her mind was quicker than ever and so was her tongue. It was becoming a habit with Wendell to drop in every few days at the Dixwells'. If Fanny was not at home there was always somebody interesting to talk to — Dr. Bowditch, maybe, or Professor Agassiz or Mr. Dixwell himself. Sometimes, turning in at the white wicket gate, Wendell met old Professor Sophocles coming out with his empty egg basket, his blue cloak and gray beard blowing in the breeze. Fanny loved Professor Sophocles. Mr. Longfellow said that to look at him made Diogenes possible. If you asked Sophocles whether he had read the paper today, he invariably replied, "No! Is this *statement* day or *contradiction* day?"

Fanny liked the Dürer article. She liked the Plato too — but wasn't there room for a trifle more investigation on this subject? . . . At the Athenaeum the Holmes library card grew thick with titles: Grote's *History of Greece*, Whewell's *Platonic Dialogues*, Lewes and W. A. Butler on the history of philosophy, Plutarch's *Morals*, Fichte and Comte and Spinoza. R. A. Vaughan's *Hours with the Mystics* affected him profoundly; he read it again and again. At the University Library, Xenophon was gone for a month; Wendell Holmes paid the fine. At the University Bookshop, John Bartlett — whose collection of *Familiar Quotations* had become so popular — sold Wendell a German edition of Plato he had despaired of ever getting off his shelves. Six volumes of it.

"Can you read it?" Fanny Dixwell demanded suspiciously.

Wendell laughed. "No — but I can spell it out. . . . Fanny, you attack a man's vanity like a — like a she-wolf. You are a shebus and a witch, and something in that gray-green eye tells me you were born on a Friday night with the moon at the quarter."

Fanny Dixwell was used to being a surprise. This was not the

Fanny Dixwell at Seventeen Reading to
Five Brothers and Sisters

first time she had been accused of a quality slightly fey. Often she withheld her surprises; not every man accepted them as gracefully as Wendell Holmes. She smiled, looking slantwise at Wendell, her strong fine hands clasped in her lap, her bright eyes quizzical. "You are cleverer than I, Wendell Holmes," she said softly. "But sometimes I think it is going to take you a long time to grow up."

CHAPTER THIRTEEN

Lincoln's election. War. Class Day
at Harvard.

NOVEMBER, 1860 . . . By election day the trees along
Cambridge lanes were stripped of leaves; in the Dixwells' garden
the chrysanthemum leaves were brittle and on the road to Boston
the mud was frosted into ruts. Westward to Albany and beyond,
in mill towns, prairie towns, mining towns, the nights were bright
with rockets, torchlight processions, and all the paraphernalia of the
most intensely felt Presidential election since Jackson's.

Wendell Holmes lacked sixteen months of voting age and was
sorry for it. Lincoln did not need his vote, that was becoming
pretty certain. But Wendell would have liked to give testimony
at college as to where he stood. His classmates were by no means
united for Lincoln. Neither was the faculty. President Felton was
not opposed to slavery; neither was Benjamin Peirce the mathematician who had friends among the Southern planters. Harvard had
always taken the conservative side. Ten years ago when Webster
had hedged on the issue in his Seventh of March speech, only Emerson, Sumner, and Lowell had stood against him. And when Emerson
spoke in Cambridge against the Fugitive Slave Act, the law students
had hissed and hooted; their professors, too, were all on the conservative side.

To Harvard undergraduates the issue was still a sort of political
lark. An anti-slavery meeting was scheduled in Tremont Temple;
a crowd of Wendell's friends decided to go. They were tired of
seeing every Abolitionist speaker forced off the platform, they said.

If there was to be a roughhouse they were going to see that some of it came from the anti-slavery side. Wendell Holmes went along. He liked a fight as well as anyone. But he began to feel very differently when they got off the horsecar on the Boston side and Henry Bowditch took off his hat and began stuffing it with handkerchiefs. "To soften things," he said.

Fists are one thing, brickbats another. A sudden picture crossed Wendell's mind: Mr. Higginson, coming in the door at Montgomery Place, a bloody bandage round his head . . . There had been a sound of bells tolling . . . When you were a boy you thought fighting was just noise and fun. But this business wasn't fun. It was ugly, ominous.

Election day fell on the seventh — a morning of pale blue, cloudless sky. Men stood in groups on the street corners, talking. They did not ask, "Will Lincoln win?" They asked, "Will the cotton states secede when they see a Black Republican in the White House?"

That night there were processions, torchlight, fireworks. Up Beacon Street marched the Black Republicans. The Somerset Club was dark; its members sat behind closed doors. The "anarchical doctrines of the Black Republicans had prevailed." But in spite of a big majority in the Electoral College, Lincoln won only forty per cent of the popular vote. He was to be a minority President.

It had been a lurid, red-painted, bitter campaign. Boston turned with relief to other matters. Five days after election the Harvard Museum of Comparative Zoology was inaugurated and the city papers ran the whole ceremony on the front page. It was Professor Agassiz's triumph. For years he had begged an appropriation from the hard-fisted farmers, shopkeepers, millowners, and lawyers that made up the Massachusetts General Court. It had been unfortunate for Agassiz that Darwin's *Origin of Species* was published in '59. Few people on this side of the water read it — but the rumor had gone round. . . . "What," one of the Court members demanded, "has Agassiz with his pickled periwinkles and pólypuses done that is really useful?" A liberal member answered bravely: "The religious world owes the professor a debt of gratitude for triumphantly combating that new-fangled and monstrous teaching that we are descended from monkeys."

"I thank God," the first speaker roared, "that I have only to go to His word — not to any French professor of atheism — for that!"

But the Museum was a fact now, and Boston was proud of it. Lincoln's inauguration was still far off; it was good to think of other things. Threat was in the air, but if the Southern states were going to make one of their wild gestures they would surely wait till March. Charles Francis Adams (Harvard '56) was in Washington visiting his father; he wrote home that the House was a disorderly body, filled with fire-eating, long-haired Southerners spoiling for a fight. Jefferson Davis, though, was an attractive figure — courteous, but not to be trifled with. Boston's one-time hero, Charles Sumner, had become almost unbalanced in his morbid excitement; it was a good thing Seward was at hand to take charge. Lincoln was still in the West, "perambulating the country, kissing little girls and growing whiskers."

But the Southern states did not wait till March to make their gesture. Just before Christmas, South Carolina seceded. For a day the North was badly shocked, then recovered, shrugging the thing off as so much Southern braggadocio. South Carolina would come crawling back at the first show of muskets. Dr. Holmes wrote a poem inviting her back. It was called "Brother Jonathan's Lament for Sister Caroline," and like most of the doctor's poems it went straight to the public heart. Critics called it a gem of patriotism, touching and truthful.

> Oh Caroline, Caroline, child of the sun,
> We can never forget that our hearts have been one, —
> Our foreheads both sprinkled in Liberty's name,
> From the fountain of blood with the finger of flame!
>
> You were always too ready to fire at a touch;
> But we said, "She is hasty, — she does not mean much."
> We have scowled, when you uttered some turbulent threat;
> But Friendship still whispered, "Forgive and forget."
>
> Go, then, our rash sister! afar and aloof,
> Run wild in the sunshine away from our roof;
> But when your heart aches and your feet have grown sore,
> Remember the pathway that leads to our door!

Down the street from the Holmeses lived a man who did not think things would solve themselves quite so charmingly. A short, heavy man in his forties, spectacled, with curly dark hair, dimpled chin, and enormous, cheerful energy. A Free-Soiler from way back, John Albion Andrew, who had beaten Ben Butler at the autumn polls and was going to be Governor of Massachusetts. That part of Boston represented by the Somerset Club called Andrew radical, dreamer, fanatic. Dr. Holmes liked him and wanted to propose him for membership in the Saturday Club. But it was too soon — Andrew had still to prove himself. In a howling January snowstorm he was inaugurated. The very same day, he sent out a call for the Massachusetts militia, dispatching through the blizzard a messenger to Maine and New Hampshire to persuade their governors to do likewise. Trouble was coming and we had better be ready when it came. On his staff the Governor put Mrs. Holmes's cousin, Harry Lee, the handsome, witty banker who in spite of his origin and business connections had been a Free-Soiler himself since '48. Andrew sent a man to England to see about new rifles; he talked about getting an appropriation for overcoats for the militia until on Boston Common the word *overcoat* became a bitter joke, slang for warmonger.

The town laughed at John Andrew. One by one, to the sound of its mirth, the cotton states slipped out of the Union. Mississippi, Florida, Alabama, Georgia, Louisiana, Texas. The action put them, everyone said, entirely in the wrong; they would soon find themselves strangling in their own lariat, longing for rescue. The Abolitionists kissed the states a glad good-bye. "Let the Union slide," said the newspapers.

The whole country waited for Lincoln — with hope, with apprehension, with scorn. He was an absolutely unknown quantity. In February, Dr. Holmes wrote a long letter to his friend John Motley, now United States Minister in Vienna. Society in Boston, said the doctor, was nearly as gay as usual. The Saturday Club dinners were feasts of wit, and he had sold stocks at a profit to pay for the house on Charles Street. What made people uncomfortable, though, was the terrible uncertainty of opinion — "I had almost said of principles. We have had predictions that New England was to be left out in the cold if a new confederacy was formed, and that the grass was to grow in the streets of Boston. . . . From the impracticable Abolitionist, as bent on total separation from the South as Carolina is on secession from the North, to the Hunker, or Submissionist, or whatever you would call the wretch who would sacrifice everything and beg the South's pardon for offending it, you find all shades of opinion in our streets.

"If Mr. Seward or Mr. Adams moves in favor of compromise, the whole Republican party sways, like a field of grain, before the breath of either of them. If Mr. Lincoln says he shall execute the laws and collect the revenue, though the heavens cave in, the backs of the Republicans stiffen again, and they take down the old Revolutionary king's arms, and begin to ask whether they can be altered to carry minié bullets. . . . Nobody knows where he stands but Wendell Phillips and his out-and-outers."

Dr. Holmes's son grew restless. Walking down Cambridge Street he ran smack into a company of militia. Men Wendell knew — older men like Higginson — went down to the Market-shed on Washington Street three nights a week to learn the manual of arms. The Home Guard was asking for volunteers; the Fourth Battalion would go out to Fort Independence to guard the harbor if they procured enough enlistments. . . . The Legislature had granted the appropriation for Andrew's despised overcoats; woolen mills were bidding for contracts. Dr. Holmes, stopping at the State House to see Harry Lee, said the Governor had hung samples of shoddy cloth on the gas fixtures in his office, each piece marked with the name of the guilty firm. Everyone who went in walked over and read the names.

The day before Inauguration was Sunday. Down in Washington, young Charles Francis Adams dined with the Sewards. Seward was always critical of Lincoln, but today he made a remark that struck Adams forcefully. "The President," he said, "has a curious vein of sentiment running through his thought, which is his most valuable mental attribute."

The country looked fearfully toward the morrow. The word *assassination* lurked in every mind. In Washington the first days of March had been warm and muggy, but Monday broke clear and beautiful. A few drops of rain fell, just enough to lay the deep dust on Pennsylvania Avenue.

On Boston Common the elms, blown bare of snow, swayed toward a sky astoundingly blue. Walking up Beacon Hill, people bent their heads to the blast, wondering what the day would bring forth, wondering if the new President would be alive at nightfall. . . .

That evening around their supper tables, men breathed freely once more. Father Abraham, too, was eating his supper comfortably down in the White House. Surely it was a portent, a sign of peace! Boston told itself a bit shamefacedly to forget its fears and go about its business as usual. Throughout March, 1861, all was quiet in the North. But Boston knew that down in Charleston Harbor, Fort Sumter's provisions were running low and that the dangerous, decisive question of relief or evacuation must be faced. So far, however, there was nothing to disrupt family life. At 21 Charles Street, the day revolved as usual. Neddy Holmes went off to school at Dixwell's, Amelia and her mother busied themselves around the house. Dr. Holmes walked to the Medical School, stopping along Cambridge Street to joke with the school children, give them words to spell – a penny if they got it right.

On the first of April, Wendell Holmes walked across Harvard Yard to the University Library and took out two books by Ruskin. In May he was scheduled for a disquisition on *Pre-Raphaelitism;* it was high time to get ready.

On the ninth, Lincoln sent provisions to Fort Sumter. On Friday the twelfth, Confederate forces bombarded the fort.

The country knew instantly what it meant. That evening, the *Post* carried a headline: *Civil War is upon us!* Three days later – on Monday – Lincoln sent out the call for 75,000 militia.

Governor John Andrew had not waited for the call. On Sunday night, acting on a report received by the press, he had telegraphed the President – "The quota of troops required of Massachusetts is ready. How will you have them proceed?" The answer came back, "Send them by rail."

It rained on Monday night, a cold, sleety drive. Under it the Massachusetts regiments began to arrive in Boston for transfer south. Many a mother, watching from the window as the boys marched up to the State House for supplies and food, thanked God for the despised word *overcoat*. John Andrew was vindicated. People who had laughed at the overcoat-begger, the musket-kisser, now praised the farsighted leader. "The only loyal pilot," said Dr. Holmes, "whose hand was on the tiller when the black squall struck the great fleet of the Union." In that first week after Sumter, Massachusetts sent out five regiments of infantry, one battalion of riflemen, and one battery of artillery, clothed, drilled, and equipped at the state's expense. It was an extraordinary record, matched nowhere in the Union.

The city was lined with flags. People got up before dawn to stand in the streets and cheer the regiments marching to the station. *"Oh, that will be joyful,"* the boys sang, their boots ringing against cobblestones —

> "Oh, that will be joyful
> When we meet at Fort Monroe."

A few days later, the Sixth Massachusetts reached Baltimore. Crossing town they were stoned and shot at; four were killed, forty-one wounded. The Mayor of Baltimore, horrified, telegraphed Governor Andrew. "Are we to have a war of sections? God forbid." In its front-page editorial the *Boston Post* asked sorrowfully, *"So soon?* Is it possible that the young and strong, who but yesterday we sent forth armed . . . ?"

It was possible. At Harvard, President Felton, Professor Peirce, were Southern sympathizers no longer. At the Law School old Professor Washburn, once Governor of Massachusetts, got out his musket and a military cap left over in the family from the Mexican War, and marched up and down half the night in front of Cambridge Arsenal. The students petitioned to organize a company of dragoons. They would use their own private ponies. Could they form a Drill Club, a company of Flying Artillery? Out in Galena, Illinois, a one-time army captain who had resigned to avoid a courtmartial for drunkenness spoke at a town meeting. He was a clerk in his father's store, named Ulysses S. Grant. "I don't know anything about making speeches," he said. "That is not in my line. But we are forming a company in Galena and mean to do what we can for putting down the rebellion. If any of you feel like enlisting, I will give you all the information and help that I can."

On the twenty-fourth of April, Wendell Holmes joined the Fourth Battalion, New England Guard. Norwood Hallowell[1] was already in it; so were Robeson[2] and Henry Abbott.[3] Captain Stevenson[4] told them all to be at the Armory by noon and to bring along towels, brushes, and one extra pair of shoes. The state would do the rest. At noon on the twenty-fifth,[5] Wendell Holmes signed his name and climbed into his Zouave trousers — light blue and baggy, tucked into gaiters. His tunic was dark blue, his red cap highly becoming. Dr. Holmes thought so anyway; the doctor came to the Armory to see the boys off. He busied about, talking ten to the dozen, greeting the new recruits by name. "Ah, young Abbott! How does your father feel about your enlisting? Wish I were young enough to come along." Everyone was glad to see Dr. Holmes. Everyone, that is, but his son. Catching his father's eye upon him, Wendell recognized only too well that eager, abstracted stare. Surely, some things were sacred, exempt from the rapacious literary eye? Surely his father would not take advantage of war itself to make word pictures?

(In a few months, the first word picture would flaunt itself in the *Atlantic*: "*If the young Zouave of the family looks smart in his new uniform, its respectable head is content, though he himself grow seedy as a caraway-umbel late in the season. He will cheerfully calm the perturbed nap of his old beaver by patient brushing in place of buying a new one, if only the Lieutenant's jaunty cap is what it should be.*")

But in April, 1861, Wendell Holmes was not a lieutenant. He was a simple private and he wished his father would mind his own business.

Out at Fort Independence he was put on garrison duty, drilled six hours a day. There were forty-three guns mounted. Any dark night, one of Jeff Davis's privateer schooners, armed to the gunwales, might loom round the point. The Harvard boys with the Battalion were to be graduated in spite of enlistment. Holmes and Hallowell were to take their examinations in June with the rest of the class, they carried a bagful of books to the Island. Just before they left college the two had been elected Class Poet and Class Orator; their respective creations would have to be hammered out in barracks.

On an evening early in May, Holmes put the finishing touches to his paper for the Harvard Elocutionary Exhibition. He could not get leave to go over to Cambridge and read it — "render his disquisition," the phrase was. But in spite of war, hell, and extra guard duty, the disquisition on Pre-Raphaelitism was finished and delivered duly.

About a week later, Governor Andrew began calling for three-year enlistments — up to now it had been three months. Out at the fort, soldiering was more a lark than a business; on Sundays half of feminine Boston rowed out to see its sons and brothers and sweethearts, bringing cakes, wine, tobacco, and once a handsome silk flag they had embroidered with the insignia of the Battalion. In the militia, officers were badly needed. Up at the State House Colonel Harry

Lee said garrison duty at the fort would qualify a man for a commission. Everyone knew it was to be a short war — ninety days at the most would put the Rebels in their place.

Boston was full of rumor, most of it pretty depressing. The word *treason* was whispered in the streets. How could men tell friend from foe? A blacksmith down near the wharves told somebody that for two cents he'd be a Secesh himself. The neighbors made him put a flag over his shop; they posted placards denouncing him. . . . It was said that somebody had been tampering with the waterworks at Cochituate . . . *Sabotage!* . . . Movements of troops across the city were a daily occurrence. On the sidewalks men stopped, took off their hats. *"Those boys won't run"* — it was the current slogan. Mrs. Lincoln came up from the Capital to see her son Robert, a freshman at Harvard. The newspapers began printing letters from soldiers south of Washington. The boys at Fort Monroe were asking for applesauce from home, to wash down their salt pork. . . . Dr. Holmes's "Army Hymn" — unsigned — appeared on the front page of the *Post:* —

O Lord of Hosts! Almighty King!
Behold the sacrifice we bring!

On the twenty-fifth of May, Wendell's service at the fort was completed. The Battalion returned to Boston in grand style on the steamship *Nelly Baker*, with the Germania Band playing on deck. How many times in summer Wendell had gone down to Nahant in the *Nelly!* Now he carried a gun, wore sky-blue harem pants, and wondered if Fanny Dixwell would be on the Common to see the Battalion parade before they disbanded . . . Marching from the wharf the band played "Yankee Doodle," the crowds cheered. On Beacon Street little boys, darting among the soldiers, begged leave to fill their canteens with water from the hydrant on the corner at Charles Street.

Wendell Holmes went up to the State House and told Cousin Harry Lee he was volunteering for three years' enlistment and would like a commission in the new Harvard Regiment he had heard about. The regiment was not formed yet, Colonel Lee replied; Wendell would have to wait. Applications for commissions were pouring in; the Governor was at a loss on what basis to make the selections. None of these youngsters had army experience; how could anyone tell which would fight and which would run? A surprisingly large number were Harvard graduates. The Governor was not a Harvard man, but Harry Lee was. "Leave this to me," Lee told the Governor firmly. "I don't know all these boys but I've known most of their fathers or uncles or grandfathers. . . . Here – this young fellow's grandfather was a first-rate captain at Louisburg. Why isn't that as good a yardstick as anything?"

It was not sentiment but common sense. If you could not commission a man for what he knew, why not commission him for what he was capable of learning? In a surprisingly short time Harry Lee's method of selection would be more than justified.

Commencement at Harvard was not until the middle of July; Wendell fully expected to be on the outskirts of Richmond by then. But as the weeks wore on and he was not called it became plain he would be at Class Day to read his poem, and so would Hallowell for his oration. Class Day was still – as in Abiel Holmes's time – the great fête of the year. Everybody Wendell knew would be in the Meeting-house to hear the son of Dr. Holmes (Class Poet of '29) read his poem.

On the morning of June 21, the class of '61, in gowns and high beaver hats, met in front of Holworthy Hall. It was a fine day, the air clear and soft. Across Harvard Yard the elms cast brief morning shadows. Under his gown Wendell Holmes clutched his poem. At the fort he had written it in a hurry and had not even made a fair copy; he hoped he would not stumble when he got up to read. The band played a march; the procession started. Hallowell and Holmes walked together. They had both sworn to burn their pieces when the day was over. Put away in lavender in the family archives, these Class Day effusions read to the next generation like comic pieces, Wendell said. Like caricatures of poems, caricatures of orations.

Marching into the Meeting-house, the seniors took their seats on the platform. Holmes, looking down at the audience, saw his family right out in front – his father and mother, Amelia and Neddy, and Aunt Ann Upham who had come up from Salem for the occasion. Just behind them was that woman, Mrs. Somebody, who wrote for the *New York Tribune*. Wendell had seen her Class Day reports and loathed them. They dripped with sentiment.

Professor Hedge had stopped praying. Norwood Hallowell got up and walked forward to give his oration. Wendell scarcely heard him. The rhythm of his own poem was decidedly shaky in spots. Would he be able to read so as to cover this up? Otherwise his father would seize upon it, worry him about it for weeks. He had not shown the poem to anyone at home. He would destroy it quickly, before his father or the *Tribune* woman could get hold of it. . . .

Hallowell finished and sat down. The Pierian Sodality struck up a rather uncertain hymn. When it ceased the audience saw a tall young man, gray-eyed, with a high color and serious eyes, step to the front. ". . . and Oliver," said the class president, "whom also the Class honoreth, for he speaketh with the verse that pleaseth."

The audience smiled, nudged each other, and craned their necks to see how Dr. and Mrs. Holmes were taking it.

In all the Class Archives, all the treasured, faded scrapbooks, Wendell's poem is nowhere to be found. But while he read it the *Tribune* pencil scribbled industriously . . . *Poet* . . . *compares the student leaving college to a steamer leaving port* . . . *felicitous figure* . . . *O. W. Holmes Junior a worthy scion of his father. On national matters his tone hopeful. Poem contains short lyric showing unmistakeable poetic ability* . . . *Dr. Holmes proud of his Poet Son* . . .

These notes, spread to a full column, did not reach the Poet's eye until the morrow. Just now, perspiring freely, Holmes finished and sat down, grinning back at a wildly applauding audience. The Class Ode was sung, there was another prayer. Audience and performers, in a high state of pleasure, poured out of the Meeting-house and went visiting round the Yard in the seniors' rooms, drinking punch and eating ices. The *Tribune* lady went too. Dr. Holmes's[6] feast in his son's room was royal, she noted. "Lobster salad for a battalion, ice cream like the pyramids of Egypt, wine like the over-flowing of the Nile, the Doctor's presence joyous as Apollo." About four in the afternoon the band, sitting outside under the trees, struck up dance music. The Lancers . . . quadrilles.

People poured from the college buildings, girls in light summer dresses, seniors in black gowns. Dr. Holmes in his frock coat and gray trousers danced like a Maenad. His silk hat rolled under a tree and disappeared entirely. There was a great time finding it. A sprinkling of uniforms showed in the crowd. Bob Shaw,[7] class of '60, Robeson of '61, very smart in their light blue trousers with the red stripe down the side, their dark coats with the brass buttons. They

O. W. Holmes Jr.
Boston

Oliver Wendell Holmes, Jr.

At the time of his graduation from Harvard in 1861

wore white gloves, their shiny new swords clanked around their knees. With little delighted screams the girls said they could not dance with long terrifying swords tangled in their skirts.

Wendell's sister Amelia looked pretty as a picture in her pink bonnet and white silk dress trimmed all down the skirt with rose-buds. She danced every dance and never stopped chattering even to get her breath. Fanny Dixwell wore gray, with a touch of red at her throat. She was surrounded by beaux; Wendell could hardly get a word with her. How handsome she looked when she was animated, Wendell thought suddenly. It had not occurred to him before, to consider whether Fanny Dixwell were handsome or homely. But today, everything stood out in sharp relief; there was something in the air that made every face, every sound, every word spoken, every bar of old familiar music, etch itself deeply, terribly in the mind. It was not only that Wendell Holmes was leaving college. He would come back from this war, he told himself, and Holworthy Hall would still be standing. The elms before his grandfather's house would still reach toward the sky. . . . But when he returned he would be a boy no longer. Wendell Holmes knew it and his heart ached strangely within him.

They were singing the class song: *"Classmates as the hasting moments . . ."*

The rings formed round the tree. Hand in hand, freshmen outside, then sophomores, juniors, with the seniors inside close to the tree. Wendell found himself clasping Norwood Hallowell's hand as though his life depended on this firm answering grasp. Round and round the tree they danced, singing, marking time, swinging their clasped hands in the ancient ceremony. Faster and faster until the rings broke and the boys leaped scrambling for the wreath of flowers that encircled the tree above their heads.

Wendell got a rose and flung it across the crowd to Fanny. His breath came hard; he stood stock-still in the scrambling, shouting crowd and was amazed to find himself weeping.

PART III

The Soldier. 1861-1864

CHAPTER FOURTEEN

The Twentieth Regiment.
Ball's Bluff.

J ULY, 1861 . . . At the State House, Cousin Harry Lee said the so-called Harvard Regiment was forming fast; he would try to get a commission for Wendell. It was not really a Harvard regiment; it was the Twentieth Massachusetts Infantry and its members were by no means all Harvard men. But when friends enlisted together they were permitted to stay together, and Harvard seemed to prefer the Twentieth. Massachusetts men objected strongly to being led by anyone born or bred outside the Commonwealth. The Colonel of the Twentieth, William Raymond Lee (no relation to Cousin Harry), was not a Harvard man, he was a "tough West Pointer" — but he was Boston born and bred. Lieutenant Colonel Palfrey (Harvard '51) was Boston to the bone. Wendell's cousin James Lowell [1] had a first lieutenancy; William Putnam [2] and Henry Abbott were second lieutenants; Bartlett,[3] '62, was a captain.

It was hard to wait. Wendell occupied himself with finishing up all odds and ends from the school year. One of these was to write his autobiography for the Class Book. *"State pedigree on your father's side very fully,"* the instructions said, *"and give in briefer form your mother's ancestral line."*

This was easy. Abiel Holmes was in the biographical dictionaries; so were the Jacksons. The Wendells and Olivers could be found in the *King's Chapel Burying-Ground* book. Wendell said so. With a flourish he added some of his great-grandmothers — Dorothy Quincy, Anne Bradstreet, who had been called the Tenth Muse. . . .

"*State prizes you have taken,*" the instructions went on, "*articles you have written, journeys you have made, remarkable risks or accidents you have met with, and other events or curious experiences in your life.*"

Wendell set down the prize for the Plato article and a Greek prize that he had won half-and-half with a junior. . . . But — "*journeys — risks, accidents, curious experiences*"? . . . He had been to Pittsfield, Massachusetts, by the cars. He had been to Nahant by the steamer *Nelly Baker* and once by way of the Lodges' carryall. The cars had not gone off the rails, the *Nelly* had not gone aground, the horses had not foundered. As for curious experiences, his life held none unless you could count the time he went fishing in the Housatonic and brought up an old straw hat of Uncle John's with a crawfish hanging to the brim. You could hardly put that in a class book. It all seemed pretty trivial, considering the turn life was taking now. Well, a man had to put down something. Wendell dipped his pen: —

Our family has been in the habit of receiving a college education and I came of course in my turn, as my grandfathers, fathers and uncles have been before me. . . . I have never had any business but that of a student before coming to College. . . . When the war broke out I joined the "4th Battalion of Infantry" and went down to Fort Independence expecting when drilled to go south (as a private). While at the Fort and after we were ordered up I had to patch up a Class Poem as quickly and as well as I could under the circumstances, since I had been elected to that office before going (2nd term Senior). We stayed about a month at the Fort and then came to Boston and on Class day (a week and a half ago) I delivered my Poem side by side with my friend Hallowell who was orator and who had also been at the Fort. The tendencies of the family and of myself have a strong natural bent to literature, &c. At present I am trying for a commission in one of the Massachusetts Regiments, however, and hope to go South before very long. If I survive the war I expect to study law as my profession or at least for a starting point.

(in haste)

O. W. HOLMES, JR.

July 2nd, 1861.

[and then in pencil]

N. B. I may say I don't believe in gushing much in these College Biog's. and think a dry statement much fitter. Also I am too busy now to say more if I would.

Eight miles south of Boston the railroad cars jerked to a stop at Readville Station. Lieutenant Holmes got down and walked across a grassy plain to where a line of white tents blazed in the July sun. There were shouts of welcome. Hallowell, Abbott, Putnam, Lowell, ran out to meet him.

Holmes found his company small. Recruiting had gone badly in Massachusetts since the initial enthusiasm of Governor Andrew's first call. Even the disastrous news of Bull Run did not bring in many new recruits. But if Company A was small, it was more than large enough for Lieutenant Holmes to handle. He was green as grass and very nervous — far more used to taking suggestions from his elders than to giving out commands himself. Each time a new batch of Nantucket men came in, Holmes prayed he would not get them in his company. All these farmer boys were independent; they had the Yankee attitude. "Why shouldn't a man go where he pleased when his day's work was done and spend his own money without asking leave of any God-damn officer?" When drill was over the men simply departed — without leave — across the plain to Mill Village and got thoroughly drunk on whiskey.

The Nantucket men were strapping big fellows. One day twenty of them arrived. One, named Kelly, was a giant. Surgeon Bryant (Harvard, '40), examining him, whistled with admiration, called Holmes to look over this newest prize. But it was hard for New England to get used to this war. New England had seen little of soldiering since 1812, and even then it had been more a matter of sailors than soldiers. With Major Paul Revere, Holmes went to Mill Village, heard the Major swear at the innkeeper and the innkeeper swear back. Then with drawn pistol he watched an outraged innkeeper empty twenty barrels of liquor into the street. . . . If the new recruits were not getting drunk they were off swimming, without leave, in the Neponset River. One was drowned. But as time went on, even these intractable souls seemed preferable to the latest acquisitions — toothless, flat-footed country boys who arrived in shoals and had to be sent home as unfit. July slipped into August,

August was nearly September, and still the ranks were not filled.

Governor Andrew did not forget his boys of the Twentieth. New rifles arrived, fine new Enfields, very different from the old smoothbore muskets the men had been using. The company that called itself "Andrew's Sharpshooters" showed off every morning on the target range. And on a day late in August the Governor and his staff, including Cousin Harry Lee, came out from Boston to review the Regiment. Dr. and Mrs. Holmes came too, and a bevy of Boston ladies carrying a fine white silk standard they had made for the Twentieth. On one side were the arms of the Commonwealth and on the other the words *Fide et constantia.* Over the plain, brown now and dusty with summer, the ladies picked their dainty, full-skirted way. The Governor made a speech which nobody heard because the wind blew so hard, and then Governor and ladies and Holmeses and everyone's cousins and friends went back to Boston, leaving the Regiment to eat its beans and bacon and to wonder when its marching orders would come.

They came on the second of September. The Regiment was to go straight to Groton, Connecticut; take steamer for New York, thence to Washington and points south. No marching through Boston, no parades on the Common with bands playing and the whole town out to cheer. In Company A, young Kelly from Nantucket fingered his Enfield lovingly. He had tied a rope to it — "to bring back southern traitors," he explained.

In Boston, the Holmes family learned from the newspapers the whereabouts of Wendell's Regiment. . . . The boys were in New York. They had marched up Broadway. . . . They had got across Baltimore without a shot fired. . . . They were in Washington. General Scott had reviewed them from a balcony. . . . They were marching to camp somewhere in Maryland. General Lander had asked especially to have the Twentieth Massachusetts assigned to his brigade. Colonel Lee was so pleased he wrote Governor Andrew about it. Lander was a dashing veteran of the Indian campaigns, a fine figure on a horse, said Lee; the men were crazy about him.

Camp was laid in a wheatfield about two miles from Edwards Ferry on the Potomac. Several weeks after they had settled in, the men sent Andrew six loaves of bread baked from their field ovens. No other regiment had fresh bread, they said proudly. Andrew's Sharpshooters got uppity and refused to take part in target practice. They knew how to shoot without being told, they said. Colonel Lee listened to their complaints — and read them out of the Regiment.

September, October. . . . The Regiment still camped on its hillside, golden now with autumn. A mile away across the river the rebels moved soft-footed among the trees. Their aim was good; now and then a man did not return from guard duty and the Regiment was reminded that this was a war and not a training camp. Once, walking on the towpath by the canal, Holmes heard a Southern voice call across the water, "When are you fellas going to Richmond?" A Yankee voice called back, "The day before you bastards go to Washington."

On Sunday, October twentieth, the observation corps went through its routine as usual. As usual, pickets walked slowly along the banks of the canal. The day was warm and clear, the camp very quiet in the Sunday sunshine. There was nothing to let the Regiment know that before another day was over they would be in the midst of one of the worst battles of the war, across the Potomac up on Ball's Bluff.

After dinner, Lieutenant Holmes sat in the door of his tent, looking downhill toward the river. Clouds moved across the sun and on the riverbank the maples flamed yellow even in shadow. That morning, Colonel Palfrey had read divine service. Holmes was not interested in religion except to rebel against when it was dogmatic, or to discuss as a philosophic system. But there had been something about those words, read in a familiar accent, that went to the heart. In the family pew at King's Chapel, Wendell's father and mother sat reading the same words, making the same responses. It was good to have one hour of the week when a soldier knew exactly where his people were, and could be with them in spirit.

Above the riverbank a hawk wheeled slowly. At home they were just sitting down to Sunday dinner. Cold roast goose, it would be, or cold roast mutton and pork, cooked the day before to save Sunday work. Fish salad maybe, and some of his mother's good onion pickle. Crab-apple pie for dessert, and pumpkin pie and cheese and fruit and candy. After dinner his father would go upstairs for a nap, or to his study . . . His father, Wendell remembered now, was called freethinker by the orthodox. He was even called atheist; the whole family had seen angry letters from readers to whom religion meant orthodoxy or nothing. Yet Wendell had never known him to miss a Sunday at King's Chapel. What had the Autocrat said? "There is a little plant called *Reverence* in the corner of my Soul's garden, which I love to have watered about once a week."

But a man couldn't force those pleasant sentiments. Either you had religion or you didn't have it. . . . Over the river the hawk swooped, then rose again. . . . In battle, did a man call upon God? So far, thought Wendell Holmes, this war had been something of a picnic for himself and his friends. He had always been very susceptible to pain. These farmer boys in the ranks — did they sweat for fear they might lose their nerve and make fools of themselves? They didn't talk about it. Big Kelly, for instance. Nobody could imagine Kelly crying if he were hurt. . . . Battle would surely come before long. The Twentieth wasn't down here for target practice. Yesterday there had been talk of trouble around Leesburg across the river, about eight miles back where the Rebels had a large force. Well, if trouble was coming it might as well come soon. . . .

The quiet was broken by a bugle. It was the call to arms. From everywhere, men ran to position, grabbing up their equipment. That rumor about Leesburg must have meant real business, Holmes thought, running to his tent.

It was more than the call to arms. It was the call to battle.

In a field above a cliff on the Virginia side of the river, the Twentieth lay in the high grass and waited for the rest of the Brigade to arrive. Ball's Bluff, the place was called. Across the field the enemy waited too, hidden by thick trees. It had taken the men half the night to cross the river in four leaky old scows they had picked up. The current ran very deep and swift. In the middle of the river there was an island, a thin strip of land about two miles long. If we have to retreat, Colonel Lee had said, make for that island.

Retreat? Nobody in the Twentieth was thinking of retreat. They were thinking of glory. Holmes heard Colonel Baker congratulate Colonel Lee on the prospect of a battle . . . The lines were formed. At command, Holmes's company cocked their rifles, fired straight into the wood.

After that things happened too fast for Holmes to ask himself if he were scared. Charging out of the woods the Rebels yelled, high and savage, like Indians. Up from the river came the Tammany

Regiment, and the California, single file in the smoke, scattering like Indians. Holmes had not fired twice when a spent ball hit him in the stomach. When he got his wind he struggled up. . . . Over by the grove they were fighting hand-to-hand now. Going down on one knee, Holmes aimed . . . The blow came again, in the chest this time. Wendell fell, vomited, lay with his eyes shut. The pain in his chest was terrible. In his tunic pocket was a bottle of laudanum. Cautiously he lifted a hand to see if he could reach it . . . Why, he had no shirt on! His breast was wet and slippery.

Wendell fainted. Around him the battle went on and on. . . .

Boston, half crazy with anxiety, waited for news. There had been an engagement, the *Post* said, somewhere down by Leesburg in Virginia. Colonel Baker was killed, Colonel Lee, Major Revere and his brother not accounted for. . . . Two days later the *Post* listed the regiments engaged at Ball's Bluff — no word as to defeat or victory, no casualties named. Mrs. Holmes went dumbly about the house, her face blank, stricken. Her husband could find no comforting word. On Friday — five days after the battle — word came by telegram from Harry Lee, who had gone down to Edwards Ferry. Wendell had been hit in the chest. He was in the field hospital, and doing well. He would travel to Philadelphia with Hallowell when able. They were not to worry.

That same day, the *Post* carried a full account of the battle. Reading it, Dr. Holmes turned white and carried the paper downstairs where his wife would not find him. The whole thing had been the most horrible defeat for the North. *Worse than a crime — a blunder!* said the headlines. The boys had fought all day. Toward dusk they had been driven back, down a steep bluff to the river. Falling, leaping, rolling to the water's edge. Trying to swim, calling for help in the swift current. A skiff filled with wounded capsized. Every man was drowned. The river ran blood; in the scows the men slipped, fell on wounded bodies . . . There had been no plan apparently, for rescue; there were no boats, no rafts . . .

Captain Putnam, right arm amputated . . . Captain Peirson, raking wound in the back . . . Captain Dreher, carriage painter, Salem, shot in both thighs . . . *O. W. Holmes, Company A, 24, law student, Boston, wounded in abdomen.*

But Harry Lee's telegram had said in the chest! Besides, Wendell wasn't twenty-four. He was twenty. *Law student.* Wendell must have given that classification himself. Or perhaps they got it from his papers? . . . *J. J. Lowell, law student, wounded in thigh* . . . Why, that was Charles Russell Lowell's young brother, three classes ahead of Wendell at Harvard.

Next day the *Post* had the lists again, a little different this time. "O. W. Holmes, wounded, not fatal. Lowell and Holmes doing well."

Dr. Holmes took the paper to his wife. "Tom Dwight is going down to Edwards Ferry," he said. "And Gay and some others. Perhaps I should cut my classes at the Medical School and go with them?"

Mrs. Holmes shook her head. They had more doctors than food at Edwards Ferry, she reminded her husband. The Sanitary Commission had sent twenty nurses down with Harry Lee. Dr. Holmes would be of more use in Boston. If he went away, who would take over his training classes at the Commission? "I am going there now," Amelia Holmes said. "Shall we walk down together?"

Two weeks later, Wendell Holmes was able to leave the hospital, which by now was filled with wailing relatives who hampered the doctors at every turn. Norwood Hallowell took Wendell to Philadelphia and put him to bed in the hospitable old house on Walnut Street. A week later Dr. Holmes came to fetch him. He found his son white as a sheet, barely able to walk, but in surprisingly good spirits and very glad to see his father. He could travel, Wendell said. Yes, he wanted to go home right away. Dr. Holmes engaged six seats on the cars to Boston and had a mattress spread across them. Leaning on his father's arm, Wendell climbed into the train. . . . How tractable he was! Dr. Holmes marveled, looking down at the face on the bed, the eyes closed, the lashes dark against the pallor. Something must have happened to Wendell on that bloody field, something besides fighting. The pride and testiness of youth were gone, and with them some anger that had been there, something rebellious.

But the boy would not talk. Dr. Holmes itched to know all. What was it like when those minié balls whined by your ear? Was it true the Rebels yelled when they went into battle? Where had Dr. Revere and his brother been when they were captured? . . . Above

all was it true that William Putnam had died in the hospital? Will —
the golden-haired, the blue-eyed, tall and straight, the handsomest
man in Harvard College?

It was true, Wendell replied wearily. On the trip in the canal
barge to the hospital he himself had fainted. When he opened his
eyes in a hospital cot, Surgeon Bryant and an officer were standing
by the next bed. Bryant said, "He was a beautiful boy." Wendell
had asked the boy's name. It was William Lowell Putnam.

At 21 Charles Street, Wendell was carried upstairs and put to
bed. Mrs. Holmes was a skillful nurse. She took the bread poultice
off the wound; when Dr. Bigelow came, brought basin and towels
and calmed the patient, who was extremely apprehensive, preferring
what he had seen of battle to lying here being poked at. Bigelow
etherized him and probed the wound. The ball had passed right
through the chest, missing heart and lungs by a fraction. When Wendell came to he was nervous, started when anyone approached the
bed. Dr. Holmes gave him laudanum. Next morning he was bright
and natural, demanded to see his sister and Neddy. Where were his
friends? Was Henry Ropes at home? Had anybody heard from
John Gray lately? How about Fanny Dixwell? Didn't people in
these parts come to ask after their friends when they had been
wounded on a battlefield?

"Wendell is a great pet in his character of young hero with
wounds in the heart," Dr. Holmes wrote John Motley in Vienna.
"He receives visits *en grand seigneur*. I envy my white Othello with
a semicircle of young Desdemonas about him listening to the often
told story which they will have over again. Wendell's experience was
pretty well for a youngster of twenty. A most narrow escape from
instant death."

The reticence of the first weeks had left Wendell entirely. The
more he talked the healthier he became. He was still very white, but
the haunted look had left his eyes and returned only at night or
when he was tired. It was as though telling these things exorcised
the horror, chased away the demon altogether. Wendell actually
laughed when he told them. Up there on the bluff he had thought
he was dying, he said. In the *Children of the New Forest* they had
all died to slow music . . . He had wondered why the music didn't
begin. . . . After that he remembered nothing until he came to
in the scow in the middle of the river. Somebody's leg was lying

across his and he tried to work his leg free. The man that was poling them slipped and let out a curse.

"What did he say?" Neddy asked quickly. It was late afternoon. Wendell sat by the library fire. Neddy lay on the floor, his chin propped in his hands. Henry Ropes was there, smoking his pipe. Amelia and Fanny Dixwell sat over by the west window, knitting.

"Never mind what he said," Wendell replied. "The army knows all the cusswords."

When the scow scraped bottom — Wendell went on — the man next to him groaned. Sir Philip Sidney would have said, "Put that man ashore first."

Wendell grinned at his audience. "I decided to keep still and let matters take their course."

He had been lucky to get across the river at all. Norwood Hallo-well had swum over, his sword hanging from his neck. Crownie — Caspar Crowninshield, Harvard, 1860 — Crownie had swum over in his uniform, carrying his watch in his mouth. Bullets hit the water all round him, but it was getting dark and the Rebs missed. General Lander had caught a ball in the leg. In hospital at Edwards Ferry a wounded Secesh officer told Lander that fewer Massachusetts officers would have been killed if they hadn't been too proud to surrender. Lander wrote a poem about it.

Wendell reached in his pocket. "Here — I copied it. Pretty good for an old Indian fighter."

Fanny Dixwell put down her knitting and crossed the room. "Let me read it, Wendell."

Mrs. Holmes, wearily climbing the stairs in her street clothes with her arms full of lint from the Sanitary Commission, heard Fanny's soft familiar voice and smiled. Reaching the living-room door she paused silently. Fanny was leaning forward to catch the fading light from the west windows: —

> Aye, deem us proud, for we are more
> Than proud of all our mighty dead;
> Proud of the bleak and rock-bound shore,
> A crowned oppressor cannot tread.
>
> . . . . .
>
> *Pride*, 'tis our watchword; "clear the boats,
> "Holmes, Putnam, Bartlett, Peirson, — Here,"
> And while this crazy wherry floats,
> "Let's save our wounded," cries Revere.

Old State — some souls are rudely sped —
This record for thy Twentieth Corps, —
Imprisoned, wounded, dying, dead,
It only asks, "Has Sparta more?"

Mrs. Holmes turned and walked upstairs to her room. Tears were in her eyes, tears not of grief but of thankfulness. She had been all day at the Commission. They had made her head of the Boston branch, a position of much responsibility. The Commission was auxiliary to the Army Medical Corps. It fitted up hospital ships, organized hospital units, and equipped them with bandages, medicines, supplies. It taught company officers how to care for their men, sent men and women to nurse the wounded, and dispatched everything to the troops from bread and beef to coffee and laudanum.

Unhooking her whaleboned bodice, Mrs. Holmes sighed. This morning the *Post* had carried an account of eight hundred Rebel prisoners received at Fort Warren in the harbor. And right in the next column was a ridiculous squib that she could not forget. It ran over and over, maddeningly, in her mind . . . "Why do women like stays? . . . Because they feel *so-laced* by them."

How crazy it all was, this war, at home as well as on the battlefield! Here in Boston, bitterness far outran — according to Wendell — anything felt at the front. The *Liberator* printed horrible stories of Southern atrocities. Dr. Holmes said every war gave rise to these tales; what angered him was the rank treason one met on Boston Common itself. Recruiting called up more quarrels than soldiers. Ben Butler wanted to raise troops one way, Governor Andrew another. Andrew took his complaints to the White House and Lincoln listened gravely. "General Butler," he said at last, "is cross-eyed; I guess he don't see things the way other people do."

In the Virginia field nothing happened; General George McClellan gave out new reasons for delay. "What are you waiting for, tardy George?" they sang on the streets. Lincoln remarked that if General McClellan did not want to use the army he would like to *borrow* it. . . . "The President is not equal to the occasion," Charles Francis Adams wrote his brother Henry in London. "The Secretary of War is corrupt and the Secretary of the Navy is incompetent. With the rebels showing us what we can do, we ought to be ashamed not to do more."

For Dr. and Mrs. Holmes, this winter of 1861–1862, there was at least certainty of principle, certainty of their own course of action, and that was a relief. There was also, it was true, this unremitting ache in the breast, this knowledge that the young laughter upstairs, the young soldier safe within the warm walls of home, was being mended only to be target for another bullet that might be more accurate than the last. How gay the young were in the face of all this! How gay and how regardless. The old could not ape this young carelessness. The old were bowed down, weighted with consciousness of the future. But the old could keep the faith, and that was important. *"Faith,"* Dr. Holmes wrote Motley not long afterward, "faith is the only thing that keeps a man up in times like these. . . . If I never see peace and freedom in this land, I shall have faith that my children will see it. If they do not live long enough to see it, I believe their children will. . . . I won't say to you, 'Be of good courage,' because men of ideas are not put down by accidents of a day or a year."

By the New Year, Wendell's wound was healed. His orders came, but when he opened them he found he was to stay home indefinitely on recruiting duty. He traveled all over Massachusetts. John Ropes's young brother Henry joined the Twentieth, and Norwood Hallowell's brother Ned.[4] Colonel Lee and Major Revere were in a Southern prison, hostages for the Rebel privateers captured by the Federal fleet. If the Southern pirates were hung, Lee and Revere would hang too. The sisters of Lowell and Putnam, who had been wounded at Ball's Bluff, sent a memorial flag down to the Twentieth Regiment. *"Stand in the evil day,"* it said on one side.

Dr. Holmes was roused to anger at the tone of the British press. John Bright and the labor men seemed the only people in Europe who sympathized with the Northern cause. Everyone else saw the North fighting for industrial conquest, the South for "independence." The word *Union* — so magic with symbolism for Americans — abroad was totally uncomprehended. Why, England asked, should the South be coerced into a union disadvantageous to her? The West End of London and the rich manufacturing interests wanted to keep the war going till they had sold off their surplus cotton at Lancashire.

"The West end is right!" Dr. Holmes wrote to Motley, his heart hot with anger. "Not by aggression, but by the naked fact of existence, we are an eternal danger and an unsleeping threat to every

Captain Oliver Wendell Holmes, Jr.

government that founds itself on anything but the will of the governed. We begin to understand ourselves and what we represent, now that we find who are our enemies, and why, and how they would garrote us now that our hands are on these felons' throats. . . . I do believe Hell is empty of Devils for the last year, this planet has been so full of them helping the secession liars."

There was a great split over making government paper legal tender, the letter went on to say. "But I believe our people are worked up to the *paying* point, which, I take it, is to the fighting point as boiling heat (212°) to blood heat (98°)." People who had met Father Abraham considered him honest enough, but simply incompetent and without plan. The emancipationists were roaring for action. The black man, they said, was the life of the South; take him away and the whole lazy structure would collapse. The *Tribune* attacked McClellan, everyone grumbled at delays. "But I believe the wisest heads are as yet reasonably patient. They know that the Virginia roads are impracticable at this particular time. They know the enlistment period of many of the rebel troops is about to expire — *before this very month is out.*"

Since Christmas the war news from the West had been good, with Federal victories in Kentucky, Tennessee, Arkansas. The Western generals were very unpopular in the East — but there was no denying they got things done. The Eastern generals Wendell Holmes had known seemed to be petering out. The dashing Lander was dead of a chill he took in camp in Virginia. General Stone was in a Federal prison, blamed for the Ball's Bluff disaster — unjustly, the men of the Twentieth said.

On the eighth of March, 1862, Wendell Holmes had his twenty-first birthday. It was Sunday, and the family walked down to King's Chapel, picking their way through mud and half-melted snow. All day the city talked excitedly about the rebel ship *Merrimac* down in Norfolk Harbor. The *Merrimac* carried ten guns; she was fitted with an iron ram and a roof of iron plates and she was spreading destruction right and left. If something didn't stop her she would be at the gates of Washington. Stanton urged Welles to block the channel by sinking loaded canal boats. Welles refused. The *Monitor* could defend Hampton Roads, he said. . . . In God's name, the country asked, what was the *Monitor?* Some newfangled little craft with armored deck and a revolving gun turret. A Swede had designed her. Nobody but Gideon Welles and the Swede believed in her.

But by Sunday night the *Monitor* had chased the *Merrimac* back to Norfolk. Boston got its breath again. . . . There was other war news: the Rebels had retreated from Manassas, McClellan had ordered the whole army to advance. To Wendell Holmes this meant that his Regiment would be moving rapidly southward. On the twenty-third of March his orders came. He was to rejoin the Regiment at Hampton, Virginia, with the rank of captain.

This time Wendell Holmes — in misery and fatigue, in boredom and horror, in exaltation and in the black depression of sickness — would learn what war really meant to soldiers in the field.

CHAPTER FIFTEEN

The Seven Days. Antietam.
Dr. Holmes hunts for a wounded captain.

CAPTAIN HOLMES found his regiment on the Virginia Peninsula a mile down the road from Hampton. The greetings were loud and heartfelt. Hallowell had grown a beard; Captain Putnam [1] was minus an arm. Down here the weather was bright and amazingly warm, the trees were budding. Out in the harbor lay the *Monitor*, looking small and insignificant; her turret would not reach the deck of a small ship. Was this the mighty vessel that had chased the *Merrimac* down the Roads?

And now began the march north and west, up the Peninsula to find Stonewall Jackson and fight him down to Richmond. Through swamp and tangled thicket, dragging musket and knapsack the men struggled, their light blue uniforms coated with mud. There was work eternally to be done: guns mounted, earthworks dug. The rains began; the men stood in water by day and lay in it by night. They devised beds on poles, shelters on stilts, and still they were never dry. Once, marching eleven hours, they made exactly half a mile, sinking down exhausted under a black and heavy sky. The enemy was always near; at dawn the sharpshooters got to work. Captain Bartlett lost a leg. Scurvy broke out, and dysentery; the men lay in misery on the ground. May, June, July . . . The men stole watermelons from the fields, ransacked the country for berries, and ate them green where they found them. It was a wild and desolate country. To Wendell Holmes, marching endlessly under the steaming sun, all faculties of the soul seemed to depart one after the other, leaving only a dumb animal power to set the teeth and persist — a blind belief that somewhere at least there was rest and water. By the time they met the enemy face to face, a third of the Regiment was sick. Cabot, Curtis, Mason, Tilden, and a score of others were sent back by ambulance to the James River, moaning, half delirious in the swinging, bumpy caravan.

Wendell Holmes was sick too, but he managed to keep on his feet, rising at dawn from his damp blankets, numb with misery and fatigue . . . *Fair Oaks, Gaines Mills, Garnets, Goldings, Glendale, Malvern.* . . . Battle after battle across plowed fields, cornfields, thicket and wood. At Fair Oaks the men charged with fixed bayonets across a field of mud, sinking knee-deep at every step. Queer things happened, incongruous as a dream. At Gainesville, just as the lines formed for battle, mail from the North arrived and the newsboys ran along the front lines crying their wares. . . . At Glendale, looking down the line just before they charged, Holmes caught Jim Lowell's eye. The cousins saluted and ran toward the enemy. Wendell looked down the line again. Jim was gone. That night on picket duty in a black and unknown wood, Holmes heard bullets spat against the trees, felt his foot on a dead man's body.

In wood and field, with rifle, bayonet, and pistol, the boys of the Twentieth fought the enemy. Hand to hand sometimes, rolling on the ground together. What swift and cunning thinking a man must acquire, to keep alive! It was out of no book that Wendell Holmes learned, when a Rebel soldier bore down on him, to reach for his pistol, not his saber. The saber was too hard to come at. Half the time the Rebels were not dressed in gray. The ones from the frontier settlements wore homespun, dyed with butternut. It was hard to distinguish them against the shrub.

Back at Harrison's Landing on the James River, after four months of fighting, Captain Holmes lay under the hot southern stars, too tired to sleep. . . . What a mess the Regiment was now! Hallowell wounded, Curtis and Henry Abbott too. Colonels Lee and Palfrey badly hurt. Sixteen thousand Federal troops killed or missing on the Peninsula since June.

War was not chivalry. War was not gallantry, heroism, adventure. War was terrible and dull, and a man had better not try to make sense of it. A man had better just keep at it day by day, doing the next job that lay before him.

*　　*　　*

At home in Boston the citizens were more bewildered even than the soldiers in the field. What kind of war was this? they asked. The Abolitionists had an answer. It was a war against slavery — if only Lincoln would come out and say so. Was Abraham a President or a *turtle!* screamed Wendell Phillips from his platform. . . . "Let's send Phillips to the Fort in Boston harbor where they keep the Secesh prisoners," the *Tribune* answered grimly. "Such a move would be worth a hundred thousand armed men to the Union cause." A Virginia Senator defined the struggle better than anyone else. "A war of sentiment and opinion by one form of society against another form of society."

Recruiting went very badly. "Old Abe has called out 300,000 men by draft . . ." a Bostonian [2] wrote to his brother abroad. "They say the Maine quota is full. . . . The regular topic is the quota of this town, and the quota of that, — how much a town is in advance of its quota and so on. . . . Governor Andrew is sentimentally opposed to a regular draft. . . . But people are getting into better spirit. 'They have just found out that this is not a picnic,' as I heard someone say in the cars today."

Dr. Holmes, walking down Beacon Street, met young men not in uniform and his blood rose within him. He went home and wrote a poem. To contemporary ears it was a clarion call: —

Listen, young heroes! your country is calling!
Time strikes the hour for the brave and the true!
Now, while the foremost are fighting and falling,
Fill up the ranks that have opened for you!

.   .   .   .   .   .

From the hot plains where they perish outnumbered,
Furrowed and ridged by the battle-field's plough,
Comes the loud summons; too long you have slumbered,
Hear the last Angel-trump, — Never or now!

On the nineteenth of August, old Mrs. Holmes died in the Gambrel-roofed House. She was ninety-three; it was time for her to go. Oliver Holmes was sad — but John was heartbroken. He had cared for his mother like a child; indeed, in these last years she had called herself his daughter. "It was a pity to look on him in his first grief," Dr. Holmes wrote to Motley. Sitting in the empty rooms, his head in his hands, John Holmes told his brother he had thought to keep his mother until she was a hundred or more. Why had she died? —

Had he neglected anything? Had he perhaps not fed her enough these last days? Had he better have closed her bedroom window against the night air? She had asked to have it open. Just a little open, so she could hear people passing. She could see and hear like a young person; she had kept all her faculties to the last. Only at the end her memory failed, she had wandered a little. Her two sons had been alone with her when she died in the old room with the flowered wallpaper, the great dark bed . . . "Abiel!" she had whispered. "*Abiel!*" Once she had called for her mother, and once she spoke over and over a name the brothers could not recognize.

When she was gone the brothers walked downstairs together, wandered through the empty rooms. Along this wide dark planking, ghosts walked . . . Their father, gathering his sermon notes to go over to the Meeting-house. Grandfather Wendell with his ruffled shirtfront, climbing the long staircase slowly, his hand on the banister. When you walked across the Square with Grandfather, everyone lifted his hat. . . .

Strange, thought Oliver Holmes, how at the death of a parent a man becomes a boy again for a moment — a terrible, poignant moment filled with all the grief of childhood and none of its joy. . . . He looked furtively at his brother. How John limped! He used his cane even in the house now. And how lined his face! Why did John look suddenly so old when he was three years younger than himself? . . . Fifty! Was it possible John was fifty? Surely it was only yesterday he had taken John by the hand and led him up Gallows Hill to that forbidden hanging. John had screamed with excitement, but he himself had been sick scared. . . .

John sat down and filled his pipe. . . . "We'll have to sell this house," he said. "The college will buy it. They've wanted it for years."

He was silent, then looked up with a sigh. "Do you remember," he said — "Do you remember . . ."

Wendell Holmes was at Alexandria when he had the news of his grandmother's death . . . One less thing to come home to, one less thing to be certain of. But in these times of violence, the death of an old woman, peacefully in her bed, seemed an easy thing, natural and right. The longer he was in this war, the more Wendell Holmes was convinced that not death was the horror, but the loss of a young man's chance to live. Never to have your chance, never to show the world — to show yourself what you could do! . . . One by one his friends were killed; the Regiment was decimated. On the thirtieth of August, Holmes heard the guns roar at Manassas. Daniel Webster's son was killed that day.

The Army of the Potomac moved northwest to Fairfax Courthouse. How good it was to be out of the wilderness of the Peninsula! It was cool and dry at last; at the end of a day's march there was no longer the heartbreaking search through the swamps for firewood and stakes to tie the horses to. This was loyal country; the farmers were willing to sell eggs and vegetables to the men. Marching into Frederick the Twentieth was cheered by the citizens; girls waved flags and handkerchiefs. General Lee's army had only just left town. His soldiers were barefoot, people said. Ragged, dirty, and always hungry.

McClellan, disgraced after the disasters of the Peninsula, was returned to command. The men waited for his coming. They adored the Chief, longed for the sight of him. What was the matter with their high command, the ranks asked angrily. The Rebel generals — Lee and Jackson — stayed with their army. Whereas the fifty-odd Federal generals were forever being swapped about, nobody knew why. The soldiers distrusted all of them except McClellan. *Mac* knew how to get an army ready for battle. Never mind the Seven Days. Never mind about Fair Oaks and Malvern Hill. If Little Mac led them, they could *fight*.

On the fifteenth of September McClellan appeared, riding slowly by his army where it stood on the dusty road to Boonsboro. The men cheered and cheered again, yelling as if their hearts would break. That night and the next, the Army of the Potomac slept well on its hillsides above Antietam Creek. Captain Holmes had a whiskey with Henry Abbott, smoked a cigar he had bought in Frederick. He had never been so tired in his life. Beyond him where he lay, the corn leaned black against the stars, stacked and ready for the barn.

Before another night came down, that corn would be trampled and broken, stained with the blood of twenty thousand men.

For Wendell Holmes, Antietam was one more battle among half a score of battles he had been through these four months. Horrible, exhausting, leading nowhither — but to be gone through to the very topmost level of a man's ability. The ideals of chivalry, the ideals of glory before Ball's Bluff, were replaced now by the fatality of the seasoned campaigner. . . . After Antietam, the thing that remained closest in Holmes's memory was a mistake he made. An injustice, perpetrated in the heat and smoke of battle. . . .

The Twentieth moved across country by the Hagerstown Pike. Ahead lay the West Wood; firing began. Holmes's company was ordered forward at double-quick. Holmes got them through the wood and out to a cornfield beyond. The morning was misty, smoke from the guns lay heavy. Holmes lost his bearings completely. A trooper belonging to the Twentieth turned and fired — as Holmes thought — straight into the ranks of his own company. Holmes roared at him, but the man, down on one knee, kept on firing calmly. Holmes recognized him; it was an Irishman from Company G. "You damn fool!" Holmes shouted. With the flat of his saber he hit the man on the back of the neck, knocking him over. There was a sudden cry — "The enemy is behind us!" Holmes turned swiftly. That Irishman had been right all the time! . . . The enemy poured in on their rear. In rows, men fell among the corn; all about them other men rushed by to the rear, stumbling over the dead bodies of their comrades. The ranks of the Twentieth did not break. What was left of them "retired to the right" — the official account says laconically — "at ordinary step, with arms at the shoulder."

Captain Holmes did not retire. He lay on the ground where he had fallen, shot through the neck. A voice spoke above him. "You're a Christian, aren't you?" Holmes tried to open his eyes; the blackness closed on him again. "Well then, *that's* all right!" the voice said, and passed on. It was the regimental chaplain; no man with a bloody hole in his neck could live; better that he should die a Christian. Another voice spoke; this time Holmes did not hear it. "I've no time to waste on dead men." It was an army surgeon; with him was a captain from Ohio named Leduc. Stooping over Wendell, Leduc spoke sharply to the surgeon. "I know this man. He's a valuable officer. I command you to do what you can for him."

Whatever the surgeon did, Holmes was unconscious of it; it was Leduc himself who told the story. The next thing Holmes knew, he was on his feet. There was someone on each side of him, holding him up. It was Leduc and a farmer's boy in a ragged straw hat.

"We'll have to get off the field," Leduc said. "There's a farm-house if we can reach it." Holmes took a step, stumbled, found he could walk. As a matter of fact, he was not nearly so badly wounded as at Ball's Bluff. The bullet had gone sidewise through his neck, missing windpipe and jugular vein, and had come out at the back, cutting the seam of his coat collar.

The taste of brandy was in his mouth, he was suddenly entirely conscious. The pain in his neck was awful; his collar stuck fast to his skin and he couldn't turn his head. Smoke hung in the air; the firing seemed to be moving west, to the wood. Holmes wondered where his men were . . . At Ball's Bluff it hadn't been like this . . . *New England Never Runs* . . . Phrases from an article in *Harper's Weekly* came back, flamboyant and idiotic. "In front of fearful fire those young men stood serene, each man a hero. . . . Lieutenant Holmes — 'wounded in the breast.' Not in the back; no, not in the back. In the breast is Massachusetts wounded, if she is struck. For-ward she falls, if she falls dead."

Well, he wasn't wounded in the breast this time. This time he was hit in the back and bolting as fast as he could. Damn glad to bolt, too, even if it wasn't so pretty for the papers. . . .

In the farmhouse the floor was covered with wounded men. "Holmes!" someone said weakly. It was Norwood Hallowell, half sitting, half lying against the wall, holding a shattered left arm. "Have you seen my brother Ned?" Hallowell asked. Wendell said no. He lay on the floor and waited with the rest. Leduc's brown pill had made him drowsy. Flies buzzed and settled and buzzed again. Like thunder the guns roared, over by Sharpsburg; the bat-tle must be moving northward. On the wall a clock ticked, loud and strong. Wendell's eye fastened on it. There was an octagonal clock like that at home in the kitchen. No . . . it was long ago at Pittsfield, at Canoe Meadow. He had greatly desired to take the clock apart; once he had got so far as opening the pendulum door when his grandmother came in and caught him.

Late in the afternoon the surgeon arrived and looked at Hallowell, who by now had drifted into a stupor. "I could save this arm," the surgeon said, "if I could find a thin piece of wood for a splint." Wendell roused. "Look in that wall clock," he said. "Behind the pendulum. There should be a piece of wood the shape you want." When the surgeon put it on, Hallowell scarcely moved, but he tried to speak. "He's asking for his brother," Wendell said. Outside there was a commotion of men and horses. "The ambulances are here," the surgeon said. Hallowell was carried out. Before Hallowell fainted, he and Holmes had arranged to stick together, go to Philadelphia when they could travel. . . . It was turning dusk when Holmes was called, tried to stand, felt sick, felt the ambulance sway and jolt beneath him and did not care. His eyes closed. Keedysville, the driver had said. They were going to Keedysville.

That night the telegrams went north from the battlefield. Boston waited for them, and Philadelphia. Norwood Hallowell's father got the news first; Philadelphia was much nearer the battlefield. Norwood wounded, Ned unaccounted for. . . . Mr. Hallowell caught the morning train to Baltimore, thence to Frederick and Hagerstown to bring home his sons.

It was midnight when the messenger knocked at the Holmes door in Boston. Dr. Holmes let him in, reached for the telegram. The family stood round; Mrs. Holmes, Amelia, and the maids in their wrappers, Neddy in his nightshirt, shivering, wide-eyed.

HAGERSTOWN 17TH [Dr. Holmes read aloud] CAPTAIN HOLMES WOUNDED SHOT THROUGH THE NECK THOUGHT NOT MORTAL AT KEEDYSVILLE   WILLIAM G LEDUC

Dr. Holmes looked up. "If I start tomorrow I can reach Philadelphia by Friday. The Hallowells will have news. I can plan my journey from there."

On the train next day he found Dwight, whose son was also wounded, and Dr. Gay the surgeon, bound for the battlefield. There were thousands and thousands of wounded, Gay said. . . .

Thousands and thousands of wounded. That meant thousands and thousands of dead. "Let us not talk," Dr. Holmes said suddenly to his companions. "Perhaps it would be better to sit silently."

Dwight and Gay had known Holmes all their lives; this was the first time they had heard him ask for silence. . . . They reached New York late at night and went to a hotel. The train for Philadelphia did not leave until morning.

Meanwhile, Mr. Hallowell had reached Hagerstown a whole day before them. By lavish bribery he procured a hack and drove to Keedysville over roads choked with mule teams, ambulances, wounded soldiers trudging slowly, wearily to the railroad. Norwood waited for his father in a cottage at Keedysville, half delirious by now, his arm full of maggots. Ned Hallowell wandered into the room, looking for his brother. All night Ned had roamed the battlefield turning up the faces of dead men, stooping with his lantern. Ned's face was flushed with the fever of oncoming typhoid; he stood now over his brother's cot and looked at him vaguely. Norwood's eyes were closed. "They told me thee was dead," Ned said, and wandered off.

An hour later his father found him outside lying on the grass, and led him back. In the cot next to Norwood was Colonel Palfrey, with a badly wounded arm. Wendell Holmes had been with Norwood, Palfrey said. In a farmhouse by the battlefield before they came to Keedysville. Holmes was wounded in the neck; Norwood said he had walked into the farmhouse but he was a little vague about it. They must look for Holmes. . . .

Somehow Mr. Hallowell got the three out of the house and into his hack. All the way to Hagerstown young Ned pulled at the curtains, starting at the sight of every uniformed man. He was a deserter, he whispered to his father. They were after him to shoot him! At every village, Mr. Hallowell inquired for Wendell Holmes. A tall man, he said. A captain, wounded in the neck . . . At Hagerstown the train stood on the track; it was to leave at six. Mr. Hallowell put his sons and the Colonel into a freight car and climbed in beside them. Across the track was a house with the door open; through the door Mr. Hallowell saw a rocking chair. Darting over he made off with the chair, pursued by a woman uttering loud cries. Mr. Hallowell pushed money in her hand, then reached down and pulled into the car a little black boy who was begging to be taken North. No Quaker could resist such an appeal.

It was growing dusk. The car gave a jerk and another jerk. A whistle sounded. Slowly the train moved northward through the night. Mr. Hallowell rocked in his chair; over in the corner the little black boy crouched silent in the darkness, Colonel Palfrey moaned and begged to be put off the train.

It was too bad about Wendell Holmes, Mr. Hallowell thought wearily . . . Had Norwood really seen him there in the farmhouse by the battlefield? The boy was so stupefied he was almost as incoherent as Ned. Well, at home they would prepare a fourth bed anyway. Unless something very bad happened, Wendell would surely arrive in Philadelphia on the morrow.

Next morning about ten o'clock, Dr. Holmes's train from New York stopped just outside of Philadelphia. The Schuylkill bridge was out with the rains. The doctor took a boat to the wharf and rode uptown in a cab. Eagerly he hurried up the white steps of the Hallowells' old house on Walnut Street. Norwood and the Colonel were fast asleep, Neddy delirious with typhoid. No word from Wendell, Mr. Hallowell said sadly.

And now began for Dr. Holmes a crazy journey that was to last six days, a bewildered search after his son that led him by rail, hired hack, and teamster through Baltimore, Frederick, Middletown, Keedysville, back to Philadelphia and on to Harrisburg. The things he saw on his journey, the things he heard, were etched by anxiety upon his memory. The ruined bridge over the Monocacy, the girders lying all crushed on the bank. A shallow grave near by, with two hands sticking up — belonging to the boy who fired the explosion. The long journey from Frederick with the hired team and James Grayden the bearded driver. And on the far side of Frederick the terrible procession of wounded, a never-ending, dolorous stream. Pale young faces haggard with suffering or flushed with fever. Leaning from the high front seat of the wagon, Dr. Holmes scanned the faces. That tall boy ahead? . . . No, his hair was too light. That long figure lying by the roadside? . . . No, no, not Wendell. . . .

Full in the middle of the road rolled the army wagons, six mules to a wagon, turning aside for no man. From his driver's seat, Grayden cursed them, pulling back his team . . . At Middletown that night the churches were crowded with wounded, lying on boards laid over the tops of pews. Holding his lantern high, Dr. Holmes searched among the ragged shapes, his physician's eye noting the terrible mutilation. He heard no groan and no complaint.

Next day at Keedysville on the tree-lined street, a medical officer pointed to a cottage. "Captain Holmes? He's in there. Doing well, too."

Dr. Holmes waited a moment, braced himself, then walked to the cottage. An old woman opened the door. "Captain Holmes?" she said. "Oh, he was taken to Hagerstown yesterday in a milk cart."

Back then, over the long road to Frederick. Back by the cars to Baltimore, to Philadelphia, and up the cobblestones of Walnut Street. Surely, Wendell would be sleeping now in the white chamber where he had slept away his fever after Ball's Bluff.

Wendell's bed was empty. No word had come. Board the cars then, for Harrisburg; Wendell must have tried to reach Philadelphia by the Cumberland Railroad. But what had stopped him on his journey? The doctor's heart beat slow within him now. Wounds that seem to be healing take on sudden, formidable symptoms. Was Wendell lying helpless in some wayside barn, racked with fever?

It was Tuesday night when the doctor reached Harrisburg. Six full days since the battle. Late Wednesday morning a message came. Captain Holmes was seen on Friday, in Hagerstown, at the house of a well-known Union sympathizer, Mrs. Kennedy.

Dr. Holmes wired immediately, but at the army hospital they told him there was small chance of anything but official business getting through. Seeking out the Chief Army Hospital Inspector, Dr. Holmes persuaded him to send an urgent message. The answer came that night: —

CAPTAIN HOLMES STILL HERE   LEAVES SEVEN TOMORROW FOR HARRISBURG PENNA   IS DOING WELL   MRS HOWARD KENNEDY

Sitting by the stove in the hotel parlor, Dr. Holmes lighted his pipe, put the message in his pocket, and looked round for someone to talk to. For six days and nights he had been strung to the highest pitch; a man could not just unstring himself and go off to bed. The hotel clerk, a mild young man, had seen Dr. Holmes's name in the register. Was he really that famous author from Boston? From the look of him no one would imagine it. No bumps on his forehead, nothing of the dandy about his get-up. . . .

That night Dr. Holmes slept like a baby. Waiting on the platform next morning for Wendell's train he talked to anyone who would listen — to prospective passengers for Philadelphia, to the station-master, to a brakeman sitting on a box. For eight days he had searched, and now the search was to end. . . . *My son!* thought the doctor luxuriously. *Even my first-born, whom I have sought in many cities.*

He looked up, a light in his eye. . . . Not a bad figure that, under the circumstances. Very apt indeed. Automatically the doctor reached in his vest pocket for his notebook. After all, this had been a thrilling journey. Would not *Atlantic* readers like to share it with him? This search for the Captain had been no purely personal affair; thousands of fathers had gone to the battlefield, looking for their sons. Thousands would want to know all about it, not from the hard pen of a *Tribune* reporter but from the sympathetic pen of — well — of the Autocrat of the Breakfast-Table.

The train came so quietly Dr. Holmes was almost startled to see it. "Careful!" he thought. "The boy hates scenes. No *hysterica passio* now, no swelling upward of the mother. . . ."

Climbing the high steps, Dr. Holmes turned into the first car. On the right of the aisle, in the fourth seat, sat Wendell Holmes. His father smiled, put out his hand.

"How are you, Wendell?"

"How are you, Father?"

CHAPTER SIXTEEN

Father and son. Holmes's third wound.

IT was not easy, Dr. Holmes found that day on the train to Philadelphia, to talk to his son. In his faded blue uniform, the bandage round his neck, Wendell sat opposite his father and responded in monosyllables.

"So you were at the Kennedys'," his father began. "I've heard of Mrs. Kennedy. How long were you there? Were other officers convalescing at her house? Why didn't we hear from you, Wendell?"

He had telegraphed twice, Wendell replied. Once to Boston, once to the Hallowells in Philadelphia. Obviously, the messages had not gone through. . . . Yes, the Kennedys had been good to him. He had been there since — well, since the day he got to Hagerstown in the milk cart. The Saturday after the battle. . . . How did he happen to go to the Kennedys'? . . . Oh, Wendell said indifferently, Mrs. Kennedy's sister saw him sitting on the curb and sent one of the young Kennedy boys across the street to ask him in.

"On the curb?" Dr. Holmes repeated. "Wendell, why were you — what made you sit on the curb?"

"I was sick," Wendell replied shortly. "My neck hurt. I was trying to walk across town to the railroad station. I sat down, that's all."

And why, his tone implied, should a man not sit down on the curb when he was tired? Why, in a strange town, should he not be led into a house by strangers; why should they not bathe him, dress his wound? And why should he not remain with them five days, making no effort to return home and no real effort to inform a family, crazy with anxiety, of his whereabouts and safety?

"This woman that beckoned you from the lawn — did you tell her your name?" Dr. Holmes ventured after a time.

Wendell did not look up. "I told her my full name, all three of them. . . . Yes, Dad, she had read the *Autocrat*. It was on the parlor table when I came in."

Dr. Holmes suppressed a pleased smile. . . . But looking once more on his son, his heart contracted. How white the boy was, and how thin! He must have lost thirty pounds. Was it from dysentery, exhaustion, the shock of battle? His uniform hung on him; the trousers were frayed, and the cuffs. Some careful hand had been at it, to press and mend . . . It was cold in the car, and drafty; the stove at the far end had no fire in it. Every time the cars jerked, which was often, Wendell winced, his hand rose to his neck. Dr. Holmes forced himself to silence. Up here in the Pennsylvania mountains the leaves were scarlet and gold. The brakes screamed as they crept downhill. Dr. Holmes stared at his son, whose eyes were closed. "Wendell!" he said suddenly, unable to contain himself longer. "Who bandaged your neck?"

Wendell jumped. His father repeated the question. Wendell stretched his neck gingerly and touched the bandage, smiling for the first time since they had sat down together in the train.

"Jones," he said. "Jones bandaged it." He closed his eyes.

(Not until many days later would his father learn — from hearing Wendell tell it to Fanny Dixwell — that Jones's first name was Ellen, and she was an extremely pretty girl of eighteen.)

Father and son reached Philadelphia that night and went to the Hallowells'. The household was gloomy with two sick boys and Colonel Palfrey still in bed and suffering. But it was much easier to be with Wendell when other people were around. Wendell was civil to Mr. and Mrs. Hallowell, very gentle with his comrades-at-arms who lay in bed. Before they took the train for New York, Dr. Holmes called on the president of the railroad, a friend of his; when they boarded the cars Wendell found a couch spread. To persuade him to lie on it required tact, but once his head touched the pillow, he went off to sleep as if he were drugged. At New York his father roused him, got him off the train and over to the Fifth Avenue Hotel. In the lobby they were directed not to a stairway but to something called a "vertical railway," in which they sat on cushioned seats and were pulled upward. "Like a cork with a giant corkscrew, eh, Wendy, my boy?"

No wounded man, no tired boy, ever had so lively a father, or one so full of metaphor. It was impossible for Dr. Holmes to keep his spirits down. If he could not talk to his son he could talk to the hotel clerks, to the waiters, the elevator man, and often enough — to his son's embarrassment — to strangers who came up and asked if he were not the Autocrat of the Breakfast-Table? Dr. Holmes went walking in Central Park; when he came in, glowing, he said it could not compare with Boston Common and the Public Garden. For reply Wendell remarked that it would be a good idea to have some whiskey before dinner. Whiskey had kept him going for six months, he said. Whiskey had kept him·from dying of cramps on the Peninsula, whiskey had kept his feet dry and his bowels from taking away all the blood in him. And whiskey was going to be the comfort of his declining years — which, he finished grimly, seemed to have begun some months ago on the Chickahominy.

They reached Boston Monday night. To Dr. Holmes the sight of his own doorplate had never been so welcome. Mrs. Holmes and Amelia took Wendell upstairs and put him to bed. After supper the doctor went to his study, closed the door, poked up the fire, sat down at his desk and reached for his pen. . . . "*Fling open,*" he wrote, "*the window-blinds of the chamber that looks out on the waters and towards the western sun! Let the joyous light shine in upon the pictures that hang upon its walls and the shelves thick-set with the names of poets and philosophers and sacred teachers, in whose pages our boys learn that life is noble only when it is held cheap by the side of honor and of duty. Lay him in his own bed, and let him sleep off his aches and weariness. So comes down another night over this household, unbroken by any messenger of evil tidings, — a night of peaceful rest and grateful thoughts; for this our son and brother was dead and is alive again, and was lost and is found.*"

Leaning back in his chair, the doctor read over what he had written. It would make a good concluding paragraph for his piece "My Hunt after the Captain." In the morning he would call on Lowell and ask what he thought of the idea for the *Atlantic*. The article was timely, people still talked of nothing but Antietam field.

He could finish the piece in three days if he kept at it. Reaching in his vest pocket the doctor took out a sheaf of small papers, written closely on both sides. He had begun making notes when they got to Philadelphia. At night after Wendell was in bed, in the cars while Wendell slept. Once, looking up, he had caught his son's eye upon him with a very peculiar expression, but the boy had said nothing, asked no questions. How sensitive the young were, and how changeable! The last time Wendell came home wounded, after Ball's Bluff, he had found nothing more pleasurable than to tell his experiences to the whole of female Boston. Now he would not say a word. A pity, too; the boy must have had extraordinary experiences in these six months of fighting. Perhaps rest and sleep would alter this strange attitude.

But rest and sleep did not alter Wendell's silence. He sat in his room or before the library fire, smoking. "Let him alone," Mrs. Holmes told her husband. "He does not want to talk. I don't think he is well at all. Let him alone."

To Wendell it seemed incredible that people would ask for stories of the battlefield as for tales of a circus, or of a boat race on the river Charles. He had forgotten his own eager garrulousness after Ball's Bluff — a battle in which he had not seen ten minutes of fighting before being carried unconscious from the field. What he knew now of battlefields was better forgotten, but Wendell could not forget. Dead men sprawled among the corn, naked, stripped of trousers and boots, eyes staring, limbs flung out in awful abandon. For those boots and trousers the Rebels had fought like tigers. If the North fought for "victory," for "Union," "freedom," the South fought for shoes to put on its bleeding feet, pants for its legs, and fought no less bravely. Here on the streets they called the Rebels cowards. They were not cowards.

Cowardice, gallantry, chivalry — how wearily a soldier, returned from the field, met such words! At home they thought of battle as if it were fought on Boston Common. As if a man came down the steps of his house pulling on his gloves, smoking a cigar — then got on his horse and charged a battery up Beacon Street while the ladies waved handkerchiefs from a balcony. What really happened was that you spent the night on the wet ground with your bowels open and fought on a breakfast of salt meat and dirty water.

Wendell had heard his father talk of Antietam battlefield; apparently he had gone out there while waiting for the evening train from Frederick. He had brought home souvenirs — a Rebel canteen, a note that said, *"tell John that nancy's folks are all well and has a verry good Little Crop of corn a growing."* Half a dozen times, Wendell had heard his father tell the story; he strongly suspected it had been written down in some kind of memoir his father made of the trip.

The visitors who came to Charles Street to pay their respects to the wounded hero were charmed with this story. But when they turned to the hero himself they were offended by what he said. "War?" Captain Holmes repeated coldly, his gray eyes remote. "War is an organized bore."

The visitors went down the steps shaking their heads. "Captain Holmes used to be so agreeable. How changed he is! Is it possible," they asked one another doubtfully, "that he is going over to the *radicals?* How hard for his dear father and mother!"

Only to his friends and comrades-at-arms could Wendell talk — and there were plenty of these. The streets seemed peopled with them, wounded or home on leave. Just around the corner was John Ropes, whose brother Henry was with the Twentieth; Ropes collected for John Gray in Virginia every item he could about the Northern Army. To these men it was not necessary to say you hated war. They all hated it — except perhaps Henry Abbott, who was a born soldier with a genius for battle strategy and tactics. Abbott was home on sick leave too. Wendell admired him enormously. The man seemed able to act without thinking — and act always rightly.

For Wendell Holmes, most acts were preceded by thought and afterward reviewed intellectually, step by step. The surgeon of the Twentieth had told him men were divided into two kinds — external men and internal men. Internal men considered ideas more interesting than things. Holmes knew well which category he belonged in — and admired excessively the opposite, those robust creatures who acted and did not need to think. Abbott, Crowninshield — born soldiers, filled with health and a kind of blessed immediacy, a capacity for living in the present and the present only. It was a gift, that quality. A man could not cultivate it. It came at birth, and to Wendell Holmes its possessor was a god.

There had been good reason for Surgeon Bryant to tell about the internal men. Bryant was older; he was Harvard, '40. Down on the Peninsula last summer after the Seven Days battles, Holmes, staggering on his feet with dysentery, had almost lost connection, for a time, with reality. He had walked round camp in a daze, his eyes dead, his lips loose and quivering. One night Bryant came to his tent, sat down, asked a simple question — and the dam burst. Holmes wept as he had not known a man could weep, shuddering, torn in two. When he finished, the fear was gone. "It is all right," Bryant said. "It's all right to cry. Crownie doesn't have to cry because Crownie doesn't see things ahead or behind, either. He can't. He isn't capable of it. The world is divided into two kinds of men, Holmes," Bryant had said — "internal men . . ."

On the fifteenth of November, Wendell's orders came. He had been home six weeks, his wound was healed. He wanted to go, although he still felt strangely weak and irritable. All these weeks, news from the front had been disheartening. McClellan removed from command, Burnside in his place. The home news was no better. Lincoln had announced the Emancipation Proclamation, to take effect next January. New England approved but most of the other Northern states did not; the newspapers argued and the Abolitionists were in a fury with the whole business, which was not nearly drastic enough to suit them. Drafting had begun in Boston and it was a mess, half carried out, then suspended after seven hundred men were taken. What was the matter with Governor Andrew, Holmes wondered. Was he afraid of a riot? The Democratic newspapers published some doggerel verses; one of them stuck disagreeably in Wendell's brain: —

> New England's sick! New England famed!
> She's writhing on a bed of pain;
> And all the doctors have proclaimed
> Her illness, *"nigger on the brain."*

The most disagreeable episode of his stay at home had not been a national matter at all, but something highly personal. Proof sheets of the *Atlantic* had arrived; Wendell's father with a pleased smile had turned them over to his son. Carrying the story upstairs to his room after the family was in bed, Wendell read them, his flesh crawling. He tried to skip, tried to stop reading, but continued in horrid fascination to the end . . . *"for this our son and brother was dead and is alive again, and was lost and is found . . . Lay him in his own bed, and let him sleep off his aches and weariness. . . ."*

Oh my God! thought Captain Holmes, blushing to the roots of his hair. What if Company A should get hold of this?

In the first car, on the fourth seat to the right, I saw my Captain; there I saw him, even my first-born, whom I had sought through many cities.

"How are you, Boy?"

"How are you, Dad?"

Boy? . . . His father had never called him "Boy" in his life. What would the Twentieth Regiment think of *that* for a salutation? And the details of the battlefield. That gimlet eye had missed nothing. How could a man be so infernally curious about every stick and stone, every sound and sight? . . . *"tell John that nancy's folks has a verry good Little Crop of corn a growing."* Those notes his father made on the train must have been calculated straight to this article. As far as description went it was all true, too. Those army wagons, bearing down the road, changing their course for no man. . . .

It was extraordinary how fast the *Atlantic Monthly* traveled. From Sharpsburg, Virginia, with the Forty-first Massachusetts, John Gray [1] wrote home to his mother: —

I was much obliged for the *Atlantic Monthly*. The little doctor's conceit and pertness appears more fully than in anything else of his I ever read (though I should make such a statement with hesitation) and I should think his "Hunt" would be considered too long by those who take no personal interest in the persons and things described, and he certainly talks more freely about the appearance and character of those he meets than he has any right to do; but I was very much interested in it and his description of the people and country is wonderfully correct and graphic, considering what a cursory view of them he must have had.

But if the young disapproved the "Hunt," the old loved it. New England read it aloud to the family, read it from the school desk and the lecture platform. It told people what they wanted to know about Antietam battlefield and told them in a tone they were familiar with — a kindly tone, filled with sentiment. A father's tone, with none of the nonchalance of youth, so baffling to middle age in the face of danger and horror. There was no need for Wendell Holmes to tell his father what he thought of this latest performance of the literary mind. Dr. Holmes knew what his son thought — and ignored it cheerfully. If Wendell did not like the *Atlantic* he could read Hobbes's *Leviathan*. The young were ridiculously sensitive; why should not a man desire to share his experiences with a waiting world?

Wendell went down to Falmouth, traveling with Henry Abbott. Snow had fallen; winter quarters on the Rappahannock were bleak. Before a week was out he was down again with dysentery. He did not send the news to his father but to Hallowell, still invalided in Philadelphia.

"You will think, I know, of my first-born in the midst of the scenes his regiment has been going through," Dr. Holmes wrote Motley on the seventeenth of December. "He is suffering from dysentery, I am afraid pretty sick, but we are impatiently waiting to hear from him. A note of two or three lines, written in pencil to a friend in Philadelphia on the 10th, was the first news we had of his being ill, and is the last thing we have heard from him to the present moment. He cannot have been in the fights, and therefore must have been really 'down' as he says in his note. The experience no doubt brought on with aggravated symptoms the trouble from which he suffered so severely on the Chickahominy, but which did not keep him from being on duty until the last of the battles — Malvern Hill — had been fought."

When the Regiment crossed the river to attack Fredericksburg they went without Captain Holmes; he was in the hospital. Arthur Dehon was killed. "The truest of friends," Wendell wrote of him — but he did not write it to his father.

In truth it was a terrible time. The Army of the Potomac reached its lowest state of demoralization that winter. After the crushing defeat at Fredericksburg the men deserted in droves. Their families sent parcels of civilian clothes to make deserting easier. Even Abraham Lincoln despaired. "We are on the brink of destruction," he wrote a friend. "It appears to me the Almighty is against us, and I can hardly see a ray of hope." General Burnside was removed, General Hooker put in his place.

Holmes, on his feet again and out of the hospital, looked at his men and was suddenly surprised to see how young they were. Before he joined the army he had thought soldiers were old men, white-bearded like the Revolutionary veterans he had seen as a boy in parades on the Fourth of July. But these soldiers had the down of youth on their cheeks, the wide, homesick eyes of boys. "Farewell, Mother!" they sang by their camp fires, —

> Farewell Mother, you may never
> See your darling boy again.

Holmes himself felt as old as the oldest general in the army. Authority had become natural to him. Late in January the Regiment left its bare and windy hill and took quarters in the comfortable houses around Falmouth; Holmes and Henry Abbott and Charles Whittier lived at the house of a Miss Dunbar. Holmes was made Provost Marshal of the town; white gloves and a paper collar were issued to him and he was told to keep order. Northward in Stafford, John Gray was pleased; Ropes had complained bitterly to him because the army was appointing Provost Marshals who were not "gentlemen." Colonel Palfrey, he had said, would be more suitable than these ex-barbers and ex-carpenters. Now Falmouth had a gentleman marshal — and the gentleman worked hard at his job.

It was not an easy assignment. Holmes found it impossible to prevent the men from fraternizing with the enemy. They sent little sailing rafts, laden with coffee, across the river; the rafts came back carrying tobacco. As spring came on the shad began to run and from Falmouth to Fredericksburg both armies, crazy for fresh fish, set out seines. In the evening the men went out in rowboats and hauled in their catch under the eyes of the enemy walking with loaded rifles. Nobody got shot, nobody stole from the enemy's nets. But it was not a situation to give ease to those in authority. Holmes was on duty, or felt himself on duty, day and night.

March, April . . . In front of the Dunbar house the tall horse chestnuts put out pink shoots and above the lawn, ivy-covered tree trunks rose to a delicious spread of shade. Across the river a broad, rich valley lay unplowed, unsown. Why should a farmer plant when he knew not who would reap his harvest?

For the army, for Wendell Holmes, the coming of spring meant but one thing — the renewal of battle. When the roads were open it would be their business to cross over and take Chancellorsville, fifteen miles below Fredericksburg.

On the first of May, shots came echoing down the river. Holmes heard them, standing on the bank, his eyes and ears straining to the southwest. By afternoon the shots had increased to the roar that meant a real battle. All that night the Regiment, throwing out pontoon bridges, crossed the river.

The plank road to Chancellorsville lay under the hills called Marye's Heights. Up this road in the early mist Captain Holmes's company advanced. It was still quiet, firing had not begun. At the canal, knowing he was in full view of the enemy's guns from the hills beyond, Holmes ordered his men sharply to lie down. He had not finished speaking when the first shell came over — and tore the cape from his overcoat. He threw himself down full length, grabbed a rifle from one of his men, and sighted it at the enemy.

When the next volley came Holmes's head went down, he buried his face in the grass. His long legs were crossed, one ankle over the other. There was a lull while the enemy took range. The next shells will be lower, Wendell thought. They were. Shrapnel that missed his head caught the heel of the foot that was uppermost. A terrific blow, tearing ligament and tendons.

It was Holmes's third and last wound. It would keep him out of the war for nine months, it would trouble him for years to come.

But Holmes, lying face down in the grass below the hills called Marye's Heights, knew nothing of this. *My leg is gone,* he thought, and fainted.

CHAPTER SEVENTEEN

Ten months at home. The Wilderness.
Holmes is mustered out.

Dr. Holmes in Boston to Dr. Hunt in Philadelphia

21 CHARLES STREET,
May 25, 1863

MY DEAR DR. HUNT, — Wendell has been doing very well, but of course without any notable change. There has been very little pain, no mark of inflammation, nothing but what belongs to the healing process. Dr. Bigelow probed the wound yesterday and found one portion of bone movable, and another part fixed but denuded. He is in excellent spirits, not at all nervous, as when he was last wounded, is very reasonably tractable, avoids stimulants, smokes *not* enormously, feeds pretty well, and has kept tolerably quiet until to-day, when Dr. Bigelow let him ride out, and is, on the whole, a quite endurable patient.

Dr. Bigelow has done nothing but keep the wound open as you did. He makes him use a little plug of *carrot* for that purpose, which is handy enough, and seems to agree very well with the wound. . . . I pinched W.'s heel a little the other day and asked him into what vegetable I had turned his carrot. No answer.

Why, into a Pa's nip! was my response. . . .

Good-by, my kind friend and my son's friend, whom I have delicately commemorated in my "*Hunt* after the Captain."

P. S. I have at last found a man who has asked me about W.'s heel *without referring to Achilles!*

How good it was to have Wendell at home when he was like this — gay, good-natured, even tolerating a little pun now and then!

Once more Wendell received his friends. John Ropes came often —
a lawyer full-fledged now, in Barrister's Hall. He wrote down to
Gray in Virginia that Holmes was "very entertaining, as usual,"
and that as usual Mrs. Holmes chased them all out of the house at
eleven.

It was not easy to find out what was really happening in
Virginia. People were impatient with Stanton's new order of military censorship. Holmes knew only that his regiment was moving
northward to meet the threatened Rebel invasion of Pennsylvania.
Fighting Joe Hooker had resigned; gloomily the North looked about
for a general it could trust. Lincoln appointed Meade. The country
showed little enthusiasm over the choice. ("I'm not Napoleon,"
Meade used to tell his staff.) Out West Ulysses Grant, Major General of Volunteers, was besieging Vicksburg on the Mississippi.

But if military news was censored, civilian criticism of the government was not. The nation roared disapproval. Lincoln's use of
Presidential wartime powers had long ago roused the anger of real
patriots, men loyal to the Union who could not know Lincoln's
character. His general suspension of the Act of Habeas Corpus in
military and disaffected areas had seemed the last straw. Wendell
Phillips called him "a more unlimited despot than the world knows
this side of China." Many who were not Abolitionists agreed with
him. Better to risk defeat at the hands of the enemy than to submit to an arbitrary government here at home. At the Law School
Professor Parker had denounced the President.

Dr. Holmes did not like this kind of talk. "Mean sympathizers
with the traitors are about in the streets under many aspects," he had
written Motley. "You can generally tell the more doubtful ones by
the circumstance that they have a great budget of complaints against
the government. . . . I do not think strange of this in old men. . . .
But to meet *young* men who have breathed this American Air without taking the contagious fever of liberty, whose hands lie as cold
and flabby in yours as the fins of a fish, on the morning of a victory —
this is the hardest thing to bear. Oh, if the bullets would only go to
the hearts that have no warm human blood in them! But the most
generous of our youth are the price that we must pay for the new
heaven and the new earth which are to be born of this fiery up-
heaval."

Wendell Holmes had little need to defend his country or his

President by word of mouth; in time of war, disaffected citizens seldom address their complaints to wounded soldiers. He was going to be home a long time and he knew it; of all his wounds this was slowest to mend. He filled his room with books from the Athenaeum and read avidly, hungry for ideas that went beyond and outside war. As usual when he was home, the family card at the Athenaeum changed its aspect completely. Instead of the *belles-lettres* and outlines of anatomy that Dr. Holmes took out, the card was crowded with titles by Spencer and the Mills: *Social Statics*, then the *First Principles* (volume one of the ten-volume Synthesis of Philosophy). Wendell read John Stuart Mill's huge *System of Logic* and went back greedily for more, bringing home the *Dissertations and Discussions* and James Mill's *Analysis of the Phenomena of the Mind.*

John Ropes was just the man to discuss all this with, although he was pretty well absorbed just now with the practical details of the law and with what went on daily down in Barrister's Hall. Various British visitors of distinction came to town. Leslie Stephen, a tutor at Cambridge and a literary man who belonged to a famous legal family; his father, grandfather, and brother were all deep in the law. Wendell Holmes was drawn to him at once. The literary scene was changed. Emerson was away much of the time, lecturing against slavery. Lowell had given up the *Atlantic* and was planning to edit the *North American Review*, becoming more and more interested in Republican politics. For once Dr. Holmes was not writing a book; he was too busy at the Medical School and in his duties at the Sanitary Commission. Only Longfellow pursued the life of pure literature; he was absorbed in his translation of Dante. There was much talk about it: Dr. Holmes heard most of it read aloud by Longfellow himself as he finished the various cantos.

By June 27 the whole of the Rebel Army was in Pennsylvania. Lee's headquarters were at Chambersburg. The North took the news with extraordinary calm; Lincoln sent for no reinforcements from the West. On the first of July the two armies met at Gettysburg. On the Fourth, news came that Meade had turned the Rebels back. John Ropes's young brother was killed — Henry, whom Wendell Holmes himself had enlisted in the Twentieth. Sumner Paine was killed — another Holmes recruit.

That day, Dr. Holmes made a speech before the city authorities. At home, he said, men complained of hardship. Yet on the streets one could buy imported delicacies — bananas and pineapples — and in a shop window he had seen peaches displayed for twenty-four dollars a dozen —

There are those who profess to fear that our government is becoming a mere irresponsible tyranny. If there are any who really believe that our present Chief Magistrate means to found a dynasty for himself and family, — that a *coup d'état* is in preparation by which he is to become ABRAHAM, DEI GRATIA REX, — they cannot have duly pondered his letter of June 12th. . . . We must be patient, as our fathers were patient; even in our worst calamities, we must remember that defeat itself may be a gain where it costs our enemy more in relation to his strength than it costs ourselves.

That same day, news came of Grant's success at Vicksburg. But it was not easy to rejoice at victory when one's comrades lay dead and dying on the field. It rained hard that night; Boston thought of the thousands lying on Gettysburg plain. Next day an official envelope arrived; Captain Holmes was promoted to a Lieutenant Colonelship. It was an empty honor, impossible to accept; the Twentieth scarcely existed. The thing to do was to go out and recruit; as soon as his foot permitted, Holmes planned to go all over the Commonwealth and see what he could raise in the way of a new company for the Twentieth.

Day after day the bodies of his friends returned to the city — "Packed in ice," the newspapers announced, proud of the new arrangement. With Norwood Hallowell and six other officers, Holmes served as pallbearer for Henry Ropes in King's Chapel. Slowly the eight, their swords swinging at their knees, walked up the aisle behind the coffin. . . . Waiting here in the city, seeing one by one the bodies of his friends come home, standing while the muffled drums beat farewell, with no tear permitted, no relaxing of the soldier's brow, the soldier's mouth — how much more awful than any fighting in the field! Worse by far than the mud and flies of the Peninsula, the picketing at night in the black woods at Fair Oaks.

The news of Gettysburg was scarcely a week old when in Boston the draft riots began. In Cooper Street east of the Common, the crowd fought savagely. Men were killed that afternoon; the wounded lay on the streets until their friends carried them away. Heat came down and stayed over the city like a pall. Captain Holmes's military collar was stiff against a scarred neck; even the visor of his blue forage cap reflected heat on his forehead, made him want to push the cap back on the thick dark hair. No one left town for the country. Mrs. Holmes and Amelia worked all day at the Commission, packing lint and doing up bundles. It seemed to Wendell that they sat up and sewed all night.

In August, Holmes went off recruiting, traveling full across the state to Pittsfield. The old town welcomed him; his list swelled with new names. How good it was to see the Housatonic again, cold and swift along its rocky bed! Greylock Mountain rose solid against the sky and in front of the old Holmes house the single pine tree spread its branches.

September, October, November . . . Abraham Lincoln went up to Gettysburg to say a few words on the battlefield in honor of the new Soldiers' Cemetery. Edward Everett came down from Boston on a like errand. Next day Wendell read their speeches in the newspaper, agreeing with his friends that the Bostonian had by far the better of it. After Gettysburg, Lee had escaped to Virginia; it was rumored he would invade Pennsylvania again when spring opened the roads.

Nearly three years of war, and the enemy undefeated. New Orleans captured by Farragut, Vicksburg captured by Grant — but the Rebels were not beaten while Lee's army roamed the roads. Wendell Holmes was restless. He knew he was not ready for active duty. He felt well enough, but he tired easily and when he was tired a tremor ran through him, vicious and uncontrollable, not to be put down by strength of will or any self-reproach. John Gray, home on furlough from the Twelfth Massachusetts Infantry, looked at Holmes and shook his head. "The Twentieth can do without you for a while, Wendell," he said. John Gray had been graduated from Harvard Law School the year war broke out. He had a brilliant mind; Holmes enjoyed him enormously. Mr. George Shattuck had moved into his new house on Marlborough Street and liked to entertain young lawyers. Gray, Ropes, and Holmes went there often. Shattuck was a big hearty man, with a crisp dark beard, enormously kind. He was a superb trial lawyer; he made the practice of law seem exciting. Holmes went up to the courthouse to see him in action and was convinced that his oratory carried away not only the jury but the judge. Walking home afterwards with Ropes — "When the war is over," Holmes began . . .

When the war is over. It was a refrain enchanting, illusory as the *Once upon a time* that begins all fairy tales.

Wendell had been home eight months; it was already January. Why didn't his orders come, he wondered. Was Cousin Harry Lee trying to get him a staff commission? He went up to the Athenaeum and got out books on strategy and tactics: Hooper's *Waterloo*, Barnard's report on the Peninsular Campaign.

Early in January, 1864, his orders came. Holmes was appointed Aid-de-Camp on the staff of Brigadier General Wright, commanding the First Division, Sixth Corps, stationed at Rappahannock. "I am very glad, at any rate, he is on staff duty," Gray wrote Ropes from the South. "I did not think when at home that he was fit to go back to his regiment."

For Holmes and his family, this was the hardest farewell of the war. It was true his three-year service would be over in July — but July was six months off. In a war, six months can mean forever. His parents had little comfort from the knowledge that Wendell was going on staff duty. Plenty of generals had been killed in this war. Since that July day of 1861 when Holmes went out to Readville in his lieutenant's uniform, the war had changed its character altogether. From being high adventure it had become a business — grim, impersonal, a movement of masses, with statistics of casualties prophesied ahead in official bulletins. Statistically the chances of Wendell's safe return this time were slim. His father and mother were aware of it.

This time Wendell would not be returning to old friends, classmates, comrades-at-arms. What was left of the Twentieth Regiment would be in Wright's corps on the Rapidan, but there was almost nothing left of it. The number of casualties to date almost exactly equaled the roster of the regiment when Holmes had joined in July, 1861. Of the twenty lieutenants Holmes had known, only five remained; they were captains and majors. Major Henry Abbott, aged twenty-one, commanded the regiment. The last time Holmes had gone back to war, he and Abbott had traveled down to Virginia together. Now Holmes was going alone. . . . At breakfast on the day of his departure he was persistently hilarious, joking, teasing Neddy, inquiring of Amelia whether she had mended the tear in his overcoat pocket. Dr. Holmes was the silent one. He sat looking at his plate, not daring to catch his wife's eye at the far end of the table. Dr. Holmes's sister was there, Aunt Ann Upham, come from Salem to say good-bye to Wendell.

There was a special breakfast that morning with Wendell's favorite dishes. Mutton chops, codfish cakes, hot cakes and maple syrup. Nobody but Neddy seemed hungry; now and then silence fell. The long windows in the dining room were frosted thick; in the middle of breakfast a huge icicle crashed from the roof. "This is the coldest winter," Aunt Ann remarked suddenly, "that Boston has known in years."

Everyone was suddenly voluble. In the kitchen the milk had been frozen solid on the table when Annie came downstairs. Dr. Holmes had been down to Park Street corner the day before with his pocket thermometer; it measured fifteen below. Had Wendell heard Tom Appleton's remark about Park Street corner? Appleton said if it was true God tempers the wind, he wished somebody would tether a shorn lamb on the steps of Park Street Church. . . .

Mrs. Holmes looked at her son gravely. "You had better take your fur coat," she said. "They will never get the cars warm in this weather."

What would he do with a fur coat in Virginia? Wendell asked. And besides, if he left his good new coat in Washington it might get lost before July. . . . It ended by his taking his Grandfather Abiel's huge old black cloak with the sealskin lining. It was the warmest coat in the family but it was also extremely queer-looking. Neddy laughed when his brother tried it on over his army overcoat.

Nobody was coming to the station; they knew Wendell hated those scenes under the big glass-domed roof, with weeping relatives crowding round. The family stood in the hallway to say good-bye. Over the hatrack the portrait of Grandfather Abiel looked down — young, handsome, with flowing dark hair.

Dr. Holmes put out his hand. "Good-bye, Wendell," he said.

Wendell shook hands with his father, stooped to kiss his mother, and went quickly out the door and down the steps to the waiting cab. Neddy ran after him, helped him put his things in the cab. "Go into the house," Wendell said, "before you freeze to death."

Looking at his brother he saw the boy was crying uncontrollably. The cab started. Wendell leaned out, waving a long, blue-coated arm.

Life is action and passion; therefore it is required of a man that he should share the passion and action of his time at peril of being judged not to have lived.

On the banks of the Rapidan, Holmes found the Army of the Potomac, found the Sixth Corps and Wright's headquarters, found the Twentieth Regiment with Henry Abbott wearing the gold maple leaf on his shoulder. The few veterans who remained with the Regiment were more homesick than the new recruits. It seemed to the army that it had been in the field forever, forever marching and fighting, forever tired, dirty, depressed. Holmes was instantly surrounded and questioned. What was it like at home? What had he had to eat, what had his mother and sister said, how had his mother and sister *looked?* Strangers asked these questions — eager, sick with longing. Have you got a picture of your sister? one big private asked Holmes gravely. No, Holmes replied. But if you come to my quarters tonight I can tell you how Boston Common looks in one of the coldest Januaries it ever went through.

The last batch of recruits had been Germans from Pennsylvania. Here on the banks of the Rapidan, homesick for their farms they sang German songs, while veterans from New England gathered round the fires to listen, touched by the sweetness of this foreign music.

Holmes was twenty-three that spring. His birthday brought news of Grant's appointment as Lieutenant General. Three days later, Grant was made Commander-in-Chief, and just before April took headquarters at Culpeper Courthouse, five miles from where Holmes was stationed. All that month the reorganization of the Army of the Potomac went on. For the last time, Holmes saw spring come to Virginia, saw the peach trees blossom and the land, starved for lack of planting, powdered into dust by wagons passing ceaselessly down from the North.

It was a time of waiting. Holmes longed to talk philosophy, talk anything that was not war. He did, to anyone who would listen, arguing passionately. "The universe is spatially limited!" he told Henry Abbott one night at headquarters. It was not, Abbott insisted. They shouted at each other; Holmes seized pencil and paper. He would prove it by calculus. The other officers laughed, egging them on. Holmes sprang to his feet, roaring at Abbott. The tent flap opened; it was a messenger from the Colonel across the field. They were making too much noise in here. What in God's name were they celebrating at two in the morning? This was a war, not a lecture forum.

On the fourth of May the army crossed the Rapidan to fight in the crazy thickets, the mud and swollen streams of the Wilderness . . . Spottsylvania, North Anna, Cold Harbor. General Sedgwick was killed. Wright — Holmes's general — took permanent command of the Corps. Holmes's old commander of the Home Guard, Major Stevenson, was killed. Henry Abbott, terribly wounded, was left behind in the hospital to die. For Holmes this was the worst blow of all. At twenty-two, Abbott knew more about life than most men of fifty. A Puritan, Holmes called him, without the Puritan's austerity. And in battle, how debonair! In the narrow streets of Frederick he had moved forward toward a hidden enemy, swinging his sword on one finger as if it were a cane.

Holmes had loved Henry Abbott. But there was no time to mourn; there was time only to press on southward. At Cold Harbor, Holmes saw nine thousand men fall in three hours, with hardly a dent made in the Confederate line. Wherever it went, the Army of the Potomac dug itself in. The old warfare of open fields and woods was gone forever.

Grant sat down before Petersburg to begin the siege that was to last a year. Suddenly, news came that Jubal Early was leading his Rebel troops down the Shenandoah Valley, advancing on Washington, burning and looting his way through Maryland. Grant ordered Wright to take three brigades north to defend the Capital. At City Point on the James River, Holmes followed his general on the steamer; they reached Alexandria early on the morning of July 11. On the wharf a group of officers and civilians waited. One, in a beaver hat, towered above the rest. From the decks the men recognized Lincoln. A roar went up. Father Abraham had come down to welcome the troops. He touched his hat, waved, and the men cheered again and again.

Out the Seventh Street Road to Fort Stevens marched Wright's brigades in the hot July morning. Lincoln went with them in a carriage with his wife. Holmes rode with Wright and the other staff officers. Some Washington ladies came all the way to the fort, but all visitors left that night. Only Lincoln himself came back to the fort next day. Below the parapets, on rolling ground Early's troops lay waiting. Wright decided to attack immediately.

The President climbed a parapet. He had never seen a battle. What he had seen, year after year, week after week, was the young recruits, marching by the White House, singing. He had seen them return in ambulances over the long bridge to the crowded hospitals where he had gone to visit them, standing hat in hand by their beds. Now he was to see them in action.

The firing began. "You had better get out of the fire," General Wright said. The President did not move. Even without his tall hat he stood six feet four, a splendid target. Below him on the dusty ground, men ran forward and fell sprawling on their faces. This was the thing for which Lincoln felt responsible. This was the thing he had dreaded, this was the picture he had seen so often at dead of night and that had caused him to leave his bed and pace the floor until morning. . . . On the parapet five feet from him a man fell. Three feet away, so close Lincoln could have touched him, an officer fell dead.

"Get down, you fool!" a young voice shouted. Automatically the President stepped back. It was Wendell Holmes, angry and terrified. From the protection of the bulwark, Lincoln looked down at the white face, streaked with dirt, the brown hair wild. . . . "Captain," he said, "I am glad you know how to talk to a civilian."

It was the only time Holmes spoke to his President — and it was the last fighting he would ever see. That night in the heat he slept fitfully. Next morning when the sun rose through the mist, standing on the parapet with General Wright, Holmes saw that Jubal Early was gone with all his troops. He had taken herds of cattle with him and provisions — and he had escaped.

July, 1864 . . . Holmes's term of enlistment was over. He had served his three years. There was nothing to do but go home and be mustered out with the rest of the Regiment. If the war lasted all winter he could, he told himself wearily, re-enlist in the spring. He was certainly no good to any man's army the way he felt now. He had never been so tired in his life. *Died of exhaustion.* His father had once said that of all the curt phrases in the casualty lists, that was the worst. In the past three years Holmes had wondered more than once why he did not die of exhaustion. Maybe he would yet, he thought wryly. A dogged, restless fatigue had enveloped him for weeks — ever since Cold Harbor. It kept him from sleeping, kept him from sitting still when he had a chance to sit still, kept him from everything except — unfortunately — thinking.

Well, the business now was to get home to Boston. Holmes went to the Abbott House, where he had stored his winter clothes on the way through to Virginia last February. Everything was gone. Somebody had walked off with all of it, including Grandfather Abiel's sealskin cloak. Holmes was furious. Climbing into the cars in the July heat he could think of nothing else. Of all the dirty tricks! He hoped fervently the bastard that took that cloak was shot dead in it somewhere south of the Pamunkey. The cars were cindery and hot, they jerked and banged. Had there ever been a time when each jerk or motion was not registered with a stab inside his head? How many times had he taken the cars thus after a battle? Edwards Ferry, Hagerstown, Frederick. Always before, he had been sick or wounded. Couches had been laid, hands reached to help him. Dr. Hunt, on those journeys from Philadelphia. His father, talking and talking, making bad puns. . . .

There was a class dinner scheduled in a week or two at Young's Hotel. As Class Poet, Holmes knew what would be expected of him. Out of eighty-one members, more than fifty had been under arms, many were still fighting. Holmes would still be in uniform, it would be August before the Twentieth was mustered out. How in God's name could a man make a Class Poem in the middle of a war? You couldn't be funny with a third of the class dead or crippled or down with dysentery or tuberculosis. . . . A poem for the Class of '61! — Arthur Dehon was dead, so were Robeson and Henry Doolittle. Bob Shaw was buried in a trench with his Negro troops. They weren't all '61, but in a war you forgot distinctions that in other times seemed important. . . . Gazing wearily out of the car window, Holmes did not see the green Susquehanna Valley passing by. He saw Jack Lowell in the line at Glendale, his hand up in a salute as the order came to advance. He saw Ed Revere at Antietam, kneeling by the wounded with his surgeon's kit while the rest of them charged by. Norwood Hallowell, lying on that farmhouse floor while the wall clock ticked.

How fought our brothers, and how died, the story
You bid me tell . . .

He might start the poem that way and just give it to them, straight . . . How many of them had been in the war as long as he? He had scarcely missed a battle in the whole Virginia campaign . . . Ball's Bluff, Fair Oaks, the Peninsula. Harrison's Landing on the James. Mud and flies and dysentery. The hospital tents below Alexandria, Falmouth in the spring with the shad rising in the river, the men seining under the enemy's guns. Marye's Heights. That morning, lying in the grass, he had thought his foot blown off entirely; he had decided not to look.

Norwood Hallowell was still in it, a colonel of colored troops with Grant at Petersburg. What a hellish row people had raised at the beginning, about enlisting Negroes. How many fighting faiths a war upset! Well, the issue was clear now. It was the Union; everyone knew that, even the Abolitionists, although they were too stubborn to acknowledge it.

It would be strange to be out of it, to lay aside this old blue uniform with the tarnished shoulder straps, the red sash, the wide shabby hat with the clover on the front. Even the clanking sword that at first had been so awkward was part of him now. With wry amusement, Holmes recalled the first time he had tried to use his saber. Down at Edwards Ferry he had been sent on horseback to carry dispatches. On the road he met a Rebel captain. They tried to get their sabers out. Both got thoroughly tangled up, wheeled, drew their pistols, rode close and pressed the muzzle to the other's side. Neither pistol went off.

No one but a soldier would understand that story. Would he, Holmes wondered, be able to talk to the people at home? He had learned a language they could not speak.

"*Don't call me hero,*" Holmes said long after the war was over. "*I trust I did my duty as a soldier respectably, but I was not born for it and did nothing remarkable in that way.*"

It was true. But it is true also that to do one's duty as a soldier respectably has its own peculiar definition. Holmes was not a soldier born. Yet during those years the soldier's creed became part of him, part of his blood and bone, engendering its own philosophy. Again and again, in public and in private, Holmes gave testimony to what he had learned at Antietam wood and in the bloody earth-works at Spottsylvania: —

> To ride boldly at what is in front of you, be it fence or enemy; to pray, not for comfort, but for combat; to remember that duty is not to be proved in the evil day, but then to be obeyed unquestioning; to love glory more than the temptations of wallowing ease, but to know that one's final judge and only rival is oneself. For high and dangerous action teaches us to believe as right beyond dispute things for which our doubting minds are slow to find words of proof. Out of heroism grows faith in the worth of heroism. The proof comes later, and even may never come.

War can make cynics; it can make a "lost generation." . . . Or perhaps like life itself, war merely makes cynics of cynics — and saints of saints.

"Through our great good fortune," said Wendell Holmes, *"in our youth our hearts were touched with fire. It was given us to learn at the outset that life is a profound and passionate thing. While we are permitted to scorn nothing but indifference, and do not pretend to undervalue the worldly rewards of ambition, we have seen with our own eyes, beyond and above the gold fields, the snowy heights of honor, and it is for us to bear the report to those who come after us. But, above all, we have learned that whether a man accepts from Fortune her spade and will look downward and dig, or from Aspiration her axe and cord and will scale the ice, the one and only success which it is his to command is to bring to his work a mighty heart."*

CHAPTER EIGHTEEN

Law School.

SEPTEMBER,[1] 1864 . . . A young man walks up the steps of Dane Hall on Harvard Square, up between the white columns, through the wide doors, and takes his seat in the lecture room of Judge Joel Parker. He is eager, but he is also more than a little confused. He is by no means sure of himself. He has only the stubborn, hazy conviction that the law is what he is going to do next and do with all his might. Within the boundaries of this conviction he is slated for hours, days, years of doubt and bitter uncertainty.

Law student, Holmes had written with a flourish three years ago in his army identification papers. On his return from the war in July of 1864 he would have liked to go over to Cambridge immediately and enroll in the Law School. But he hesitated. It was a serious step. Was the law really his objective in life — not merely the "starting point" he had called it in his class autobiography? There was one other possibility: philosophy, with the eventual goal a professorship at Harvard. Since his undergraduate days and the prize essay on Plato, Holmes's passion for philosophy had grown steadily deeper. Metaphysics, dialectics, formal logic, theories of government and theories of sovereignty: these things fascinated him. And in 1864, these were the things that lay behind the law.

The question was, should such knowledge be pursued with only itself as goal, or was it better to have a focus, a boundary, some clinical application outside the classroom such as a money-making law practice that brought a man up against the world and the living problems of the world? Mr. Robert Morse, who had a very good law practice on Pemberton Square, said Wendell was born for the law.

Wendell received this statement with skepticism. The only thing he felt born for was to use his powers to the full. Even more clearly than when he was in the army, Holmes recognized that his powers were intellectual, that he was an "internal" man, to whom ideas were more interesting than things. For three years, he had lived a life as external as it would be possible to live. He had slept on the ground, had killed men with his own hand, saved men's lives by his own hand. Now he was free, and the life of pure scholarship beckoned. But if he embraced it, if he followed in the footsteps of such a man as Emerson, might he not, at forty, find himself dwelling in a cloud land of pure speculation, his own vital force dilute in this rarefied region?

All his youth he had looked up to Emerson as the wisest man he knew. When you were young you found your hero, never doubting that you could pattern yourself upon him, follow after him. But life changed you. Or at least, the things that happened brought you to yourself. Behind Emerson's highest flights of writing, behind his most magnetic utterances, one could discern always a moral purpose. Not a narrow purpose; of all men Emerson was most tolerant.

But examining himself, Holmes felt no such crusader's impulse. Merely, he desired to use his brain, drive it to its fullest capacity. He desired to examine and understand the laws of social being, the pattern men followed in their lives. In the law, if one dug far enough, would not one find recorded all the customs of mankind? In Wendell Holmes's day, anthropology did not exist as a science or as a study. Neither did sociology. Political economy existed — but it was a dry subject, filled with statistics. What had Disraeli called it? *The dismal science.*

You heard stories of great men and how they chose their professions. Jeremy Bentham as a young man had examined himself severely to see if he had a *genius* for anything. The answer had come clearly — "a genius for legislation." Bentham had followed that voice and because of it the course of English history had changed and was still changing. But were these stories true, about great men? Did not luck have a lot to do with it? It seemed to Wendell Holmes that success in a chosen profession depended as much upon luck as upon logic.

At home he said nothing of his plans, aware that his father had long ago studied the law and hated it. Dr. Holmes liked philosophy no better, having the scientist's mistrust for abstract speculation. It seemed to him that lawyers went about solving their problems — and what dreary problems! — in a manner both unreal and devious. He had a quotation from Gulliver about lawyers that he loved to air. "*It is a maxim among . . . lawyers, that whatever hath been done before may legally be done again: and therefore . . .*" Recollection of it kept Wendell's lips sealed. He had no wish to be preached at concerning the uselessness of lawyers and philosophers in a hard, practical world.

"What are you going to do?" Dr. Holmes asked continually. "What about science? Science is the coming thing. What about teaching? It's true the professor's chair has an insulating quality that cuts it off from contact with reality. I've said that rather well in the *Autocrat*. But combined with writing or some more practical application, teaching is a very satisfactory way to make a living."

He had talked until his wife cautioned him to be still, let Wendell alone, give him a chance for a rest and a few months' vacation before making his decision. If the war was not over by spring the boy would probably re-enlist whether he was physically fit or not. Let him have a winter free of responsibility. Give him time to look round, get flesh on his bones, heal up his nervous system.

On the first of August, Holmes was mustered out of the Twentieth Regiment in a ceremony on the Common with the other three-year men.[2] He carried the title of Lieutenant Colonel, brevetted for "gallant and meritorious service at the battle of Chancellorsville." Afterward the Regiment marched around Faneuil Hall behind the brass band, ending up at the Apollo Gardens for beer and an excellent supper provided by the Citizens' Committee. Wendell sat with Captain Magnitzky, an older man, a Pole from out near Lowell who had volunteered as a private and served right through the war. Wendell was immensely fond of him. "Do not look so troubled," Magnitzky told him now. "You have done your part. You were a good soldier, Colonel Holmes. And you were not born for it. In six months, eight months, if we do not beat the Rebels you can perhaps re-enlist. Now it is time for you to forget soldiering and be a scholar. It is time for you to do for a little while the things you were born to do."

A few days later, Holmes went out to Concord to see Emerson. In the warm summer afternoon the two sat under the elms, talking earnestly. Emerson said nothing definite. He never gave advice, having too much respect for a man's freedom. He talked eloquently, passionately, about his beliefs, about the world that lay ahead after this war and the part a young man might take in rebuilding that world. Holmes was stirred. But traveling home by the cars in the summer twilight, he knew that Emerson had not reached him as once he would have reached him. About it all there had been something remote. Wendell's teeth needed a harder bite, something tougher to cut on. "You are a lawyer," Dr. Johnson had said to — somebody or other.[3] *"Lawyers know life practically. A bookish man should always have them to converse with. They have what he wants."*

Next morning Holmes knocked on the door of his father's study. "I am going to the Law School," he said without preamble.

Dr. Holmes looked up from his desk. "What is the use of that?" he said. "What's the use of that, Wendell? A lawyer can't be a great man."

The remark was instinctive. But if he had tried, Dr. Holmes could not have devised a statement more provocative to his son. *A lawyer can't be a great man.* To Wendell the statement combined a paternal cocksureness concerning the universe and its arrangements with a bland assurance that any son of Dr. Oliver Wendell Holmes could be a great man if he started out right. The words struck home, pointed, steel-shafted. If there had been doubts, they were resolved now. Wendell would go over to Cambridge and sign his name on the rolls at Dane Hall, not for a starting point but as a profession that would last a lifetime. . . .

His father looked at him sharply. Had Wendell heard what Dean Swift had to say about lawyers? Before Wendell could reply, Dr. Holmes reached for a book on his desk. "Here!" he said. "Gulliver is talking to the Houyhnhnms. *'It is a maxim among these lawyers, that whatever hath been done before, may legally be done again: and therefore they take special care to record all the decisions formerly made against common justice, and the general reason of mankind. These, under the name of precedents, they produce as authorities, to justify the most iniquitous opinions; and the judges never fail of directing accordingly.'"*

Highly pleased with the aptness of the allusion, the doctor returned *Gulliver* to its place. Uncle John, he continued, had tried the law and abandoned it. Had Wendell discussed a law career with Uncle John?

Wendell had, but he saw no reason for telling his father about it. Uncle John did not hate the law, he merely laughed at it. "So," Uncle John had said, "you will be nursemaid to the ambulatory will, with all its little codicils running around after it? . . . Wendell, it does not matter what career you choose. If a man is adequate in native force he probably will be happy, no matter what fate has in store for him. I think you have that adequacy. There is no reason why you should not apply it to the law as well as to anything."

Wendell Holmes did not repeat this to his father. Leaving the book-lined study, leaving Gulliver and Dr. Holmes, he went over to Cambridge and signed his name in the rolls. . . . But his father's words went with him. *A lawyer can't be a great man.* When he was ninety, Wendell Holmes would quote that phrase, adding that his father had kicked him upstairs into the law and he supposed he should be grateful.

But what Dr. Holmes had said about the law was not, Wendell knew in all fairness, dictated wholly by the personal prejudice of a man who had tried a profession and failed. There was tradition behind his remark. Not so very long ago, America had despised lawyers. Colonial America had looked upon them as mere tradesmen who earned a questionable living by cleverness and chicanery. Paid attorneys were barred from the courts, rigidly restricted as to fees and procedure. Later, lawyers rose to power simply because America desired to fit the English common law to its own local needs, and lawyers were the only men who could do it. Lawyers drafted the Constitution. John Adams was trained in the law. So were Jefferson, Madison, Monroe, John Quincy Adams. With truth, Burke had remarked in Parliament that the American Union was governed by lawyers.

Even so, the public was slow to separate statesmen from lawyers and continued to mistrust the latter. The American law had had of necessity a slow growth. The grandfather of one of Holmes's classmates — James Kent Stone — became Chancellor of New York in 1814. For the nine years that Chancellor Kent held office, not a single decision or opinion of his American predecessors was cited to him or even suggested. Now in 1864 the traditional English material, worked over for a hundred years, was becoming available in its American form. The Harvard Law School was not yet fifty years old; it had amounted to little until Judge Story had come there in '29, determined that a lawyer should have training beyond the customary apprenticeship in a lawyer's office. Two years of such apprenticeship — unless you were lucky enough to get into the office of a man of genius — usually resulted in nothing more than a good scrivener's handwriting.

But it was hard to alter custom. In 1864, the Harvard Law School was conducted very much like a lawyer's office. The three lecturers had all been practising lawyers; they shared the outlook of their day as to how their various subjects should be taught. They were all elderly men who never heard of teaching law by the case system or indeed by any system other than giving the student a text to read and commenting on it. As the life of the law lies in its application, this system was not only dull but remote. There were no requirements for admission. It was not necessary to be a college graduate or take an examination. The student could enter at any time during the winter, sit down with the others and try to catch up. When Holmes signed the register he paid exactly what a student in a law office paid: one hundred dollars for the year. At the end of eighteen months he would receive, without examination, a certificate called LL.B. which would not, of course, admit him to the bar.

Wendell Holmes had no complaint to make concerning this system. How could he, when nothing existed with which to compare it? He had read a fair amount of social theory: Montesquieu and Plato, Hume, Locke, Hobbes, John Mill, Spencer. Long ago, Thomas Jefferson had advised the law student to make all knowledge his province, to read the natural sciences, history, *belles-lettres*, criticism, rhetoric, oratory — and read from dawn until bedtime. It was a program to appeal to Wendell Holmes. Profession of the law was not a way to make money on Court Street. The law was a door opening into knowledge. It was a window, opening out on all mankind.

Sitting in Judge Parker's lecture room on a bright day of September, Holmes took out his notebook as the Judge began to speak. It was a large class; the war had not caused college enrollments to fall off. The last undergraduate class at Harvard had in fact been much larger than Wendell's own class of '61. George Morison sat just across the aisle, Sedgwick next to him, both Boston men. Peter Olney, Robert Lincoln. Strange to be a student once more — to sit, notebook in hand, waiting for the professor's voice. What an impressive-looking man Judge Parker was! Senior professor of the Law School, he had been Chief Justice of New Hampshire. His black eye shot lightning, his features were strong, he carried himself very straight. When he strode through the room and onto the platform he looked as if he were going to walk right on through the other side. He was sixty-nine; he had lectured at the school for sixteen years. A good fight was meat and drink to Parker. He was much concerned with politics and for the past two years had bitterly condemned Lincoln's use of wartime powers. Everyone knew what Judge Parker had said to the president of Dartmouth. "Sir!" roared Parker. "This modern education is all a humbug!"

President Lord had only sighed. "Judge Parker," he replied, "it is."

There was no other way to converse with Judge Parker. His knowledge of the law was vast. It was also exact, formal, and involved to the point of obscurity. Holmes had been warned not to try to understand Parker's lectures. Just get what he said into a notebook and then learn it by heart. Wendell had been scornful of this. He was no undergraduate trying to skim through college. He was a man of twenty-three who had been to the wars and desired knowledge.

But after the first twenty minutes of Joel Parker, Holmes was not so scornful of his adviser. He could not make sense of one word the Judge was saying. Holmes glanced around. Everyone else had stopped writing too. Morison looked dazed, Sedgwick's eye was glassy. Only Peter Olney leaned forward, intent, frowning. Was this the frown of understanding or the anxious pucker that goes with hopeless incomprehension? Holmes hoped it was the latter. Only last night, Harry James had told him that he had sat through an entire winter of lectures at the Law School without understanding a single word. Then he had joyfully abandoned the law. Father, Uncle John, Harry James . . . not stupid men. . . .

At home that night Wendell Holmes was unusually silent. Next day Professor Parsons lectured. And Professor Parsons, fortunately, was a different matter altogether. At sixty-seven, Parsons seemed years younger than Judge Parker. He was ruddy-cheeked and big. He liked to tell a good story and he was interested in many things outside the law — the *Free Press* which he had edited for years; Swedenborgianism, to which he was almost as ardent a convert as Mr. Henry James the elder. Parsons hated the more technical parts of the law, such as pleading and property, and did not hesitate to say so. His father had been Chief Justice of Massachusetts, his own book on contracts was getting ready its fifth edition and was so much used in the courts that a student was heard to ask if there was a statute making Parsons an authority. Even so he seemed more *litterateur* than lawyer. Holmes was drawn to him immediately.

Parsons always gave his first lecture of the year on the ethics of the profession and it always opened with the same words. The students grinned with anticipation: *"If a young lawyer pays for his sign the first year and his office rent the next, he can tell himself he is doing very well."* . . .

The third professor, Emory Washburn, was a strikingly hand-some man in his early sixties. In the early days of the war Holmes had been much impressed by seeing him march up and down, gun on shoulder, guarding Cambridge Arsenal with his students. Like the other two professors, Washburn was descended from a long line of patriots. He himself had been state Senator, Judge, Whig Governor of the Commonwealth. This summer Holmes had twice seen him walking behind soldiers' funerals in the uniform of the Home Guard. The bushy gray eyebrows and side whiskers of the former Governor looked strange under a private's cap, and some-how touching. "Oh, I like to help when I can," Washburn said. He was the best lecturer in the school, he could breathe life even into Coke on Littleton and the dreadful logic of Fearne on Contin-gent Remainders. When he laughed you could hear him across the Yard, and the students loved him. Holmes said it was Washburn who taught him the meaning of the phrase, *enthusiasm of the lec-ture room*. Non-law students, seen mounting the steps of Dane Hall, explained that they were going in to hear Washburn talk law for a while.

So far, so good. Under teachers of first-rate minds, strong char-acters and contagious personalities, Holmes could start off with enthusiasm. He lived at his father's house on Charles Street, going back and forth to Boston in the crowded horsecars over the West

Bridge, carrying large brown books to study at home — Spence and Fearne and Austin. Austin's *Jurisprudence* was new. Its second edition, published in London in 1861, had taken sudden fire from discussion of the impending Reform Bill. Austin was a Utilitarian. Lawyers said his book attempted to untangle law from ethics, to separate old theories of political sovereignty from the historical foundations of society. But the book made very unpleasant reading. Later, in London, Frederick Pollock[4] said that Austin "dogmatized overmuch," and with typical Pollockian candor declared the author to be "uncouth and excessive," his literary manner so repulsive that even at his most accurate it was difficult to believe what he said.

Not all the books Holmes studied were British. From the Law School itself came some of the best ones: Story's commentaries, Greenleaf on Evidence, Stearns on Real Actions, Parsons on Contracts. For American jurisprudence Holmes had a book he liked: Walker's *Introduction to American Law*. It was, he said afterward, one of the two books that gave him a glimpse of what he was seeking — the law in its general, historical aspect. The other was the first volume of Spence's *Equitable Jurisdiction*.

Timothy Walker, a student at the Law School under Judge Story, had written his book as a very young man, apologizing in the preface because somebody older and wiser had not written it instead. In it he examined American law from the Bill of Rights to Civil Procedure, discussed the conflict of laws and from state to state quoted case and precedent to support him. The student was advised to shun delights and live laborious days. "Genius without toil," Holmes read on page nineteen, "may, to some extent, distinguish a man elsewhere; but here he must labor, or he cannot succeed. No quickness of intuition can supply the place of patient investigation. A clear mind might determine at once what the law ought to be, but actual inspection alone can determine what the law is."

Wendell Holmes did not spurn this investigation. He reveled in it, pursued it mightily. In the students' law club — the Marshall Club, it was called — he argued cases with Olney and Lincoln. At home he continued the argument until his father, rebelling, said if Wendell went on talking law he would get out his fiddle and play against him right here in the library.

> Come you of the law, who can talk, if you please,
> Till the man in the moon will allow it's a cheese.

Did Wendell remember, his father demanded, those very apt lines from his poem written long ago for the Berkshire Jubilee? Wendell laughed. How much pleasanter his father was to get on with, now that the decision was made and he was actually committed to the law! Wendell had not looked forward to living at home. After being a captain in the army, how could he submit even outwardly to his father's authority? Yet he had no choice. He had no money, he was twenty-three. It was his business to get through Law School as cheaply as possible.

Neddy was a sophomore at Harvard, he came home only for holidays. Wendell's sister Amelia was twenty-one — a tiny, brisk creature, very congenial with her father. But Mrs. Holmes's pleasure in having her eldest son once more under her roof was extreme. It touched Dr. Holmes, made him suddenly more tolerant. When Mrs. Holmes heard Wendell's voice she came quickly into the room and sat down, watching him with an expression of such bright pleasure that Wendell turned instinctively, addressing the rest of his remarks to her. Once, while Wendell was speaking, his father got up and, putting an arm over his wife's shoulder, patted her gently, then left the room.

Mrs. Holmes was interested in every detail her son brought home from the Law School. She did not want to talk about the war, she said. She had had enough of war. Wendell had earned the right to use his mind. Let him use it then, while the chance was given him. The Rebels were not beaten; God knew what lay ahead. Mrs. Holmes was especially interested in the Marshall Club debates. Wendell had a talent for speaking, she said. Dr. Holmes did not agree, but for once he kept silence. The law was a bowl of sawdust; Wendell had undertaken to swallow it down. Let him swallow it then. His father wished him well. But what exactly was that phrase? *Sawdust without butter* . . . Some English barrister had said it to a young aspirant. *"If you can eat sawdust without butter, young man, you will be a success in the law."* He must look the phrase up, have it ready for Wendell next time the boy began to orate on the virtues of jurisprudence over against medicine, as a mind trainer.

John Ropes, coming in one evening, found Wendell sparring with his father and was hugely amused. At the end of October he wrote John Gray that Wendell seemed well and happy and had just written a sonnet for the *Transcript* — "really strong and good," Ropes added.

Actually, the sonnet sounds like bad Matthew Arnold. But compared with most of the poems in the papers and magazines of the period, it was sterling work.[5] In the same issue was a poem called "A Sea-Shell." "Cool lips of shell, sing, sea-shell warm and sweet!" . . . Even the *Atlantic Monthly* gave space, under the name of poetry, to effusions so sentimental one is astonished to see the famous names appended to them.

Wendell published his sonnet anonymously. He had loved Henry Abbott, it was good to relieve himself of this burden of debt to a comrade-at-arms: —

H. L. A.

Twentieth Massachusetts Volunteers

He steered unquestioning nor turning back,
Into the darkness and the unknown sea;
He vanished in the starless night, and we
Saw but the shining of his luminous wake.
Thou sawest light, but ah, our sky seemed black,
And all too hard the inscrutable decree,
Yet noble heart, full soon we follow thee,
Lit by the deeds that flamed along thy track. . . .

To Holmes, out of the war himself, it seemed particularly terrible to see soldiers' funerals along the streets. Day after day the muffled drums, the slow processions over Beacon Hill. The war news itself was very favorable. Atlanta captured, Jubal Early routed in Virginia. It was a good thing, too, with a Presidential election only a few weeks off. If news from the front had continued bad, Lincoln supporters would have had a hard time putting a stop to the premature peace talk. Faneuil Hall in September had been the scene of a tremendous Democratic rally. Orators reminded the people that four years of war had failed to save the Union — and that Lincoln started the war.

On the Republican side, George Shattuck was very active. Holmes liked to see him in the public forum, vigorous, confident, with his handsome gray head, his skillful oratory of the trial lawyer. As election day approached, victory looked safe for Lincoln. Higginson was home, honorably discharged from the army, looking white and wobbly, but campaigning passionately for Lincoln. On

November 8, a day of rain and wind, it was decided. "Lincoln will walk the course, God bless him!" Professor Asa Gray of Harvard wrote his friend, Charles Darwin. "Homely, ungainly Lincoln is the representative man of the country." By the middle of December, Sherman was within five miles of Savannah. It began to look as though the end were in sight. News from the front was almost pushed off the newspapers by advertisements of new petroleum and coal companies. In the early mornings Wendell saw smartly turned out broughams lining the sidewalks downtown. Ladies in furs, waiting for the brokers' offices to open so they might be first in line.

One evening in December, Mr. Robert Morse stopped in to see Wendell. He had a proposition to make. How would Wendell like to come into his office for the rest of the winter, part time of course, and see a little practical application of all this theory he was reading in Cambridge? Might do him good to handle a real writ, acquire a practical conviction of the difference between assumpsit and trover. After all, lawyers weren't made in libraries. The old apprentice system had had its points.

Wendell did not hesitate. Next Monday afternoon he sat on a high stool behind a desk in Barrister's Hall and copied wills, deeds, trusts, for three hours. He could not pretend it was invigorating work. But as the weeks wore on he was continually surprised at the speed with which Morse moved when a question was brought to him. At law school it had seemed that such questions would require weeks of argument, reference, and cross reference before a decision was reached. It left Wendell open-mouthed, he told the family at supper, to see the swift certainty with which a master of his business turned it off.

Dr. Holmes, helping himself to butter from the dish on the table, paused, knife in hand. "*Sawdust!*" he murmured. "*Sawdust without butter.*" He looked up. The old gleam was in his eye. "Wendell, have you heard what the English judge said to the young man who asked how a person could recognize a real vocation for the law?"

Under the table Neddy kicked his brother swiftly. Across the table Amelia watched, her brown eyes quick as a bird's. Mrs. Holmes poured Wendell's tea, handing it to him serenely. Wendell looked at his mother; their eyes met without expression.

"No, Father," Wendell said gravely. "I haven't heard. What did the judge say to the young man who wanted to be a lawyer?"

CHAPTER NINETEEN

The war ends. Holmes asks himself
some questions about the law.

John C. Ropes to John C. Gray, Jr.

BOSTON, 21 BARRISTER'S HALL
31 *January*, 1865

When are you coming home on a leave? Soon, I hope.
Holmes and I were talking about you on Sunday evening over
a gin toddy and some cigars, and wishing you would come in to
join us. Why can't you? Wendell, by the way, is working hard
at the law, and judging by the fondness he has for talking over
his points he is much interested in it. He will master the theoretical part easily enough, I doubt not.

Talking over his points. Wendell Holmes could not talk enough.
What he learned in the morning he was irresistibly impelled to communicate at night, and the nights seemed all too short for his purpose. Charles Street was a continual Babel of tongues. Amelia's
friends, sewing in the living room at tea time, Neddy's friends from
Harvard, Dr. Holmes's friends, Mr. James Freeman Clarke, John
Osborne Sargent, Professor Gray, and the rest. Even these did not
talk the language that Wendell Holmes was so laboriously learning.
It was not only the law he desired to talk about. It was the cosmos
itself, all the problems of the universe. Wendell brought home young
men studying law or medicine at Harvard, drew them upstairs to his
room under the flaring gas lamp. William James and Henry Bowditch, both medical students. Charles Peirce the black-eyed, ferocious

young philosopher, son of Professor Benjamin Peirce. T. S. Perry, Chauncey Wright, John Ropes; John Gray when he came home on leave from the army. Men who were not embarrassed by the largest, angriest topics: the universe, the cosmos, all the *isms* from Kantian idealism to Comtian positivism. Whiskey and glasses were on the table, the air was blue with pipe smoke. Tonight, they told each other eagerly when they met in the Harvard Yard under a dry morning light — tonight we will take the cosmos and twist it by the tail.

When John Gray came home from Virginia the talk turned on the war. In February, Charleston fell. Two weeks later, Lincoln was inaugurated. There was disappointment at the President's address. He had simply got up and observed there wasn't much to be said on this second occasion of taking the oath. If it was God's will the struggle should continue, then *"with malice toward none; with charity for all; with firmness in the right, as God gives us to see the right, let us strive on to finish the work we are in; to bind up the nation's wounds; to care for him who shall have borne the battle"* . . . and to achieve a *"just and lasting peace among ourselves, and with all nations."*

This was all very fine, but why, the papers said, didn't Lincoln say *how* things were to be resolved? Why did he give no program? Now of all times, the nation looked for a program. A little tact and diplomacy would have won the less rebellious states. The President could have got back Georgia and North Carolina by a word. People were deathly tired of war. But Grant was not tired of it, waiting in front of Richmond. Lincoln went down to see what was going on. Grant, he said, had promised to show him Richmond. When the day came he wanted to be on hand.

For Wendell Holmes there was only one attitude. If a man could not be in the war, he could hope fervently for victory, could dream of days to come when thought would seem as important as action, contemplation as justifiable as bustle. Rapidly, in Virginia, events moved toward this consummation. "Victory, Victory! The Rebellion Crumbling!" the news headlines said on April third. . . . *"We took Richmond this morning,"* General Weitzel telegraphed. *"I captured many guns."*

At Dixwell's School the boys heard the news at closing time. They raced up Boylston Place to the Common, shouting at the top of their lungs. Wendell Holmes's joy was tempered by the caution of a man who had been through many battles and knew that even the fall of Richmond was not final victory. Nothing meant victory except the surrender of Lee's army. For seven days the people waited; their talk was all of Richmond. Where was Jeff Davis? How did he get away, on foot or on horseback? Where was Lee? . . . It was said the Fourth Massachusetts pickets were the first soldiers to enter the city at dawn on Monday. The people ran after them, asking if they had anything to eat. "Jeff Davis has *not* sold his furniture," a news correspondent wrote. "It is here in his house where I am writing."

On Monday, April 10, the news came for which the people had waited. "Praise God!" the headlines said. "Surrender of Lee and his whole army." In Boston that day, nobody did anything but shout, dance, pray, and make speeches. By night the city was crazy with fireworks. The Holmes family walked downtown to hear Dana make a speech. On Washington Street they met the Faneuil Hall marketmen parading in their white frocks, singing "John Brown." Dana was at his best that night. He knew better than to mention the word *Grant*. No orator could get beyond that magic word. At the sound of it people went mad with joy. Dana was very serious. "We want to say something that will cross three thousand miles of water," he began. "For the first time in history, a self-governing republic is capable of maintaining itself against internal rebellion. What monarchy could have carried through this war as we have carried it? Could our army have fought for a country owned by any one man or by any number of men or families?"

Three thousand miles of water . . . Yankee faces turned grimly, triumphantly to the eastward. England! England had not helped to win this war. England had all but put her stakes on the South. England had not believed the North could do it. She had not *wanted* it done. "The West end is right," Dr. Holmes had written two years ago, "*not by aggression, but by the naked fact of existence, we are an eternal danger and an unsleeping threat to every government that founds itself on anything but the will of the governed.*" It was the older men who felt this, spoke of it among themselves. England would have no more to say in our internal affairs, Dr. Holmes told his son triumphantly, walking home late that night from the victory meeting. . . . "England?" Wendell repeated vaguely. "Who cares about England? It's Lee that won't have anything more to say in our affairs."

Dr. Holmes was silent. He had been deeply stirred not only by events in Virginia but by events of long ago. There had been another night . . . another victory. In Cambridge the colleges had been illumined in the early winter dusk. He had run all the way home from school, out of breath from yelling "Hurrah for America!" . . . *1815–1865* . . . With what extraordinary clarity it all came back! There was a magic continuity somewhere, if he could stop long enough to catch it. Three wars, two of them terrible wars, before a man could say "these United States." We had withstood two revolutions. We had proved ourselves. We were a nation — let come what may . . . Tonight the speaker who came before Dana had mentioned "the President of the United States." The crowd had gone crazy. It was not Lincoln they cheered. It was those two words. *United States.* The man next to Dr. Holmes had burst into tears. "Yes, Sir!" the speaker had continued. "Thank God, President of the *United* States!"

In the streets beyond the Common they were singing, the refrain came over the hill. "*The Union forever, Hurrah boys hurrah!*" Around the Holmes family as they walked, people took it up. Mrs. Holmes had her husband's arm. Neddy and Wendell walked ahead with long strides, marching in step. Wendell's arm was across his brother's shoulder, his voice was loud and healthy. And as usual, his father noted, he sang off key. Mrs. Holmes pressed her husband's arm; Dr. Holmes became aware that she was talking to herself, saying something over and over, quietly. Tears streamed down her face.

"The war is over," she was saying. "Thank God, thank God, the war is over."

In the autumn of 1865, Holmes resumed his studies at the Law School. Now in his second year his mind was clearer, he looked at his courses with a dispassionate eye and found them wanting. In the catalogue, "Instruction for the Bar" was listed briefly: "*Various branches of the Common Law, and of Equity. Admiralty; Commercial, International and Constitutional Law; and the Jurisprudence of the United States.*" Holmes still had no fault to find with his teachers. They were admirable men.

But when you had mastered the subjects they presented, where did it lead? Holmes had thought to make all knowledge his province, walking from ignorance to light through a door labeled *The Law*. Now he found himself wandering in a maze of technicalities, a nightmare of doors that opened only to close silently upon themselves, with no progress made, no path revealed. With one or two exceptions the books that were put into his hand gave no perspective beyond the intricate learning they presented, appeasing not at all Holmes's curiosity, his passion for an ordered intellectual vision of the connection of events. Any man of ambition is willing to labor unceasingly to master the tools of his profession — provided the tools are adequate to the job that will follow.

The trouble was that in 1865, the tools of legal education were dishearteningly inadequate. Holmes came to the study of law at an in-between time. Jefferson had advised the law student to make all knowledge his province. But the broad humanism of Jefferson had disappeared, to be replaced by the specialization that comes inevitably to any growing profession — a specialization that for a time remains disordered, swamped in its own technical detail. Holmes had expected the detail. All the learned professions must be entered through a mass of dry technicalities. The would-be doctor, burning to discover new paths to healing, must learn every bone, every joint and muscle in his body and spend long hours mastering the technique of a simple handling of tools. And yet — a tool in the hand is a live thing; even a list of two hundred and six namable bones has a hard, quick, common-sense relation to life. These bones are inside the student's own frame.

But the dry bones of the law refuse to come to life so easily. Tomes and tomes of musty reading, all relating to the past, to time and things — rarely to people — which to the student seem not only dead but never to have existed. In 1865, the law was not presented to the student with its sociological implications; he was not taught history, economics, or given any sense of continuity in the law, of past, present, or future.

Holmes was tough-minded, yet in the long line of American jurists he was not alone in his bewilderment. Judge Story himself had suffered vast disappointment. Coming eagerly to the study of law there was put into his hand, straight off, that scourge of all law students, *Coke on Littleton*. Opening it, Story's heart sank within him. "Intricate, crabbed, and obsolete learning," he said. "You may judge . . . how I was surprised and startled on opening works, where nothing was presented but dry and technical principles, the dark and mysterious elements of the feudal system, the subtle refinements and intricacies of the middle ages of the common law, and the repulsive and almost unintelligible forms of processes and pleadings. . . . I took it up, and after trying it day after day with very little success, I sat myself down and wept bitterly."

Chancellor Kent, Judge Taney, Daniel Webster, recorded a like bewilderment. "Why," said Webster, "disgust and discourage a boy by telling him that he must break into his profession, through such a wall as this? I really often despaired. I thought I never could make myself a lawyer and was almost going back to the business of school-keeping."

Webster and Story were admitted to the Massachusetts bar in the early 1800's. Students who came after them fared little better, being nourished upon such books as Puffendorf's *Latin History of England*, Grotius, Wood's *Institutes of the Laws of England*, Hawkins's *Pleas of the Crown*, Bacon's *Elements*, Juvenal. Often enough it was necessary to stop short in the middle and go back to a study of Latin grammar, or spell out for themselves from the Norman-French. Long after he was a judge, Dwight Foster told T. W. Higginson that the real objection to study of the law was not that it was uninteresting. It was eminently interesting. But it filled the mind with knowledge that could not be carried into another stage of existence. The first law professorship at Harvard was founded in 1815; Story came to his long professorship in 1829. Through sheer genius for teaching, he accomplished much.

But the times were not yet ripe. Year after year the same ancient books were given the student, the same rules to learn by rote. Wendell Holmes came to Law School only six years before Christopher Columbus Langdell brought the case system of study to Harvard. But when Holmes was in school, in 1865, the case system was as unknown to Cambridge as the telephone. Holmes had to learn the law the way his grandfather, Judge Jackson, had learned it, by fumbling through detached and unrelated books on legal specialties and by studying such meager reports as the U. S. courts had lately gathered. The temple of the law, Dr. Holmes had said, was very cold and cheerless about the threshold. With violence, his son repudiated this statement. But the farther he went in the law the stronger grew his own doubts. And as always, doubt engendered challenge. Durant, of the class of '42, a highly successful lawyer in the city, said the law was simply a system of fossilized injustice, with not enough intellectual interest to occupy an intelligent man for an hour. Holmes himself gave testimony to the hardships of his search: —

"One found oneself plunged in a thick fog of details — in a black and frozen night, in which were no flowers, no spring, no easy joys. Voices of authority warned that in the crush of that ice any craft might sink. One heard Burke saying that law sharpens the mind by narrowing it. One heard in Thackeray of a lawyer bending all the powers of a great mind to a mean profession. One saw that artists and poets shrank from it as from an alien world. . . ."

And yet, observing Holmes at twenty-four as he pursues his way through the law, one has the impression that the blind seeking, the lack of compass, chart, and rudder, was for him a not unfavorable circumstance. Lack of tools may cause the weak to abandon their project. But to the strong it is a constant, irksome challenge. Chancellor Kent said he owed his reputation to the fact that when studying law during the war (1779) he had but one book — Blackstone — and that one book he mastered. Paucity of material forced him to be not only thorough but imaginative, to exercise his mind far beyond the program.

As for tools, had not Holmes's forefathers made their own? When John Holmes the Connecticut Go-Outer desired clapboards, he made a sawmill. Abiel Holmes, yearning to read the history of his country and finding none available, sat down and wrote his own *Annals of America*, taking twenty-six years to do it. Wendell's father, angered by the mysterious death of young mothers in childbed, sought through uncharted regions of a medical tradition that knew no Lister, no Pasteur, no germ theory, and no antisepsis until he found the contagiousness of puerperal fever. What pioneer ever had chart and a lighthouse to steer by?

Wendell Holmes could not know that in the field of historical jurisprudence he was to be a pioneer. He sought a perspective based on that ordered precedent which is history. No wonder he could not find it. He was himself to be its spokesman.

PART IV

The Lawyer. 1866-1882

CHAPTER TWENTY

William James. Fanny Dixwell. Wendell Holmes plays with his mind.

William James in Boston to Thomas W. Ward in New York
BOSTON, *Mar.* 27, 1866

The only fellow here I care anything about is Holmes, who is on the whole a first-rate article, and one which improves by wear. He is perhaps too exclusively intellectual, but sees things so easily and clearly and talks so admirably that it's a treat to be with him.

James was boarding near the Medical School, waiting for his family to move from Boston to Cambridge. Not only was the attraction mutual between him and Wendell, but Dr. Holmes also was charmed with this student of medicine whose imagination went so far beyond the facts of anatomy. In class, James was not brilliant. But recalling his own student days, Dr. Holmes was by no means convinced that brilliance was necessary in the beginning, when the whole task was one of mastering terminology. "My nature," the doctor liked to say, "is to snatch at all the fruits of knowledge and take a bite out of the sunny side — after that let in the pigs." When it fell upon him to examine James in anatomy, Dr. Holmes asked him two questions about the *nervus petrosis superficialis minor*, then closed the book and remarked heartily, "If you know that you know everything. And now tell me, just when will your father bring his family to Quincy Street?"

Dr. Holmes would have agreed with James that Wendell was too exclusively intellectual. But the doctor would not have used such flattering terms. He would have said that Wendell took himself too seriously, that for a man of twenty-five he had far too little sense of the amenities. Half of Dr. Holmes's success in life lay in the charm with which he imparted his knowledge. Mrs. Holmes insisted that Wendell also had a talent for speaking, for expression, a talent for debate that would be much to his advantage as a lawyer. Dr. Holmes did not agree. His son was quick; there was no denying it. Like lightning his mind penetrated to the meaning of a subject, like lightning reduced it to manageable terms. But the terms themselves were cold, ruthless, intellectual. Once he seized upon a subject, Wendell could not let it go. He worried it until the bare bones showed. If someone broke in with a pun, a quip, Wendell not only did not laugh but he ignored it and talked on without so much as a decent interval. Nobody could stop him.

"Wendell puts a *but* at the end of every sentence," John Gray said, "so he can keep on without a pause." There was fire in Wendell's eye while he talked; even his father saw it. Wendell shouted, waving his arms, striding up and down, banging out his pipe against the mantel as if his pipe were the common enemy and he must smash it. But the words he spoke were cold, logical. "*Feeling* counts," James said one night. The doctor applauded. Wendell's reply was quick. "To know is not less than to feel," he said.

But it was not to his father that Wendell Holmes expounded his views on the universe. Upstairs under the gas lamp that smelled and sputtered, he and James argued passionately about the existence of an external world — a question that has occupied philosophers since the beginning. Holmes attacked the problem with all the freshness, all the confidence of youth. And because this was the 1860's, he attacked it in Kantian terms. . . . A table exists. A man exists. But do they exist as fact or idea? Is a table a thing you lay plates upon, touch, bump into? Or is it merely the idea-of-table? The *Ding an sich*, the table as essence? Who was right, the nominalists, the realists, the Platonic idealists? What about Hegel? What about the argument *a priori*? Hegel said *a priori* was the only way to think, from the general to the particular, with pure ideas untainted by fact. Newton and his apple — theory evolved from witnessed fact — was the mere work of vulgar minds. . . .

When the night was not long enough to settle their questions,

Holmes and James sat down and wrote to each other. "Why I'm blest if I'm a Materialist," James began one day in pencil, not pausing for salutation. "I think it would take me ten or twelve years of hard study to form any opinion as to the truth of your second premise. — I send the above remarks . . . because they were what I was groping for the other evening, but could not say till you were gone and I in bed. To conclude:

"Corruptio optimistorum pessima!"

The young men liked to air their Latin; they had a hearty, unabashed pleasure in the sound of their own voices.

"I am just in from town in the keen, cold and eke beauteous moonlight," James wrote his sister. " '. . . where have I been?' 'To C. S. Peirce's lecture, which I could not understand a word of, but rather enjoyed the sensation of listening to for an hour.' I then turned to O. W. Holmes's and wrangled with him for another hour."

On evenings when Chauncey Wright and Charles Peirce joined them, Holmes was hard put to it to hold his own. Peirce had a kind of grim common sense that was wanting in most philosophers. At twenty-six he was smart, fiercely combative. His angry black eyes, his square chin, gave him the look of a man of action. His lectures at Cambridge were making the town angry. He stood and hurled at his audience unintelligible phrases about the Firstness of Firstness, Secondness and Thirdness and then suddenly said something that woke up the hall like a fire gong. "The demonstrations of the metaphysicians are all *moonshine!*" he had shouted the other night. "Classical German philosophy is of little weight except as suggestion." This was heresy to a generation that had evolved its moral values from Kant.

Peirce was saturated through and through — he proclaimed often and loudly — with the spirit of the physical sciences, against which the logic of the metaphysicians was but a reedy tool. Healthy tonic, this, for Wendell Holmes to whom the logic of the metaphysicians was a dangerously fascinating instrument. Chauncey Wright was another with the scientific outlook. He was a mathematician, older than the others, having been graduated from Harvard in '52. His championship of John Mill was soon to be followed by as fervent a championship of Darwin. Wright carried the Darwinian theory actually into the activities of the mind. The most elaborate psychical activities, he said, could be traced back to conscious processes in the animal kingdom. It was Wright who taught Holmes never to say *necessary* about the universe. "How could you know," he asked Holmes, his extraordinary pale blue eyes alight with a cold passion — "how could *you* know what the universe considers necessary?"

The *Origin of Species* was only six years old. In America its repercussions, delayed by the tumult of the Civil War, were just being felt. Chauncey Wright was far in advance of his time; Darwin himself urged Wright to publish his articles in England. Boston and Cambridge had not gone nearly so far as to carry the Darwinian theory to the activities of the mind. What upset America was the threat to Genesis I. The Harvard Divinity School was in a ferment. One of its professors lectured on the topic: "Can a man believe in Darwinism and remain a Christian?" From a Boston pulpit a preacher shouted, "If I could not believe that Joshua made the sun stand still in the heavens, I should lose faith in the Bible and in God!"

Such young men as William Lawrence (later Bishop of Massachusetts) were soon to suffer spiritual torments. In the Lawrence family Bible, opposite Genesis I, was penciled firmly the date of creation: *March 2, 4004.* William Lawrence had always believed it. And on a bright morning he went to hear Agassiz lecture on the new glacial theory . . . "Shentlemen!" said Agassiz in his robust foreign voice. "The world is older than we have been taught to believe. Draw a silk handkerchief once a year over Plymouth Rock until the rock is a pebble. *So long has the world existed.*"

Young Lawrence felt ill, troubled beyond expression. There was no longer one world as heretofore, but two: the world of everyday common sense where answers to questions were straight — and that other, religious world where faith played havoc with common sense. It was a false situation, Lawrence said. Unreal, offensive to the moral sense.

Holmes knew the Lawrence family well. At Nahant last summer Dr. Holmes had rented the cottage next to them. But in these torments endured by the faithful, Wendell Holmes had no part. To him it mattered not at all that Darwin made the Garden of Eden a myth and Jonah's whale a monster to frighten children. In all the long discursive philosophical letters between James and Holmes, neither Darwin nor Darwinism is mentioned. For Holmes the core had been taken out of Christian theology a generation ago, when the Unitarians disavowed the doctrine of original sin. Man lost his fear of hell-fire — and on that day gave back Christian doctrine to the preacher as irrelevant to life. After that, disbelief in Genesis I was a small thing. Wendell Holmes had achieved it without the least struggle. He was born to it. His father's frantic efforts to free himself from Calvinism had never freed Dr. Holmes. But they freed his son.

It was, in truth, a time of extraordinary intellectual and spiritual ferment. The English-speaking world was going through a complete rebirth in science, theology, economics, sociology, and last of all, law. New terminologies were forming everywhere; it was no wonder Wendell Holmes sat up all night practising them upon his friends. Very soon, his ideas were to have but one focus. Very soon the terminology of the law would exclude from his mind every other subject — and his friends would be driven from him by this passionate single-mindedness. But just now he was trying his wings, was exercising tongue and brain upon every subject, every person available.

William James to Tom Ward

Boston, *March* 27, 1866

. . . I made the acquaintance the other day of Miss Fanny Dixwell of Cambridge (the eldest), do you know her? She is decidedly A 1, and (so far) the best girl I have known. I should like if possible to confine my whole life to her, Ellen Hooper, Sara Sedgwick, Holmes, Harry, and the Medical School, for an indefinite period, letting no breath of extraneous air enter.

Within the week, James wrote even more revealingly about Fanny Dixwell, this time to his brother Wilkinson: —

Miss Dixwell . . . is about as fine as they make 'em. That villain Wendell Holmes has been keeping her all to himself out at Cambridge for the last eight years; but I hope I may enjoy her acquaintance now. She is A 1, if anyone ever was.

That villain Wendell Holmes would have been astonished at this description of his relationship with Fanny Dixwell. He saw Fanny two or three times a week. She was perhaps his most intimate friend. He had known her since they were children. Eight years ago when he was a freshman at Harvard he had formed the habit of dropping in at the big frame house on Garden Street after classes, in the evening or whenever he happened to be near. Going to the Dixwells' was almost like dropping in on one's family. Often enough he and Uncle John met at the white wicket gate and walked up the Dixwells' path together. Fanny was twenty-five. She was the girl a fellow could take his troubles to, talk to by the hour. She was the girl a man could count on as his partner for the sleighing party, the summer picnic, the country walk. She was always stimulating, never demanding. Holmes saw plenty of girls: Susie Shaw, handsome and clever, who was getting ready to enter the women's college at Oxford. Minnie Temple, who rumor had it was in love with John Gray. Wendell said it was James that Minnie had her eye on; Gray said it was Holmes.

The Dixwells' house itself was full of girls. After Fanny came Esther, then Susan, then one brother, John. Then Arria, then Mary Catherine who at twelve was an imp, casting eyes at every man that entered. Dixwells were noisy and merry and unpredictable. In Cambridge you did not ask why a member of that family had done thus and so. It was understood that nobody was entitled to a *why* about a Dixwell. Mrs. Dixwell was a comfortable, lively, handsome woman. Uncle John Holmes adored her. On her wedding day, he had brought her a little white silk bag containing eight one-dollar gold pieces. Mrs. Dixwell liked to tell about it. She was always trying to marry off John Holmes and getting nowhere. John lived just off Garden Street now, in a little alley that bore the grandiloquent name of Appian Way. His house wore an air of dilapidation; it was filled with cats, books, birds in cages; his mother's old housekeeper took care of him. "You should move to better quarters, John," Mrs. Dixwell told him severely.

"Oh, I can't move to better quarters," John Holmes replied gravely, "until I have a better half."

The remark went all over Boston. Tom Appleton heard it and took it to London, and the first thing Boston knew, it read the words in London *Punch*, under a drawing of a slim, whiskered young man who did not look like John Holmes at all.

The Scientific Club met every week at the Dixwells'. If Wendell happened to call on Wednesday night he ran into the professors Wolcott Gibbs, Agassiz, Asa Gray, Jeffries Wyman. They were all very old friends. Mrs. Dixwell had a wedding-day story about Gray, too. He was passionately fond of flowers and hated to pick them. Mrs. Dixwell said he must love her very much because on her wedding day he had appeared with two sprays of white lilac broken from his own bush. Sometimes when there was an evening party in Cambridge, Wendell spent the night at the Dixwells'. On these occasions Mr. Dixwell had a stock remark he always made next morning. Walking briskly into the breakfast room he would take his place at the head of the long table, beam at the company through his spectacles, and remark heartily, "Well! Did the evening's enjoyment bear the morning's reflection?"

Wendell loved it, felt as much at home as he did on Charles Street. This spring he talked much to Fanny about his approaching trip to England. He had been planning it for years; he was to sail early in May when his course at the Law School was over. Fanny herself had never been abroad; her travels were limited to summer trips to Nahant, or Mattapoisett on Buzzard's Bay. "I am to meet John Stuart Mill in London," Holmes told her eagerly. "And Hughes, the jurist, the fellow that wrote *Tom Brown.* I have letters from Motley and Sumner. Leslie Stephen will cross over with me to Switzerland. He has some really tough climbing mapped out. Do you remember my telling you about it in the spring of '63 when Stephen was in Boston?"

After the manner of women listening to masculine plans they may not share, Fanny's expression and words were enthusiastic. It would be splendid, she said, the clear color high in her cheeks. Wendell needed to get away, see other countries, meet other men and women. "Mind you stand up for this country," she said, "with your fancy friends in the West End of London. Stephen and Hughes and Mill were on our side in the war. But your father tells me you will have *entrée* to some very big houses. Do you think you will be able to hold your own?"

At home that evening, Wendell repeated Fanny's words. "She says they will spoil me in London. Fanny says I will lose my Yankee ways and come home with an Oxford lisp."

Around the table a queer little silence fell. It was Neddy who broke it. Neddy was a junior at Harvard now, and often went to the Dixwells' to see Susie. Neddy was too bright for his bones, the family said. He had grown very fast, he was thin as a rail and much bothered by asthma. He read omnivorously and brought home marks that his brother and father had never equaled in their undergraduate days. Wendell loved him. He had a precise way of speaking, his voice was quiet, a little husky. "You are not very discerning about Fanny Dixwell, Brother," Neddy said now, reaching a long arm for the bread platter across the table. "It's not necessary to ask me what I mean. You just aren't very discerning about her, that's all."

Wendell grinned. He did not want to know what Neddy meant. Neddy was at an age to see romance everywhere. Today as Wendell came out of Dane Hall at his usual hour of one o'clock, Fanny Dixwell had happened to be walking just across the street. She had hailed him, invited him to supper tomorrow night. Susie Shaw was coming, she said. Wendell would enjoy talking to her about Oxford . . . Fanny was the best friend a man ever had.

"Not smart about the girls — I?" Wendell said to his brother. "Young fellow, when you learn to manage the ladies as well as I do, you can start giving advice to your old Uncle Wendell."

Dr. and Mrs. Holmes smiled, their eyes meeting down the length of the table. But as the family rose from supper and made its way up the long stairs to the library, Mrs. Holmes told herself with a slightly troubled air that Neddy had been right. Fanny Dixwell was a marvelous girl, a girl among thousands. She was devoted to Wendell. For how many years had they been close friends? People linked their names. Wendell did not seem aware of it, he was totally unconcerned. He had more girls than you could count on ten fingers. Stepping into the library, stooping to turn up the flame in the lamp on the center table, Mrs. Holmes told herself again that Neddy was right. Wendell was *not* very discerning about Fanny Dixwell.

Toward the middle of May, Holmes sailed for England. Before he left Boston, George Shattuck asked him to come into his office next winter and read for his Bar examination. Holmes accepted gladly. The firm of Chandler, Shattuck and Thayer was famous as a training ground. Holmes looked forward to Shattuck's practical wisdom, his skill in handling men, and to Thayer's scholarship.

He had a summer's grace before him, a summer's holiday. In his pocket were good introductions — some of them from Motley, procured of course by Dr. Holmes. "Oliver Wendell H., Jr.," the doctor had written his old friend, "is a presentable youth, with fair antecedents, and is more familiar with Mill's writings than most fellows of his years. If it like your Excellency to send me two brief notes for him . . ."

Wendell Holmes was by no means sure he was going to like the British. Dr. Holmes, in spite of deep indignation at England's attitude during the war, was fascinated with the visiting Englishmen who came to Boston. The M. P., he said, was better company than the M. C. People used to society were plastic, receptive, lighter in hand than our own average countrymen. "Politically," the Autocrat had written, "I go for *equality*, and socially for *the* quality." People of the world, the doctor insisted, carried with them a pleasing simplicity, almost an innocence, not found in our hard-featured Yankee.

Dr. Holmes's son was suspicious of this. His father's books were very popular in England; what author was not susceptible to flattery? But Wendell himself had been much attracted to the English visitors he met in Boston, especially Leslie Stephen. Stephen's grandfather was an abolitionist, author of the famous *Slavery Delineated*. Leslie himself had remarked that the best Yankee was about the best of mankind. John Stuart Mill had been one of our staunchest Northern supporters. But Holmes knew he would find many who felt differently. Charles Eliot, recently home from London, said the English were insufferably arrogant; on the streets they pointed at his scarred cheek. Mr. Charles Francis Adams told a story of a Londoner at an evening party who came up to him just after the Bull Run disaster and remarked, smiling, how well the *Southerners* fought. "Yes," Adams replied. "They too are Americans."

Suppose, Holmes thought, he himself were attacked like this at a dinner party among men older than he, distinguished, worldly men? Would he be able to hold his own? He had never been anywhere. Were cultivated people the same the world over?

At his first London dinner party he was put to the test. General Hamley [1] sat opposite, veteran of the Crimean campaign, professor of military history at Sandhurst and by all odds the highest authority on military tactics in England. The general was crusty and made it plain he looked upon our Northern army as guerilla fighters, undisciplined but lucky, fit only for shooting Indians from behind trees.

"Colonel Holmes," the General asked sharply while the company listened. "Can you train your men to fight in line?"

"Why General Hamley," Holmes replied, "you can train monkeys to fight in line."

The company smiled. They liked this young soldier, spirited, modest, quick-witted. Holmes was a success in London. He was making friends. When he was older he would come back and match wits with these worldly ones. But now he was young, he had come abroad not to shine but to absorb light, not to triumph but to learn. Traveling out from London to Blackheath Park to call on John Stuart Mill, Holmes wondered if the sage, now sixty, would be like the only sage he knew at home. Uncle Waldo Emerson, benign and rugged. Mill on *Liberty*, Mill on *Utilitarianism*, Holmes knew almost by heart. The practical or utilitarian individualism of Mill appealed to him deeply. *Do good because it results in the happiness of the greatest number:* this was the philosophy of Bentham and the Mills. To Holmes it was far more acceptable than Kantian idealism with its *Do good because good is high.* With what vast reluctance the world had turned from theology to transcendentalism to practical ethics! Modern political economy had almost begun with the Mills, father and son. Not so very long ago, John Mill had stood up in Parliament, stubborn, conscientious, with his "greatest good for the greatest number," and Disraeli from the Conservative bench had breathed, "Ah — the nursery governess!" Holmes had heard the story — who had not heard it? Yet the impending Reform Bill of '67 would be only the latest of a series of acts that were changing the face of England. John Mill was more than a little responsible.

About him there would be, Holmes knew, no worldly atmosphere, no artifice, no "taste." Mill's master, Jeremy Bentham, had loathed the word *taste.* It implied a separation from the moral standard. Traveling out of town, watching the green English fields move by, Holmes reflected that there was more than a little of the Puritan about these Utilitarians. They made one think of Uncle John Holmes, smoking his five-cent cigars "so his taste would not become too refined" . . . of John Adams in Paris, writing home to Braintree how he could not help suspecting that "the more elegance the less virtue in all times and countries." . . . *"The Devil is dead,"* Uncle John had said. *"Men have to find new devils to fight."* John

Mill said he was an atheist. Even so, he was most certainly to be reckoned among the Evangelicals. England rocked with the results of his practical middle-class morality. Atheist Evangelicals like Mill, muscular trades-union Churchmen like Hughes — such men were known not for their wit but for their works. Holmes liked wit, he was accustomed to it. His father and his father's friends avoided solemnity; they had had too much of it in their youth.

But if Holmes liked wit he was even more stirred by intellectual power. It would be extraordinary to meet a man who by sheer persuasion of thought had influenced the actual legislation of his country. Wendell Holmes was never to believe wholeheartedly in the power of legislation to change men's lives. But he was to be the apostle of a jurisprudence that recognized the social function of the law, a jurisprudence based upon what he himself was to call, in one of his nicest phrases, "the felt necessities of the time." Of all men living in 1865, perhaps John Mill's philosophy came nearest this idea.

Behind the high wall at Blackheath Park, Holmes found the sage of Utilitarianism different indeed from the sage of Concord. This face beneath the bald head and curly side hair was not benign but mobile, extremely restless. Here was none of Emerson's repose. But there was (Holmes thought of his father's words) an extraordinary simplicity, the scholar's innocence perhaps. Amazing to meet a giant intellect that knew no arrogance, a reformer lacking the crusader's egotism.

Holmes went from Mill to Leslie Stephen and his brother Fitz James the jurist. Fitz James was older than Leslie; he had already published his lectures on English criminal law. He had been a pupil of Henry Maine himself. Maine's *Ancient Law*, published in '61, Holmes had not been able to come at in America; the war had made it difficult to get the new foreign books.

Holmes and the Stephen brothers crossed the Channel, headed for Switzerland. For Holmes the next weeks were an adventure and a delight beyond all expectation. Leslie Stephen had been right: these snowy heights could cure a man of any wound, any memory of war and death and blood. The Balmhorn, Mönchen and Mönchjoch, Tschingel Pass, and across the Col du Géant[2] — Everything was forgotten but the climb itself. The careful measuring of each footstep on the glacial pass, the rope against one's back, the danger always present to enhance one's consciousness in this panorama of color and wine-bright air.

How good to hurl oneself against these magnificent heights, to put out all one's effort and feel body and spirit respond! In war — in Virginia — on the Peninsula, Holmes had called upon these same reserves again and again. But always with the spur of grim necessity, never for the pure pleasure of the task, never with this splendid detachment. Harvard oarsmen, gasping for breath in that last eighth of a mile — was it this that drove them, this sense of the body triumphing? No wonder Crowninshield spoke of rowing as other men speak of their god. The chivalry and courage of sport carried an aristocracy all their own.

Wendell Holmes was never to become either sportsman or mountain climber. From these weeks in Switzerland he carried away a lasting friendship with the Stephen brothers, a sense of the poetry of sheer useless effort, and the materials for a story that sixty years later was to give him much delight — the story of an Englishman who came to Boston, went to Cambridge to the Law School Library and asked to see Holmes's portrait. "Ah yes, the great judge!" the librarian said. "I don't know about *that*," the Englishman replied. "But O. W. Holmes was one of the very first members of the Alpine Club. I am here to pay my respects."

In September of 1866, Holmes sailed for Boston. It was good to be going home. What tales he had for Fanny, for Bill James, John Gray! In his trunk below decks was Henry Maine's book on *Ancient Law*. Maine himself was in India now as legal adviser to the Council. But some day — Holmes told himself as the steamer plowed steadily westward — some day Maine would be back again in London. Some day Wendell Holmes would meet Maine and talk with him, meet Joseph Chamberlain, the young Birmingham liberal that Hughes admired.

Leslie Stephen and Fitz James — John Mill, Tom Hughes — Serious, thoughtful faces to carry forever in one's mind. Older men whose whole concern was the study and observation of society. Scholars, statesmen, men of the world. And of those wise men he had met on his travels, not one, Holmes reflected as the steamer rose, then dipped to a gray horizon — not one had said a lawyer could not be a great man.

CHAPTER TWENTY-ONE

Holmes reads law. He is examined
for the Bar.

WENDELL HOLMES, returning to Boston in September,
1866, expected somehow to find the whole face of nature changed.
What had happened to him was important, exciting. Like many a
returning traveler he never doubted the·excitement would be reflected everywhere.

But it was not reflected. Here at home, things were remarkably
the same. Dr. Holmes went off to Grove Street every day to lecture.
He had ceased — mercifully — to play the violin, but he was writing
a new novel and burned to talk about it. Neddy, a senior at Harvard,
came home over the week ends. Amelia was brisk and cheerful,
helping her mother with the housekeeping, going to her Sewing
Circle [1] and to such festivities as the season afforded.

The supper table listened for a night or two to the elder brother's
adventures abroad, then turned eagerly to its own affairs. They had
been to Nahant in the summer, in a cottage near Longfellow and
Agassiz. Dr. Holmes had suffered his usual Nahant asthma. The
Indians had been a real nuisance, coming in swarms for the fishing,
pitching their dirty tents right against the Lodges' hedge over on
the Point.

Ben Butler down in Washington wanted to impeach the President, Neddy interposed. But of course, Wendell never had been
interested in politics. In England, had he continued his absurd habit
of not reading the newspapers? . . . "Your grandfather, Judge
Jackson, never read the newspapers," Mrs. Holmes said quickly.

"At least, during the three years he was reading law I know he never looked at a paper. He told me himself."

Dr. Holmes laughed. Wendell would never lack a champion while his mother lived, he said. . . . But even his esteemed father-in-law, Judge Jackson, had the defects of his qualities. Would the Judge's daughter permit him to recall the contemporary estimate of her father?

"I remember very well," Mrs. Holmes replied serenely. "You have often reminded me. *'Law knowledge, 100 per cent adequate. Political knowledge, 30 per cent. Classical knowledge, 10 per cent. Talent, 80. Integrity, 100. Practice of law, 100 . . .*" Mrs. Holmes paused, smiling. "*Wit, 0,*" she finished.

Never mind about Grandfather Jackson, Neddy went on. Even if Wendell didn't read newspapers, he would be interested in what was going on in Boston. Laboring men here and all over the country were combining against their employers. The Eight-hour Movement was the talk everywhere. Cousin Wendell Phillips had thrown himself into it, and orated away on platforms about how ten hours of work ruined a man's soul. There had been a printers' strike in Boston during the summer. There seemed to be an actual trend toward Federal socialism. Somebody had even suggested publishing income returns in the newspapers. It would be a sad day when our government ceased to protect the privacy of individuals. But anyway, a boss blacksmith told the commissioners at the State House that a man working only eight hours could be of more value to an employer than one who worked ten. He said when a man got too tired he used tobacco and liquor. Pure nonsense of course. A harness maker had stood up and said he couldn't fail to notice that the men who worked shorter hours were always the more intelligent. . . . What did John Mill in London say about the Eight-hour Movement?

Nobody waited for Wendell's reply. Fourteen chapters of his new novel were finished, Dr. Holmes said eagerly. *The Guardian Angel,* he was going to call it. It was a kind of sequel to *Elsie Venner,* on the same theme of heredity. But he was taking a hard crack at the old-fashioned, hell-fire type of clergy. Dr. Bellamy Stoker, the villain of the story, had three sermons on hell — his *sweating* sermon, his *fainting* sermon, and his *convulsion-fit* sermon. He hadn't made that up, the doctor added quickly. He had got it from an actual instance in a town in Maine back in his lecture-circuit days. The *Atlantic* would probably publish the novel serially.

"You had better be careful," Wendell told his father. "There was trouble enough about *Elsie* and the *Autocrat*. People will be calling you a Free-thinker all over again."

Dr. Holmes rubbed his small hands delightedly. "In New England they weld iron bands around the sapling elms to keep them within bounds. Your Uncle John and I, Wendell, were banded with iron in our youth. My books help me to get the iron of Calvinism out of my soul."

"Uncle John," Neddy said irrelevantly, "only goes abroad so he can have the extreme pleasure of coming back to Boston. In Venice he used to go every day to some perfectly commonplace spot and stand there. He said it reminded him of the junction of Broadway and Cambridge Streets in Cambridge. . . . Mr. Appleton told me."

Boston people were hopelessly provincial, Dr. Holmes said genially. Had Wendell noticed it, after being abroad? As he had once written Motley, your Boston man carries the Common in his head as a unit of space, the State House as the standard of architecture, and measures off men in Edward Everetts as with a yardstick. He himself had often been accused of provincialism. But he was not at all sure, for a literary man, that it was a weakness.

"They are still trying to name the new hotel," Amelia said, complacently pursuing her own line of conversation. "It is nearly finished and it is enormous. It will have a passenger elevator as big as a room. They cannot decide between The Hub Hotel and Everett House. Father, if they name it The Hub you will have to be godfather and assist at the christening. Wasn't it you who called Boston the hub of the universe?"

Neddy fixed his sister with a cold eye. Quite a long time ago he had asked his brother a question about the eight-hour day. Was it never possible, he asked, to get an answer from this family before somebody started their irrelevant *chatter*?

Looking around the table, Wendell was amused. He had no slightest intention of telling this supper table what John Mill thought about the Eight-hour Movement. He had already told Fanny Dixwell, before he had been home forty-eight hours, every word Mill had said. Fanny did not interrupt a man to tell stories of her own. She listened attentively, her comments and questions intelligent. This family could not hold its peace for two consecutive moments. Yet, listening now to their talk, Wendell recognized, with the fresh eye of the returned traveler, that his family, while undoubtedly irritating, was very far from dull. This was not the wit of London dinner tables, but whatever it was, it had life. *Provinciality!* There was something good about it, something vigorous and plain.

"Mother!" Wendell said suddenly. His strong voice came out easily above the rest. "Did you hear what Saint Peter said to the Boston man at the pearly gates?" *

Surprisingly, the table was silent, waiting.[2]

On a Monday morning, Holmes went down to Court Street to the office of Chandler, Shattuck and Thayer. Mr. Shattuck greeted him with enormous heartiness. Peleg Chandler,[3] the senior partner, came out. Gray whiskers grew all around under his chin; his wing collar came up to his ears. He shook Wendell's hand. "How is your father?" he said. "No candidate from this office ever failed a Bar examination, my boy." He bowed slightly and disappeared.

George Shattuck winked. It would take a half-wit to fail the Bar examination, he said. If Holmes had sat three years in this office he would be admitted without examination. As it was, he had been to Law School instead, and the Commonwealth took no account of law schools. "Make sure you don't know too much," Shattuck said. "The examiners don't like smart young men from the Law School. I've known them to fail a man because he tried to show off. I've also known them to drive a nice little bargain, promising not to ask the candidate any question he couldn't answer if the candidate would do the same by them."

A client came in. George Shattuck vanished. Holmes stood at a loss, looking at the rows of familiar brown books on the shelves. A heavy film of dust lay over most of them. There was dust on the long windows. In the street below, a market dray rumbled past, and from the wharf near by a steamer whistle sounded.

The inner door opened. James Bradley Thayer[4] came out. He was ten years older than Holmes. He had got his LL.B. at Harvard in '56. Rumor said he was aiming for a professorship at the Law School. He wore his fine dark hair rather long, he had the dreamy, gentle eye of the scholar. Shattuck, it appeared, had turned over the student end of the office to Thayer. "Sit down," Thayer said. "Now, what are you after, Holmes? Admission to the Bar or perhaps a trifle more education with it? No thinking will be required

* Answer: *"You won't like it here."*

at the Court House. Judge Shaw used to make them think, but the rules are changed. Only memory is required. . . . But they can lay it on pretty thick, in spite of what Shattuck says. If you get old Asaph Churchill [5] he is partial to Coke. Wasn't Churchill in college with your father? Do you know the rule in Shelley's Case?"

That autumn, Holmes's card at the Athenaeum listed *Coke on Littleton*, Austin's *Jurisprudence*, Stephen's history of English criminal law, Gibbon, Humboldt, Mill's *Logic* again, Bracton's *Relation to the Roman Law*, Montesquieu's *Spirit of the Laws*. Holmes was fascinated by Montesquieu. Here was a lonely scholar, sitting in a library — yet his book had done as much to remodel the world as any material product of the eighteenth century. Montesquieu was an authority for the writers of the *Federalist*. He was the precursor of Burke, of modern political economy, of Adam Smith and the Mills.

Sitting in the outer room of Chandler, Shattuck and Thayer, the *Esprit des Lois* open on his knee, Holmes was struck anew with the awful power of ideas to change a world. Montesquieu commanded the future more surely from his study than Napoleon from his throne. A valid idea was worth a regiment any day. The man of action has the present, yes — but does not the thinker control the future?

Perhaps a man had to fight in a war to find that out. When you were twenty it was the Henry Abbotts, the Caspar Crowninshields — external men all — who seemed to rule the world.

But this picture Montesquieu drew of the government of England — was it valid? Montesquieu divided it into three distinct parts, the legislative, executive, judicial. Surely that was a fiction, even two centuries ago! Holmes got up, knocked on Thayer's door. . . . "Find out for yourself," Thayer said. "Read Bagehot. How well do you know Stephens on English criminal law? Have you read Reeves?"

An enormous impatience began to possess Wendell Holmes. He could not find what he wanted fast enough. On his card at the Athenaeum appeared Bagehot on *The English Constitution*, Argyll's *Reign of Law*, Gladstone's *Reform Speeches*, McCosh on *Mill's Philosophy*. Holmes read Lecky, Phillimore's *Principles and Maxims of Jurisprudence*, Forsyth's *History of Trial by Jury*, Reeves's *History of English Law*, Palgrave's *English Commonwealth*. It seemed no more than a drop in the bucket of knowledge. His age had begun to worry him. He was nearly twenty-six. He had lost three years by the war. Men younger than he were well along now in law offices, done years ago with such puerilities as Bar examinations.

"When will you come up for examination?" Dr. Holmes asked just before Christmas. He had asked at least three times in the past month. "In the January term of Court," Wendell replied.

It was, actually, the twenty-seventh of February before George Shattuck wrote the conventional letter of recommendation, testifying to his good moral character. Holmes took it to the courthouse. His petition was filed. Asaph Churchill and Charles W. Huntington were appointed his examiners.

On a Wednesday morning, by appointment, Holmes walked up a flight of dark stairs to Mr. Churchill's office. He felt more curious than apprehensive. "Good morning, Holmes," Churchill said. "How is your father? We were at college together. Afterward, I believe he was not so successful at law as at writing verse. . . . You gentlemen from the Law School have the advantage of us. Huntington, here, and I got our law the hard way, in a lawyer's office."

Behind Churchill, Charles Huntington [6] grinned broadly. He was a much younger man, graduate of Harvard in '54, but he had not been to Law School. Asaph Churchill motioned Holmes to be seated across the big desk. He put on his glasses. His face was serious but Holmes was conscious that Churchill was enjoying himself. "We might as well begin," Churchill said. "Huntington, with your permission . . . Now, Holmes, who owns the land between high and low water mark?"

"In Massachusetts and nowhere else," Holmes replied with equal gravity, "the land belongs to the owner of the adjoining land. . . ."

An hour later, Holmes walked out on Court Street. He felt exhilarated. They had let him off too easily, he thought. After one or two routine questions, the three had simply sat and talked law. But it was not bad fun, being examined for the Bar. He could have got through with a third of his knowledge, a fifth of it. There were six hundred lawyers in Boston. Had they all slipped through so easily?

He turned in at 4 Court Street. George Shattuck whacked him on the shoulder. "Did you know the rule in Shelley's Case, my boy?" he said. "Chandler will take you to court Monday to be sworn in. Like to go myself, but I have a client coming. This will call for celebration. Come to my house Monday evening. Bring Ropes and Gray. I will ask Parkman and Warner and Green. I have a receipt for a new gin toddy. There is nothing better for drinking the healths of newborn counsellors at law."

Monday morning was dark and gusty, with a threat of rain. Peleg Chandler, his ears entirely hidden inside his shirt collar, walked to the courthouse with Holmes. It was barely a block, on the same side of the street. The pillared granite portico was dark and high. Holmes always entered the place with a quick sensation, not so much of excitement as recognition. This courthouse was a part of him, of his background and childhood. Here Judge Loring had sentenced the runaway slaves, Sims and Burns. Manacled to these very benches, they had waited the verdict. Up these wide granite stairs, Higginson had led the mob that tried to rescue Sims. Holmes had been eight years old. He had stood at his bedroom window on Montgomery Place, three blocks away. There had been shouts, feet running on Tremont Street. . . .

Entering the wide doorway with Peleg Chandler, Holmes did not think of these things. Merely, he was conscious of them. They were part of him, and what he was about to do would make these remembered things, this dark high hallway, even more a part of him. . . .

Holmes and Chandler were early. Court sat at nine-thirty. Behind the Judge's Bench the new oaken panels shone yellow in the gaslight. There were five lawyers in court, they sat facing the Bench. Holmes recognized two of them; they nodded to him. Peleg Chandler walked back and took his seat with the spectators.

Judge Lord came in, thrust back his coattails, and sat down, looking toward Holmes, who sat alone on the petitioners' bench. Lord was nearsighted; he raised his bearded chin, his face straining slightly toward Holmes.

". . . *and God save the Commonwealth and this Honorable Court*," the crier finished.

There was a rustling of papers among the members of the Bar. The Clerk stood up. His voice was loud, monotonous: "The Court will attend to the taking of the oath."

Holmes came forward. It was like graduation, like walking up for your diploma, like the Brevet-Colonelship given him three years ago on the Common. It was absurd to feel so solemn. But Holmes did feel solemn. He liked ceremony. You did your work, and someone in a black gown handed you a piece of paper, bowed to you. . . .

The five lawyers stood up, so did the spectators. The room was silent. Holmes swore true faith and allegiance to the Commonwealth, swore to support the Constitution of Massachusetts and of the United States. Then with his hand on the Bible he took the Attorneys' Oath: —

> *I solemnly swear that I will do no falsehood nor consent to the doing of any in Court; I will not wittingly or willingly promote or sue any false, groundless or unlawful suit, nor give aid or consent to the same; I will delay no man for lucre or malice; but I will conduct myself in the office of an attorney within the Courts according to the best of my knowledge and discretion, and with all good fidelity as well to the Courts as my clients. So help me God.*

Judge Lord smiled, inclined his head. "Come and sign the Bar Book," Peleg Chandler said. It was in the next room, on a high desk against the wall. At the bottom of the page was room for one more name. There were twelve names inscribed in this January term of court. Most of them, Holmes noted, were from the Law School. Horace Graves, Josiah Bellows . . .

Jan Term 1867

Jan 7. Michael Henry Mac namara
" 12 George Milton Reed
" 22 Erastus Barton Powers
" " Thomas Stanly Wilson
. 25 Andrew Coyle Bradley
, 28 Horace Graves

. 30 *Jacob Murray Baker J*
„ 31 *Marquis Fayette Dickinson Jr.*
Feb 12 *Robert Hamsa. Pollock.* ✓
„ 19 *Josiah G. Bellows* ✓
„ 25 *Charles Willard Turner* +
„ 26 *Edward Payson Nettleton* *dead*
Mar 4 *Oliver Wendell Holmes Jr.*

Holmes signed his name carefully. There was no flourish to the way he did it. Peleg Chandler peered over his shoulder. "Horace Graves," he read. "Promising fellow, Graves. I knew his father. Well well, Holmes! You can have a sign on your door now. Be sure you bring us in some clients."

For Peleg Chandler, this was unusually facetious. Holmes put down the pen, turned, and followed Shattuck's senior partner to the door. On the portico, rain drove through the pillars, wind blew back the skirts of Chandler's overcoat. Turning up his coat collar, Holmes descended the steps and followed Peleg Chandler down the gray slope of Court Street.

A week later, the secretary of the class of '61, Harvard University, received a small card in the mail: —

OLIVER WENDELL HOLMES, JR. [it read]
Counsellor at Law
4 Court Street, Boston.

CHAPTER TWENTY-TWO

Counsellor at Law. "To know is not
less than to feel."

OLIVER WENDELL HOLMES, JR., Counsellor at Law, was not overwhelmed with business. What had Washburn said, at the Law School? "If a young lawyer pays for his sign the first year and his rent the next, he can tell himself he is doing very well." Holmes was a businessman now, committed to business and the making of money. And this, he told himself a trifle gloomily, was an idea he must learn to live with.

All summer he stayed in town, going every day to the office, with an occasional week end with the Lodges at Nahant. All his friends were out of town it seemed — and Wendell Holmes had need of company. If to Shattuck the practice of law was exciting, to Holmes it was quite horrifyingly dull. This was no sudden discovery; Holmes had long suspected it. But it was not something a young lawyer could go around confessing to his friends. He could have told it to William James.

But James, unfortunately, was in Germany. He had sailed quite suddenly in April. "To study physiology," he said. In reality he had gone in search of health. He was ashamed of his share in the family "nerves." Backache, insomnia, eye trouble, deep depression: the symptoms seemed unmanly. He confided in no one, not even his family.

Holmes missed him greatly. James's very sensitiveness, the over-acute perceptions that made him ill, drew Holmes to him. In September James wrote, confessing his complete prostration — inability to work, study, sometimes even to read. To Holmes, loving action above all else, this was a purgatory almost inconceivable. He knew James to be no moody neurotic but a man like himself, ambitious, desiring work and the companionship of his fellows. It touched him that James, from his lonely exile, should turn to him, confessing the whole story.

You had better believe [James wrote] I have thought of you with affection at intervals since I have been away, and prized your qualities of head, heart and person, and my price-less luck in possessing your confidence and friendship in a way I never did at home; and cursed myself that I didn't make more of you when I was by you, but, like the base Indian, threw evening after evening away which I might have spent in your bosom, sitting in your whitely-lit-up room, drinking in your profound wisdom, your golden jibes, your costly imagery, listening to your shuddering laughter, baptizing myself afresh, in short, in your friendship. . . .

But pray, my dear old Wendell, let me have *one* letter from you — tell me how your law business gets on, of your ad-ventures, thoughts, discoveries (even though but of mares' nests, they will be interesting to your William); books read, good stories heard, girls fallen in love with — nothing can fail to please me, except your failing to write. . . .

. . . Give my very best regards to your father, mother and sister. And believe me ever your friend,

WM. JAMES.

P. S. Why can't you write me the result of your study of the *vis viva* question? I have not thought of it since I left. I wish very much you would, if the trouble be not too great. . . .

Vis viva — the vital forces? Holmes sat down, wrote page after page. Then he lit a cigar, tilted back his chair, read over what he had written — and tore it up. Easy enough to see that force is not destroyed — but not easy to master the formula. Translating mathe-matics into English was no simple exercise.

In November, as Junior Counsel to Shattuck, Holmes tried his first case in court. The widow of a passenger on the New York Central claimed $5000 from the railroad. Shattuck and Holmes were counsel for the plaintiff. Holmes sat at a long table below the judge's desk while Shattuck talked; occasionally he jumped up to hand Shattuck a needed paper. Shattuck, he observed, was nothing short of magnificent. Needing the excitement of advocacy to waken his interest, Shattuck's mind, once roused, moved like lightning, like lightning struck and struck again. A stranger, coming into court, would have thought, watching him, that Shattuck was arguing for some great principle, some question of American rights, free speech, honor.

They lost the case. But Judge Hoar, delivering his opinion, leaned his handsome, bearded face across the bench and said the argument of the plaintiff had been both ingenious and impressive.

Walking back from the office late that afternoon, Holmes reflected on all this. He had worked hard on the case, preparing his statement of facts, looking up law. Yet even in court, he had been a trifle bored. If the excitement of advocacy awakened George Shattuck's powers, it by no means awakened the powers of Wendell Holmes. How small a goal lay at the end of these huge legal efforts! Better, like the scholar, to have no goal at all, pursuing doggedly the unknown end. . . .

"So you lost the case?" Fanny Dixwell said the next time she saw him.

Wendell had come over to Cambridge in the horsecars, stopping by prearrangement for Uncle John on the way. They had had tea with the Dixwells. Now they sat round the library fire: Fanny's younger sisters, Arria, and Mary Catherine. John Dixwell, a sophomore at Harvard, had left the house directly after tea on business of his own. Mr. and Mrs. Dixwell got out the cribbage board. Uncle John was to be umpire.

Fanny sat quietly, her hands in her lap. "You lost the case?" she repeated.

"Yes," Wendell said. "Shattuck was magnificent." He was silent. John Holmes looked thoughtfully at his nephew. A generation ago, John had sat in a law office himself, for two mortal years. Twenty-four months too many, he often said. Tonight, Wendell was telling of his first case in court. Wendell was very far from being a reserved character. Yet all he had to say now was that Shattuck had been magnificent. . . . Wendell would never make a lawyer. Clients meant nothing to him. His father had better stop pushing him.

Frère de mon frère. John Holmes had not the writer's urge to communicate what he saw, yet he had the writer's interest in the human drama. He turned his eyes now to Fanny. She was looking at Wendell, who sat smoking, his eyes on the fire.

Fanny inquired no further concerning the lost case. "Wendell," she said, "I meant to ask you long ago, did you answer Bill James's letter? About — what was that thing he wanted to know about?"

"*Vis viva?*" Wendell said. "No. I tried three times. All I could wring out was diluted moonshine. It wouldn't come right. There seems to be an insufficiency of facts."

Fanny made a gesture of impatience. "Bill James is your friend," she said. "He is alone and he is ill. I think I have written him more letters than you have. He loves you. Write to him without *vis viva.*"

Wendell shrugged. Fanny got up, went to the table for something. In a moment she turned to John Holmes, her color high. "Mr. Holmes," she said. Her voice was urgent. "Has your nephew, all his life, professed to care more for ideas than he cares for people?"

Wendell Holmes to William James

BOSTON, *Dec.* 15, 1867

DEAR BILL, —

I shall begin with no apologies for my delay in writing except to tell you that since seeing you I have written three long letters to you at different intervals on *vis viva,* each of which I was compelled to destroy because on reflection it appeared either unsound or incomplete. But I was talking yesterday with Fanny Dixwell and she told me to fire away anyhow — that she thought it would please you to hear from me even without *vis viva.* So here goes. Writing is so unnatural to me that I have never before dared to try it to you unless in connection with a subject. Ah! dear Bill, do me justice. My expressions of esteem are not hollow nor hyperbolical — nor put in to cover my neglect.

In spite of my many friends I am almost alone in my thoughts and inner feelings. And whether I ever see you much or not, I think I can never fail to derive a secret comfort and companionship from the thought of you. I believe I shall always respect and love you whether we see much or little of each other. . . .

For two or three months I debauched o' nights in philosophy. But now it is law-law-law. My *magnum opus* was reading the *Critique of Pure Reason.* . . .

And Holmes is off to paragraphs of pure logic — exercise that for him was obviously salutary, rousing him as the excitement of advocacy could arouse George Shattuck. Yet even as he wrote, even as he quoted, Holmes was aware that it was only exercise. . . .

In Berlin, James did not wait for this letter. He was lonely and ill; he sat down in his student's room and unburdened himself to his friend on many pages.

> . . . I suppose you are sinking ever deeper into the sloughs of the law [he wrote] — yet I ween the Eternal Mystery still from time to time gives her goad another turn in the raw she once established between your ribs. Don't let it heal over yet.
>
> When I get home let's establish a philosophical society to have regular meetings and discuss none but the very tallest and broadest questions — to be composed of none but the very topmost cream of Boston manhood. It will give each one a chance to air his own opinion in a grammatical form, and to sneer and chuckle when he goes home at what damned fools all the other members are — and may grow into something very important after a sufficient number of years. . . .
>
> . . . I don't know whether you take it as a compliment that I should only write to you when in the dismalest of dumps — perhaps you ought to — you, the one emergent peak, to which I cling when all the rest of the world has sunk beneath the wave. . . .
>
> Good-bye! Keep the same bold front as ever to the Common Enemy — and don't forget your ally,
>
> W. J.

Holmes had this letter early in February, 1868. It was April before he replied. He had become fascinated with the legal end of President Johnson's impeachment, which was in full swing. The trial, begun in March, was to last nearly three months. Holmes wrote to Charles Sumner in Congress, asking for the pamphlet account of the impeachment; it was hard, he said, to get the facts in convenient form.

February, March, April . . . On Boston Common the gaunt outlines of the elm branches softened. Color crept slowly down the giant oaks, the cracks along the sidewalks showed a brilliant, yellow green. Piles of blackened, muddy snow still lay in the gutters, high as a man's waist. But Holmes, swinging down Beacon Hill from the office in the late afternoon, raised his head and felt his step quicken, the blood move faster in his veins. On Saturday he would take Fanny for a walk in Cambridge, up around the Fresh Pond. Arbutus would be out under the leaves, and bloodroot. For how many Aprils had they gone together to search for it? . . . Holmes did not ask himself this question. Merely, it was spring, high time Fanny sent him a message about the bloodroot being up, in the woods around Cambridge.

That night, Holmes could not keep his mind upon the law. He got up from his desk, went to the window, flung it open. Air poured in from the river, soft, caressing. How strange, for the northern animal, this sudden armistice with winter! To be permitted, suddenly, to cease the long defense, to breathe deeply, let all one's senses go out to meet air and earth and sky. It made a man want to sing, shout, caper, write poetry.

Wendell Holmes could not keep a tune, and as for poetry, he was under no illusion about his talents there. Well, a man could always write letters. Bill James would put up with anything. Returning to his desk, Holmes shoved aside books and pamphlets, seized his pen: —

Wendell Holmes to William James

BOSTON, *April* 19, 1868

DEAR BILL, —

The icy teeth have melted out of the air and winter has snapped at us for the last time. Now are the waters beneath my window of a deeper and more significant blue. . . . Now do the fields burn with green fire. . . . Now couples, walking round Boston Common Sundays after sunset, draw near to each other in the dark spaces between the gas lights and think themselves unseen. Now are the roads around Cambridge filled with collegians with new hats and sticks and shining schoolboy faces. Now the young man seeks the maiden nothing loath to be pursued. Spring is here, Bill, and I turn to thee, — not with more affection than during the long grind of the winter, but desiring if it may be to say a word to thee once more.

Since I wrote in December I have worked at nothing but the law. Philosophy has hibernated in torpid slumber, and I have lain "sluttishly soaking and gurgling in the devil's pickle," as Carlyle says. It has been necessary, — if a man chooses a profession he cannot forever content himself in picking out the plums with fastidious dilettantism and give the rest of the loaf to the poor, but must eat his way manfully through crust and crumb — soft, unpleasant, inner parts which, within one, swell, causing discomfort in the bowels. Such has been my cowardice that I have been almost glad that you weren't here, lest you should be disgusted to find me inaccessible to ideas and impressions of more spiritual significance but alien to my studies. . . .

And the winter has been a success, I think, both for the simple discipline of the work and because I now go on with an ever increasing conviction that law as well as any other series of facts in this world may be approached in the interests of science and may be studied, yes and practiced, with the preservation of one's ideals. I should even say that they grew robust under the regimen, — more than that I do not ask. To finish the search of mankind, to discover the *ne plus ultra* which is the demand of ingenuous youth, one finds is not allotted to an individual. To reconcile oneself to life — to dimly apprehend that this dream disturbing the sleep of the cosm is not the result of a dyspepsy, but is well — to suspect some of the divine harmonies, though you cannot note them like a score of music — these things, methinks, furnish vanishing points which give a kind of perspective to the chaos of events. Perhaps I am fortunate in what I have often made a reproach to myself.

Harry never lets up on his high aims, — somehow it connects itself with the absence of humor in him which himself avows. *I do.* There are not infrequent times when a bottle of wine, a good dinner, a girl of some trivial sort can fill the hour for me. So for longer spaces, work, — of which only at the beginning and the end do I perceive the philosophic *nexus*, and while performing forget the Great Task Master's Eye. This makes life easier though perhaps it does not deserve approval. . . .

Mrs. Holmes, if she could have looked over her son's shoulder, would have smiled at this. *A bottle of wine, a girl of some trivial sort.* When had Wendell Holmes sought any but the Susie Shaws, the Minnie Temples, Ellen Hoopers? Girls whose fathers were his parents' friends. Pretty girls, preferably witty as well. And if dull, they must be even prettier. . . .

Holmes's pen went on and on . . . "Let me give another example of 'if *A* is *B*, then *C* is *D*' (in my last letter) which does not denote a causal connection."

And Holmes is off to three pages of logic, out of which he springs quite naturally to ask after his friend's health: —

> Dear old Bill, I haven't said anything about your illness to you — there is nothing, perhaps, which particularly belongs to me to say. But for God's sake don't lose that courage with which you have faced "the common enemy" (as you will have it). Would that I could give back the spirits which you have given to me so often. At all events doubt not of my love.

At this point the spring went quite definitely to Wendell Holmes's head. The rest of his letter has nothing to do with logic, with what *C* is to *D* if *A* is to *B*. The rest of the letter is so long that Holmes could have papered his room with it. He simply plunged into what he may have thought was poetry and laved himself in it, snorting and rolling with all the abandon of a colt in a pasture. What we give here is only a fraction of the whole: —

> Let me not be sad. . . . There is a new fire in the earth and sky. I, who through the long winter have felt the wrinkles deepening in my face and a stoop settling in my back — I, who have said to myself that my life henceforth must and should be given only to severe thought, and have said to youth, "*procul esto*," . . . I feel the mighty quickening of the spring. . . .
>
> I saw a butterfly today . . .
>
> O! passionate breezes! O! rejoicing hills!
>
> Sing, sparrow — kissing with thy feet the topmost tassels of the pines.
>
> Cease not thy too much sound, O! robin. Squirrels grind thy scissors in the woods. Creak, blackbirds. Croak, frogs. Caw, high-flying crows, who have seen the breaking of the ice in northern rivers and the seaward moving booms. . . .
>
> Dear Bill, to whom should I vent this madness but to you? Goodbye. You know my sentiments — I will not repeat them. Affectionately yours,
>
> O. W. HOLMES.
>
> *Apr.* 25. It is snowing again. S'help me.

William James, in Dresden, was astonished by all this, more perhaps by the extraordinary length of the letter than by its manner, which he accepted, he said, as a pleasing expression of its author's "fiery personality." The thee's and thou's, after all, were used by such tough-minded writers as Carlyle. To contemporary minds there was something pleasingly classical about this mode of expression. It was a proper scholarly concomitant of spring and the sprouting of the larches.

James answered immediately. He spoke affectionately, but he spoke frankly too, as though the craziness of Holmes's letter had released something in him, a doubt that he had had of his friend. Wendell had always been so logical a thinker, so very orderly in his mental processes! It put lesser minds to shame, made them uncomfortable. But this, about spring, was not orderly at all. It was crazy and reckless. It smacked of a good digestion, a strong tumultuous circulation of the blood. Oh, there was something full of gusto about this Wendell Holmes! How he loved life!

When a man took such pleasure in being alive, in eating and drinking and walking and *thinking* — surely, he could not be accused of lacking heart.

". . . The ground of my friendship for you," James wrote, "is more a sort of physical relish for your wit and wisdom, and passive enjoyment of the entertainment they afford, than anything else." Even so, he confessed that he had often felt constraint with Holmes — felt himself forced into a position of self-defense, as though Holmes threatened to overrun his territory, injure his proprietorship. But the devils of egotism and jealousy are subtle. Probably, James said, the whole thing was due to them.

Holmes was more amused than surprised at all this. It was not the first time he had been accused of what James called a "too cosmic-centric consciousness." There was truth in what James had hinted. *To know is not less than to feel,* Holmes had told his father. Yet this desire to think always economically, avoiding the loose ends of sentiment, altruism — this is a path that can lead very far from the heart, far from friendship and sympathy with one's fellow man. Holmes had learned that sympathy on the soldier's field, won it dearly, at high cost. Now he was in danger of losing it. He was embarking upon the least attractive phase of his long career. He was setting out on a journey that left no room for friendship, perhaps no room for love. He was digging himself a pit, a trough. He was building a bridge on the other side of which, he thought, lay knowledge.

And on this bridge was no room for any man but Wendell Holmes.

CHAPTER TWENTY-THREE

Kent's Commentaries. Holmes sails for the Pole.

O NE saw that artists and poets shrank from [the law] as from an alien world. . . .

And yet one said to oneself, law is human — it is a part of man, and of one world with all the rest. There must be a drift, if one will go prepared and have patience, which will bring one out to daylight and a worthy end. . . . Most men of the college-bred type in some form or other have to go through that experience of sailing for the ice and letting themselves be frozen in.

In the first stage one has companions, cold and black though it be, and if he sticks to it, he finds at last that there is a drift as was foretold. When he has found that he has learned the first part of his lesson, that one is safe in trusting to courage and to time.

But he has not yet learned all. So far his trials have been those of his companions. But if he is a man of high ambitions he must leave even his fellow-adventurers and go forth into a deeper solitude and greater trials. He must start for the pole. In plain words he must face the loneliness of original work. No one can cut new paths in company. He does that alone.*

What now began to happen to Holmes did not happen in a day or a year. It would be absurd to dramatize it, to see him suddenly entering the lonely, bitter solitude of the scholar. On the contrary, his life for the next few years pursued a normal, even humdrum outward course. Each morning he went down to Shattuck's office,

* O. W. Holmes, from a speech at Brown University Commencement, 1897.

each evening returned. Around him the town, the nation, recovering from battle and heroism, pursued also its daily course, desiring nothing so much as business as usual — and more business and more.

1868 . . . A Presidential year. By the end of October the torchlight processions had begun. "Grant and Colfax," the banners read. *Union and Peace. . . . Freedom and Grant!* The Republicans were very sure of themselves. New England expressed herself as filled with — in capital letters — Great Hopes. . . . Grant won by a huge majority. "A Time to Crow!" the *Boston Transcript* said. . . . A time to crow, and the first thing for Grant to do was to "make every department strictly accountable for its expenditures."

It was a good idea, a nice little suggestion to carry through eight years of the most corrupt administration the nation would experience for many generations. But the word *Grantism* had not yet been coined. Money was the watchword, and if the South was filled with poverty and apprehension, the North was filled with business and optimism. "Culture" raised its head once more. Boston referred to itself as "this Athens of the Union." Lecture forums hummed. Instead of war news, casualty lists, the newspapers published leisurely "Travel Letters from the Yo-Semite Valley." Josh Billings, Petroleum Nasby, wrote their dialect humor and everybody laughed when Nasby went to the "Anteetum Dedicashun."

America enjoyed her leisure, found new uses for it. *Sport* began to fill the news sheets. The Harvard crew went to England, and Boston was indignant because the men of Oxford desired the men of Harvard to row the British way. Sprawled across the newspapers were advertisements of gold mines, shares in Western silver mines, petroleum companies and, above all, railroad ventures. *Ladies' Dress* received public attention. Hoop skirts were going out, bustles coming in. "A morning dress of Bismarck velvet is *de rigueur*. . . . L'Elite Patent Bustle has a spring, so it will not cause that drooping and bulging so annoying to the wearer."

In New York State a new university was inaugurated, with Andrew D. White as president. Professor Agassiz went down to make a speech. Cornell, the college was called, after its founder. At Harvard, President Hill resigned and Charles Eliot's name came up immediately. The Overseers were alarmed. Eliot believed in the new "practical" education; under him, science, chemistry, would take up a large part of the curriculum. Dana [1] and Parker [2] protested. A

classical education, they said, was the important distinction between
a man who had been to college and a man who had not. Anything
that diminished the importance of this distinction was essentially
revolutionary and tended to anarchy.

And on Court Street, Wendell Holmes observed George Shattuck
receiving his clients, and marveled. Shattuck actually seemed to like
personal responsibility, liked to shoulder the troubles of his fellow
men. Bewildered people came to him, their faces lined with anxiety.
Listening to them, advising them, Shattuck's bearded face was cheerful, kind. Only his fingers, Holmes noted, twitched in his lap as he
talked.

But Holmes's admiration held no trace of envy. He had little
desire for personal influence over the lives of his fellows. It was a
far different power he craved. The man of action has the present,
but the thinker commands the future from his study. . . . Holmes
took Bagehot's works from the Athenaeum again, Henry Maine,
Ortolan's *Roman Law*, Reeves and Stephens and Bracton, Baine,
Herschel, and Lecky. Lecky's *History of European Morals* was
brand-new and already the center of controversy.

William James was home from Europe. "John Ropes told me the
other night," James wrote to Henry Bowditch, "he had never known
of anyone in the law who studied anything like as hard as Wendell.
(This must lead to Chief Justice, U. S. Supreme Court.) Wendell
amuses me by being composed of at least two and a half different
people rolled into one, and the way he keeps them together in one
tight skin, without quarrelling any more than they do, is remarkable.
I like him and esteem him exceedingly. . . ."

"Wendell Holmes," James wrote his brother Harry, "has skipped
many Saturdays often by my request, but comes pretty regular. He
is very affectionate *to* me and *of* you. . . . I think he improves surely
every year, and has that in him which makes you sure his fire won't
burn out before the age of thirty as 'most everyone else's seems to."

Burn out? Wendell Holmes had barely begun to live. That autumn
he seized eagerly upon a fresh task in the law. A new edition of
Kent's *Commentaries on American Law* was due; the chosen editor,
James Bradley Thayer, asked Holmes to help him. The last edition
— the eleventh — had been published in 1867. To make a twelfth
edition would be a long, exhaustive, exact study. Holmes would
have to do his part of it in the evenings, in his spare time. As the

weeks passed, Thayer turned the job over to his assistant entirely. Holmes was pleased, but the magnitude of the undertaking affected him visibly. "Wendell Holmes is hard at work," James wrote to Bowditch. "I fear too hard, having undertaken a two years' job to edit Kent's *Commentaries;* and being ambitious of excellence he says the time is too short for the amount of work he is resolved to put into it, and it weighs heavy on his soul."

Holmes worked and searched, wrestled with his footnotes to Kent as Luther had wrestled with his devils, was obsessed with the work, pursued by it, and, above all, unsure whether this quarry, if brought down, would repay the long hunting. Was the law really "worthy a whole intelligence"? Even now, he was not sure he had chosen the right course for his life's work. *The law is part of the universe,* Holmes told himself, sitting at his desk, staring at the rows of books on the wall before him. *If the universe can be thought about, one part must reveal it as much as another to one who can see that part. It is only a question if you have the eyes.*

If you have the eyes . . . What Holmes was doing now was to look upon the common law analytically, in the light of history. Not, What are our rights under God, but, What laws have actually been used? Why were they made? How and when did they lose their force?

For America it was pioneer work. Nothing so searching and critical had been done before. Since Kent died, in 1847, his *Commentaries* had gone through five posthumous editions. Holmes went back, checked all footnotes with the sixth edition. To bring the work down through twenty-five years meant keeping the whole in mind always, in order to let bear upon any part of it such new decisions in England and America as might be pertinent. Examining a case, Holmes went to the original report, examined it painstakingly, re-writing the footnotes until they were up to date.

And the farther he went, the more absorbed he became. He began to study the German jurists; Savigny's *Roman Law* was on his library card. The great Savigny had been dead less than a decade; scholars hailed him as the father of a new jurisprudence. Savigny's disciple, Professor Vangerow in Heidelberg, by no means held with the British and Scotch notion that metaphysics, logic, philosophy, lay behind the law. *History* lay behind it — analysis not by logic, reason, or even legal precedent, but analysis by social history, custom, and the original uses of the law. When one of his pupils asked him for a book on the philosophy of law, Vangerow raised his eyebrows coldly. "I doubt," he said, "that that kind of reading will help you at all."

At the Metaphysical Club[8] on Quincy Street, Holmes was curt, opinionated. Standing with his arm on the mantel, gesticulating with his pipe, he told off James and Wright, tried even to demolish Charles Peirce and could not. Always, Holmes's arguments came back to the law. There were other proofs in the world, James said angrily. There was the utilitarian proof of result, consequence. There were also men's feelings, their intuitions. . . .

Holmes's eyes narrowed, the congenital Irish lip grew even stiffer and longer. He agreed about testing law by result. But behind all intuition — all poetry — were the facts. It was well to explore the facts. "The law is not the place for the artist or the poet," Holmes said dryly. "The law is the calling of thinkers."

To his listeners it was pure arrogance and it was insufferable. "The more I live in the world," James wrote his brother Henry, "the more the coldblooded, conscious egotism and conceit of people afflict me and T.S.P. is sweetly free of them. All the noble qualities of Wendell Holmes, for instance, are poisoned by them, and friendly as I want to be towards him, as yet the good he has done me is more in presenting me something to kick away from or react against than to follow and embrace. I have seen him but sparingly since the spring, but expect he will be here tonight. . . ."

Holmes himself cared not in the least what impression he was creating. If anyone had told him he was conceited, he would have laughed. Conceited, with a world of knowledge as yet barely opened, with a job ahead that he might not be able to finish, a job that might prove too big for him?

"If you would wax thin and savage, like a half-fed spider, — be a lawyer." . . . So Dr. Holmes had written, long ago. Observing his son, the doctor was reminded of this lighthearted remark, tossed off when he himself had just given up trying to be a lawyer. Dr. Holmes at present was in a spasm of pleasure over his new house. He had bought land on Beacon Street, west, in the new filled-in Back Bay area, and was building on it. The yard behind led down to the river, his study upstairs would look out to Cambridge spires and eastward to Bunker Hill itself. A view over all creation, the doctor said. What more could man aspire to? His son's reaction to

all this was so apathetic as to be, in the doctor's eye, downright disagreeable.

All during the summer of 1870, the doctor watched his house go up. Everyone was building, money was plentiful. Trouble was brewing in Europe but it did not make stocks go down at home. Napoleon III was getting ready to declare war on Prussia, or so the Boston papers read the signs. "The Gallic cock is crowing lustily," the *Transcript* said. "Will it dare attack the Prussian eagle?" By the middle of September Napoleon had lost his throne, Marshal Mac-Mahon was captured with all his army, there was revolution in France. Boston showed enormous interest in the war. Headlines told the news as if it were a novel: Eugénie had gone to Notre-Dame to pray for France . . . Eugénie had denounced her husband as a coward . . . Paris was besieged . . . Paris was starving.

And in America there was a business boom. Mining stocks soared, railroads reached iron fingers across the continent. The golden spike was driven, East and West locked hands in trade. Martin Van Buren, could he have seen it, would have smiled sardonically. So had canals been dug in his day, to make men rich and make them free. Turnpikes opened, rivers dredged, companies formed, promotion rampant . . . And what had followed but panic, starvation, men begging for bread, begging for work?

1837 . . . 1857 . . . 1873 . . . At America's heels was another panic. The era of Big Business had begun, the era of the Bosses, of Jim Fisk and Simon Cameron, Tweed and Tammany and Slippery Dick Connolly, Roscoe Conkling and Jay Gould — the era of the railroad kings whose gold could buy up government. Expansion was the watchword, caution and thrift were the virtues of weaklings.

In the autumn of 1870, Dr. Holmes's new house was ready, the family moved in. Wendell's room was in the third story, communicating with his brother Ned's. These windows also looked across the river, to Bunker Hill and the spires of Cambridge. But to Wendell Holmes the view by no means comprised all creation, nor half of it. For him the whole of creation lay in the green lawyer's bag that contained his Kent. Each night it was carried up three long flights of stairs, carried down in the morning and set, at mealtimes, carefully by the front door. From kitchen to attic the household knew its place and had instructions to save it in case of fire.

In the autumn of 1870, Holmes left Chandler, Shattuck and Thayer and opened a law office with his brother Ned, who had done amazingly well in the Law School, graduating with honors. Wendell had secured a position for him as secretary to Charles Sumner in Washington and he had filled it for a year. Now he was home again and it was good to have him. He looked taller and thinner than ever, he wheezed with asthma when he ran upstairs. But in the firm of Holmes and Holmes, the younger brother was by far the more interested partner. For Wendell the office business only retarded the real business of life, which was to work on Kent. Moreover he was invited, that winter, to lecture at Harvard on Constitutional Law.

This was Charles Eliot's doing. Eliot had taken up his duties as president in the spring of '69. And he had — as Dr. Holmes wrote Motley — turned the University over like a flapjack. This grave young man behaved as if he had been *born* president of Harvard. "How is it," an elderly professor demanded in Medical Faculty Meeting, "that we have been going on so well in the same ordinary path for eighty years, and now within *three or four months* it is proposed to change all our modes of carrying on the school?"

"I can answer . . . very easily," Eliot replied. "There is a new president."

Eliot reached into Boston and brought new men to his teaching staff, fresh minds with the skeptical scientific outlook that he liked. Wendell Holmes, John Gray,[4] Henry Adams, John Fiske.

Holmes was enormously pleased with his appointment. It was by no means a professorship — merely an instructorship. But the work fitted exactly with the research he was doing on Kent. During the summer he had written an article for the *American Law Review:* "Codes, and the Arrangement of the Law." It was published in October and resulted in Holmes being made editor of the *Review.* This meant preparation of frequent articles, book reviews, editorials. It meant keeping up with the latest law books, with all important decisions here and abroad. In the November term of court, Holmes paused long enough to argue his first case alone. He won it. (It was what lawyers call a case in tort for the obstruction of an easement.)

Dr. Holmes expressed himself as gratified. But at home it was Ned who talked about the case. Wendell seemed to look upon the whole thing merely as a chore to be done. Now it was over and he could forget it. Ned's attitude seemed to the doctor far more sensible. Ned had an added incentive to money-making; he was engaged to be married. Wendell preferred not to think about this, either. The object of Ned's affection was a Wigglesworth, affinity incomprehensible to his brother. It was a huge tribe, Boston to the bone, all solemn, nearly all rich. There had been a Wigglesworth in Wendell's class at college, there was always a Wigglesworth at Harvard. If Ned actually married this girl, he would be lost to his brother forever. Wendell knew it and tried to think some act of God would intervene.

And on top of this melancholy affair, Wendell's sister Amelia became engaged to a widower, John Turner Welles Sargent, who was even more rigid than the Wigglesworths. In Amelia such a move might have been predicted. But Ned was a man of parts. Something unnatural had got into the boy, Wendell complained gloomily to John Gray. Under the influence of this woman, with her money and her Wigglesworth thrift, Ned was becoming correct to the point of dullness. He talked about stocks, about "getting on in the world." Horrid phrase! What had Herbert Spencer said, at thirty-nine? *"I don't mean to get on. I don't think getting on is worth the bother . . ."*

Getting on! It only retarded the real purpose of life, only stifled the flame that burned steadily, driving a man by day and by night. There was so much to do, so much to learn. At the Law School, Holmes found two students to help with the routine research on Kent. Henry Parkman [5] and Joseph Warner,[6] young men working for their degrees, who seized eagerly upon the job. Even so, Holmes could not get through what he had to do. His abstraction became noticeable; he was pale, irritable. At his mother's urgency he went out sometimes in the evening. And when he had been half an hour in a roomful of people, he longed desperately for escape, longed to get back to Kent, to the desk under the gas light with the green bag spilling its contents on the floor.

"Wendell Holmes," William James reported to his brother Harry, "spent an evening here this week. He grows more and more concentrated upon his law. His mind resembles a stiff spring, which has to be abducted violently from it, and which every instant it is left to itself flies tight back."

Slowly, steadily, the tension mounted. Mrs. James, kind, perceptive, used to brilliant sons, nervous sons — and very fond of Holmes — wrote to her son Harry: —

Wendell Holmes dined with us a few days ago. His whole life, soul and body, is utterly absorbed in his *last* work upon his Kent. He carries about his manuscript in his green bag and never loses sight of it for a moment. He started to go to Will's room to wash his hands, but came back for his bag, and when we went to dinner, Will said, "Don't you want to take your bag with you?" He said, "Yes, I always do so at home." His pallid face, and this fearful grip upon his work, makes him a melancholy sight.

Wendell Holmes had started for the Pole.

CHAPTER TWENTY-FOUR

Mr. and Mrs. Oliver Wendell
Holmes, Junior.

IN the autumn of 1871, the tall new brownstone house on Beacon Street became suddenly very empty. Amelia Holmes had married her widower in the spring; in October, Ned married Henrietta Wigglesworth. No one was left but Wendell and his parents. In the third floor back, most of Ned's furniture was gone from the adjoining room. Ned's desk, the tree where his clothes had hung so neatly, each garment on its especial hook. In the evening, getting up from his study table, Wendell closed the door between the rooms, hardly knowing what he was doing, aware only of a sense of oppression.

At mealtimes especially, Wendell missed his brother and sister. There was no one to divert the flow of Dr. Holmes's conversation. The doctor was wrapped in his latest work, *The Poet at the Breakfast-Table*, successor to the *Autocrat* and the *Professor*.[1] It was to appear serially in the *Atlantic*; the doctor was being handsomely paid. With satisfaction he mentioned the sum. A shadow passed over Wendell's face. At thirty, he was entirely dependent on his father financially. The lecture fees at Harvard, the work on the *Law Review*, brought next to nothing. The law practice with Ned was negligible.

None of this actually worried Wendell Holmes. None of it indeed took actual shape in his mind, it was felt only as a vague, increasing oppression. He worked too hard to ask questions about himself. He worked by day and by night, and the only people who could make him stop were John Holmes and Fanny Dixwell. When Amelia had lived at home, Fanny had stopped in often for tea and stayed all evening, or run in for lunch when she was in Boston. Now she did not come at all. Wendell was vaguely irritated. Must the whole world change its course because of a Sargent and a Wigglesworth?

He complained bitterly to Fanny. The whole thing was unreasonable, he said. "What's the matter with you, Fanny? Don't you ever come to Boston? You used to. Was Amelia the only person on Beacon Street worth seeing? I haven't seen you for a week."

"A week?" Fanny said. Her voice was quiet, a little tired. She had not seen Wendell since Christmas afternoon, more than three weeks ago, when he had stopped in with his Uncle John. When he was an undergraduate at Harvard he had run in nearly every day. When he was at Law School it had been the same. And when that had ceased, Amelia Holmes had made it possible for Fanny to go herself to the Holmeses'. Now the last tie was gone. . . . Twelve years of such a tie, broken now by circumstance, by the simple fact of the Charles River lying between them. Fanny knew she would not be the first woman to lose a man when fate brought up this challenge of inconvenience. And when had Wendell Holmes ever put himself out for anyone? Obviously, he did not even realize what was happening.

"Three weeks since I've seen you?" he was saying. "That's absurd, Fanny. By the way, Uncle John is driving over for tea Sunday. Will you come with him? Mother sent all kinds of messages. She said to tell you she was very lonely now, without a daughter."

Fanny looked at Wendell strangely and looked away. She was pale, thin. The clear high color that was natural to her had left her cheeks. Yes, she told Wendell. She would come to tea Sunday with Uncle John.

Next Sunday John Holmes took his nephew to the third story after tea, under pretext of looking out some especial tobacco he said Wendell was concealing from him. All the way upstairs he limped badly, holding his knee. Wendell, following him, was puzzled. He watched his uncle let himself down gingerly in the worn leather chair, stretching out his bad leg. John Holmes grunted. "I'm getting as lame as a battered game cock," he said. "Wendell, I didn't climb these penitential stairs for tobacco. I came about you — and Fanny Dixwell. The best girl in Cambridge. There is no higher praise. She is in love with you. . . . Yes, that is what I said. She is pining away — Fanny, of all people! I am not the only one to notice it. Why, she is ordinarily as spirited as a race horse!"

John Holmes looked up, frowning. "What is the matter with you, man? Haven't you *looked* at Fanny lately? Her eyes — as if someone had whipped her. She is thirty. Thirty-one maybe. So are you. Wendell, you have loved that girl for years. We've waited patiently, all of us, for you to find it out. But there is an end to patience. We don't like it. *I* don't like it."

John Holmes paused. Wendell's back was turned, he stood by the window, his hands in his pockets. At the first words he had whipped round, crossed the room. The back of his neck was scarlet, even his ears were red. Not a sound came from him. He could not have spoken if his life depended on it. His surprise went deep, a shock that pierced beyond discomfort. . . .

Fanny, in love with him? Fanny, *pining?* Why, Fanny couldn't pine for anyone! Fanny was the one who had always told him off, pricked his bubble, brought him back to earth. Fanny was a leader. She ran her family, all those sisters. She ran *him*, Wendell Holmes. Told him what to do when he was hesitant, laughed him out of it when he was nervous, involved. There had never been need to tell Fanny what he was thinking. She knew it before he spoke. Sometimes she knew it too quickly, so that it set him back a little in his own esteem. She was quick as lightning . . . and she was warm, generous. Her voice reached him as no music had ever reached him.

It reached him now, in a whirling flash of memory . . . *"Has Wendell always cared more for* ideas *than he does for* people?" . . . *"Bill James is your friend. Write to him without vis viva. Sometimes I think, sometimes I wonder . . . Don't you love* anybody, *Wendell Holmes?"*

Wendell turned from the window. When he stepped forward he almost stumbled. Whatever he said to Uncle John, he could not remember a word of it afterward.

Wendell Holmes to Mrs. Kennedy in Hagerstown, Maryland [2]

March 11, 1872

My dear Mrs. Kennedy,

It is with a sort of trembling that I write after such an interval to the dear and respected friend who was my good Samaritan long ago. But I must send a line to ask your good wishes.

I am engaged to Miss F. B. Dixwell who has been for many years my most intimate friend and who will now I hope soon be my wife.

On the seventeenth of June Fanny Bowditch Dixwell married Oliver Wendell Holmes, Junior. There had been some discussion about the church. Tradition pointed to a Unitarian one. Fanny did not care, she said, "So long as we can invite all your old girls, Wendell." In the end they chose Christ Church. Phillips Brooks was the clergyman.

There was no time for a long honeymoon. Chancellor Kent, Fanny observed, was no respecter of romance. But she was grateful that Wendell had not, like Chief Baron Palles,[3] taken *Fearne on Contingent Remainders* on his wedding trip.

By September the two were settled with the senior Holmeses at 296 Beacon Street. They had the third floor to themselves. There had been no choice of where they would live; there was no money for a separate establishment. Dr. Holmes was enormously pleased to have a new daughter under his roof. A fresh audience was a godsend, he said. His wife and son knew all his stories by heart. "You may find me a trifle egotistical," he told Fanny, beaming on her, his eyes bright as buttons, the crow's-feet deep around his eyes. "The reason I have to take so much interest in myself, my dear, is because I have a good deal to do. I must put my spirit into it — and that makes a person more or less of an egoist."

Fanny had always gotten on well with Dr. Holmes. Before she came to live in his house she had been continually amused by his industry and his vanity. Now, amusement gave way to a kind of amazement. *More or less of an egoist*, Dr. Holmes had said. There was no *less* about it. Nor was there any doubt that Dr. Holmes was a genuine celebrity. Letters came to him from all over the country and from abroad, too, huge piles of them, day after day. Requests for speeches, requests for poems to be read at banquets, at cornerstone ceremonies. Extraordinarily personal letters, enclosing poems to be criticized; asking the Autocrat if the writer should marry a girl older than himself; if it was wrong for a woman to leave a brutal husband and whether the doctor advised voting for Grant or Greeley in November?

Most of the letters were flattering to a degree. Dr. Holmes read them aloud, laughing delightedly. "I purr very loud over a good honest letter that says pretty things to me," he told Fanny. "A man bears superlatives about his own productions with wonderful fortitude. Self-love, my dear, is a cup without any bottom, and you might pour the Great Lakes all through it and never fill it up."

Was ever vain man so disarming? "Your father is like a child," Fanny told her husband. "His vanity is harmless and charming."

Wendell's expression was unfathomable. A moment later his face softened. Fanny seemed actually to enjoy the old man. "Fanny," Wendell said, "if I go up to our rooms early tonight, right after tea, will you stay with them an hour or so? I don't want to use my *Law Review* article, straight, for my lecture at the Law School tomorrow. I want to work over it."

Fanny Holmes was happy, that winter. How splendid to be of use to Wendell, daily, hourly almost! To make things smoother for him at home, make them all laugh at table, ease this tension between father and son. For a clever man, Dr. Holmes asked his son the most tactless questions, Fanny observed, that father ever propounded. Again and again . . . "Wendell, did that last case bring you much of a fee?" . . . "Wendell, don't you think Eliot should give you a full professorship next year, on the basis of these lectures at the Law School?"

It was not greediness on the doctor's part, Fanny knew. This family cared no more for money than the Dixwells did. They lived comfortably enough. But there was no luxury, no talk of luxury, and no desire for it. Merely, Dr. Holmes was trying to show an interest in his son's career. Prodding him . . . And Wendell did not need prodding. Fanny knew his ambition; it was deep and endless as a well. But it was the slow ambition of a scholar; it could not be hurried. There was about Wendell's ambition a silence and a kind of ferocity. It was Fanny's instinct to hold him back. *Do not hurry,* she wanted to say. *There is time, Wendell, there is time. Do not be afraid.* And here was his father prodding him as one prods a lazy man. Mrs. Holmes intervened always, at first. Fanny noted it and was grateful. But Fanny was far quicker than Mrs. Holmes. Moreover Fanny was new, in the household. She could be impudent with impunity.

And she was impudent, again and again. She was Wendell's wife; it was her business, now, not another woman's, to rescue her husband. It was her business to make peace in this house, for Wendell Holmes.[4]

But as the winter advanced, there were times when she despaired. There were times also when she wondered if the situation were not mostly of Wendell's making. He who was so genial, friendly, within these walls never lowered his defenses. It was as though he felt himself threatened, as though any slightest yielding would constitute for him a dangerous defeat. Yet his father was never malicious. There was no real threat here, Fanny told herself. Wendell was too remote from his father for rivalry. Their minds were wholly different. Wendell's talents, the quality of his brain, all his values, were totally apart from his father. There was no *harm* in Dr. Holmes, Fanny told herself again and again. She was even sure he loved his son.

And yet, and yet . . . Was a threat valid only when it was plain to the eye of the beholder? They must get out of this house. She would not let Wendell know it. They would be here, of necessity, a year, two years longer. But all the while she would be planning, looking for a place they could afford. Even one room, anywhere, would be better than this.

And they must go before she herself should begin to hate the doctor. So far, she did not hate him. "It is not reasonable to hate a bee simply because it *buzzes*," she told Wendell, laughing, imitating her father-in-law. "B-z-z, bzzz, at supper tonight. Has anyone counted how many words a minute your father can achieve, at his best?"

Wendell laughed. Fanny's heart warmed at the sound. To make Wendell laugh at his father was a triumph, a victory.

But Fanny knew, and Wendell knew, that there was no real chance of their setting up their own home until Wendell were offered a professorship at Harvard or a partnership in some old, established law firm. George Shattuck had been made a Harvard Overseer. He came often to see the Holmeses in the evenings, urging Wendell to get along with his edition of Kent. "It is good to be thorough, to take pains," Shattuck said. "But there comes a time, Holmes, when a book has to be finished."

In the spring of '73, it was finished. "I have devoted more than three years," Holmes said in his preface, "to the attempt to bring this work down through the quarter of a century which has elapsed since the author's death. While it has been in progress I have tried to keep the various subjects before my mind, so far as to see the bearing upon them of any new decision in this country or in England. Almost all my more important notes have been partially or wholly rewritten — many of them more than once — in the light of cases which have appeared since their first preparation; and every case cited has been carefully examined in the original report."

Shattuck was delighted. "It is a work to be proud of," he said. "It will make your reputation, combined with your work on the *Law Review*. How many articles for the *Review* have you done, altogether, these three years?"

"Counting book notices?" Wendell said. "Oh, six signed articles. About sixty book reviews and editorial pieces. My last article will be out in July. 'Theory of Torts.' "

"Well, well, Holmes!" Shattuck said. "We're both lawyers, you and I. It's the business of a lawyer to know law. You've heard me say that before. I notice you are pretty free with your references — from Bracton to Reeves. You learn your law in libraries. I learn mine in court. Give me a jury and a judge any day, to make *my* wheels turn."

Wendell Holmes knew well enough that George Shattuck had not approved all his *Review* articles. There had been one, after the gas stokers' strike in London and resultant discussion on both sides of the Atlantic, when Holmes, taking issue with Herbert Spencer, had said plainly that the development of legislation cannot be explained theoretically, by logical deduction from axioms. "The fact is," Holmes wrote, "that legislation . . . is empirical. It is necessarily made a means by which a body, having the power, puts burdens which are disagreeable to them on the shoulders of somebody else."

Empirical. It was the new word. *Legislation is empirical. . . .* President Eliot would like Holmes's article, Shattuck knew. Eliot insisted that law was a science and should be taught as a science. So did the new Dean of the Law School, Christopher Columbus Langdell. *Empiricism* — how the clever young men were fluent with these phrases! The theoretical young men. . . .

"Not my kind of law," Shattuck said. "Not my way of looking at things at all. But keep it up, my boy. You seem to be going somewhere. Shoot off plenty of ammunition and you'll be bound to hit the target."

He was not trying to hit a target, Holmes told Fanny that night. Why did men always assume that one had an end in view, some definite goal?

Fanny made no reply. To her the goal, the target, loomed large, and very definite indeed. To get out of this house, find money for their own home. Why could not George Shattuck do something for Wendell besides advising and approving? Shattuck had left Chandler and Thayer, was practising alone — and looking for a partner, John Ropes said. Business was high and booming, everyone had more money than they used to have. Dr. Holmes mentioned with satisfaction that his railroad shares were yielding double what he had expected.

One evening in June, Shattuck came in to call. His manner was especially hearty. Fanny led the way upstairs to their sitting room, her heart beating a little faster than usual. Shattuck sat down ceremoniously, cleared his throat. "Holmes," he said. "You have heard that I am reorganizing the firm. You are done with Kent, done with the *Law Review*. How about coming into my office next fall, as partner? You and I and Bill Munroe.[5] . . . Oh, you won't bring us any clients. We all know that. But you will have your uses. It's even possible you know things about the law we business lawyers have missed. . . . Wendell, I never told you, but I think you are headed for a very distinguished career."

"Thank you, Shattuck," Wendell said.

Shattuck gave him no time to say more. He got up, crossed the room, laid a hand on Wendell's shoulder. He turned to Fanny. "Do you think we can keep his nose out of Bracton and the *lex Salica* long enough to do a little business, Mrs. Fanny? Seems to me you young people might have uses for a little money of your own."

Shattuck looked round the little sitting room. Fanny sat speechless, her eyes shining. Wendell leaned forward, pipe in his hand. He smiled at Fanny, his eyes on her face. Shattuck, Munroe and Holmes? The office again on Court Street, day after day. It was what he ought to do. It was right. It had to come. If it had not come, he would have had to go out and make it come. But the fact gave him no joy, no lift whatever beyond a kindliness toward Shattuck. Only the look on Fanny's face could compensate for what the years would be now, day in and day out. . . .

"*Shattuck, Holmes and Munroe,*" Mr. Shattuck was saying heartily. "Well, how does it sound, my boy? How does it sound?"

September, 1873 . . . In Philadelphia, the brokerage firm of Jay Cooke and Company closed its doors, completely insolvent. The East was shocked, unbelieving at first. Jay Cooke had controlled the Northern Pacific Syndicate. . . . What did this mean? Was anything wrong with the railroad companies? . . . The nation soon learned what it meant. Panic broke. One after another, banks closed, commercial houses failed. Prices fell, farmers sold their grain below production cost.

Two million men out of work . . . three million . . . In Boston that winter Wendell Holmes, walking to the office, saw men sleeping in areaways, or huddled on steps. Misery in the nation, corruption in high places. President Grant did not seem to know an honest man from a rogue. Jay Gould, Jim Fisk, bought Senators as Western cattlemen bought steers. Frantically, men tried to devise quick remedies. Greenbacks, cheap money . . . Silver, more silver, would restore the national credit. In Boston, Elias Nason lectured on "Greenbacks," Mrs. Livermore on the "Battle for Money."

The bad times did not affect Dr. Holmes's household [6] in any direct way. But it put off to a more remote future Fanny's hopes of her own home. One more winter, and they should have saved enough to start out by themselves. Dr. Holmes talked about his railroad shares, but he did not really care. His interest in the depression was more literary than financial. At the Centennial Dinner of the Proprietors of the Long Wharf he read a poem of his own that he thought put the situation very neatly. When people began to talk about railroad stock, about Jay Cooke, about scandal and the Gold Ring, Dr. Holmes fidgeted with eagerness until he could quote one of his verses: —

With my rights (or my wrongs) in the "Erie" — alas!
With my claims on the mournful and "Mutual Mass.";
With my "Phil. Wil. and Balt.," with my "C.B. and Q.,"
But I never, no never, will sell out of YOU.

That winter, Fanny Holmes scoured the houses around the Common for rooms they could afford. Her brother John Dixwell, graduated now from Medical School and living on the crest of Beacon Hill near the Athenaeum, found them for her. Number 10 Beacon Street, the address was. The rooms were upstairs, over a drugstore, but they were pleasant and sunny and above all they were cheap.

They could have the rooms in the autumn, the landlord said. Painting was to be done, and refurbishing, a gas ring installed. Mrs. Holmes could cook breakfast. Their other meals would have to be eaten outside. . . . Mrs. Holmes herself, standing by the sunny rear window that looked downhill across the old Granary Burying Ground to Tremont Street, saw no drawbacks whatever to the arrangement. Her strong, fine hands clasped tightly before her, her eyes shining, she surveyed the future. Here she would live with Wendell, the two of them alone, their kingdom undisputed.

Outside, pigeons swooped from the Athenaeum roof, their wings flashed in the sun. A faint rumble of traffic carried through from Beacon Street. Here, thought Fanny Holmes, would be paradise, and she the mistress of it.

CHAPTER TWENTY-FIVE

Holmes works at the office. He prepares
a little book on The Common Law.

THAT summer of 1874, by some unexpected windfall Holmes got money enough to take his wife abroad. Ever since his first trip in '66 he had longed to return, cement the friendships he had made, meet new friends.

And he did meet them. One man especially was to prove of enormous benefit to him — a barrister named Frederick Pollock, four years younger than himself, son of Sir Frederick Pollock. "Wendell Holmes (son of Oliver) . . . came to sit by my side in Judge's Chambers," the elder Pollock recorded.[1]

For Holmes the trip was a huge success. He returned to Boston braced with the stimulus of fresh minds, pleased moreover with the dining out in London — social triumphs that grew directly from his former visit, his earlier friendships. But Fanny Holmes returned with a far different impression. She had seen Europe and cherished but one ambition concerning it — never to go again. For her the trip had been a nightmare. On the ocean she was not seasick, but for days after she landed, the houses of London swayed in the sky, the pavement sloped gapingly beneath her feet. Moreover she was shy of these great ones who invited her husband to dine. The women especially left her tongue-tied — sensation novel to Fanny Dixwell Holmes, and not one she enjoyed. She was, in fact, desperately shy and could not shake it off. All her wit, her quickness, left her and with it, she knew, her charm.

Fanny said nothing of this to her husband. Merely, she began to beg off in the evenings, persuaded Wendell to go alone. He must remember, she said, her well-known capacity for amusing herself. In the daytime if Holmes went to judges' chambers or elsewhere with men friends, Fanny poked assiduously around London by herself. At night when Wendell returned, she had gay stories of her adventures to tell. But what she really longed for was September and home, for Boston Common with the elms all dusty in the heat, for their cab from the station rattling homeward over the cobblestones, the lamp on the table lighted, Wendell at his desk, writing, studying. . . .

And when at last the ocean was crossed and they were home again, Fanny was content. Here in Boston, the two went out very little. Since the war, a fashionable society had developed that gave balls, wore full dress, went to Newport in summer, and got itself written about fulsomely in the illustrated weeklies. "*Mrs. H—— has a turnout which is perfectly lovely. A shell-shaped phaeton, with ebony-colored 'tiger' and blue and gold livery, drawn by two little black ponies, whitefaced and whitefooted, with gold-plated harness. Sunny mornings a fringed canopy protects the occupants from the heat, and altogether, there is not a more graceful establishment at Newport.*"

The Holmes family knew these people, were related to many of them. But they had never belonged to the fashionable group; they had no interest in belonging. Fanny and Wendell lived frugally in their second-floor rooms — but to neither of them did it seem frugality. It seemed adventure. They were both over thirty, yet for the first time in their lives they were free of the parental nest, independent financially, domestically. They could come and go as they pleased, with no questions asked. Even after a year, two years, it still seemed a miracle to Wendell Holmes that he could put on his hat, start down the stairs without his father's voice following him: "*Wendy — where are you going?*" Fanny never asked this question; she knew well what it meant to her husband not to have it asked.

Almost every night the two walked down to the Parker House for supper; often they met friends who dined with them. They liked this; it meant gayety, a bottle of wine. Fanny wore her new gray cloak. It was edged with brown fur and came nearly to the ground; she carried her little round muff. There was a flash of scarlet in her bonnet. Wendell thought he had never seen a woman who held herself so well. Sometimes after dinner their friends came home with them for an hour or two. Boston was the fifth largest city in the Union, with a population of almost three hundred thousand. But it was small enough so that on streets around the Common, Fanny and Wendell Holmes knew half the people they met. Their relatives lived all around them. But what had once seemed oppressive was delightful, now that they had their own home and could choose their visitors for themselves. Wendell went once or twice a week to his men's dining clubs, Fanny to her Sewing Circle. They lived quietly; they were a young couple making their way, laying the groundwork for what was to come.

At the office of Shattuck, Holmes and Munroe, practice was of a mixed sort. The cases related to questions in equity, contracts, torts, mortgages, bankruptcy, and the like. None of the cases involved criminal law, very few were concerned with large sums of money. In only one case was a question of constitutional law presented — raised by Shattuck and Holmes, and overruled.

But Shattuck had prophesied rightly when he said Holmes would not bring in many clients. The fact was that Holmes was bored with the office, bored relentlessly with the practice of law. Was this, he asked himself, to be his life, forever, year after year? Was all his study, all his preparation, to end with this greedy watch for clients, the practice of the shopkeeper's art, the sharp conflict over often sordid interests? Could these things make out a life?

They could make a life for George Shattuck. Holmes still admired Shattuck, still loved him. But Shattuck looked upon the thing with a far different eye. Shattuck kindled to these matters, warmed to the clients, to their troubles, their anxieties over a few hundred dollars. Holmes did not. He was nothing more than a glorified law clerk, he told himself.

Slowly, painstakingly — and withal passionately — Holmes began to make his escape. And he did not escape out of the law but into it. Since 1873 he had written no articles for the *Law Review*. Now he began again. A long article, "Primitive Notions in Modern Law," appeared in April of '76. Holmes took enormous pains with it; the material was too big for one article; he planned a second that would take all next winter to write.

The work was a godsend. The thought of it carried him through the day. The moment he walked out of his office door, fatigue dropped from him; he strode quickly, eagerly, up the hill, around the narrow brick pavement of Pemberton Square, like a man whose day is not ended but just beginning.

Fanny Holmes, watching this double life of the law, wondered how long a man could stand it, even a man as invincibly healthy as Wendell Holmes. At thirty-five he was as lean as ever, his color high and fresh. He had let his mustache grow to cavalry proportions; with obvious satisfaction he asked Fanny if it did not give him the look of a buccaneer? He held himself magnificently, he had never lost his army bearing. And the look of a man was more becoming to him, somehow, than the look of a boy that he had worn for so long. The deep gray eyes shone with purpose, with a hard masculine ambition. Was she, Fanny asked herself half fearfully, half proudly, going to find herself married to one of those men who grow handsomer with age instead of homelier?

Once more it was William James who recorded this change in Holmes — less a change than a development. And it followed with surprising fidelity the pattern James had drawn so long ago. Fanny had rented a small cottage at Mattapoisett for the summer, a remote, unfashionable spot on Buzzards Bay. Holmes brought his friends sometimes for week ends.

William James to his brother Henry, in London

CAMBRIDGE, *July 5* [1876]

I spent three very pleasant days with the Holmes's at Mattapoisett. I fell quite in love with she; and he exemplified in the most ridiculous way Michelet's *"mariage de l'homme et de la terre."* I told him that he looked like Millet's peasant figures as he stooped over his little plants in his flannel shirt and trousers. He is a powerful battery, formed like a planing machine to gouge a deep self-beneficial groove through life; and his virtues and faults were thrown into singular relief by the lonesomeness of the shore, which as it makes every object, rock or shrub, stand out so vividly, seemed also to put him and his wife under a sort of lens.

To the discerning eye then, "she" was adorable — he a powerful machine, gouging his groove through life. . . . Slowly, the plane made deeper cuts, slowly its gains were consolidated. The actual events, the landmarks of success, were in no way spectacular — but they were significant. In that same year of '76, Holmes was made an Overseer at Harvard. It was a position of great trust, Harvard men everywhere looked up to it. And Holmes loved Harvard College. "Every limb of it," he said. It was good to go to the meetings with Shattuck, have a voice in Harvard affairs. "Your father never was Overseer," Fanny reminded her husband, a light in her eye. "Professors can't be Overseers," Wendell replied. "You know that, Fanny." Nevertheless there was chaffing about it between father and son. "We talked over Medical School affairs at the last Overseers' Meeting," Wendell told his father, grinning. (This was pure fabrication of course.) "I told them," Wendell went on, "to make allowances for the Anatomy Department. 'After all,' I said, 'Dr. Holmes is busy with his writing. Something of temperament must be allowed to artists.'"

Dr. Holmes laughed, rubbing his hands together with a quick, circular motion. "My poem for the Centennial at Philadelphia is worth six of my lectures on the brachial plexus," he said. " 'Welcome to the Nations,' I call it . . .

> Welcome! a shout like the war trumpet's swell . . .
> Welcome! it quivers from Liberty's bell.

"I end with a note of peace," the doctor went on quickly. (Experience with his son had told him these poems must be recited quickly or not at all.)

> Hushed is our strife, in the land of the free . . .
> Thrones of the continents! isles of the sea!

"Very nice," Dr. Holmes's son remarked dryly.

But observing the nation that autumn, Wendell saw more of strife than of peace. After nearly eight years of *Grantism*, of shady politics, bribery and corruption, the country was getting ready to elect a new President. The politicians had got out the bloody shirt again, and were waving it. The Republicans contested their nominee bitterly, turned down James G. Blaine — Plumed Knight from Maine; turned down Roscoe Conkling — golden-haired, golden-voiced boss of his party in New York. General Hayes from Ohio, "the clear-eyed reformer," got the nomination.

But when the votes were counted, nobody could tell whether Hayes or Tilden had won. December passed, and January — and still the country did not know. Panic threatened, troops were called out. The people had a right to suspect dirty work. Boss Tweed was in jail, but for one rascal in jail there were ten at large. The robber barons strode across the continent, railroad lines in their fists. Freight wars raged; on the roads themselves brakemen, firemen grumbled, getting ready for a nation-wide strike. . . .

January, February — and still no one knew who was to be President. Who ran this country anyway, the people asked. Simon Cameron, Matthew Quay, Conkling, Platt? Commodore Vanderbilt, Jay Gould — the political bosses or the railroad promoters? Not the people, certainly. In March, Hayes became President. By the time he was inaugurated the country was bored with the whole affair, surprised when Hayes turned with vigor on the bosses, refused to support the spoils system, talked Civil Service reform.

In the autumn of '78, a seat on the District Bench fell vacant; Holmes's friends of the Boston Bar recommended him for the place. An older man got the judgeship. But for Holmes the incident was more encouraging than not. The Bar had spoken out in his praise. His articles in the *Law Review* were bearing fruit at last; his name was known beyond the confines of Shattuck, Holmes and Munroe.

Three articles had appeared in the *Review* since '76: "Primitive Notions in Modern Law" (I and II) and "Possession." "Common Carriers and the Common Law," "Trespass and Negligence," were to follow. Each piece, as it came out, Holmes sent to Pollock in England, some of them also to Henry Maine, Albert Dicey. Pollock wrote back enthusiastically — as far, that is, as Pollock ever showed enthusiasm. These articles, he said, were important for scientific understanding of the law. Holmes replied that as soon as he had accumulated enough material, he hoped to rewrite the articles in the form of a book.

Shortly afterward, Holmes was invited to give a course of lectures at the Lowell Institute in Boston. Twelve lectures, there would be, based on his *Law Review* articles. Holmes had nearly a year to prepare them; they were to be delivered during the winter of 1880–1881.

It was the focus he needed. Twelve lectures — there would be material enough here, certainly, for a book on the common law. Now at last, Holmes had a definite program. For some fifteen years he had studied, selecting, evaluing from immense stores of material, relying for authenticity on his scholar's intuition. Much of the time, during these long years, he had had no definite end in view, being motivated only by intensest interest in the search. *"No man can go far,"* he had learned to say, *"who never sets down his foot until he knows the sidewalk is under it. No man has earned the right to intellectual ambition until he has learned to lay his course by a star which he has never seen, — to dig by the divining rod for springs which he may never reach."*

And now these springs were within his reach. The Lowell Lectures and the book that grew from them would embody all Holmes had learned in fifteen years of study. He was thirty-nine. And he had a conviction — or superstition — that if a man was to make his mark in life, he must do it before he was forty. By then a man has found his dominant, leading conceptions; the rest of life is working out details.

The Common Law, he would call his book; the lectures would bear the same title. And by the time the twelve lectures were delivered, Holmes would have passed his fortieth birthday — March 8, 1881. His book must be out by then or it would never be out. He was sure of it. The thought drove him day and night. These Lowell Lectures were not intended for lawyers alone but for the general public. The material would have to be recast in a form comprehensible to laymen. No easy task — but it was the kind of work Holmes was pre-eminently fitted to do. He had always disliked what he called "the jargon of specialists"; it implied a kind of snobbism. Moreover, Holmes had a capacity for seeing things in the large, for viewing trends and the shape of things to come. Specific cases he had begun to call "the small change of legal thought." Fourteen years in the market, fourteen years of dealing in this small change, had given Holmes a familiarity with it, a facility. Now he could deal in larger, simpler, less fractional figures.

And he was no longer harried by doubt as to whether he had found his life's work, whether the law was "worthy a whole intelligence." He had said the law was not the place for artists and poets; the law was the calling of thinkers. He still believed it. And yet — how close to mankind was this abstraction called the law! As in a magic mirror it reflected not only our own lives but the lives of all men that have been — it made the tales of novelists, the loves of Daphnis and Chloe, seem pale indeed. . . . This story that unfolded night after night, this story culled slowly, painstakingly, from ancient documents, from Bracton and Gaius and the *lex Salica*, from reports of tribes living centuries ago in the German forests — was not this the tale of what men have most believed, most wanted?

Like a challenge the question rang in Holmes's brain. He looked up from his desk. It would be good if in his lectures he could answer that question concerning the law as a profession! If it were an audience of law students he could even put the question baldly. He could say right out that no other calling gave such scope to realize the spontaneous energy of one's soul — no other calling let one plunge so deep in the stream of life, so share its passions, its battles, its despair and its triumph.

But as Lowell Lecturer he would not be speaking to law students but to lawyers and professors of law. John Gray, James Bradley Thayer, Ames,[2] Christopher Columbus Langdell himself very likely. It was not Holmes's business to inspire such an audience concerning the value of law as a study. It was his business to describe certain basic forms of law in the light of their past growth. It was his business to present a general view of the common law, alternately referring to history and to existing theories of legislation.

He would warn his hearers at the outset that he was going to use another approach than the one they expected, which was the approach of logic, syllogism.

"*The law,*" he would say — and say it in the first two minutes — "*embodies the story of a nation's development through many centuries, and it cannot be dealt with as if it contained only the axioms and corollaries of a book of mathematics. . . . The life of the law has not been logic: it has been experience. The felt necessities of the time, the prevalent moral and political theories, intuitions of public policy, avowed or unconscious, even the prejudices which judges share with their fellow-men, have had a good deal more to do than the syllogism in determining the rules by which men should be governed.*"

So wrote Wendell Holmes, and what he wrote was new. He was deprecating formalism; he was saying that judicial decision does not derive wholly from precedent. He was saying that a good judge unconsciously predicts a law according to the result it will have upon the community at large.

Charles Peirce already had a word for this, not in law but in philosophy. *Pragmatism*,[3] he called it. In an article in *Popular Science Monthly*, published in 1878, Peirce had said that beliefs were nothing more than *rules for action.*

It was a conception that developed quite naturally out of the spirit of the times, out of a century of applied science. Practical ethics had come with the steam engine, the spinning jenny, the multiple reaper. A rising standard of living was the people's concern now. Quite as well as Abiel Holmes's Calvinism, it served as a religion. Goodness was proved by its works, defined by convenience in the present rather than sanctity in the past.

Wendell Holmes may or may not have been familiar with the word *pragmatism*. It was not necessary for him to know the word. Eight years ago, in the *Law Review*, Holmes had said that legislation was empirical. Now he was developing that conception. He was looking at the law pragmatically; he was saying that judge-made law is predicted according to its effects, not developed entirely by formality, according to precedent.

Some day, as a judge on the Bench, Holmes would act out his beliefs. Now he merely struggled to present them. Looking at the law with the merciless eye of the scientist, he presented no rule, no belief, without its cause, the train of facts that led to it. And this thoroughness did not make the book get finished faster. It seemed to Holmes that the work crawled. The days and nights disappeared — engulfed, swallowed, gone without leaving more than one new page written, two new pages. He became more and more abstracted, lost weight, looked white, drawn. Wendell Holmes, his friends said, was heading for a nervous breakdown.

Fanny was frightened. She had seen Wendell look this way before, years ago when he was working on Kent. But that had not been nearly so significant or so dangerous. Wendell had been a young bachelor then, with no office job to take his strength all day. He had been able to afford such intensity, such extravagance of intellectual absorption. He had sailed for the Pole, and neither solitude nor strain had harmed him.

But now it was different. Now he was nearly forty. This was in a sense his last chance. If he failed now — To Fanny it was unthinkable that he should fail. What she feared was not failure but illness, some nameless, sudden collapse. It was time for Wendell to take his place in the world. Yet intellectually, he was still remarkably alone, and he had had little recognition. Except for Pollock, Dicey, and the men in England with whom he corresponded, the articles in the *Law Review* had not really brought him into communication with his fellows. At Harvard, Langdell, although modern in his teaching methods, was a legal formalist, very academic in his viewpoint. Even John Gray and Thayer were not wholly to be counted on.

The fact that Wendell loved his work, was following his own bent, his own inclination, did not ease the strain but only enhanced it. Wendell's mother was worried about him too. Dr. Holmes was not. He deprecated the whole business. Good brains make their owners live longer, he said cheerfully. Benjamin Peirce had said so, years ago when Agassiz had his breakdown. Weir Mitchell in Philadelphia had agreed with Peirce — provided, Mitchell said, the owners of the brains rest frequently from their work. Dr. Holmes had experimented at the time, to see how soon his own brain tired when he was writing. He had recorded his reactions for Dr. Mitchell. "I never felt actual *fatigue*," he told Fanny now with relish. "Just a kind of disgust. . . . Tell Wendell to go out every evening after work and take a brisk walk around the Common. Twice round, and back across the Long Path. It's been my remedy for years, my dear. I'm seventy-one, and as spry as ever."

Fanny walked home through the summer twilight in a fury of resentment. *Seventy-one, and as spry as ever.* It was true. The doctor was tough as weathered timber, old shoe leather. Suppose Wendell broke down, was unable to go on? Suppose . . .

There was only one way Fanny could help her husband, and it had nothing to do with walks around the Common. She could divert him, make him laugh, keep him in touch with earth — pull him back, by fair means or foul, from this place of solitude and strain where he lost himself night after night.

It was a role for which she was well suited. Wendell had always loved her stories. Now Fanny thought them up deliberately, saved them, broke in at night when she knew her husband was nearing his limit of strength. He never rebuked her. . . . Did Wendell realize, Fanny demanded one evening, that her sister Mary was actually going to *marry* George Wigglesworth — had finally made up her mind? Could they endure the double Wigglesworth connection? Wendell's brother and her sister, fallen into the same pit! Tom Appleton had stopped Mary on Garden Street and demanded point-blank if she knew what she was doing, embracing a name like that. . . . Ned Holmes's son was seven years old. Did Wendell realize he was the uncle of a half-grown Wigglesworth? The tribe was alarmingly prolific; Boston would soon be peopled with Wigglesworths. "Look out on the Common any time of day, and what do you see?" Fanny demanded bitterly. "A squirrel and a Wigglesworth." And that reminded her, did Wendell remember what Charles Kingsley, stuttering his way through the literary clubs of Boston, had called Dr. Holmes? "An inspired j-jackdaw!"

Wendell threw back his head, laughed aloud and felt the better for it. There had been a telephone put in at the Chief of Police's office, Fanny went on, unfolding her newspaper. A telephone! Did Wendell hear what she was saying? A speaking tube like the Lovers' Telegraph at the Philadelphia Centennial, only this one was screwed to the wall. She would have one put in here at 10 Beacon Street if Wendell wouldn't listen to her any other way. . . . There was a flying machine on the Common! Sitting right there by the Frog Pond. She had walked round it. For one of the new five-cent nickel pieces she would have climbed up and sat in it—policeman or no policeman. Had Wendell seen it?

Wendell had not seen it. "Sarah Bernhardt is coming to the Globe," Fanny continued. "The comedians, Robson and Crane, are there now, in something called *Sharps and Flats*. I am going if I have to go alone."

Fanny had no intention of going alone. She had small interest in Robson and Crane, but she had seen Wendell laugh at worse comedians than these. It would be worth sitting through even the trained dogs to see him roar, his shoulders shaking, tears in his eyes. For ten rows each way, people would turn their heads as they always did. At first this had embarrassed Fanny. Now she was beyond caring. If she could not find the means to make her husband relax, she would soon, she told herself, have no husband at all.

But Wendell Holmes would not go to see Robson and Crane. He had not time, he said brusquely, irritably. Didn't Fanny realize it was October? The publishers must have the book in their hands by January at the very least.

And after January would come February, and after February, March. On March 8 he would be forty . . . Forty! Sitting at his desk, Holmes shook his head, staring at the sheet of white paper before him. If a man could not finish a book in ten years, if he could not get his ideas in order by the time he was forty, would he ever get them in order? Long ago, he had worried for fear the law was not worthy a whole intelligence. Now the question was ironically reversed. Would his own capacity measure up to the task he had set himself? This vision of the law, this ordered intellectual sequence of events — could he set it down for others to see, as clearly as he himself saw it?

Looking up, Holmes fastened haggard eyes on his wife and waited for her answer. He had not asked the question aloud, but he thought he had. He did not know that he had asked this question, or some form of it, every night now for a month.

Fanny did not seem disturbed. She pulled bright silk through the tapestry work on her knee, cut off her thread and looked cheerfully at her husband. "It took Adam Smith ten years to write the *Wealth of Nations*," she said.

She smiled. And there was in her smile something of reassurance, something of confidence or of love — perhaps something merely of dailiness, or the homely, simple thing she had said, that caused her husband to smile back at her, the strain to leave his face.

Drawing a long, comfortable sigh, Holmes bent once more over his desk. In the room there was no sound but the scratching of a pen. Outside, horses' hoofs struck against cobblestones. Wheels lumbered heavily, turning the corner on Park and Beacon Streets. In Park Church belfry the clock struck twelve, midnight.

CHAPTER TWENTY-SIX

Holmes lectures on the Common Law.
He presents his father with a book, and is made
a full professor at the Law School.

ON a November afternoon of 1880, at the Lowell Institute,[1] Holmes gave the first of his lectures on the Common Law. The bare, gas-lighted hall was perhaps three-quarters full. There was a sprinkling of law students, and most of their professors. John Gray and James Barr Ames, James Bradley Thayer. Dean Christopher Columbus Langdell was there, his long dark beard flowing over his shirt front, his fine eyes level and searching behind his spectacles. Langdell, as Holmes well knew, was all for logic and hated references to anything outside of it, but he was a superb teacher. A noble old swell, Holmes called him, and said he loved him for his idealist devotion to his work.

President Eliot was there, sitting straight in his chair, his arms folded. There were not many practising lawyers present. Run-of-the-mill lawyers were still suspicious of historical analyses of the law. Shattuck was there of course, and Munroe and Captain Magnitzky from the office. Henry Parkman and Joseph Warner who had helped with Kent's *Commentaries*. Fessenden and Brooks Adams, young Louis Brandeis.

There was also a contingent from the world of banking and large business affairs. Higginsons, Lees, Wigglesworths — friends of the Holmes family. The rest of the audience was made up of the usual Institute followers, elderly men and women who pursued culture even in its more formidable aspects. That these lectures on the Common Law would be formidable they had not a doubt. But surely a son of Dr. Holmes would leaven the lump with a quip or two, some homely, local reference to make them smile? Many of them recalled the winter of '53 when the doctor himself had been Lowell Lecturer. His subject had been the English Poets, but the really pleasing part of each lecture had been the end, when the doctor recited some of his own verses. . . . It was gratifying, now, to have Dr. Holmes's son as lecturer. Boston liked its rewards to stay in the family, among people one knew — not be given out to strangers. And to be Lowell Lecturer was a distinction envied by scholars.

When Holmes walked out on the platform there was a stir; the audience turned to look at Dr. Holmes sitting near the front, to see how he was taking it. The doctor was smiling broadly, whispering to his wife. The family, the audience noted, took up almost a whole row. The heavy-set man with the cane they recognized as the doctor's brother, Mr. John Holmes from Cambridge. The lecturer's wife was there, Edward Holmes the lawyer, the lecturer's sister, and various unidentified inlaws and cousins. All of them sat motionless, staring at the platform, except the doctor, who turned to nod to his friends, wave a greeting.

Dr. Holmes's feelings this afternoon were mixed. Long ago, he had become convinced that Wendell would never make a public speaker. Wendell's manner was not easy; when he was interested in a subject he was uncompromising, making no effort to charm his audience. When Wendell's mother demurred at this, the doctor had ended by saying a trifle irritably that Wendell's neck was too thin for platforms. Public speakers should be robust.

The doctor thought of it now. Wendell had begun to speak. His voice was certainly agreeable; it was soft but it had resonance, and carried well. His neck was indubitably thin, even at forty. He was thin all over, with the figure of a man of twenty-five; he held his shoulders like a soldier. He had no notes and spoke slowly, continuously, as though telling a story that he himself found enormously interesting. *"The life of the law has not been logic; it has been experience,"* the quiet voice went on, gathering depth.

George Shattuck turned his head abruptly and looked at Professor Langdell. What Holmes had just said was in direct opposition to Langdell's beliefs. Shattuck's own outlook on the law was more like Langdell's than like Holmes's. But this had not deterred Shattuck from saying openly that Holmes should have a Harvard professorship — and a judgeship later on. If it was the business of a lawyer to know law (this was Shattuck's favorite phrase) it was the business of a professor and a judge to know even more law. Wendell Holmes knew more law, perhaps, than any man in Massachusetts. . . .

Langdell's expression was unfathomable behind beard and glasses. But President Eliot had unfolded his arms; he leaned forward, his face raised toward the speaker. Holmes had walked round from behind the lectern and was standing at the edge of the platform; his voice rang with the slow, quiet assurance of a man who speaks from a conviction born of knowledge, and who knows that only time is needed to bring other men to his view. *"The very considerations which judges most rarely mention, and always with an apology, are the secret root from which the law draws all the juices of life. I mean, of course, considerations of what is expedient for the community concerned."*

In the audience a Wigglesworth, a Lee, a Higginson — bankers all — stirred a trifle uneasily. "Expedient *for the community concerned.*" What did the lecturer mean by "the community"? The bankers and businessmen, who were the rightful leaders — or the mass of people? If the latter, it was a notion no man of business would tolerate for a moment. It smacked of government interference, legislative interference. . . . Anathema to an audience reared in the atmosphere of *laissez faire*, an audience that had never heard of the social function of property, an audience to whom governmental interference meant an assault on liberty and to whom a measles sign on the front door would have been an affront to the castle which was a man's home.

So far, however, the lecturer had said nothing actually anarchistic. Merely, a suspicion was born. But surely, this fellow Holmes belonged in the right camp! He was a Wendell, an Oliver, a Holmes, a Jackson. Maybe these were just the notions of a theoretically-minded man. Holmes had never made any real money in the law. . . .

When it was over, Eliot, Langdell, and Ames moved up the aisle toward the platform. So did Louis Brandeis. Wigglesworths and Higginsons, after shaking Dr. Holmes by the hand, disappeared. The bulk of the audience filed out onto dark November streets, looked at its watches and thought about supper. Dr. Holmes's son was a pretty good lecturer certainly, although a trifle learned for everyday consumption. But after all, was not the law the dryest subject on earth? The lecturer, obviously, did not think so. The lecturer was plainly in love with the law.

It was this quality, perhaps, that brought the audience back, day after day until the twelve lectures were done. The lectures did not become successively easier to understand. On the contrary, the subject matter as announced in the program was quite horrible. "Theory of Torts," "Contracts," "Trespass and Negligence." Fortunately, the lecturer did not scorn homely illustration. Speaking one night of criminal intent . . . "The law," he said, "does not punish every act which is done with the intent to bring about a crime. If a man starts from Boston to Cambridge for the purpose of committing a murder . . ."

The audience, which had been settling into a stupor, roused itself delightedly and looked at its neighbor. "From Boston to Cambridge." The audience knew every stone of that journey. Murder! Was Mr. Holmes going to refer to the Parkman murder, that had happened in the Medical School right beneath his father's classroom?

Mr. Holmes had no such intention. "Public policy," he continued, "that is to say, legislative considerations are at the bottom of the matter." And he was off again to the point he had stressed before.

As he progressed into the more specialized phases of the law, Holmes tried to simplify the problems. "I gave a light touch to the question of bilateral contract in my Eighth Lecture," he wrote Pollock.

It was not light enough. But until the end the audience remained loyal, sat solidly in its seats and left at the time appointed. When it was over the general conviction was that the whole thing had been learned, elevating, and dry. What Eliot and Langdell thought would become apparent later on. What the Wigglesworths and Higginsons and Lees thought — what indeed, the entire non-legal audience thought, was a matter of indifference to Wendell Holmes. He was not a professional lecturer; he was a man with an idea; he was a scholar who needed a channel for his scholarship.

What he did care about enormously was the book that he was making out of the lectures, and the response to this book he might expect from the legal world. By January, 1881, the book was finished and in the printer's hands. On the third of March — five days before his fortieth birthday — Wendell and Fanny Holmes walked down Beacon Street to the parental mansion. Under Holmes's arm was a new, brown-covered book. *The Common Law*. He handed it to his father. On the flyleaf was written: —

O. W. Holmes,
from his affectionate son, O. W. Holmes, Jr.
March 3, 1881.

How many books on Wendell Holmes's shelves bore a like inscription — but reversed! The inscriptions went all the way back to 1848, when Wendell was seven. Each of his father's works as they came out. But Dr. Holmes had never abbreviated the names; he had written them in full, with a flourish. *"Oliver Wendell Holmes, Jr., from his loving father, Oliver Wendell Holmes."* Most fathers would have stopped with the word *father*. But not the doctor. Posterity, he knew, would want to know who this father was. It had never ceased to irritate Wendell Holmes. Now at last the inscription was reversed, now the son could pay the father in his own coin. And the event was scheduled just in the nick of time; five more days, and Wendell Holmes would be forty.

On the evening of her husband's birthday — March 8, 1881 — Fanny Holmes brought out a bottle of champagne. She and Holmes drank it, toasting *The Common Law*, toasting its author. Draining his glass, Holmes picked up the empty bottle, carried it to the sink. He held the cork a moment in his fingers, turned it over. Outside, March winds, whirling up the hill across the stones in Granary Burying Ground, shook the windows. . . .

Forty years old, and his work well started. There had been black months — but never inactive months. *If a man gets a year's life out of a year, he can ask no more*. . . . Holmes had declared himself, had told what he knew, what he believed. He had arrived at a viewpoint and had expressed it in print. He would stand or fall by the declaration. Forty years old. It was a day to remember, a day of true celebration. With a quick motion, a half smile, Holmes, before he turned back to his wife, put the champagne cork in his pocket.

"The only reward which I have promised myself is that a few men will say well done."

They did say it. The *London Spectator* called the book "the most original work of legal speculation which has appeared in English since the publication of Sir Henry Maine's *Ancient Law*." Of all legal historians, Maine was the one Holmes admired most. John Austin's book — a necessity for students — was tedious, often mistaken. But Maine could make the student feel as if his whole road were strewn with diamonds. And now men who really knew compared Holmes with Maine. Pollock, too, wrote at length in the *Saturday Review*, and in the new edition of his own book discussed Holmes's chapters on Contract.

But this did not come all at once. It was, indeed, very slow in coming. More than a month after he had sent his book to England, Holmes wrote Pollock, "I hope you will read my book . . . I fancy it is an accident whether it falls into the hands of people who will realize that the work is at least a serious one."

It was not an accident. Merely, the wheels in such matters grind very slowly. Practising lawyers, as was to be expected, cared nothing for the book. Practising lawyers still believed that law could best be learned by rule of thumb, and that most law professors were little better than impostors. Not even scholars accepted the book unanimously; one famous library committee refused it shelf room. Granted, that the author had made exhaustive study of his points; from its very beginnings he knew the common law. But his viewpoint, the method of his presentation, were suspect. The old method had been to trot out antiquarian knowledge and follow it with theory. And here was an unknown American — not even a professor at a university — placing upon the table leading notions of English law, and with scalpel in hand laying open the body. The very words he used looked strange upon the page: *experience, expediency, necessity, life.* Heretofore the pages of legal histories had been black with far different words: *logic, rule, syllogism.* The time-honored way was to deduce the *corpus* from *a priori* postulates, fit part to part in beautiful, neat, logical cohesion. Whereas *O. W. Holmes, Jr.* wrote lightly of "the humble error of supposing the science of law to reside in the *elegantia juris*, or logical cohesion of part with part."

Already, Holmes was suspect. But already, also, among the initiated he had made his mark. He had entered the arena and waited now for what was to come. One deep conviction remained: he knew himself to be only at the beginning. The years of study had completed nothing. They had merely opened a door.

January, 1882 . . . A Harvard graduate named William Weld announced to President Eliot that he had some money to dispose of. He would like it to go to the Law School. Four professors were not enough for a school of the scope and standing of this one. Would ninety thousand dollars endow a fifth professorship?

Charles Eliot smiled, reaching out his hand. Already Eliot, in an era of Big Business, was known as one of the biggest businessmen of them all. Some people said, indeed, that there was no more love of learning in Eliot than there was in Jay Gould. But the men of business, the men of money, had confidence in Eliot. Like themselves he was tough-minded, recognized expediency as one of the high gods. In the University, he commanded an almost doglike following. This young man who twelve years ago had — as Dr. Holmes said — turned the University over like a flapjack, now led the University by drawing strings — and led it to glory. The great white paladin of the business world, they called Charles Eliot in '82.

Ninety thousand dollars for the Law School. Eliot had not countersigned the check before he knew where the new salary was going. Oliver Wendell Holmes, Junior, was the man for the place. Brilliant, and with the scientific outlook. A man who would produce books as well as teach — a combination that Eliot insisted upon. A Harvard graduate, son and grandson of Harvard graduates, married to a Dixwell, his roots in good Massachusetts soil. A man of solid, distinguished background who would settle down in Cambridge, teach thirty years, then die and leave what money he had to the University in the best Harvard tradition.

When Holmes was notified of the appointment he went straight to his law partner. Shattuck was in no way surprised. Shattuck was not at the moment a Harvard Overseer, but he knew everything that went on. "Take the job," he said instantly. "It is your kind of job and your kind of life, Holmes. You can keep up some kind of connection here at the office. But you will never make money in the law; your heart is not in the right place to make money. I always suspected it, but after I sat through those Lowell Lectures I was sure of it."

Shattuck paused, then went on vigorously. "On the Massachusetts

Supreme Court, Otis Lord is sick. He can't last much longer. You are the man to succeed him. And don't tell me you haven't thought of it yourself, my boy.".

Shattuck grinned through his beard. He had not been well lately. He looked old. But he had lost none of his spirit. "Don't let Eliot tie you to more than a year's contract," he went on. "Have it in writing that if you are offered a judgeship you can resign. It's highly unusual. Eliot won't like it. He's not an easy man to bargain with. But I have never observed that the Holmes family lacked stubbornness, itself."

Holmes laughed. But he followed Shattuck's advice about the Law School contract. Eliot agreed to the proviso. After all, a Harvard professorship was a thing seldom relinquished. Once it was tasted, Holmes would surely desire to continue a career so distinguished, so secure. Eliot, in short, was getting the man he wanted for the place he wanted him. That was enough.

Holmes looked forward eagerly to his new job. The Law School, he well knew, was a very different place from the days when he himself had gone there to "read law" behind the white painted pillars of Dane Hall, entering with no academic requirement and leaving after three years, without examination. Langdell's "case system" was well established now, but it had taken ten years of battle to establish it. Holmes approved the case system. Law only ends with a theory; it begins with a concrete case. Naturally, a student remembers an actual instance more vividly than a general principle. . . .

But in September, when he walked into his classroom, Holmes was anything but sure of himself or of the case system. In his own day, Parker, Parsons, and Washburn had handed out the textbook, asked rote questions, and disappeared to their businesses across the river. Now the student depended neither on textbook nor on lecture; he was handed a book of cases and plunged into the fray. . . . "Mr. Codman," Holmes heard himself saying, "will you state the facts in the case of *I. de S.* v. *W. de S.?*"

This was a first-year class in torts. And to Holmes's eye the students, sitting in rows before him, looked like so many babies, thick-haired, round-cheeked . . . But Mr. Codman, his wide blue eyes snapping, went ahead without hesitation, and stated the facts with accuracy.

"Mr. Hoar, will you give the plaintiff's argument?"

"Mr. Parker, do you agree with them?"

The whole thing was exhilarating. Holmes enjoyed his classes. Besides torts, he taught jurisprudence, suretyship and mortgages, and agency and carriers. When test papers fell due, Holmes made them stiffer than the students had been used to, asking no rote questions marked A, B, and C. Instead, he gave a searching question that required a full answer, a discussion more like the form of law examinations today.

Years ago, Holmes had become convinced that no man could actually teach another anything. All a teacher could do was to let his students be partners in his work — impart as it were a ferment, as Parsons, Washburn, Emerson, had once imparted a ferment to Wendell Holmes. But the trouble was, as you got older you realized that most men were incapable of receiving this contagion. ＿＿＿ ard enough," Holmes told his students, "you will ＿＿＿ ou want."

＿king again on their faces — healthy, stolid, indifferent, ＿ous — Holmes knew that he had lied. These boys could learn, ㅡ hey could reason, memorize. But among the rows of faces, how many, when he flung out a challenge — how many showed an answering light? Two, perhaps three. . . . Suppose, Holmes thought, that he told them the rest of this half-truth — told them that WANTING is born in a man or it isn't there and never will be. Wasn't it a deception, to stimulate a man to want?

It was a deception that Wendell Holmes achieved only too easily. His very presence was stimulating — his quick step and erect bearing, the fire that burned in his gray eye. His colleagues on the faculty watched to see what he would do — Langdell, and Holmes's old friend John Gray. Thayer was still abroad on his sabbatical. In his forties, Gray was handsomer than ever; the dark trimmed beard, peppered now with white, became him. He was a big man, wore his tweeds and loud ties with a traveled, worldly air. "Gray's transcendental ties," they called them around Cambridge. Besides being a superb teacher, Gray was a constant producer of books, articles on law. His older brother, Horace, was on the Supreme Court in Washington. Boston said proudly that Horace Gray was the biggest, most imposing-looking Justice ever to sit on the Bench.

John Gray talked sometimes about the Bench versus teaching as a career. He was quite frank that for Holmes he would have pre-

ferred the former. It had more of action. Most scholars fled the life
of action because it interfered with scholarship. But Holmes, Gray
observed, had always sought action almost as though he were driven
to it by a conscience that loved too much its opposite. It was a
natural corollary that Holmes should profess admiration for the self-
made men, the captains of industry that roared and swaggered now
in Chester Arthur's administration, although it was hard to tell if
Holmes was being ironic or truthful about this. From Rockefeller
to James J. Hill, were not these men of enterprise, Holmes demanded. Didn't they represent the free American system? And besides, why not look upon them in terms of the consumer, in terms
of cheaper oil, better transportation?

Measures to curb these industrial giants, these robber barons, had
barely been suggested, as yet. But suggestion was in the air. There
was another man on the Law School Faculty who sometimes debated
social questions with Holmes — a very young man, Louis Dembitz
Brandeis, aged twenty-six, who was lecturing on evidence that year.
Brandeis came from Kentucky; he had gone through the Law
School in two years instead of three, earning his living while he
did it. In '77, the Corporation, by special vote, had granted him his
LL.B. although he was below the required age of twenty-one. He
had gone out West immediately, to practise law, but his classmate
Samuel Warren had called him back to Boston to start a joint
partnership: the firm of Warren and Brandeis was already doing
well.

It was an extraordinary record, but it took no second glance to
establish the fact that here was an extraordinary man. Tall, extremely thin, black-haired, with blazing blue eyes, Brandeis was
like an electric wire that trembled with a highly charged energy.
But with it he was quiet, possessing a quality of gentleness that sat
strangely upon a man so young. Perhaps it was not gentleness but
compassion; Brandeis was deeply stirred by social injustice; already
the slums of Lowell, Lawrence, were making him restless for reform.
Like Holmes, he came of a long line of liberty-loving ancestors.
Brandeis's parents had come over from Bohemia in 1848 to escape
the political troubles. They had the sensitiveness, the wide intellectual
and artistic background, of the cultivated European Jew. Their
carved dark furniture, their square piano and bright-colored china,
had gone down the river to Kentucky on a raft. All their money

was lost after the Civil War. But they had sent Louis to the Dresden *Realschule* when he was sixteen, thinking he might go through the German universities. He had come home again to be an American. "There is more freedom in Kentucky," he said.

Holmes was enormously drawn to this young man. There was a sympathetic quality to their minds. Both were brilliant, incisive, thoroughly independent. Brandeis had a passion for thoroughness; his mastery over facts, statistics, was stupendous. "If you can't solve it by law you can solve it by mathematics," he said. Holmes was not so sure. He laughed a little at this young passion for the facts, but he respected it too. The kind of facts that Holmes liked to master did not lie in contemporary pamphlets concerning the population of Lowell, the technical problems of Boston's water system.

And Brandeis in his turn was drawn to this scholar with the soldier's bearing who carried three historic names, who did not know what poverty meant, what persecution meant, yet who understood intuitively things that he, Brandeis, had had to learn through suffering, learn by the feel and bitter taste of life.

Standing on the platform facing his students, Holmes told them they could be anything, if they wanted to hard enough. Brandeis had wanted to; wanting had been born in Louis Brandeis. Holmes did not say his name. But it made him impatient with the students, this contrast, as Thayer and Gray were seldom impatient. Holmes was not a born teacher. With the slow and especially with the indifferent, he was often bitingly cynical. He did not suffer fools gladly. But any man who reached out to him received his reward. *The ferment of genius in its creative moments is quickly imparted.* . . .

Going back and forth to Cambridge in the horsecars, that autumn of 1882, Professor Wendell Holmes thought about the Law School, about his students, wondered if this was to be his life henceforth. He had been a teacher only three months. Yet there was something in the very familiarity of the scene that made the months seem like years. This Square . . . The Harvard Yard . . . How little time it seemed since he had been a student himself! How little time before that, when, climbing out of the omnibus on Sunday afternoons, he had run across the Square ahead of his father, waving to his Uncle John who stood under the elm by the door of the Gambrel-roofed House. . . .

CHAPTER TWENTY-SEVEN

A Judge with a sense of history.
And a brief summary of the con-
ditions that confronted him.

T HE *place for a man who is complete in all his powers is in*
the fight. The professor, the man of letters, gives up one-half of
life that his protected talent may grow and flower in peace. But
to make up your mind at your peril upon a living question, for
purposes of action, calls upon your whole nature.

O. W. H., JR.*

On the morning of December 8, 1882, Professor Holmes was called
out of his classroom. In the foyer stood George Shattuck, hat in
hand, his beard bristling, his eye alight with news.

"Otis Lord has sent in his resignation," he said. "Governor Long
wants you for the judgeship. He has to submit your name to the
Council by twelve o'clock, and he has to have your consent first."

Shattuck took out his watch. "It's eleven now," he said, and grinned
through his beard.

Outside, a bell sounded; students poured from the classrooms,
laughing, talking, pushing past the two men. . . . The Supreme
Court! So it had come at last. In his heart, Holmes had hoped always
— but he had never really expected it. It left him stunned, speechless.
It was a stroke of lightning that in one second wiped out the past,
changed his whole future. . . .

* From Holmes's speech to the New York State Bar Association, Jan. 1899.

"Why are you standing there?" Shattuck asked. He was almost as excited as Holmes. "An hour is not long to get ourselves to Eliot's office and then across the river to the courthouse."

Holmes got his hat and coat. The two walked down the steps of Dane Hall, turned left on Harvard Square toward the president's house. The sky was a brilliant blue. Gusts of dry snow, blowing along the bricks, touched their faces.

"How do you think Eliot will take this?" Holmes asked. "Once before, I left Harvard on short notice. When I joined the Home Guard in April of my senior year there was a row because I didn't call on President Felton for permission. How do you think Eliot will take this?"

"Badly," Shattuck replied, his voice cheerful with the prospect of imminent battle.

Holmes looked at him gratefully. In every crisis of his life, Shattuck had somehow appeared on the scene, to stand behind him. Shattuck had said to go ahead and edit Kent and make a job of it. "Get done with it, my boy. Thoroughness is all very well, but there comes a time when a book must be finished." Shattuck had said to write *The Common Law* and make a job of *that*. Why, George Shattuck had done more for him than anyone else in his life, outside of his family.

It would be good to say so, to tell Shattuck now, while the impact of this huge event still dislocated the barriers between them, pulled down the reserve of years of daily business encounters. Holmes looked round. His long stride had left Shattuck three paces behind. He waited.

"Shattuck!" he said. He laid his hand on the older man's arm. "I want to say something . . . I want to tell you . . ."

"God Almighty!" Shattuck said, panting. In the clear air his breath emerged in steamy blasts. "Holmes, you have a stride like an antelope. . . . Here, we're at the president's gate." He shook off Holmes's hand. "Good-bye, my boy, you won't be long. I'll meet you in the car shed on the Square." He paused. His face, red with cold and the exertion of walking, was suddenly serious. "You have a philosophy, Holmes, about the judicial function and the common law. Until now you've talked about it." He looked sharply at Holmes. "Now you must live it through."

*   *   *

One week later, on December 15, Holmes was formally appointed to the Court. His resignation was accepted at Harvard on January 8. There was some reason for Eliot's displeasure. The Weld Professorship was an important chair; ordinarily, a resigning professor gave the Corporation at least time to fill his place before leaving college. James Bradley Thayer was named Holmes's successor, shifted from the Royall Professorship, which was given to John Gray. Ames was also angry. The salary of a professor in the Law School was $4500. Holmes had no right, Ames said, to take six months' salary for three months' work.

Holmes was little disturbed by any of it. On the third of January, 1883, he took his seat in the Supreme Court, the youngest of seven judges. He was forty-one. Field was fifty. The other five — Morton, Devens, Colburn, the two Allens — were white-haired, white-bearded. Charles Devens (Harvard, '38) had commanded the Fifteenth Massachusetts Infantry and fought through the same battles as Holmes. Devens knew Holmes well, trusted him as one soldier trusts another.

But the other five had no especial reason to trust him. For a judge, Holmes was young, he was known as a man erudite rather than judicial — what practical men call a "theoretical fellow." His record consisted of a respectable but thoroughly undistinguished law practice, numerous learned articles in the *Law Review*, editorship of the twelfth edition of Kent, a course of Lowell Lectures that one or two of the judges had attended, and his recent book on *The Common Law*, which the judges understood had been well spoken of in England. Beyond this, he had been a professor at the Law School for three months.

It was not the usual road by which men came to the Supreme Court. Charles Allen, it was true, had compiled the fourteen volumes called *Allen's Reports*, Field had taught mathematics at Dartmouth for a brief period in his youth. But *Allen's Reports*, Field's mathematics, were not to be compared with the huge original research done by Holmes, and the Court knew it. All six judges had arrived on the Bench the usual way, through years of law practice, an appointment to the Superior Court, or a place in the State Legislature. *Experience* was what made a judge — not scholarship or theoretical conceptions of the judicial function.

There was precedent, of course, for a close Harvard connection with the Bench. Isaac Parker had been Royall Professor of Law during most of his years on the Massachusetts Supreme Court. And the greatest of them all in Massachusetts, Joseph Story, had taught sixteen years at the Harvard Law School while he was Associate Justice of the United States Supreme Court. But these men were dead; they belonged almost to legend. Oliver Wendell Holmes, Junior, was not only alive but radiating health, energy. His hair was dark and thick and shiny, his cavalry mustache swept magnificently outward. His very quietness gave the impression of a man lying in wait, ready, biding his time.

The other judges all knew Holmes's father, of course. Who did not know the Sage of Boston? Local newspapers no longer referred to "Dr. Holmes, the author." When they desired to quote him they simply wrote, "*as Dr. Holmes says.*" The doctor was as much part of the local scene as the State House itself, and had been there certainly longer than the statue of George Washington. But the comfortable conservatism of Dr. Holmes was no guarantee against the possible conduct of a son who did not resemble his father in a single feature. In its Declaration of Rights, the Massachusetts Constitution adjures its judges to be as "free, impartial and independent as the lot of humanity permits." The Justices Morton, Field, Allen, Colburn, and Devens were united in their interpretation of this freedom and this impartiality. It did not really occur to them that Justice Holmes would see another side of the question. Merely, they were uneasy, watchful.

Not long after Holmes took his seat on the Bench, he was the guest of honor at a public dinner. The Mayor was there, and seated next to him at the speakers' table, Dr. Holmes. The doctor was in particularly fine fettle; he laughed, joked, talked incessantly. On both sides of him, men leaned forward to catch what he was saying. Laughing, they repeated his words to their neighbors.

Mr. Justice Holmes, observing this tableau, moved a trifle apprehensively as the table was cleared, the cigars lighted, and men pushed back their chairs. From time to time he had caught his father looking at him, and there was no mistaking the gleam in that parental eye. Holmes had seen it too often. His father was going to make a speech — and this time the son feared he was to be the subject.

Mayor Palmer got up. "Dr. Oliver Wendell Holmes!" he said. "The father who went in search of a captain, and finding him presents now his son, the Judge!"

Dr. Holmes was on his feet, beaming. From his hand trailed a long, narrow slip of paper. The company applauded wholeheartedly. Adjusting his spectacles, Dr. Holmes threw an arch glance at his son. The company, catching it, applauded more heartily than ever. Clearing his throat, the doctor began: —

> His Honor's father yet remains
> His proud parental posture firm in,
> But, while his right he still maintains
> To wield the household rod and reins,
> He bows before the filial ermine.

The audience howled delightedly, its eye fixed now on the poet, now on the Judge. Wendell Holmes, smiling carefully, looked at the tablecloth.

> The mighty monarch whose renown
> Fills up the stately page historic,
> Has howled to waken half the town,
> And finished off by gulping down
> His castor oil or paregoric.

> The justice who, in gown and cap,
> Condemns a wretch to strangulation,
> Has scratched his nurse and spilled his pap,
> And sprawled across his mother's lap
> For wholesome law's administration.

The poem went on and on; it rang every bell, harped on every strain. If his father left out the war, he could forgive all this, Holmes thought. He could almost enjoy it . . . Amazing, how the old man could make a roomful of hardheaded businessmen respond to this kind of thing! That high old voice had all the turn and inflection of an actor's. But the Mayor's reference to that infernal *Hunt after the Captain* . . . his father would never be able to resist it . . .

> The fearless soldier who has faced —

Ah, here it was! Beneath the table, Wendell Holmes gripped his napkin in both fists . .

The serried bayonet's gleam appalling,
For nothing save a pin misplaced,
The peaceful nursery has disgraced
With hours of unheroic bawling.

Looking up, Holmes caught John Gray's eye fixed on him quizzically.

The whirligig of time goes round
And changes all things but affection . . .

The audience suddenly ceased smiling and looked gratifyingly sentimental.

. . . you did not come to weep,
Nor I my weakness to be showing;
And these gay stanzas, slight and cheap,
Have served their simple use — to keep
A father's heart from overflowing.

The high, soft old voice ceased. Dr. Holmes sat down. There were cheers, calls for a reply from the Judge.

Mr. Justice Oliver Wendell Holmes, Junior, rose slowly to his feet and faced the assemblage.

1883 . . . Chester Arthur was President. The Great Comet had come and gone, trailing down across the Boston sky. Women wore hats instead of bonnets, their dresses no longer swept the pavement but hovered a good inch above the dust. Ben Butler was defeated for a second term as Governor of Massachusetts. The *Transcript* deplored the evils of Butlerism. Harvard, when Butler had arrived in state for the Commencement exercises, frostily withheld the traditional degree.

In Tremont Temple, Henry George lectured on the Single Tax. The *Transcript* was relieved to note that at least five sixths of the audience consisted of Irish-American mechanics and laborers. The "better element" was not there. George's land scheme was a mere piece of impracticable folly. There was no doubt we were becoming overpopulated, which was all the more reason for not proposing crackpot remedies. The *Transcript* recalled that Goethe had said the masses were always childish.

Smoothly the *Transcript* disposed of Henry George, disposed also of the women who wrote begging for suffrage. It was pleasanter to give a whole double column to Tennyson's new ballad, *Launcelot and Guinevere*, and to the lady who wrote protesting the publication of "impure novels, translated from the French. We should believe that marriage has simply closed the doors upon such things." The *London Quarterly Review* had severe words for "the new school of American fiction headed by Howells and James." The *Transcript* reprinted the criticism, not yet sure of its own stand. To be genteel was safer than to be new, and raw, and suffering from growing pains.

1883 . . . America was still extremely new, roaring audibly with the pains of growth. Genteelism was a balm that scarcely penetrated the outermost skin. In Packingtown, 15,000 hogs slid squealing down the chutes each day, to emerge as lard in the nation's kettles and money in Philip Armour's pocket. Chicago worked and built and sweated above the reeking mud flats of its Lake. Detroit had 128,000 inhabitants, Chicago 500,000. San Francisco, full of color and wickedness, sprawled wantonly beside her turquoise Bay. In Pullman cars, crossing the continent, legislators flourished free passes for themselves and their friends. Two thousand passes to one lawmaker was good business for the railroad, bringing rich return in Congress for favors received. The National Labor Union was dead but the Knights of Labor, very much alive, got ready to fight the Gould railroad interests.

1883 . . . Holmes was a judge on the Bench. Badly, the Supreme Court needed men of vision. These were times of vast social change. With extraordinary rapidity, a pioneer economic individualism was giving way to the collectivism of corporate trade — and the transition was attended by groaning and travail. A country that in Holmes's youth had been rural in tone now rushed to build new cities. Jefferson's fears had come to pass. Men lived piled upon one another, struggling for survival under smoking factory chimneys of which Jefferson could not have dreamed. By 1883, the transition from a rural to an industrial economy was gathering momentum; in the '90s the ills attending it would be acute. Before Holmes went to Washington in 1902, he would see "business" swollen to a size threatening and dangerous, far too unwieldy for existing social machinery to cope with. Had Abiel Holmes been alive, once more he would have said the country was growing too fast for its heart.

But this time it was more than a change; it was a revolution. Holmes recognized it. He had studied the common law from its beginnings. He had studied the formation of great states and the causes of their dissolution. When the pattern of society changes, legislation meets the change — or the state perishes. In *The Common Law*, Holmes had said again and again that the best judge bears in mind public policy, the felt necessities of the time.

When Holmes came to the Bench, the burning issues of the day were labor's grievance against the employer, and the people's grievance against the corporations: two manifestations of the individual's battle for survival in a collectivist world. The battle was just beginning; it would rage all during Holmes's lifetime and beyond. And in court the fight hinged always around two clauses of the Constitution: the Commerce Clause and the Fourteenth Amendment that declared *"no State shall deprive any person of life, liberty or property without due process of law."* There was no way for the lawmakers of 1866 to foresee this, to foresee the emergence of a huge corporate ownership that would seek to construe "due process of law" to its own ends.

After the Civil War, America found a new symbol. Once she had looked to the Declaration of Independence. But the Declaration was a trifle vague — to a Massachusetts businessman, almost transcendental. By 1880, there was more than a suspicion that in spite of the hopes of the Fathers, political liberty would never result in economic equality. Men became less interested in being born free and equal, more interested in regulating commerce. If the Declaration had been a profession of faith, the Constitution was its working instrument, and America looked now to the Constitution.

The trouble was that the courts gave this working instrument no elasticity; they regarded it as immutable, written in stone on Sinai. Desperately, the people needed judges who possessed historical as well as judicial awareness, judges whose social prejudices were leveled by the long view of the scholar. Only such men, fearing neither socialism, capitalism, nor any other *ism*, could construe the Constitution according to the needs of the times.

Holmes was such a man. "A constitution is not intended to embody a particular economic theory," he said, "whether of paternalism . . . or of *laissez faire*. It is made for people of fundamentally differing views, and the accident of our finding certain opinions natural and familiar or novel and even shocking ought not to conclude our judgment upon the question whether statutes embodying them conflict with the Constitution of the United States. . . . Constitutional law, like other mortal contrivances, has to take some chances. . . . *The Constitution is an experiment, as all life is an experiment.*"

CHAPTER TWENTY-EIGHT

Judge in Massachusetts.

A DEBUT," Disraeli said, "should be dull." In the case of a Justice of the Supreme Court, not to be dull would be a disaster; from its judges the public desires no slightest theatrical effect, but only the effect of deepest sanity. It would be ten years before Holmes gave voice to the first of the opinions — and dissents — that were to make him famous.

That first summer of the judgeship, Wendell and Fanny Holmes left the second-floor rooms next to the Athenaeum where they had lived for so long, and took a house between Beacon Street and the river. Nine, Chestnut Street, the address was. It was a pleasant neighborhood of wide white doorways, brass knockers, brick steps with iron rails on which the brass knobs shone cheerfully. In spring, horse-chestnut trees along the curb hung white with blossoms; in summer the street drowsed in the shade, undisturbed by traffic.

Fanny loved the house. There was room at last for all her things — old silver, furniture she had acquired in ten years of married life and had had to store away at her father's house in Cambridge or at the Holmeses'. Fanny knew by now that she was to be childless forever. She did not mourn, or if she did, it was not her nature to show it. From Beacon Street she brought her two caged finches, talkative small brown birds that she addressed always by name. One day she brought home two nightingales, then a mockingbird. Every morning after breakfast she fed them, cleaned their cages, talked to them, scolding, applauding imaginary feats of generosity or acrobatics. Wendell loved to watch her. "Aren't you going to court?" Fanny would ask. "What are you waiting for, Wendell? Aren't you ever going about your business so that I can go about mine?"

"I am waiting for you," Holmes would reply. "Fanny, isn't it time for you to feed your birds?"

Holmes's salary was $6000 a year, with $500 over for traveling expenses. Fanny was able to engage a cook, a housemaid for upstairs. The cook was an Irishwoman, newly arrived, ignorant of such things as oysters browned in the pan, baked mackerel with savory stuffing, blueberry muffins, hot deep crab-apple pie with the crust all flaky round the dish edge. Instead of the gas ring for breakfast, the Parker House for supper, the Holmeses lived well. Fanny hung the parlor windows with red damask, bought a white fur rug for their bedroom. The house was bright, filled with color and sunshine.

They were about ten blocks from Dr. Holmes. Mrs. Holmes had begun to show her years; her gentleness had taken on a quality of helplessness. She stayed much in her room. Fanny went often to see her; they talked about Wendell, about how he looked sitting in court in his black frock coat and gray trousers, at the far left end of the Bench with the six other judges. Mrs. Holmes remembered the time he had gone up from Shattuck's office to argue a case in the Massachusetts Supreme Court. Instead of the conventional black, Wendell had worn a new gray cutaway coat he very much fancied. Judge Horace Gray had rebuked him.[1] It was rather a pity, Mrs. Holmes added, that the judges did not wear robes.

Holmes went to see his mother when he could, went also to call on his brother Ned, who was terribly crippled now with asthma. His heart was affected; he walked slowly up the stairs, breathing hard, his hand on the banister. Watching him, Wendell felt his own heart contract. Ned was only thirty-seven. So much brilliance and promise, so much sensitiveness, thrown away before it had had its chance. . . .

In the summer of 1884, Ned died. Holmes missed him greatly. Looking around him, now in his forties, Holmes noticed the absence of long-familiar faces. His friends had by no means begun to die of old age as yet. But things seemed to happen to them, now that the first vigorous thrust of youth was gone. People failed, dropped out of sight.

There were, fortunately, some hardy souls who looked as if they would go on forever. Uncle John Holmes, lame, stout, kindly, greatly beloved, lived on in Cambridge with his old housekeeper. Holmes saw him seldom, but the knowledge that he was there was somehow comforting. As for Dr. Holmes, at seventy-five he did not seem a day older than he had at fifty-five. He had taken to wearing brown suits with a plaid bow tie, bright Scotch colors, scarlet and green. Thirty-five years of a black coat every morning to lecture at the Medical School was black enough for one man, he said. Since his retirement from Harvard he had a running contract with the *Atlantic* which he described as very lucrative. He had lately got out a new volume of poems; he was writing a memoir of Emerson, book-length, to appear next year. His love of flattery had by no means diminished. "You know I am a trifle deaf," he would say quickly when someone praised his latest work. "Won't you please repeat that a little louder?"

Judge Holmes was too busy to go often to his father's. But when he did go, when the high dark rooms of the brownstone house received him, his wife noted the same metamorphosis that had taken place of old. Inside those rooms, crowded with lamps, bric-a-brac, all the mementoes of a long, busy life, Holmes became silent once more, watchful, ironic, restless. Observing this, Fanny marveled. Forty-odd, and a Judge of the Supreme Court! Did a son never grow up, in the presence of such a father, never attain the stature of a man?

Elsewhere, Wendell Holmes was most certainly a man — confident, mature, fulfilled. The work at court was hard and exacting; at intervals, Holmes confessed as much to Pollock. "I have been on the stretch all the time . . . I have scarcely set eyes on a soul outside the bar . . . I am a recluse . . . Some of the older judges affirm that no one can do all the work without breaking down."

The cases that came in were by no means all "big cases." An enormous amount of the work was routine. Besides the cases in the big courtroom with the other judges, besides the meetings round the table in the judges' consultation room where the Chief Justice assigned opinions to be written, Holmes held equity court by himself downstairs, handled probate jury cases, divorces, contests over wills. For a short while, before they were taken out of the Supreme Court, Holmes even handled murder cases. From time to time he went off to hold equity court all over the state — in Dedham, Springfield,

New Bedford, and as far away as Pittsfield. Sometimes he got home for Sundays, often he was away a fortnight or longer.

But he loved the work, every minute of it. The dull spots were not dull to him. His cousin John Morse observed that Wendell Holmes read the Year Books as other men read dime novels, avidly and with relish. Holmes himself said that to a judge, accretion comes slowly; a man has to be very old before he can have covered the field. Like the oyster, the judge cannot reach out and draw in the morsels he desires; he can only wait, hoping each day, each week, each month, that an interesting case will be presented.

The Democrats were getting ready to nominate Cleveland for President; the Republicans had already decided on James G. Blaine, the Plumed Knight from Maine. A sad choice for respectable Republicans — between an honest Democrat and a Knight whose plumes were by now sadly bedraggled. Cleveland's election would perhaps put an end to the spoils system. But he would be the first Democratic President since Buchanan; even the reform Republicans doubted the worth of such a sacrifice. Cabot Lodge was in the thick of it. After nine years as a student at Harvard he had — Holmes wrote Pollock — thrown over the early law and was chairman of the state Republican Committee, with a large share of credit for having beaten Ben Butler for governor and put Robinson in his place.

Holmes saw Lodge often; the younger man tried hard to draw him into the political arena. But as always, Holmes was more interested in law than politics, more interested in ideals than in the mechanics of practical reform. When he did mount a platform, what he said concerned larger, vaguer issues than elections and the character of candidates.

On Memorial Day of 1884, Holmes went up to the village of Keene, New Hampshire, to make a speech. Dr. Holmes did not want him to go, and said so. The Lowell Lectures on the Common Law had by no means changed the doctor's opinion concerning his son as a public orator. Now that Wendell was a judge, he would probably be asked to make speeches all over the state; he had better be warned and confine his orations to court. Wendell's mother did not agree. She drew her son aside, laid a light, dry old hand on his arm. "Do it, Wendell!" she whispered. "Go to Keene and talk about the war. Tell what it meant to you. Tell the young people what it can mean even to those that were born too late to be part of it."

Wendell was touched. There was a transparency now to his mother's face and figure, a look of fragility and evanescence. Mrs. Holmes was preparing for her departure; her son sensed it. It gave her, gentle though she was, a quality oracular, prophetic. . . .

The afternoon of Decoration Day, 1884, was sunny, not too warm. A breeze moved through the elms that lined Keene Common. In the center of the green patch between square white clapboard houses, the soldier's monument was garlanded with evergreens and flowers, roses, iris and columbine. Fanny drove into Keene with her husband. The Common and the four roads leading to it were bright with people in holiday clothes, men in the federal blue, boys carrying flags, women and children from all over the county. Inside the crowded hall, Judge Holmes mounted the platform; the band played what the *New Hampshire Sentinel* afterward described as a dirge, there was a vocal quartet, and Judge — once Captain — Holmes got to his feet: —

"Not long ago I heard a young man ask why people still kept up Memorial Day, and it set me thinking of the answer. . . ."

The answer Captain Holmes gave was simple and brief. He remembered his friends who had died in battle — Dehon and Putnam, Henry Abbott, Dr. Revere, spoke of them, told of bravery and comradeship. *"Through our great good fortune, in our youth our hearts were touched with fire. It was given us to learn at the outset that life is a profound and passionate thing. While we are permitted to scorn nothing but indifference, and do not pretend to undervalue the worldly rewards of ambition, we have seen with our own eyes, beyond and above the gold fields, the snowy heights of honor, and it is for us to bear the report to those who come after us. . . ."*

At home, Wendell said little of the event, which after all had been small and local and by no means world-shaking. But he gave his mother a report that pleased her. Holmes had reason to be suspicious of speechmaking, whether of the pompous variety or the merely arch; he met it with irony, a sharp and biting sarcasm. But Dr. Holmes had spoken truly when he said his son would be called upon often to speak in public. During the '80s, Holmes's utterances out of court made up for the suitable dullness of his debut on the Bench. Before the Suffolk Bar Association he talked on "The Law," talked to Harvard undergraduates on "The Profession of the Law." At the 250th anniversary of his Grandfather Abiel's church in Cambridge he talked on "The Puritan." It was good, he said, that the Puritan still lived in New England, good that this cold passion, surviving many doctrines, still lighted its flame in men who possessed more grace, but less fertility, less tenacity than their forebears.

Holmes liked to speak of these things about which he felt so deeply. He knew he did it well. He took great pains with his talks that sounded, on delivery, so spontaneous, rehearsing them to Fanny, asking her opinion. One evening, young Arthur Hill, the lawyer, and his wife stopped in to call, interrupting a rehearsal. At their insistence, Holmes kept on. What he said was so solemn, so real, and the manner of his delivery so impressive, that both the Hills were on the verge of tears.

Suddenly, Holmes broke off, turned to his wife. "Well, Fanny!" he said briskly. "How about it? Too much *tremolo?*"

In June of 1886, Yale University gave Holmes an honorary degree. It was something his Alma Mater had not seen fit to do. With Eliot it still rankled that one of his professors had chosen to quit after three months of teaching, walking out to a job he liked better. That Holmes had been within his rights and also within the terms of his contract made the taste of it no sweeter.

Holmes was pleased with the Yale degree. He believed in education quite simply and passionately; it was something upon which he never turned the shafts of his irony. Standing on the platform, parchment in hand, the Yale colors over his shoulders, he spoke to old President Porter: "I accept it proudly as an accolade," he said. "Like the little blow upon the shoulder from the sword of a master of war which in ancient days adjudged that a soldier had won his spurs and pledged his life to decline no combat in the future."

And on the very same day that Oliver Wendell Holmes, Junior, became a Doctor of Laws, over in England his father received a like honor from Oxford. Cambridge too had invited the Autocrat to cross the ocean and receive her colors. It was a double honor that came seldom to one man. Over the water sped Dr. Holmes; his daughter Amelia with him. The doctor had a wonderful time. Wrapped in his plaid shawl he watched Ormonde win the Derby as fifty years ago he had watched Plenipotentiary win. (He still considered himself a judge of horseflesh.) In London he dined out until he talked himself into a bout of asthma. His old friend the Reverend Dr. Haweis gave him an inhaling tube that looked, said the doctor, like Gabriel's trump. "You had better let me tell the Fido story tonight," Amelia said, nothing loath at the prospect.

Her father's reply was quick. "Amelia," he said, "in Boston you enjoy the reputation of being the only person who can out-talk Phillips Brooks. But the time has not arrived when you can out-talk *me*. And besides," he added, gasping, grinning at his daughter like a small, aged ape, "Fido is one of my major successes. Not even you, my dear, could do the story justice."

On the platform at Oxford the doctor looked, the English papers reported, like a small, gray-headed boy. The scarlet gown, the pink hood, engulfed him. Waiting in the gallery, the students were noisy; the Latin orations seemed interminable. "Did he come in his One-Hoss Shay?" they shouted. "Watch your Latin there, Orator! The Autocrat will catch you up!"

At last the orator turned to the little figure muffled in its scarlet: — "*Et tu, qui trans aequor Atlanticum . . .*"

The boys caught the last word; the rafters rang with cheers. Down among the audience, Amelia sat, her bright, kind, silly face upturned. Tears of happiness ran down her cheeks.

Fanny Holmes was touched too, when the travelers returned and she heard the tale in full. Even so, she could not resist a feeling of satisfaction that Wendell also had received a degree that day. Father and son were running neck and neck now. It was a race unrecognized, but to Fanny Holmes, at least, it was a race more significant than any run at Epsom Downs.

But there was sadness also in the travelers' return. They came to Beverly in July, to Dr. Holmes's small brown summer cottage under the jasmine-covered cliff. "*Beverly-by-the-Dépot*," the doctor called it, making fun of his fashionable North Shore neighbors who had their summer writing paper stamped "*Manchester-by-the-Sea*." But they found Mrs. Holmes ill, her mind affected. When the summer was over and the family moved back to town, she did not improve. It became patent she was not going to improve. She did not leave her pleasant bedroom overlooking the river, but moved about all day from bed to sofa, tranquil, contented, her white hair soft about her face. Neddy had been in to see her today, she would tell Wendell in the evening. How pleasant it had been to see him! And her

father, Judge Jackson (dead thirty years), had been in too. . . .
Dr. Holmes was deeply distressed. He went restlessly about the
house, searching he knew not what. Impossible that his wife was
not there — in the dining room, the library, coming up from the
basement kitchen or hurrying along the hall, keys at her belt. *"Don't
stop now, dear, to tell me your news. Go and get ready for tea."*
Everyone else in the world — his sons and daughter, his brother
John, his friends — had been an audience to charm, a challenge to con-
versational powers. But his wife Amelia — Amelia had been part of
himself, the kind part, the warm part, the part that for nearly fifty
years had kept him in touch with all in life that was not merely
literary. Not that she refused to listen to him; Amelia had always
and forever listened readily, quietly. Sometimes, as she sat sewing
in their bedroom, the doctor had suspected she did not even hear
what he said. But it had not mattered. She was there, present as a
man's own spirit is present to judge and to balance.

Walking now to his wife's bedroom in the late afternoon, Oliver Holmes felt his step quicken as it had quickened of old; words
accumulated, sprang to his lips. But at the threshold he had to check
himself, silence those words. It was an act of deepest disappointment,
deepest grief. He came in softly, laid a hand on his wife's hair, on
her shoulder, thin now under the white Cashmere shawl. . . .

For two winters, Mrs. Holmes lingered. In February of 1888,
she died, making her departure painlessly — "with that sweet smile
on her face," the doctor wrote a friend, "which the parting soul
sometimes leaves on the features. To the few who looked upon it,
it was like a celestial vision."

This time, Dr. Oliver Wendell Holmes was not being literary.
He had lost the thing he loved most. He was seventy-eight. Besides
his son, of his immediate family only his brother John remained.
Nearly all his friends were gone: Longfellow, Emerson, Motley,
Sam Howe, Theodore Parker, Agassiz, Asa Gray, Charles Sumner.
In the next few years the rest would go: Whittier, Bancroft, Low-
ell. Six years of life remained to Dr. Holmes.

Wendell and Fanny, looking upon the doctor, then upon the big
empty house, were more than thankful for Amelia Sargent. But for
Amelia, they would have to give up their house on Chestnut Street,
move in with the doctor. Amelia, widowed now, announced her intention of selling her house and coming home to live. She arrived

and the doctor began, miraculously, to rally. Brisk, cheerful, Amelia bustled about, busy with painters and paperhangers, doing over the house. Her taste was rich; it ran to gold appliquéd wallpaper — the newest thing, and regarded as very handsome. The house was soon gorgeous with gilt scrolls against a sepia background. Amelia put fresh lampshades in the living room — rose silk, richly fringed, a fringed cover on the sofa by the fire. She had the dark furniture polished until it shone.

Barely a year later, Amelia fell suddenly ill. Watching by the bedside, Fanny Holmes took charge, ran the house. One thought was uppermost. If Amelia went, the doctor could not be left to die slowly and alone. Not that the doctor looked like dying. In the past year he had recovered both health and spirits, went sometimes to his club, took his daily walks around the Common.

In April of 1889, Amelia died. Fanny did not hesitate. Wendell was much pressed with work; he was due in Springfield next week. "I will tend to the moving," Fanny told him promptly. "You can forget all of it. When you get in from Springfield, just take a cab from the station to your father's house."

That was all. Wendell looked at his wife gratefully, looked at her also with a measure of awe and puzzlement in his face. Was it a quality of womanhood, or was it a quality peculiar to Fanny — this ability to meet life bravely, without complaint, making great sacrifice into a small thing, pretending that a disappointment deep and bitter was a mere matter of annoyance, of securing a moving van, of danger to china and furniture? The way Fanny talked, one would have thought she did not really mind going back to 296 Beacon Street. But Wendell knew — and Fanny knew he knew — that this move was one of the bitterest things life had ever held out to her.

It was bitter also to Wendell Holmes. But he was very busy, his life more outside of home than in it. It would not be he who spent hours on end in that dark house with the old man. Wendell knew it. Fanny was a woman to whom *home* meant everything. In the past six years on Chestnut Street she had been happier than Wendell had ever seen her.

Yet there was nothing to say. In matters of duty they both belonged to a generation and a group that neither hesitated nor questioned. Wendell packed his bag to leave the city. He went slowly downstairs, Fanny behind him. At the door he paused. "Fanny!" he said. His voice was deep, troubled out of all proportion to his words. "Fanny — you will take your birds with you, of course? And your needlepoint pictures. The one of the apple orchard will look very fine, hanging at the head of the stairs . . ."

Fanny looked up. "Why yes, Wendell," she said. "The head of the stairs! That is just the place for the apple orchard. I was wondering where there was a bare space that would hold it."

CHAPTER TWENTY-NINE

*Judge Holmes dissents from his
brethren. Farewell to the doctor.*

Dr. Holmes to his old friend, Elizabeth Phelps Ward

BOSTON, *April* 13, 1889

. . . the loss of my daughter is a heavy blow and a great *disappointment* . . . I am not left alone. My daughter-in-law, a very helpful, hopeful, powerful as well as brilliant woman, is with me, and my household goes on smoothly, and not without a cheerful aspect. Her husband the Judge will soon be established in the house, and I trust we shall live as happily as we ought to, if my large allowance of years should be a little farther extended. Pray come and see me, and bring Mr. Ward with you, the next time you are in town. We shall, both Mrs. Holmes and myself, — for the Judge is a good deal away from home, — be most happy to see you.

That summer, the Judge went to England as scheduled. Fanny insisted that he go. He must not sacrifice his English connections to domestic sympathies, she said. What he learned in England, the people he met there, fed him through the Boston winters. Fanny took her father-in-law down to Beverly on the North Shore, to the little house against the cliff where he had spent so many summers.

In August, Dr. Holmes had his eightieth birthday. The schoolchildren of Beverly, dressed in white and carrying sprays of flowers, trooped up to the front porch. "We wish you a happy birthday, Dr. Holmes!" they said. From all over the world, telegrams poured in. Eleven ladies of Boston brought a huge silver loving cup, engraved with their names and a poem.

Instantly, the doctor was ready with a return poem, in eight verses: —

Count thou their number on the beads of Heaven:
Alas! the clustered Pleiads are but seven;
Nay, the nine sister Muses are too few, —
The Graces must add two.

The eleven ladies were enchanted.

A few days later, Fanny took the household back to Beacon Street. . . . "I am living here with my daughter-in-law," Dr. Holmes wrote to Whittier. "Just as I turned this leaf I heard wheels at the door, and she got out, leading in triumph her husband, His Honor, Judge Holmes of the Supreme Court of Massachusetts, just arrived from Europe by the *Scythia*. I look up to him as my magistrate, and he knows me as his father, but my arms are around his neck and his moustache is sweeping my cheek, — I feel young again at fourscore."

But how old his father looked, Wendell Holmes thought with a shock, following him to the dining room. The thick hair was snow white. The tiny figure was still erect and walked as rapidly as ever. But it swayed a little, putting out a hand to the wall for support. The face was lined with wrinkles, crisscrossed, stamped like a very map of life with the emotions, the blows and triumphs of eighty years.

Dr. Holmes looked up from his soup, caught his son's eye upon him. "I'm getting old, Wendell," he said, "I'm beginning to dissolve. It's what happens to the aged. The time will come when you will hold me up to the light and see the light through me." He smiled. "But I shan't know it," he added cheerfully.

Watching her husband, Fanny saw his face change and darken. For how many years Wendell had looked upon this man as his enemy! Now the battle was taken out of Wendell's hands. Now time itself, now fate and the forces of life were granting him a final victory. Yet here was no victory at all, but only — Fanny sensed it was a prescience that was gone as quickly as it came — only once more the same inevitable defeat. . . .

Fanny was glad that her husband was busy, away much from

home. This house was bad for him. If he needed humility — and sometimes it was borne in upon Fanny that her husband did need humility — it was not the brand of humility to be found here at home. There was a hardness to Wendell, now in his middle years, something within that made him slough off, when he could, the immediate troubles of others. Perhaps, Fanny thought, it was not hardness but a kind of invincible health, a physical and nervous drive that made such a man impatient of the delay of sorrow, old age, illness. What had William James said, that summer long ago at Mattapoisett, as he stood watching Wendell dig the garden in his shirt sleeves? "Wendell is a powerful plane, gouging his own deep, tidy groove through life. . . ."

Fanny had laughed, told James not to be so free with his metaphors. Besides, he was talking nonsense, she said. But she had not forgotten. The words came back to her now, observing Wendell, noting his growing preoccupation with everything, professional and social, that took him from home. In the afternoons when court closed he no longer hurried back but came slowly down Beacon Street, stopping by the way, arriving home at six or later. "Will you have tea?" Fanny asked him. "No," Wendell would reply. "I stopped in for tea with Miss Crosby." Or with Mrs. Codman or Mrs. Whitman.

Professionally, he was especially busy just now. In 1890, Chief Justice Morton resigned. Walbridge Field took his place. And no sooner did Field become Chief Justice than he entered upon a long illness. The fact that Holmes wrote his opinions with extraordinary quickness made it natural for him to be assigned a large share of work; the judges had long ago discovered that this quickness did not mean any carelessness or overlooking of points. Holmes had always possessed a talent for seeing to the heart of an intellectual situation; his long training in the historical phases of the law enhanced this ability, now that it was turned to practical legal problems. Lawyers were allowed two hours for oral argument. After the English fashion, Holmes liked to decide from the oral argument, not wait for the brief. He went at it zestfully, as a man goes after game. The moment the lawyer started to speak, Holmes leaned forward, listening raptly, making penciled notes. Sometimes, five minutes were not gone when he threw himself back, closed his eyes. "Holmes has made up his mind," the other judges told themselves. "Counsel hasn't stated the point yet — but Holmes has somehow got it."

Justice Holmes about 1890

Holmes's opinions, when he handed them in, did not read like other judicial opinions. They were pithy, filled with — strange juxtaposition! — both learning and common sense . . . *"If it is a bad rule, that is no reason for making a bad exception to it."* . . . *"A horse car cannot be handled like a rapier."* . . . *"A boy who is dull at fifteen probably was dull at fourteen."* . . . *"Civil proceedings in court are not scientific investigations the end of which always must be objective truth."* . . . *"The mind like any other organism gradually shapes itself to what surrounds it, and resents disturbance in the form which its life has assumed."*

Now and then Holmes lapsed ever so little into the professor. The other judges did not mind; they liked it. "It is only tautologous to say that the law knows nothing of moral rights unless they are legal rights, and from before the days of Hobbes the argument has been public property that there is no such thing as a right created by law, as against the sovereign who makes the law by which the right is created."

That was said in 1888. Only very seldom did the philosopher peer out from behind Holmes's briefs — but when it came, it came with a flash: *"All values are anticipations of the future."*

This was straight pragmatism — and brand-new. None of the other judges could have conceived it, and they were aware of this. To have such a mind on the Bench was highly stimulating, whether or no you agreed with its premises. "Holmes is like rum to the other judges," a lawyer said, and the phrase went round.

Old Justice Morton was dead. Justice Devens died in '91, then Justice William Allen. But even with three new appointments, Holmes, at fifty, was still the youngest man on the Bench. In seven years, he had dissented only twice from his brethren. Now, in 1891, a labor case came up that impelled him to utter the first of the dissenting opinions that were to mark him — to his rather ironic amusement — as a friend of labor.

An employer was indicted for withholding part of an employee's wages. A Massachusetts statute made it unlawful to "impose or exact a fine" or withhold part of the wages of a worker for imperfect work. The Court declared this statute unconstitutional, on the grounds that it violated fundamental rights by impairing the obligation of contracts.

Holmes dissented. He did not want to; then as later he disliked the position of dissenting judge. *"I have the misfortune to disagree* with my brethren," he wrote. *"I have submitted my views to them at length, and, considering the importance of the question, feel bound to make public a brief statement, notwithstanding the respect and deference I feel for the judgment of those with whom I disagree. . . .*

"I do not see that [the statute] interferes with the right of acquiring, possessing, and protecting property any more than the laws against usury or gaming. . . ."

The statement itself was clothed of course in legal formality. The public read it in the *Daily Advertiser* in the columns allotted to the court records — Massachusetts judges had given up oral delivery years ago. Holmes's statement reached the laboring men whom it affected, reached also those employers whose interests would have been injured had it not been a minority report. But even these might have forgotten the case had it not been followed by others of equal importance.

A year later, the Massachusetts House of Representatives asked the Justices' opinion as to the constitutionality of a proposed bill to enable cities and towns to purchase, sell, and distribute coal and wood as fuel. Field, Allen, Knowlton, Morton, and Lathrop said no, that cities could not sell these articles.

Holmes disagreed. If the government could support paupers and take land for railroads, why, he asked, couldn't it sell coal, wood, water, gas, electricity? *"I see no ground for denying the power of the Legislature to enact the laws mentioned in the questions proposed. The need or expediency of such legislation is not for us to consider."*

So wrote Oliver Wendell Holmes, Junior. And from State Street, Beacon Street, and Louisburg Square a roar went up. . . . "I have found myself separated from my brethren on some important constitutional questions . . ." Holmes wrote to Pollock. ". . . And among the respectable there are some who regard me as a dangerous radical! If I had seen fit to clothe my views in different language I dare say I could have been a pet of the proletariat — whereas they care nothing for me and some of the others distrust me."

Fanny Holmes was enormously entertained by this suspicion of her husband in respectable quarters. She knew well enough that he would never lift a finger to disabuse it. Even some of the family had joined the ranks of the disapproving. One evening in the library, Wendell, smoking his after-dinner cigar, saw his wife smile as she bent over her sewing. "Mary Wigglesworth stopped in today," she said. There was a veiled quality in her voice that always preceded any particularly spicy news. "George says that if you keep on this way, Wendell, with your extraordinary championship of the mill operatives, he would prefer to have his boys, as they grow older, kept away from 296 Beacon Street."

Dr. Holmes, dozing in his chair by the fire, looked up when he heard laughter, and asked what the joke was. The doctor's deafness came on with especial virulence whenever legal subjects were brought up; he was still frankly bored with the law. Wendell shook his head. "George Wigglesworth thinks I'm an anarchist," he told his father. "I think I can endure the charge. . . . Father — I stopped in at the Corner Bookstore today. *Over the Teacups* is still selling fast."

"Twenty thousand in three months!" Dr. Holmes said, sitting bolt upright, his eyes once more as bright as buttons. "My latest book, Wendell — and my last." He paused. "Although," he added, "if what Eliot said the other night at the Club is true, I really ought not to call myself too old to begin another series of papers."

There was a brief silence. Fanny looked up from her needlework. "What did President Eliot say?" she asked softly.

Wendell glanced at his wife in wonder. How many times, how many scores and hundreds of times in the past twenty years had she stepped into this same breach? There was a fund of good will in the woman, a fund of warmth and generosity that never ran out, was never exhausted.

But if the doctor's ears were failing him, there was nothing whatever the matter as yet with his brain. He should be in the twilight of dementia, he said — but if he was he had not found it out. What he minded most was the loss of his old friends. It was not easy to make new ones. Changing one's whole suit of friends left moments, he said, when a man felt naked, and shivered. What helped most was routine, and the doctor kept up a valiant daily routine, rising early in the morning, spending the forenoon answering letters, tending to his affairs. Before lunch he took his walk down Beacon Street and around the Common, his back as straight as ever, his white hair bristling from under the brim of his silk hat.

"I go to the Symphony Rehearsals," he wrote Mrs. Kellogg, "and to a five o'clock tea once in a while. . . . My two young people go to the theatre together, and I am glad to have them amuse themselves; but I rarely accompany them. Once in a while we all dine at some public table — Young's or Parker's — just for the fun of it and by way of change. Mrs. Judge knows how to make me comfortable, and does it wonderfully well. But I grow lazy, as I ought to. . . . Goodby, dear Mrs. Kellogg, brightest of your sex. . . ."

Mrs. Carolyn Kellogg, brightest of her sex, was herself well along toward eighty. The only people left who were actually older than Dr. Holmes were, he said, Fanny's father Mr. Dixwell, and Dr. William Furness in Philadelphia who had been graduated from Harvard in 1820. "I feel like my own survivor," the doctor wrote Howells.

Every Sunday Dr. Holmes managed to get down to King's Chapel for morning service. "They say I fell asleep this morning in church," he told a visitor one Sunday afternoon. "Possibly, possibly. But when I woke up, the minister was preaching very well."

In the summer of 1894, Dr. Holmes failed visibly. Something within him seemed to break and crumble, as it does with the aged. He had had a long bout of grippe; he was up and about now, and took his customary walk at noontime. But people, seeing him on Beacon Street, shook their heads. The doctor is about ready to go, they said. And perhaps because he was accepted as a public character, they said so quite bluntly to the doctor himself. After all, he knew he was famous; weren't his books read, his stories repeated, all over the continent of Europe?

Callers came daily, some of them complete strangers. Fanny never kept these admirers from her father-in-law, but let him expend himself upon them as a young man would be permitted to expend himself. One afternoon a lady caller, observing the Autocrat as he sat, benevolent and distinguished in his chair by the fire, clasped her hands and exclaimed ecstatically: —

"How superb your death notices will be!"

This was too much even for Dr. Holmes. "Have you heard," he asked the lady blandly, "of Madame and her husband in the Siege of Paris? Everyone was starving. Madame had a pet lapdog; shall we call him Fido? Finally, in desperation, she had him cooked and served, nicely garnished. Madame and her husband picked the platter clean, wiped up the gravy with their fingers for lack of bread. Madame looked at the remains and sighed.

" 'How Fido would have enjoyed those bones!' she said."

The visitor, with a sharp intake of the breath, rose hastily and left.

Wendell and Fanny Holmes watched the frail old figure day by day, tried not to help him rise when he struggled from his chair. How thick his hair was, and how bright his eye! But obviously, it was very hard for him to see, and when he sat down at the desk, his hand knotted and he could not write. On a table by the fire the pearly nautilus shell sat, gleaming with iridescent color: —

> *Build thee more stately mansions, O my soul,*
> *As the swift seasons roll!*

Abraham Lincoln had known those verses by heart. How apposite they seemed now — Fanny thought. And those other verses she had heard him quote so often: —

> *And if I should live to be*
> *The last leaf upon the tree*
> *In the spring,*
> *Let them smile, as I do now,*
> *At the old forsaken bough*
> *Where I cling.*

Did his father know, Wendell Holmes wondered, that the end was near? Surely, his medical knowledge must tell him daily, hourly, the meaning of this film before his eyes, this helplessness when the pen dropped from his fingers. On these October afternoons his father sat in his chair, gazing into the fire, his tiny wrinkled hands crossed on his knee. Outside, autumn winds ruffled the bright waters of the river; along the street, leaves scurried, golden, wine-red, driven early from the trees. "An old man ought to be sad," Wendell had written three years ago, when he himself was fifty. "I don't know whether I shall be when the wind is west and the sky clear."

"Wendell," his father said one day, suddenly, sitting thus by the fire in the October dusk. "What is it for me, King's Chapel?"

Fanny Holmes, sewing by the table, looked up.

"Wendell, what is it, I said. King's Chapel?"

"Yes, Father."

"All right then, I am satisfied. That is all I am going to say about it."

The days moved swiftly. Fanny, reading to her father-in-law at teatime, rose to draw the curtains and saw across the river, beyond the spires of Cambridge, beyond Mount Auburn and the northern range of hills, the sky alight with the colors of the setting sun. How Dr. Holmes loved that view! "I seem to look out on all creation," he had said. Could there be, for this man, a heaven that did not contain Bunker Hill and Boston Common, the State House and Harvard Yard?

Fanny moved back to her place by the lamp. Wendell came in, and the three talked quietly of the day's events. The white head sank a little lower. "Father is going to sleep," Wendell Holmes thought, and saw his wife get up and move swiftly to the old man's side. Wendell got up himself. Leaning over the chair the two waited, motionless.

The frail shoulders moved with an even breathing. The white head sank a little lower. Wendell Holmes, putting out his hand, knew suddenly that the shoulders had ceased to move.

It was extraordinary that among all the notices, the telegrams, letters, eulogies, the kindest came from England. Boston was so used to the doctor's verses and his jokes and his articles in the *Atlantic* that the city could not seem to realize that he was gone. The doctor had been so *cheerful*, Boston said, so good to meet on the paths across the Public Garden. He had had real gayety of heart.

But it was London *Punch* that struck, somehow, the notes nearest to the doctor's own chord. The nine verses dedicated "To the Autocrat" might have been written by the Autocrat himself: —

"The Last Leaf!" Can it be true,
We have turned it, and on *you*,
　　Friend of all?
Was there ever one who took
From its shelf, by chance, a book
　　Penned by you,
But was fast your friend for life,
With *one* refuge from its strife
　　Safe and true?

CHAPTER THIRTY

Fanny Holmes and her husband.
Vegelahn *v.* Guntner. *Theodore*
Roosevelt enters the scene, and the
old century is ended.

FANNY and Wendell Holmes did not leave 296 Beacon Street. No decision was made; they simply stayed on, settling the doctor's affairs, tending to the mail that poured in. Oliver Wendell Holmes, Junior, was Junior no longer. If Boston still thought of him as the son of his father, he knew himself now as Judge Holmes, the head of his house.

Here in Beacon Street, it was true, his father's presence was everywhere. In the library the *Spy* cartoon hung on the wall — Dr. Holmes in frock coat, smiling, the long upper lip and bushy eyebrows prominent in silhouette. The pearly nautilus shell lay on the mantel, beneath the oak-trimmed mirror. *Fides Invicta Triumphat,* said the wooden plaque over the fireplace. *Per Ampliora ad Altiora,* said the doctor's bookplate, staring up from the rows of first editions that lay on the long shelves around the room: Thackeray, Longfellow, Motley, Emerson, Lowell — Dr. Holmes had known all these men, they had called him friend.

And yet somehow these things were oppressive no longer. Holmes was in his father's house from choice now, not compulsion. The very presence of all these mementoes, these reminders of the Autocrat, now gave his son a sense of freedom. For the past five years since Amelia's death, Holmes had gone to absurd lengths, in this house, to avoid his father. When he went out he used the back stairs; if he went down the front way his father caught him always on the landing outside the library: *"Wendy, where are you going?"*

In that first year after the doctor's death, Wendell and Fanny were at home, of necessity, most of the time. There was a long period of mourning; Fanny wore black for her father-in-law. She was far more conscious of the house than Wendell seemed to be; with amusement she watched him settling into it, watched him gradually assume the privileges of the manor. Things he had not dared to touch he began now to use as his own. Grandfather Jackson's high desk stood in a corner of the library. Wendell had always been proud of Judge Jackson, pleased when in court he had to refer to his rulings. Now he stood at the desk to write his opinions. "Doesn't it tire you?" Fanny asked, watching him write, one knee propped against the desk. "Yes," Wendell replied. "But it's salutary. Nothing conduces to brevity like a caving in of the knees."

Downstairs, the portrait of Grandfather Abiel smiled over the balustrade, young, handsome with flowing locks and broad shoulders under the clergyman's white bib. Fanny, going down to feed her birds, looked up at him often. He was as handsome as Wendell; when he passed along Cambridge streets, the girls had turned their heads . . . "There goes Mr. Holmes."

In a little room across the hall from the portrait, Fanny kept her birds and all her china animals, the frogs and ducks and kittens she had collected, brought home, named and endowed with vivid and extravagant personalities. Now she made it her own room, papered it with a bright figured blue, had the woodwork painted white, a gay flowered rug on the floor beside the little marble fireplace. When her friends came she received them there.

It seemed a little odd to Fanny that no one, not even Wendell, asked if she minded living on here at 296 Beacon Street. No one, that is, but John Holmes. Uncle John had always been quick to understand Fanny's feelings. Long, long ago, before Wendell proposed to her, when she had been terribly in love, terribly afraid she would not see Wendell any more, now that he was through with the Law School and lived in Boston — it had been John Holmes who came to the rescue. He had had his carriage stopped — on how many Sunday afternoons! — at Garden Street, called Fanny downstairs. . . . "Will you give me the pleasure of driving to my brother's house to tea, my dear?"

Lately, a few months after Dr. Holmes's funeral, Uncle John had driven to Beacon Street; Wendell had helped him upstairs to the library. He had sat quietly, looking about the room. "Does this house oppress you, Fanny?" he had asked suddenly, in his quiet voice. He glanced at his nephew, standing straight and tall beside the fire, his hands behind his back. "You're getting gray, Wendell," he said. "Fanny, my dear, don't let the Judge get so wrapped in his business that he forgets about — the household. It's a family trait, you know." Fanny had glanced quickly at Uncle John. Their eyes met. "I like him being busy, Uncle John," she said, and John had nodded slowly, smiling at her.

How quickly the months passed, how soon one forgot these scenes that seemed, at the time, so significant. At court, Wendell was busier than ever, he seemed never to tire. There were times when it was a little wearying to keep up with this invincible quiet health, this deep-flowing energy. Wendell was helping his cousin, John Morse, Jr., edit Dr. Holmes's *Life and Letters*, which a Boston publisher was to bring out. Morse was Harvard, 1860, and he was enormously clever. It was diabolical the way he saw into people, particularly members of the Holmes tribe. "I hope he doesn't live to write *my* life," Holmes said. "Johnny knows too much."

The year the book came out — 1896 — Fanny had a long, severe illness. Rheumatic fever, the doctors called it. Her recovery was slow; week after week she remained upstairs. Wendell could not get used to it. Fanny had always been so well, almost robust. When finally she emerged from the bedroom to sit by the fire, she looked extraordinarily thin and white. The strangest manifestation of all, to her husband, was a kind of listlessness that wrapped Fanny round. She could not seem to shake it off, made indeed no effort to do so. The physician said it was the natural effects of the disease, but to Wendell Holmes it seemed anything but natural. She who had been so busy, so gay, sat idly now, her long, fine hands in her lap. As spring came on she would not go out, except sometimes into the back yard to throw crumbs to the birds or tend to her flower borders.

"You must see more people," Wendell told her, puzzled, dismayed. "Nina and John Gray want us for dinner. So does Mrs. Whitman. I saw Nina today after court."

"Go and dine without me," Fanny said. "I am tired, Wendell. An evening alone will suit me beautifully. And besides, my hair looks odd."

During the fever they had cut Fanny's hair, cropped it all round like a boy's. The result, in a day when woman's crowning glory was her hair, was indeed odd. What remained, brown on top, gray around the face, did not lie in pretty curls but bristled from her skull or lay in discouraged streaks. Fanny had always been shy; now she was implacable about being seen.

Little by little, Boston got used to Mrs. Holmes's non-appearance at dinner parties. The Judge also got used to it. Nobody, least of all her husband, knew whether Fanny minded staying home alone. She had always avoided fashionable Boston; hostesses who to Wendell now seemed beautiful and witty Fanny disposed of in words brief and pungent. And the few times she did venture out, Fanny did not make it particularly easy for her hostess. Her tongue was quick and she used it. The plain fact was that Fanny was tired, she wanted to be left alone.

"Do you think I can ask Judge Holmes for Friday without his wife?" The words were heard frequently on Chestnut Street, Louisburg Square. To obtain the Judge as an extra man became a social battle, a social triumph. This was the era when Mrs. Bell, Mrs. Pratt, Mrs. Whitman, reigned supreme in Boston. The first two were the daughters of Rufus Choate; they were sharp, witty, they had been everywhere and remained Boston to the core. Dr. Holmes had been particularly fond of Mrs. Bell; in Beverly they were to be seen driving out together, the doctor holding over them both his minikin sunshade. Mrs. Bell, who rejoiced in drawing rooms, loathed the country. "Kick a tree for me," she said to a friend who stopped in on her way out of town. To these and other hostesses, Judge Holmes was a godsend. They found his manner charming, the things he said were dry and startling. He was as fresh to society as a stranger. For how many years had he been buried in his law books, unseen except upon the street, hurrying to court or to the library, his green bag under his arm? And Boston society needed fresh material.

"I hear you have been reading *Germinal*," Mrs. Bell remarked one evening. "Boston is still 'shocked' by Zola. What do you think of him, Judge Holmes?"

"Improving, but dull," Holmes replied.

Mrs. Bell was enchanted, so were all the people to whom she repeated the remark. Holmes was definitely pleased himself. Fanny would like it. He would tell her tonight, when he got home.

Fanny liked Mrs. Bell. But her husband's wholehearted pleasure in these ladies both young and not-so-young was a continual puzzle. Wendell was wholly indiscriminate in his praise. If a woman was pretty enough, she was invariably brilliant. Again and again he exclaimed over their brilliance. Extraordinary, he said, that a woman like Mrs. Whitman, without study, without work, could arrive at large social conclusions that he himself had found only after years of conscious search!

Standing before the mirror in their room, late at night, taking off his white tie, Holmes told his wife about these things. "It is not hard to mistake worldliness for wisdom," Fanny said dryly, from the bed. She was sitting up in her long-sleeved muslin nightgown; her cropped hair had grown below her ears; it looked more incongruous than ever. Catching sight of her image in the glass across the room, she ducked out of sight.

Wendell did not notice. "Well!" he was saying heartily. "We had terrapin. The champagne was too sweet. And fresh asparagus. Nina Gray looked ravishing. But Fanny, you are right about not putting *hollandaise* on garden asparagus. . . ."

Fanny looked at her husband. Irritation rose in her like a tide. Was ever man so invincibly innocent? How was it possible to have such depth of intellect, such quickness of spirit, yet remain blind, where women were concerned, to the obvious?

Wendell was laying his dress coat over a chair, folding it with his usual meticulous care. Since he entered the room he had not stopped talking for a moment, and he had surely been home an hour. *Neglect* her? What had John Holmes said? Why, she might as well have been at the party; Wendell had repeated every word of the conversation, had described the food, the drink, the women — and just one man, who had persisted apparently in holding the floor when Wendell wanted it for himself. . . .

Wendell had turned and was standing at the foot of the bed. "Fanny," he said. "Mrs. Bell asked me what I thought of Zola, tonight. What do you think I told her, my dear?"

*   *   *

In the winter of 1896, the case of *Vegelahn* v. *Guntner and Others* reached the Massachusetts Supreme Court. Vegelahn was a shopowner; Guntner and his friends patrolled the pavement outside, informing the public that Vegelahn was unfair to his employees. There was no violence done; at no time did the pickets exceed two. But this was 1896, and Vegelahn succeeded in getting an injunction against the pickets.

It was a natural decision for the court to make. The whole country was reeling from the strikes and picketings, the violence and horror of the past ten years. In Chicago the "anarchists" of the Haymarket riots were dead. Their bombs had indubitably injured the cause of labor. But executing the men who threw the bombs had apparently not put an end to revolt. All over the country, strikes broke out with renewed violence. Against the trusts, against Standard Oil, Carnegie Steel, the Federation of Labor formed by Gompers and Strasser was powerless as a boulder against an avalanche. At Homestead in the Pennsylvania hills, Carnegie Steel — with the aid of Pinkerton — broke the worst strike America had yet seen.

The public, terrified of the strikers, was by no means wholly in sympathy with the employers. Law after law was passed to curb big business. States moved against the trusts — Louisiana against Cottonseed Oil, New York against the Sugar Trust, Ohio against Standard Oil. And one after one the states lost their suits; big business knew its "due process" clause. In 1890 the Sherman Act reaffirmed, in American form, an old principle of the English common law. But the Sherman Act got nowhere. "He mocks the people," Grover Cleveland told Congress in his last message of 1888, "who proposes that the government shall protect the rich and that they in turn will care for the laboring poor."

But in 1889 Cleveland went back to Buffalo, defeated, and in the White House Benjamin Harrison heard the shouts of the Silver men resound across the continent . . . Pro-silver, Free Silver, Bimetallism, Cheap Money. Greenbackers, Grangers, Laborites, Populists. . . . The banks failed, there was no confidence anywhere.

Grover Cleveland [1] came back to the White House. The panic of '93 swept across the country. Fortunes were lost, and men blamed it on the Democrats. In the mills, on the railroads, workmen were laid off by the thousands. Coxey and his army of unemployed converged shoeless onto the parks of Washington. In Chicago, hotbed of anarchy, the Pullman strike started in the autumn of '94, spread westward to the Coast, bitter and terrible. A workman's baby, wrapped in the American flag, was thrown in front of a locomotive driven by a scab. The baby was rescued but the public, horrified, screamed for retribution against the strikers. Eugene Debs, the mild-mannered, was put in jail.

In a year or two, business began to pick up. In Boston they excavated for the subway and began once more to worry about whether football interfered with scholarship at Harvard. The papers carried pictures of shooting big game in the Indian territories — conception new to a nation that had lately considered game as something to eat when you were hungry. The chief hunter was one T. Roosevelt, vacationing from New York politics — a Harvard man, very intimate with Cabot Lodge, and no friend of big business. He wrote to Owen Wister, "I recognize that all the time there are numerous evil forces at work . . . I am not so sure that I can afford to look at the coming years with levity."

And in Boston, in the spring of '96, the Massachusetts Court gave Vegelahn his injunction against the strikers; outside his shop the pickets marched no longer. In the past ten years the Court had seen much violence; where labor was concerned a threat had become synonymous with a crime.

Justice Holmes dissented. The patrol was legal, he said. There had been no force used, no threats to physical property. Judicial reasoning seemed to him inadequate. *"The true grounds of decision are considerations of policy and of social advantage, and it is vain to suppose that solutions can be attained merely by logic and the general propositions of law which nobody disputes."*

How many times had Oliver Wendell Holmes said that same thing in books, articles, or on the lecture platform! Then it had been theory, with no risk involved. Now he was saying it in court. This was a living question now; his words would affect men's lives.

> I have seen the suggestion made [Holmes said] that the conflict between employers and employed was not competition. But I venture to assume that none of my brethren would rely on that suggestion. If the policy on which our law is founded is too narrowly expressed in the term free competition, we may substitute free struggle for life. Certainly, the policy is not limited to struggles between persons of the same class, competing for the

same end. It applies to all conflicts of temporal interests. . . .

It is plain from the slightest consideration of practical affairs, or the most superficial reading of industrial history, that free competition means combination, and that the organization of the world, now going on so fast, means an ever increasing might and scope of combination. It seems to me futile to set our faces against this tendency. Whether beneficial on the whole, as I think it, or detrimental, it is inevitable, unless the fundamental axioms of society, and even the fundamental conditions of life, are to be changed.

One of the eternal conflicts out of which life is made up is that between the effort of every man to get the most he can for his services, and that of society, disguised under the name of capital, to get his services for the least possible return. Combination on the one side is patent and powerful. Combination on the other is the necessary and desirable counterpart, if the battle is to be carried on in a fair and equal way.

I can remember when many people thought that, apart from violence or breach of contract, strikes were wicked, as organized refusals to work. I suppose that intelligent economists and legislators have given up that notion today. I feel pretty confident that they equally will abandon the idea that an organized refusal by workmen of social intercourse with a man who shall enter their antagonist's employ is wrong, if it is dissociated from any threat of violence, and is made for the sole object of prevailing if possible in a contest with their employer about the rate of wages.

This was straight speaking and strong speaking. Holmes was well aware of what its repercussion would be, and of its effect upon his future career. He had thrown himself bodily against the vested interests; the fact that he had done it from intellectual conviction rather than from sympathy with labor would make no difference to the men at the top. In thirteen years, Holmes had moved up, on the Bench, from the end of the line to the seat on the right of Chief Justice Field. Field was deeply attached to him; again and again the two took the liberal side together. The older man made it no secret that he hoped Holmes would succeed him.

The night of the Vegelahn dissent, restless with what he had done, Holmes went out, walked up Beacon Street to the Arthur Hills'. Young Hill stood much farther to the left than Holmes; like

Brandeis, Hill desired to set right the universe, abolish the slums of Lowell, give the public its "rights" in the city's utilities, the new subway, the elevated railway.

Crossing Beacon Street in the soft June air, Holmes went up a pair of brownstone steps, rang the bell. "Arthur!" he said, in the lighted hallway of his friend's house. "I have just handed down an opinion that shuts me off forever from judicial promotion."

What Holmes did not realize was the respect and even affection with which the Court had come to look upon him. They no longer suspected him of being a theoretical fellow; in these years his erudition was proved. However mistaken, however dangerous Holmes's judicial opinions — still, they were indubitably bolstered by the actual legal thinking that is a judge's first business. Better than any one of the six, this man knew the common law. "General maxims," he had once said, in court, "are oftener an excuse for the want of accurate analysis than a help in determining the extent of a duty or the construction of a statute."

Holmes never failed to make this analysis. Moreover, neither in the Vegelahn dissent nor in the others had he defied the Court; he had been at pains to explain his stand in language that was actually deferential to his brethren. And he had done it with perfect sincerity. These men who saw him every day, who knew him well, recognized this sincerity.

When the next boycott case came up — *Plant* v. *Woods* — again the Court gave the employer his injunction against the strikers. Again Holmes dissented. But this time, he was able to state that the difference between himself and his brethren was only one of degree. "Much to my satisfaction . . . the Court has seen fit to adopt the mode of approaching the question which I believe to be the correct one." It was also significant that since the Vegelahn dissent the English courts had vindicated Holmes's stand in their own case of *Allen* v. *Flood*. Holmes mentioned this briefly.

In the summer of 1896, the social unrest of a violent decade manifested itself politically. In this Presidential year the issue turned on the tariff and on free silver versus the gold standard. At St. Louis, Mark Hanna skillfully secured the nomination of William McKinley, his friend and his god. Platt and Quay and Cabot Lodge went confidently home to their respective states. They knew politics; they told themselves they knew the people. Whether the Democrats nominated Cleveland or Bland next month, the country did not want Populism, it wanted prosperity. McKinley was to be prosperity's advance agent.

But the Democrats, meeting in Chicago in the July heat, hesitated over their financial plank. Should they compromise, or should they come out whole-hog for silver? On the fifth day a new man strode upon the platform, a young man from Nebraska, dashing, magnetic. William J. Bryan of the silver tongue — "beautiful as Apollo," the papers said. He raised his fist: *"You shall not crucify mankind upon a cross of gold. . . ."*

It was not common sense but it was oratory, and it touched dead center. Cheap money — the West could pay its debts! Bryan, Democratic nominee for President, was carried out of the hall on the shoulders of his frenzied followers. A Witches' Sabbath, Theodore Roosevelt remarked to Lodge. Mark Hanna was alarmed. But Bryan, said Roosevelt, would surely talk himself out before November.

He did, swinging round the country while McKinley sat on his front porch in Canton, Ohio, genially receiving delegations. All Bryan's golden words could not avail against Hanna's poster with his candidate's picture; under it the simple words: *McKinley, advance agent of prosperity*. Lodge and Roosevelt went on the stump together. In November, McKinley became President by the largest popular majority since Grant.

It was not the President's fault, of course, if prosperity was a little slow in spreading — if, as ever, it stagnated at the top, refusing to spread its sustenance below the customary level. Such manifestations as Coxey's Army had held no terrors for Morgan and James J. Hill, for Carnegie, Harriman, C. P. Huntington, George Baer. The Supreme Court had lately declared the income tax invalid. The lark was on the wing, McKinley in his heaven; for Business, the era of good will had begun.

Massachusetts, of course, voted wholeheartedly for McKinley — although most of Boston did not like Mark Hanna. To the Irish he was branded with the dollar sign and to Beacon Street he was unlettered — although it was rumored that at one time he had been a constant attendant at Emerson's Chautauqua lectures. McKinley had fought at Antietam; William James said Holmes would vote for anyone who had fought in the Civil War; in '88, James had been extremely annoyed when Holmes came out for Benjamin Harrison. But not even James, professor of psychology at Harvard and busy editing *The Will to Believe*, was as remote from politics as Holmes. Cabot Lodge, observing Holmes's labor dissents and the stir they made, but knowing full well that Holmes was no radical, did not cease to urge the lure of the life political. "Why don't you run for governor?" Lodge asked one day. "It's one road to a senatorship."

"Because I don't give a damn for being senator," Holmes replied, and the subject was closed. It was the law and more law that continued to interest this man. "I am occupying a 48 hours of leisure in looking into the early cases as to calling in the jury in negligence cases and the like," Holmes wrote to Pollock in May of 1898.

It was the second month of the Spanish-American War. In February, the *Maine* had been sunk in Havana Harbor, blown up under circumstances highly suspicious. President McKinley hesitated. Weeks passed, and the country grew restless. Were we going to sit by while Spain blew up our ships? McKinley could not sleep without powders. "The man has no more backbone," said Roosevelt in New York, "than a chocolate éclair." But on the eleventh of April McKinley sent his message to Congress, and eight days later we were at war.

On the plains by San Antonio, Roosevelt trained his cavalry, adjuring Lodge not to make peace until the Rough Riders got to Porto Rico. Boston businessmen took their securities inland to Springfield and Worcester; a formidable Spanish fleet would undoubtedly soon attack our coast. . . . "We are waiting to hear news of another big fight . . ." Holmes wrote to Lady Pollock from Beacon Street. "I hear the sound of music as I write these words; probably some fellows going off. . . . Such sounds . . . recall old days. It gives one a certain ache. It always seems to me that if one's body moved parallel to one's soul, one would mind campaigning less as an elderly man than as a young one. If you are killed as a young one you feel that you haven't had your chance. . . . At least that was the way I felt; but when one has had a try at life, has shown what he can do, and has come to some understanding with himself, to die a little sooner is only to lose pleasure, not to miss the point of being."

By mid-August the boys were home again. At Montauk Point, Colonel Roosevelt mustered out his Rough Riders, wrote Lodge of his plans for running for Governor of New York. And at Beverly Farms on the North Shore, Judge Holmes, aged fifty-six, got out his new bicycle and rode proudly down to the village. He had progressed far enough to be able to take one hand off the bars and wave to his friends — a matter that had bothered him greatly at first. Once, crossing the Mill-Dam on Beacon Street, he had met his old friend Robert Grant the Probate Judge, also on a bicycle. Grant had waved gayly. Holmes, his hands glued to the bars, had cursed long and loud. "Damn that fellow! He was just showing off. Next chance I get in court I'll overrule him."

Fanny went driving every day with her husband, her long starched white skirts flowing in the victoria, a veil on her sailor hat, her parasol up. Since her illness she had become very susceptible to bright light, kept the shades drawn at home. Her husband did not mind, Fanny's arrangements always seemed to him perfection. One week they drove to New Hampshire to their nephew Ned Holmes's wedding. It was a wonderful trip, Holmes wrote to Lady Pollock. The bobolinks sang in the meadows, and all the way there and back Fanny talked as she had not talked in two years. "I was more than happy," Holmes wrote. "My wife who hasn't by any means got back to where she was before her rheumatic fever, was wonderful in her resources of imaginative humor and forethought and seemed to awaken to a life and joy which she has not known for a good while."

Beacon Street, Boston, Massachusetts, was Fanny's home. Beyond Cambridge she knew indeed no other home. Was it coincidence, in the past few years, that Fanny seemed happiest away from Boston? Her old gayety, the crazy fancy that her husband adored, returned the moment they were out of sight of the people, the scenes, they knew so well. Once more she was mischievous, played tricks on Wendell, carried on absurd conversations with imaginary companions — and once more the things she said entranced her husband. Every tree, every cloud, was endowed with a personality, beneficent or malignant. At Beverly, old Mr. Emo came for them each afternoon in his livery-stable hack; one day he remarked unfavorably upon the weather. Fanny shook her head. "No no, Emo," she said earnestly, pointing with her parasol to where a black cloud floated against the sun. "Be careful! They'll hear you, up there. Don't stir up the witches."

That was the summer that Fanny bought the marmosets. Two
of them, and three flying squirrels. Beyond tearing up their master's
slippers, the marmosets were comparatively quiet. But the squirrels
— which Fanny kept in their bedroom "so they would not be
lonely" — were anything but quiet. "You look pale," a visitor remarked one day to Holmes. "The squirrels won't let me sleep," he
replied, but without complaint. "They jump on my bed and scare
me.. Fanny says they don't scare *her*. She says it simply shows their
affection. . . ."

In the autumn of 1898, Judge Charles Allen resigned. Of the six
judges who were on the Bench when Holmes came to it in 1883, only
Justice Field was left. Over in Cambridge, Uncle John Holmes
complained bitterly of his length of years. He was eighty-six. "Am
I to live forever?" he demanded. "Will nothing finish me off?" His
old housekeeper was dead; except for a servant who came by the day,
he lived quite alone, refusing all his friends' offers of care, hobbling
out onto Cambridge Common to sit sometimes in the sun. All old
men shrink, he said, but with him the shrinkage seemed acute. Very
soon, like Methuselah, he would go about complaining, "Oh dear,
oh dear — won't someone keep my shoe strings from blowing into
my eyes?"

In the winter of 1899, John Holmes died. Until the end he joked,
greeting death companionably, as he had always greeted life. He
was a long time dying; he lay motionless in the bed, scarcely breathing, seemingly comatose. Around Cambridge, the manner of his
going became legend. The nurse, it was said, bent over the bed one
afternoon, felt the patient's pulse and shook her head. She put her
hand beneath the covers. "If his feet are warm," she said to the
watcher by the bed, "he's alive. I'll just feel them. Nobody ever
died with his feet warm."

"*John Rogers did!*" John Holmes said with startling distinctness.
. . . John Rogers, burned at the stake for heresy three centuries
past.[2] . . .

John Holmes never spoke again. Wendell loved to tell the story.
Uncle John was gone, he lay in Mount Auburn beside his brother.
But it was impossible to speak of him woefully, with a long face.
There had been something gentle yet invincible about John Holmes:
Wendell had taken rebuke from him that he would have resisted
violently from his father. It came back to him now, scene after

scene . . . The time Uncle John had led him upstairs on Beacon Street, told him bluntly he was behaving badly about Fanny. . . . "The best girl in Cambridge, Wendell. Are you blind? When will you give her the chance to refuse you?" . . . And his story about the Roman emperor who had a triumph; in the middle of it a little boy had stuck out his tongue . . . *"There is always an urchin at the edge of every triumph, Wendy, to remind you that your crown isn't on straight. . . ."*

From first to last, John Holmes had been outshone by his brother. *Frère de mon frère,* he had written in a Cambridge note-book. Yet it did not matter now, Wendell Holmes knew. There had been here no defeat. . . .

In that same winter of 1899, Fanny's father died. Epes Sargent Dixwell, aged ninety-two. There had been a quality in these quiet lives that was hard to define. Thinking of it, Fanny remembered something Dr. Holmes had said, speaking one day of his own father, Abiel Holmes. *"Our elders had pith in them."* They had indeed, Fanny thought now. How different in outlook those old heroes — John and Oliver Holmes, her own father — from the prevailing spirit of the day! *Fin de siècle:* the phrase was on everyone's lips. To be *fin de siècle* was the fashionable thing; it connoted indifference, a surface sophistication — Oscar Wilde, Whistler, the young men of Oxford. There was a companion phrase in Boston: *Harvard indifference.* The magazines caricatured it: —

> This life's a hollow bubble,
> Don't you know?
> Just a painted piece of twouble,
> Don't you know?
> We come to earth to cwy,
> We gwow oldeh and we sigh,
> Oldeh still and then we die,
> Don't you know?

Four years ago, Holmes had attacked this spirit in its stronghold — on Memorial Day, in the huge new ugly Harvard building called Memorial Hall. "The Soldier's Faith," the talk was listed in the program. Holmes was scheduled for an LL.D. that Commencement, on the platform with John Gray and Sir Frederick Pollock. It was pleasant, the three old friends crowned together, and it was good to know that President Eliot had buried the hatchet. But the honor came too late, Holmes said, for him to feel any real triumph.

On the platform that hot Memorial Day, Holmes had shocked half of Boston. "What kind of a world do you want?" he demanded, as the audience fanned itself, preparing for a pleasant talk from its distinguished townsman. A world — Holmes went on — where pain is the only evil? A world cut up into five-acre lots, no man upon it who is not well-fed and housed — and lacking altogether the divine folly of honor, lacking altogether that senseless passion for knowledge that outreaches the flaming bounds of the possible?

"War, when you are at it, is horrible and dull. It is only when time has passed that you see that its message was divine. . . . In this snug, over-safe corner of the world we need it, that we may realize that our comfortable routine is no eternal necessity of things, but merely a little space of calm in the midst of the tempestuous untamed streaming of the world, and in order that we may be ready for danger."

This snug, over-safe corner of the world . . . What kind of way was that to talk about Boston, Harvard sisters, wives, sweethearts, asked each other, filing out toward Cambridge Common where the Revolutionary cannon sat square and black, painted neatly under the elms? Wasn't Boston the very cradle of liberty? Didn't Bunker Hill prove it, and Faneuil Hall and those ancient stones in the churchyard yonder, where the country's heroes lay buried?

Boston did not forget this speech. It reached, indeed, beyond Boston. Theodore Roosevelt, pondering it, sat down in New York and dashed off a note to Lodge: "By Jove, that speech of Holmes' was fine; I wish he could make Edward Atkinson learn it by heart and force him to repeat it forwards and backwards every time he makes a peace oration."

And now the century was ending. On the Massachusetts Supreme Court, at the far left of the Bench, sat a judge too young to have known the Civil War: Caleb Loring had been only ten when Holmes crossed the river at Ball's Bluff. A new generation was at hand.

Holmes was fifty-eight — a time when men have a right to think their life has reached the narrowing point. From now on his sphere would be, he thought, in the very nature of things restricted more and more. It would be well to bear this in mind, accustom oneself to this narrower life, not fight against the inevitable.

CHAPTER THIRTY - ONE

Chief Justice in Massachusetts.
Roosevelt writes to Lodge about
Holmes. Farewell to Boston.

IN July of 1899, Chief Justice Field died. The Governor immediately appointed Holmes as his successor. No one was surprised, it was the logical move.

But what did surprise Boston — and especially the judges — was the ease with which Holmes, from the very first, filled his place. The judges had known that this was a brilliant mind, a forceful and persuasive character. But Holmes was independent, impatient of slower minds. In the consultation room alone with the other judges, how would he behave? Had he the tact, the poise, to carry it, assign the opinions to be written, resolve differences, preserve judicial harmony?

Chief Justice Holmes, it seems, had all these qualities. And he loved the position, was happy in it. He was suddenly a legend in Boston. Newspaper reporters, notebook in hand, followed him up the hill to the courthouse. "His long frame is singularly youthful. He does not mind Beacon Hill, and breasts it with a long, quick step, bending forward, almost swaying in his carriage. He is sure to stop at the Athenaeum, his green bag has room for another book. His face is purity itself; he has the kindest eyes, and an illuminating smile."

Seven months after he was made Chief Justice — on March 7, 1900 — the Bar Association of Boston gave a dinner in Holmes's honor. Everybody came; there was a tremendous turnout. The Chief

Justice of Rhode Island was there, President Eliot and many of Holmes's old friends — John Gray, John Morse, Henry Higginson. Gray presided, introducing Holmes.

And when Holmes got up, the long room burst into a roar. He tried to speak, they cheered again and again. Holmes was deeply touched. He spoke briefly, went back, as was natural at the end of a century, and reviewed a past that he had shared with many of his hearers. . . .

Yesterday I was at the law school again, in the chair instead of on the benches, when my dear partner, Shattuck, came out and told me that in one hour the Governor would submit my name to the council for a judgeship, if notified of my assent. It was a stroke of lightning which changed the whole course of my life.

And the day before yesterday, gentlemen, was thirty-five years, and yesterday was more than eighteen years, ago. I have gone on feeling young, but I have noticed that I met fewer of the old to whom to show my deference, and recently I was startled by being told that ours is an old bench. Well, I accept the fact, although I find it hard to realize, and I ask myself, what is there to show for this half lifetime that has passed?

I look into my book in which I keep a docket of the decisions of the full court which fall to me to write, and find about a thousand cases. A thousand cases, many of them upon trifling or transitory matters, to represent nearly half a lifetime! A thousand cases, when one would have liked to study to the bottom and to say his say on every question which the law ever has presented, and then to go on and invent new problems which should be the test of doctrine, and then to generalize it all and write it in continuous, logical, philosophic exposition, setting forth the whole corpus with its roots in history and its justifications of expedience real or supposed!

The day after the dinner was Holmes's birthday; he was fifty-nine. It was extraordinary how young he looked. His face with its high color was lined and showed all the marks of living. But the deep gray eyes were more searching than ever and there was a quickness about him that seemed to stem from far within, from a wellspring unending and joyful. Young Judge Loring in particular looked upon his chief with amazement. One day, worried over an opinion Holmes had assigned him to write, Loring took it to Beacon Street, carrying along all the papers of the case.

Holmes glanced through the material, turning the pages. Then he got up and went to the high old desk in the corner. Standing, he wrote ten lines, handed them to Loring. The younger man was appalled. Surely, the Chief Justice was not going to let this cursory examination suffice?

But when Loring submitted the report it was accepted by the others as the opinion of the Court, and incorporated without question in the records. In ten minutes, Holmes had seen to the heart of the matter.

Fanny Holmes gave her husband a little birthday party that year, as she always did. If Wendell at fifty-nine looked forty, his wife, at sixty, looked every inch her age. And she knew it. She made no slightest effort to conceal it, to keep pace with a husband so handsome, so cavalier. She still wore always a dash of color — a red bow on the shoulder of her dark dress, turquoise beads that flashed as she moved. But her gray hair swept grimly up from her forehead, netted, pulled back so tightly that her eyebrows went up with it. Fanny had become addicted to guimpes and wore at all times a high collar of white net, boned. She paid not the slightest attention to fashion, but dressed as she pleased. And her clothes became her. Fanny Holmes had a style quite her own. When everyone else was in bonnets she wore a sailor hat, veiled, set severely on her pompadour; when they wore hats she reverted to her bonnet, tied under her chin with ribbons, perky and fresh. "Mrs. Holmes's bonnets" became a phrase around Boston. "No, no, my dear, that hat is not for you. It looks like one of Mrs. Holmes's bonnets."

But when she walked out to her carriage with Wendell, there was something invincibly distinguished about Fanny Holmes. She had got her strength back; she walked swiftly, held herself well. She looked like Garden Street, Cambridge, New England, and it did not occur to her to want to look otherwise. She not only dressed as she pleased, but now that she was sixty, Fanny Holmes did as she pleased. Twice, that winter, she and Wendell were seen running to fires along Beacon Street, moving with astonishing speed for people of their years . . . the Chief Justice of Massachusetts and his wife — "who was, you know," delighted spectators told each other, "Miss Dixwell of Cambridge, daughter of old Dicky who kept the school on Boylston Place."

The Boston subway was finished, now, and down town the

buildings soared high, steel-girdered. A few enterprising souls came to the Harvard football games in gasoline carriages; newspapers carried an advertisement of *The Locomobile Company of America.* On Cape Nome, Alaska, five thousand men made camp, searching for gold. Mr. Dooley said his say about troubles in the Transvaal, and in Washington, D. C., Admiral Dewey moved into the mansion presented to him by the people of America.

In New York, Tom Platt and the machine maneuvered Roosevelt gently out of the governorship. T. R. had been very troublesome around the city with his reforms. The Vice-Presidency was the safest place for him; McKinley was up for election again that autumn of 1900. Roosevelt would have none of it, he said. But the convention, when Lodge presented his name, came out for the ticket with a roar of acclaim, and Roosevelt accepted.

In November the party won again, hands down. This time, Bryan had built his campaign on anti-imperialism. Even the trusts and the high tariff were not so harmful, he said, as the course of empire to which the Republicans had committed the country. Nobody listened to this jeremiad. The country was enjoying the prestige it had won at Santiago, Porto Rico, and the Philippines. John Hay had imposed upon reluctant European powers his policy of the "open door" in China. America had entered a world-wide political arena, and the American people liked it.

The Republicans were in, the watchword was expansion, within our borders and without. Under the leadership of J. P. Morgan, seven great steel companies planned a merger — "the billion-dollar trust." Bryan was as good as dead; business held its head high, there was no need for dissimulation. "We are the rich," said one Frederick Townsend Martin. "We own America; we got it, God knows how, but we intend to keep it if we can by throwing all the tremendous weight of our support, our influence, our money, our political connections, our purchased Senators, our hungry Congressmen, our public-speaking demagogues into the scale against any legislature, any political platform, any Presidential campaign that threatens the integrity of our estate."

It was a boast absurd, arrogant, and dangerous — a battle of the people against the people: the tycoons themselves stemmed directly from the ranks. Theodore Roosevelt, rich himself, heard the threat and was angry. But the country was not yet aware of the man who would wield the Big Stick. Colonel Roosevelt, late of the Rough Riders, was simply McKinley's Vice-President, and the reforms he had fought for in New York were of small moment as against the billion-dollar merger.

At 49 Broadway, Boss Platt smiled. "Are you going to the inauguration?" someone asked him.

"Yes," Platt replied. "I am going down to see Theodore Roosevelt take the veil."

On the third of March, United States Steel was formed. "Who made the world, Charles?" a character in *Life* inquired. "God made the world in 4004 B.C., but it was reorganized in 1901 by James J. Hill, J. Pierpont Morgan, and John D. Rockefeller." . . . In Washington, Vice-President Roosevelt, feeling dejected, took the oath, and promptly began studying law, "as a preparation," he said, "for retirement from public life." Justice White advised him not to enroll in a Washington law school; it would look odd for a man in his position. Let Roosevelt study law by himself, then come every Saturday evening to White for quizzing.

On Boston Common the elms shook off a winter's snow. Judge Oliver Wendell Holmes, advised by the physician to spare his eyes, played solitaire in the evenings while his wife read aloud from Marcus Aurelius, the *Education Sentimentale*, George Ade's *Fables in Slang*. In July, Holmes went to England by himself. Fanny went down to Beverly, invited one of her sisters to visit her. Little Dorothy Upham, Dr. Holmes's great-niece, came too. Fanny had a gift with children. She made presents for Dorothy — a toy screen with hinges of stamps. The child was enchanted, followed her aunt around the house, curious to see what she would do next, say next.

Letters came frequently from London, filled with triumphal doings — dinner parties every night, a visit to Margot Asquith in Scotland. Wendell had met statesmen and royalty. Andrew Lang, very *fin de siècle*, insufferably insolent, had walked up to Wendell in a London drawing room. "So you are the son of the celebrated Oliver Wendell Holmes?" he drawled.

"No," Wendell replied. "He was my father."

Fanny laughed with pleasure, told the story often. A few weeks later, Wendell returned. "The Judge has come home," Fanny told her friends, "hung with jewels."

Early in September, President McKinley went to Buffalo to greet holiday throngs at the Exposition. Theodore Roosevelt, aged forty-two, was up in Keene Valley climbing mountains, enjoying the strenuous life. In Music Hall, McKinley put out his hand to greet a citizen standing in line; the man raised his hand, a shot was fired.

McKinley lived for eight days. The country as a whole was ready for Roosevelt — but the conservative Republicans were not. His first message to Congress was moderate but firm, and there was no mistaking the fact that the government was going to assume a new relation to business. The "square deal" for all parties would include labor and the public as well as capital. In words less disturbing and far more judicial, Holmes had said the same thing in the Vegelahn dissent . . . "The organization of the world, now going on so fast, means an ever-increasing might and scope of combination. . . . Combination on the one side is patent and powerful. Combination on the other is the necessary and desirable counterpoint, if the battle is to be carried on in a fair and equal way."

Roosevelt and Holmes were poles apart in temperament, differing both in their approach to social problems and in their plans for meeting these problems. Yet it was natural, reading the Vegelahn dissent, that Roosevelt should see here a Justice who would be his man, who would support the policies he believed in. Without the Court on his side, no President could be effectual. Huge issues could depend — as Roosevelt himself said — on "whether a Judge of the Supreme Court came down heads or tails."

In June, 1902, one of the Justices was ill: Horace Gray of Boston, John Gray's stepbrother. He was coming home to Nahant, he said, to rest for the summer. Justice Gray was seventy-four. During eighty-two of its one hundred and thirteen years the Supreme Court had included a Massachusetts man. Newspapers speculated, and in their prophecies the name of the Chief Justice of Massachusetts loomed large.

Henry Cabot Lodge to Theodore Roosevelt

NAHANT, MASS., *June* 5, 1902

DEAR THEODORE:

I hear on my return that Judge Gray is so much more weak that he has resigned. . . . I want of course to talk with you before you decide. I have not bothered you because I thought it would not come for some time, but I have thought it over a great deal.

Ever yrs,
H. C. Lodge

Theodore Roosevelt to Henry Cabot Lodge

Oyster Bay, N. Y.
July 10, 1902

Dear Cabot:

. . . Now as to Holmes: If it becomes necessary you can show him this letter. First of all, I wish to go over the reasons why I am in his favor. . . . His father's name entitles the son to honor; and if the father had been an utterly unknown man the son would nevertheless now have won the highest honor. . . .

The labor decisions which have been criticized by some of the big railroad men and other members of large corporations constitute to my mind a strong point in Judge Holmes' favor. The ablest lawyers and greatest judges are men whose past has naturally brought them into close relationship with the wealthiest and most powerful clients, and I am glad when I can find a judge who has been able to preserve his aloofness of mind so as to keep his broad humanity of feeling and his sympathy for the class from which he has not drawn his clients. I think it eminently desirable that our Supreme Court should show in unmistakable fashion their entire sympathy with all proper effort to secure the most favorable possible consideration for the men who most need that consideration. . . .

Now a word as to the other side. . . . In the higher sense, in the proper sense, [a man] is not in my judgment fitted for the position unless he is a party man. . . . Marshall rendered such invaluable service because he was a statesman of the national type, like Adams who appointed him, like Washington whose mantle fell upon him. Taney was a curse to our national life because he belonged to the wrong party and faithfully carried out the criminal and foolish views of the party which stood for such a construction of the Constitution as would have rendered it impossible even to preserve the national life. The Supreme Court of the sixties was good exactly in so far as its members fitly represented the spirit of Lincoln.

This is true at the present day. The majority of the present Court who have, although without satisfactory unanimity, upheld the policies of President McKinley and the Republican party in Congress, have rendered a great service to mankind and to this nation. The minority . . . have stood for such reactionary folly as would have hampered well-nigh hopelessly this people in doing efficient and honorable work for the national welfare. . . .

Now I should like to know that Judge Holmes was in entire sympathy with our views, that is with your views and mine and Judge Gray's, for instance, just as we know that ex-Attorney General Knowlton is, before I would feel justified in appointing him. . . .

Faithfully yours,
THEODORE ROOSEVELT

P. S. . . . How would it do, if [Judge Holmes] seems to be all right, to have him come down here and spend a night with me, and then I could make the announcement on the day that he left, after we have talked together?

Whether Lodge showed this quite extraordinary letter to Holmes we have no way of knowing; it seems unlikely that he would have taken such a chance. No doubt Holmes had met Roosevelt; more than once they had attended the same Harvard celebrations — a football game, a commencement exercise. But Holmes did not know Roosevelt as Lodge knew him. On the face of it, such a letter might have repelled a man of Holmes's independence and idealism. Lodge, a politician himself, knew exactly what Roosevelt meant when he made *party man* and *constructive statesman* into synonymous terms. But would Holmes understand it — Holmes, who lately, meeting by appointment some practical leaders of the people, had condemned them as "men of aims but not of ideals"?

Holmes knew the appointment was coming; he could not help but know it. He had by no means made up his mind to accept. He was happy where he was; quite frankly he enjoyed the position of Chief Justice. In Washington he would be only Associate Justice, the newest man of nine, seated once more at the far left end of the Bench. The question of money did not enter; Holmes had his father's inheritance now. As Chief Justice of Massachusetts, his salary was $8500 a year, with $500 for traveling expenses. In Washington it would be $10,000.

But if Holmes hesitated, his wife did not. From the first, she made her position clear. Holmes must accept the appointment. The more he talked, the more silent Fanny became. She had said her say — of what use to repeat it? "Wendell, you have gone as far in Massachusetts as you can go. Your family lives forever, and so will you. Are you going to *stop*, just because the calendar says 'sixty'? Break up our home — why can't we break up our home? We have done it before. That is my department. You may leave that to me."

They were at Beverly when Justice Gray resigned. Holmes, following Fanny aimlessly around the house, watched her feed her birds in their cages on the back veranda, tried again to make her speak. "Fanny, what do you want to do? Not for me, but for yourself? Won't you mind it, uprooting your whole life?" He caught her by the shoulders, turned her round. "We shall have to dine with the President. In tails, Fanny, and white satin. You will sit next to ambassadors and ministers of state."

Fanny drew a long breath. But her expression did not change. She freed herself, turned and poked her finger through the bars at the Japanese robin, chirruping at him. "The Judge is frightened, Koko," she said.

On the eleventh of August, Holmes's appointment was announced in the papers. All New England, it seemed, was pleased. Most of the accounts mentioned the Vegelahn dissent; there was a disposition to pronounce the new Justice something of a radical. The *Springfield Republican* came nearer the truth; it was much quoted by the other papers. As a Harvard man, it said, Roosevelt was in touch with the sentiment that attached to the Holmes family. Moreover, Justice Holmes had a known disposition in favor of the strenuous life "to which imperialism has invited the nation." Like Justice Gray, the new Justice would be disposed to let the United States drift along the new lines which were a departure from the old Americanism, and the divisions in the Court would remain the same. Justice Holmes's opinions were no longer criticized as being too literary; time had served to change and "largely dissipate" this early view.

But the papers dwelt upon this literary propensity; it still aroused suspicion. The new Justice was inclined to be brilliant rather than sound, the *New York Evening Post* said.

Holmes read the notices and his heart was sick within him. Twenty years on the Bench, and all the people seemed to know was that he had taken the labor side in *Vegelahn* v. *Guntner*, and that his opinions had a literary style. Holmes had always hated publicity, but beyond his father's incurable habit of making domestic events into literary ones, he had had to suffer very little from the public eye.

Fanny, reading the notices, laughed. Not one of them omitted the fact that the new Justice was the son of the Autocrat. "The play of inherited wit," Fanny read aloud one afternoon as she sat with Wendell on the veranda at tea time — "the play of inherited wit is seen in all Judge Holmes' utterances. . . . Wendell, did you know you were the Laboring Man's Hope?"

This last was from the *New York Evening Journal*. It was in large type, a headline . . . " 'Judge Holmes is a quiet, reserved man, very democratic,' " Fanny went on relentlessly. " 'He has made a friend of everyone who has met him. He is one of the ablest and most commonsense judges on the Bench. He inherited his scholarly and literary characteristics from . . .' "

Holmes gave an exclamation, loud and profane. He got up. "You she-devil, Fanny! . . . Brooks Adams is coming to ride with me at five. I think I'll go and look over my bicycle."

It was December before the Senate could confirm Holmes's appointment. He stayed on, meanwhile, as Chief Justice in Massachusetts. That autumn, walking to court or driving slowly up Beacon Hill in the hired carriage, every scene, every stick and stone of the familiar journey took on new significance. By November the leaves were gone from the trees; under a pale blue sky a few green bushes huddled against the sunny side of Beacon Street. From the brownstone houses, bay windows jutted outward, their glass dusty against the sun. People, walking on the Common, bent their heads against a sharp east wind. Sun struck the gilded dome of the State House; on the lawn before it, Daniel Webster stood grandly on his pedestal. Hoarsely, from the harbor, steamer whistles sounded.

"This month sees the end of the happiest twenty years of my life," Holmes told his colleagues of the Bar and Bench at a dinner given him in November. "And the happiest of those years have been the last. I am associated on the Bench with men every one of whom is my personal friend . . . in the consultation room all is affectionate and free. It is a good deal of a wrench to leave old friends.

"But gentleman, it is a great adventure, and that thought brings with it a mighty joy. To have one's chance to do one's share in shaping the laws of the whole country spreads over one the hush that one used to feel when awaiting the beginning of a battle.

"We will not falter. . . . We will reach the earthworks if we live, and if we fail we will leave our spirit in those who follow, and they will not turn back. All is ready. *Bugler, blow the charge.*"

Fanny Holmes had no opportunity to rise before the crowd, girding her courage to the occasion. Fanny's role was one of silence — and she did not find it easy. All her talk, her laughter, her goading on of her husband, was assumed, laid on with skill and love. She wanted to go to Washington it was true, wanted it first of all for Wendell, but also, in some vague way she could not define, wanted it for herself.

But the thought of Washington terrified her. Her mirror showed a woman old and gaunt, thin to the point of emaciation. Since her illness Fanny had not regained her plump contours; she was never to regain them. Her cheek bones stood out, there was no color to the face beneath the sparse gray hair.

Twice, during the autumn, people had mistaken her for Wendell's mother . . . *Tails and white satin, ambassadors and ministers of state.* . . . It was not the ambassadors that Fanny feared; it was their wives, their daughters. For the past few winters, Wendell had gone out in Boston by himself, leaving his wife at home. Fanny had made no complaint; the situation had been of her own making. She did not like fashionable Boston; it bored her and at the same time it defeated her. She had made her own life here at home.

In Washington, there would be no chance for this kind of easy independence. As wife of a Justice of the Supreme Court, her presence at social functions both large and small would be required. Where Wendell went, in tails and silk hat, Fanny would have to follow.

There was no concealing from herself the fact that Fanny was scared. If she could have told her husband it would have been easier, but she could not tell him. Her role must be one of calm assurance. Fanny had few close friends. One of these was a much younger woman, not Boston born, in whom Fanny could confide. One afternoon late in November, this friend, coming in, found Fanny sitting alone in the little downstairs room at 296 Beacon Street where she kept her birds.

Fanny got up, came swiftly forward. Her face was troubled, there was a kind of desperate humor in the gesture with which she put up both hands to her hair.

"Mary," she said. "Look at me. How can I go to Washington — I, who look like an abandoned farm in Maine?"

PART VI

Washington. 1902-1935

the bright shield of the Union, the eagle snarling, the red canopy over the Chief Justice's chair. All it needed, to make a perfect Guido Reni, was a fellow at each end of the Bench with a brace of wolf-hounds. . . . The very incongruity of things, here in Washington, was somehow exhilarating. That first day, when he was sworn in, for instance . . .

"We had our robes on," Holmes said. "I had already taken the first oath in the robing room and the judges had started across the hall. I was at the end of the line, of course. They go very slowly. There is always a crowd hanging round the Capitol corridors. Just as I started across the hall, a man spoke out very distinctly, in a sort of awed whisper. 'Christ!' he said. 'What dignity!' "

Fanny gasped. No, Holmes said quickly. The man wasn't joking. Let Fanny come to Court and find out for herself. The whole scene was extraordinary, the feeling of tradition behind it. And the questions that came up . . . from Arkansas, from Wisconsin and Texas — questions for statesmen, not lawyers. The whole thing was *big*. A man had no need to search within himself, to find his sense of the infinite. The infinite was right there, in that old Courtroom. . . .

Fanny Holmes looked around her, at the furniture, half unpacked. Newspapers littered the floor. In the hallway she heard Annie, the maid who had been with them since Dr. Holmes's time, complaining bitterly that the place was a shambles. What had Doherty been doing for six mortal days, the Irish voice demanded. Why hadn't he got the kitchen clean instead of playing up here with them books?

It would take weeks to get this house in order. . . . Come to Court tomorrow? Fanny looked at her husband. He had got up and was pacing the room, his hands in his pockets like a college boy, talking nineteen to the dozen about an opinion he was hoping the Chief would assign to him. . . .

"Why yes, Wendell," Fanny said. "I'll come to Court with you tomorrow. Can we drive there? Have you been able to hire a hack for every day?"

On Friday morning, in the chamber of the Supreme Court, Fanny Holmes watched the hands of the round clock above the Chief Justice's chair move toward noon. She had sat here for half an hour; the spell of the old room had settled upon her. Light came benignly from the domed ceiling, Justices in marble looked down from their pedestals. It was all as Wendell had described: overhead on the red, white, and blue shield, the stars were only twenty-six. Fanny counted them . . . Why, John Quincy Adams had been President then! This room had been in continuous use ever since, first by the Senate. Just before the Civil War it was taken over by the Supreme Court.

On a raised dais, nine tall black leather chairs faced the chamber. In that center chair, under the red canopy, Justice Taney had sat at eighty-seven, reviled and mistrusted by a country he had served for half a century. Daniel Webster had debated here, and Calhoun. It was an awesome sight for the wife of any Justice, this quiet room with the round clock ticking above the eagle. In one of those great chairs, Wendell Holmes would sit, his gray hair outlined against the cushions. . . .

There was a stir to the left; in a long black line the Justices came slowly in: Chief Justice Fuller, hale and hearty at sixty-nine, his white hair worn long, after the Western fashion. How tiny he was, in front of Harlan! John Marshall Harlan of Kentucky, the giant who had been in the Court since '77. Last of the tobacco-spitting judges, Holmes called him. Next to Harlan was White of Louisiana, the sugar planter, veteran of the Rebel army, dark-haired, with a square, stubborn head.

Slowly the nine walked to their places. Brewer of Kansas, Brown of Michigan. The Justice next to Brown was Peckham of New York, then came somebody Fanny could not place, and then, standing next to Wendell, was a man with a face like Lincoln's, whiskers all round under his chin. That was McKenna of California, the only McKinley appointee.

"*Oyez! Oyez! Oyez! . . . God Save the United States and This Honorable Court!*"

Fanny Holmes, looking up at her husband, was swept with sudden, deep emotion. It was not only that Wendell was so handsome, standing there straight and tall in his robes. But they had done right to come. Whatever might arrive, whatever fate had in store for him — and for her, in this sprawling city of strangers — they had done right to come. They had done right to leave home, break away, cut off the associations of a lifetime. Fanny Holmes had always felt it. But now she knew it and rejoiced.

Gazing up at her husband from under her prim dotted veil, Fanny felt tears surge to her eyes, hot and overflowing.

Washington in 1903 was the most exuberant place on the civilized earth. And in the center of it, in the midst of all this ferment of a new century, a new era, Theodore Roosevelt stirred the mixture with his Big Stick, busting the trusts, curbing monopoly, shaking his fist, grinning from newspaper cartoons, one eye on the matter in hand, one on the Presidential convention next year in Chicago. . . .

Newspapermen had never had a President who was such copy. Everything he did was spectacular. The Sunday afternoon hikes through Rock Creek Park, with the French Ambassador panting behind in lavender kid gloves. *"Pour l'honneur de la France,"* the Ambassador had remarked resignedly, throwing off his clothes preparatory to swimming the Creek after the President.

"America," John Morley wrote home to London, "has two extraordinary spectacles: Niagara Falls and Theodore Roosevelt." In all its history, the country had never had such a noisy man in the White House. In the corridors upstairs, Archie and Quentin rode bronco on their father's back, and in cities from Maryland to Oregon, bands played *Alice, where art thou,* and the people noted the skirts of the President's delightful daughter, worn daringly short, almost to her boot tops.

The country liked it — the plain people especially. The West, almost forgetting Bryan, was glad of a leader who was not afraid of Wall Street. But the captains of industry, captains of railroads and captains in Wall Street, looked with anger and apprehension upon the Dude Cowboy who had promised to continue unchanged the policies of his predecessor, McKinley. . . . Theodore Roosevelt was not continuing anything; he was initiating, inaugurating, changing, reforming. His manner of settling the coal strike, for instance, had been completely out of line. Swiftly and without precedent he had taken the public into his confidence by publishing in the newspapers the owners' refusal to meet with the miners. The public, furious, had compelled the owners to arbitrate.

It was the first time the public had been consulted in an industrial dispute; the result was immediate and significant. Henceforth a Commodore Vanderbilt would not flaunt his scorn so arrogantly

. . . "The public be damned." Henceforth an E. H. Harriman would not boast so openly concerning his power to buy both legislators and courts. The public conscience was aroused – and T. R. suited the public conscience perfectly. In the big new magazines, *McClure's, Collier's, Everybody's,* the muckrakers exposed the packers, the sweatshop proprietors. Lincoln Steffens was writing *The Shame of the Cities.* People read Frank Norris – *The Octopus, The Pit.* Upton Sinclair, Ida Tarbell, prepared their indictments.

Here in the White House was a man who the public knew would stand behind it. When Theodore Roosevelt did not like a thing, he set about instantly to legislate it out of existence. To him the legal and political viewpoint were one and the same; it did not occur to him that there were men – among them a new Court appointee from Massachusetts – who looked upon the thing far differently.

"What the boys like about Roosevelt," a Senator said, "is that he doesn't care a damn for the law." Neither did the country. What the country desired just now was neither legality nor reason, but revenge. Let T. R. smash somebody *big,* make an example of him – a meat packer, the sugar trust, anybody or anything so long as there was action.

The country had not long to wait. Looking round, Roosevelt seized upon the biggest, newest railroad merger of them all – the Northern Securities Company – asked his Attorney General to investigate its legality under the Sherman Act. Knox went ahead, and in February, 1902, suit against the Northern Securities Company burst upon the captains of industry like a declaration of war.

The stock market plunged downward. "Doesn't your friend," a railroad man asked Owen Wister in Philadelphia, "ever *think?*" In Washington, Henry Adams answered the question. Roosevelt, he said, from head to foot was *pure act.* . . . And on the other side of Lafayette Square, the new Justice from Massachusetts watched a trifle sardonically while his President wielded the Big Stick. The Sherman Anti-Trust Act, obviously, was going to be Roosevelt's favorite weapon . . . and Holmes had always disliked the Act. "The Sherman Act isn't fair," he said often. "It won't let the strong man win the race." Besides, mere bigness didn't make a merger illegal. How it behaved, what it did, determined its legality. Very possibly the Northern Securities case would never reach the Supreme

Court; with John G. Johnson as counsel, Morgan and Jim Hill might win their case in the lower courts. Suit was brought in St. Paul; as weeks passed, the public forgot it and turned to other matters.

Meanwhile, in Washington, Justice and Mrs. Holmes took their place in society — rather to their surprise, among the inmost circle of the Roosevelt Familiars. It was a natural affinity. The Cabot Lodges, Henry Adams, Owen Wister, Roosevelt, Holmes . . . Harvard men, with a like background and like tastes. Brilliant men, vigorous, good talkers who were ready to give an opinion on any subject on earth. Holmes had known them all in Boston except the President.

Mrs. Henry Adams was dead; Adams lived alone in the big beautiful house around the corner from the Holmeses. Adams still retained his pose of the old cardinal, turning life to dust and ashes. But underneath he was kinder, Holmes suspected, than his brother Brooks. And he was always interesting. Very often they dined informally at the White House. John Hay joined them, or the Jusserands, and they went afterward to the theater with Mrs. Roosevelt. Holmes's fervent joy in the play gave the others enormous pleasure. He was like a great boy. "Oh my God!" he would cry out. "If only I could act like that!" On January 8, 1903, Wister records one such intimate dinner at the White House when the talk bubbled over and the President, leaning his hands on the table, burst out suddenly in sheer joy, "Oh, *aren't* we having a good time!"

The Holmeses had been in Washington less than a month when this dinner party took place. To Holmes the whole situation was natural and pleasant. He took it easily; good company was relaxation after a hard day's work. But for Fanny Holmes, this association with presidents and ambassadors burst like a storm of lightning, like a tornado threatening to engulf her. That first function at the White House had not been intimate at all. It was a big formal dinner, to introduce the new Justice from Massachusetts. Fanny had approached it with trembling, a secret horror. She had dressed in silence and in silence had stepped into the cab. How magnificent Wendell looked in tails and white tie, his silk hat under his arm. *Tails and white satin . . . Ambassadors will kiss your hand.*

Fanny had not worn white satin at all, to that first ordeal. She had worn gray silk; her long stiff skirt had rustled behind her as she entered the White House. At her bosom were her favorite flowers, violets from Wendell, from under her *décolletage* rose the white net guimpe, well boned to the ears. Her gray, straight hair swept backward to its tightly braided knot, white gloves reached above her elbows.

In the Green Room, filled with chattering, laughing people, the President himself came forward, greeting Mrs. Holmes as an old friend. He had heard about her, he said genially, from the Lodges, Owen Wister; at Harvard he had, indeed, boarded for a year in a little frame house not very far from the Dixwells. . . . How uncompromising she was and how distinguished, with her look of New England, her straight back like a ramrod, her extraordinary head with the bones showing in her cheeks like a mask. The President spoke to her kindly, making conversation. Had she seen much of Washington in this first fortnight since her arrival? Had she been to Congress, met many people?

Quite a number of Congressmen's wives had called on her, Fanny replied politely. There was a veiled note in her voice that caused the President to look up, sharply. "You found the ladies pleasant?"

"Washington," Mrs. Holmes replied blandly, "is full of famous men and the women they married when they were young."

The President roared with laughter. Around them people turned inquiring heads. Mrs. Roosevelt came forward, greeting Mrs. Holmes warmly. Dinner was announced. Supreme Court Justices, of course, take precedence over everyone but ambassadors, and there were no ambassadors present. The President bowed to Fanny. Without so much as a look at her husband, moving across long carpets, under crystal chandeliers, Fanny Dixwell Holmes of Garden Street, Cambridge, laid her hand on the arm of the President of the United States and led the company in to dinner.

She was seated, of course, at the President's right. Wendell was a mile away, at the other end of the table. Roosevelt turned to Mrs. Holmes immediately, asked a question. Fanny's reply was quick. The President laughed. From across the table Fanny was aware once more of heads turned in her direction. . . .

She felt suddenly light, as free as air. Why, this was not difficult at all, this company! She could say anything, anything at all, or just sit and listen to the President. This was not a matter of trailing through brilliant rooms in the wake of a brilliant husband. In this company she was first by order of ceremony. Among all these women, so beautifully dressed and so charming, she need wait for no one to speak, for no one but her hostess to make a move.

The knowledge gave her sudden deep assurance. Fanny had always got on well with men. But here, even the women seemed eager to know her, eager to hear what she said that so amused her host. Whether they were friendly or hostile did not really matter. She was first anyway. . . . Why, one could feel at home here, could feel happy, exhilarated! It was as different from Beacon Street as heaven from hell.

All evening, Holmes watched his wife. But Fanny was marvelous! She was a huge success. This sparkling creature, easy, quick — this was the woman who for some thirty years had made life amusing, made life crackle and leap for him. Now for the first time in company he saw her let herself go, be herself, the self that never failed to fascinate.

Late that evening in the cab, leaving the White House portico, Holmes leaned forward in the darkness, tried to see his wife's face. "Fanny," he said. "You were magnificent. You captivated them all." He reached out, laid his hand over hers. "Are you happy? Fanny — tell me."

Fanny turned to her husband. Her face was grave, composed, and very tired. They rolled through the White House gates, light flashed into the carriage and was gone. "I think we shall be very much at home here, Wendell," she said. "I — find it somehow easier to go in to dinner at the head of all the company."

As the months passed, cordial relations with the White House deepened, officially as well as unofficially. In June Holmes went to England, where he had a chance to do the President a service in a very important and delicate matter.

During the winter the British had resurrected a claim to a long strip of the Alaskan coastline — convenient to the Klondike. Polite parleying, obviously, was not going to shake them loose. An arbitration commission was formed; the Americans were Lodge, Elihu Root, and ex-Senator Turner. Among the British commissioners was an old friend of Holmes's — Alverstone, Lord Chief Justice of England. Moreover, Holmes had known the British Colonial Secretary, Joseph Chamberlain, for many years.

Before the Board met, some kind of informal talk was imperative;

if the Commission came to a deadlock there would be nothing left but to shoot it out. For all the rights they had in the matter, the British might as well have claimed Nantucket Island and Roosevelt said so in a long letter to Holmes. Show this to the proper people, T. R. suggested — notably, Joseph Chamberlain.

"I wish to make one last effort," the letter said, "to bring about an agreement through the Commission. But if there is a disagreement, I wish it distinctly understood, not only that there will be no arbitration of the matter, but that in my message to Congress I shall take a position which will prevent any possibility of arbitration hereafter."

This was strong language, far too strong to have been made through any channels other than private diplomacy. It worked. When the Commission met, Lord Alverstone voted with the Americans and a dangerous business was settled.

Theodore Roosevelt, greeting Holmes in Washington next October, was well pleased with his new Justice. The Presidential handshake was hearty. What extraordinary charm the man had, Holmes thought, leaving the White House one October afternoon. That wide, infectious grin . . . There was nothing enigmatic about it, certainly. Energy like that, pugnaciousness like that, was a basic talent. And how it served the man! Roosevelt got things done, and there was evident sincerity about him. . . .

Sincerity . . . The word brought Holmes up short. It was a vague word, and suspect. What had that young Harvard fellow said the other night that was so good? *"One must always remember that T. R.'s sincerity is of a contemporary nature."* . . . Walking through the White House grounds in the clear October sunlight, Holmes quickened his step impatiently. How a man, even an old fellow like himself, got taken in by praise, by friendliness from high or low! T. R. was a politician. He had to be, it was in the nature of his job. Holmes hated politics, had no pleasure in maneuvering men.

Politics was indeed something Holmes had feared, in coming to Washington. So far, he had not had to meet it. But a Justice of the Supreme Court would do well to keep his distance and not be dazzled by qualities like sincerity, stemming from high administrative quarters. . . .

Holmes felt his frock coat over the left breast. There was one of those good cigars left. He would go up to his study and smoke it, and finish writing that second opinion he had begun on Saturday. A vast satisfaction flooded him, the President was forgotten. There were a couple of citations still to look up. . . . A good cigar and a job to do. A hard job, one to shake a man to his marrow.

In the center of Lafayette Square, golden maple leaves drifted against General Jackson, prancing on his charger. The General waved his hat. Holmes, glancing upward, grinned, and touched a finger to his forehead.

CHAPTER THIRTY-THREE

The Northern Securities case.
Theodore Roosevelt frowns.
The Lochner case.

ON December 14, 1903, the case of the *Northern Securities Company* v. *the United States* reached the Supreme Court.[1] The country turned its eyes eastward; this, obviously, was a test case. Would the Court dissolve the huge railroad merger planned by the nation's greatest businessmen, or would the merger slip through as so many other corporate plans had slipped through? Never mind legalities and technicalities. The question was whether the government of the United States lay in Wall Street or Washington. This was a good time to find out.

The Courtroom was filled, that noonday, with Congressmen, diplomats, judges, lawyers from every state in the Union. All the Justices were present except Brown, kept at home by an affliction of the eyes. Reporters noted "a fair number of ladies: Mrs. Roosevelt, Mrs. Lodge, Mrs. Knox, wife of the prosecuting Attorney General, and Mrs. Holmes." Crowded behind the bar stood the plain people, pushing in until the room would hold no more. The Northern Securities Company had a whole battery of lawyers, and when John G. Johnson of Philadelphia got up to speak, even the reporters from the radical papers conceded the rugged strength and distinction of his appearance. Beside him, the dapper little Attorney General seemed a mere David going out to battle. Reporters noted also Justice Holmes, "handsomest man on the Bench. Tall and broad-shouldered, carefully dressed, with the manners of a courtier — and the humor of his father. . . ."

But today there was time for neither humor nor courtliness. John G. Johnson stood up. In his seat, second from the end, Justice Holmes took out notebook and pencil.

This, Johnson began, was prosecution under a criminal law. Were the achievements of James J. Hill the acts of a criminal? Here was an American who had done extraordinary service to his country. Born to obscurity, almost to poverty, asking favor of no one, he had become perhaps the greatest railroad man in our nation. Through untrodden country he had laid his rails, from Minot to the Great Falls of the Missouri, through the Rocky Mountains down to tidewater on Puget Sound. Now his steamers carried American produce to China and the Far East. . . .

And through all this wild country where his railroads ran, Hill had developed the land, irrigated the dry spaces, imported fine cattle from England and gave them by the hundreds to the Western farmers to improve their stock. Here, Johnson implied, was no smug executive sitting at his desk directing the fate of thousands. Here was a man who got out and sweated, working with his hands like any good American. . . .

This of course was not law but oratory. Justice Holmes's pencil poised, waiting. Johnson, describing his hero-client, had by no means reached what Holmes was pleased to call the point of contact — "the formula — the place where the boy got his finger pinched in the machinery."

Yet what he said interested Holmes, who had always admired Jim Hill of the massive brow, the overwhelming energy, the pioneer's daring. No one, not even the Bryanites, accused Hill of dishonesty. But they accused him of power, and that was enough. In Holmes's mind the question hovered: Was power, mere bigness, illegal under the Sherman Act?

"The Northern Securities Company," Johnson's voice went on, "is enlarging commerce, not restraining it."

Holmes's pencil began to write. . . . The Court would recall, Johnson said, the favorable ruling in the anti-trust case of *Knight* v. *the United States*. . . .

From time to time, one of the Justices interrupted. Reporters came instantly awake; what a Justice said might reveal which way he was going to vote. Johnson mentioned the "thousands" involved in the transaction and Justice Harlan bent his huge bulk forward. The figures of the report, he said, spoke not of thousands but of millions.

"Yes, Your Honor," Johnson said quickly. "You see I am not given to exaggeration."

Spectators smiled. Johnson was a wizard — but Justice Harlan, it was pretty certain, would vote with the government. As for the argument of the Attorney General, people scarcely needed to listen. Was not this the public's own argument, translated into legal terms? When a trust got too big, bust it! Never mind if it called itself a merger, a trust, or a holding company. Never mind the technicalities, the laws of New Jersey and Minnesota. Bust the trust before it strangled its competitors! Prove to the people that Wall Street was not master!

The lawyers finished, gathered up their papers. The Justices rose, and the people, standing, waited for them to go, then spread noisily to the street. It might be months before a decision was announced. To hell with all these lawyers and their arguments. If the company won the case, then T. R.'s Big Stick was a willow wand and the Party had better nominate Mark Hanna for President in June.

Theodore Roosevelt himself, counting over his nine Justices, was well satisfied. He would win by a seven–two decision, or at worst a six–three. A righteously aroused public opinion would surely react upon what T. R. might have called the conscience of the Court. Let the Justices look to their conscience and settle this case as it should be settled! The atmosphere was auspicious for victory. Concerning his new judicial appointee from Massachusetts, the President had no doubts. Holmes's labor decisions in Boston, notably *Vegelahn* v. *Guntner* and the later case of *Plant* v. *Woods*, showed clearly where his sympathies lay.

The President could not have been more mistaken. To Holmes, the Supreme Court existed for the purpose of interpreting the statutes according to the Constitution of the United States — not as a whipping post for malefactors of great or little wealth. If the Northern Securities Company was proved, under the Sherman Act, to be in restraint of trade, it should be dissolved. If not, it should stand. All this pressure of public opinion served merely to cloud the issue.

Holmes, it was true, had said again and again that judges must bear in mind the economic changes in society, the "felt necessities of the time." But that was a very different matter from being stampeded by a public opinion which the exigencies of the moment dubbed "righteous." If the public would come out frankly and say it desired to sock the rich, it would be, Holmes thought, far more admirable than this pretense of using the courts to call the rich illegal simply because they were rich. As for the conscience of the Court, a court that ruled according to its "conscience" would be no court at all. Law was neither morality nor politics nor expediency nor art. Theodore Roosevelt, obviously, chose whichever definition suited the moment.

It was March before the decision was ready. In the intervening three months every precaution had been taken against leakage; the public was not even supposed to know what day to expect the decision. Nevertheless, on March 14, 1904, when the nine Justices walked to their seats at noon, they found the Courtroom jammed with spectators.

Justice Harlan began to read the majority opinion. *The Northern Securities Company was in restraint of trade. No scheme came more certainly within the words of the Sherman Anti-Trust Law. This device of Morgan and Hill would suppress free competition among railroads, and it would be impossible for Congress to protect the public against further exactions. . . .*

There was a stir in the Courtroom. The government had won! What the newspapers wanted to know was, How did the votes lie? They soon found out. The vote was five–four — in itself a surprise. But to those who considered themselves especially knowing, the greatest surprise of all was Justice Holmes's dissent. Not merely the fact that he had voted against the government, against dissolution of the Company, but his words, which were outspoken and very strong: —

> Great cases like hard cases make bad law. For great cases are called great not by reason of their real importance in shaping the law of the future but because of some accident of immediate overwhelming interest which appeals to the feelings and distorts the judgment. These immediate interests exercise a kind of hydraulic pressure which makes what previously was clear seem doubtful, and before which even well-settled principles of law will bend. . . . We must read the words before us as if

the question were whether two small exporting grocers shall go
to jail. . . .

There is a natural feeling that somehow or other the statute
meant to strike at combinations great enough to cause just
anxiety on the part of those who love their country more than
money, while it viewed such little ones as I supposed with just
indifference. This notion, it may be said, somehow breathes
from the pores of the act. . . .

In the first place, size in the case of railroads is an inevitable
incident . . . in the case of railroads it is evident that the size
of the combination is reached for other ends than those which
could make them monopolies. . . .

Of the majority of the Court, only three concurred in Harlan's
opinion. (Justice Brewer had written a separate opinion.) Holmes
was happy to know therefore — he went on — that only a minority
of his brethren had adopted an interpretation of the law which
in his opinion "would make eternal the *bellum omnium contra omnes*
and disintegrate society so far as it could into individual atoms."

If that were its intent I should regard calling such a law a
regulation of commerce as a mere pretense. It would be an attempt to reconstruct society. I am not concerned with the wisdom of such an attempt but I believe that Congress was not
entrusted by the Constitution with the power to make it and I
am deeply persuaded that it has not tried.

I am authorized to say that the Chief Justice, Mr. Justice
White and Mr. Justice Peckham concur in this dissent.

Theodore Roosevelt heard the decision of the Court and was
jubilant. The suit, he said, was one of the greatest achievements of
his administration. The Knight case had been overruled, the Northern
Securities Company was dissolved, the power of the government
against the monopolies was established. The government — Roosevelt
called it "we" — had gained the power.

But it was a crime that the decision had not been more nearly
unanimous. Justice Holmes's dissent in particular was outrageous.
What did the man mean, turning against him that way? Obviously,
Holmes had simply lost his nerve. "I could carve out of a banana,"
shouted T. R., "a judge with more backbone than that!"

Holmes himself cared nothing whatever about the Presidential reactions. He was, in fact, as angry as the President. Years later, he wrote to Pollock about it. "[The affair] broke up our incipient friendship, however, as [Roosevelt] looked on my dissent . . . as a political departure (or, I suspect, more truly, couldn't forgive anyone who stood in his way). We talked freely later but it was never the same after that, and if he had not been restrained by his friends, I am told that he would have made a fool of himself and would have excluded me from the White House. . . . I never cared a damn whether I went there or not. He was very likeable, a big figure, a rather ordinary intellect, with extraordinary gifts, a shrewd and I think pretty unscrupulous politician. He played all his cards — if not more."

In March, 1904, feeling ran high after the Northern Securities decision, not only in Washington but all over the country. Wall Street had been dreading the decision. Now that it came, stocks went down. Most certainly, this would be only the prelude; T. R. would not stop with one victory. There was to be a Presidential election in the fall. As usual the Roosevelt luck held, and his only formidable rival in the party, Mark Hanna, died in February.

In June the Republican convention met in Chicago, with Cabot Lodge much in evidence — and nominated the Trust Buster by acclamation. Five months later, Roosevelt was elected by the largest popular and electoral majority to date.

And on March 4, 1905, nine Supreme Court Justices sat on a windy platform outside the Capitol building while the President was sworn in. The older a Justice got, the more he dreaded this quadrennial exposure; it was a matter for pneumonia and the ague. Oliver Wendell Holmes, shivering, watched a trifle sardonically while Chief Justice Fuller, his white hair lifted by an icy wind, administered the oath.

The Dude Cowboy was back in the White House, with the people's mandate behind him. There would be no stopping the slaughter now. In cartoon after cartoon, newspapers took up the crusade. The fat trusts in their traditional costume of checked waistcoat and fancy watch chain — the Cheese Trust, the Meat Trust, the Sugar Trust — talk behind their hands, watching across the room nine black-gowned figures. "The Supreme Court," they whisper, "is a nervy bunch. Those judges should be abolished."

The Pure Food and Drug Act went through, the Anti-rebate law, the Employers' Liability Act. "The door to the White House," T. R. shouted, "shall swing open just as easily to the poor as to the rich — *and not one bit easier*." The Hepburn rate law went through. In Philadelphia, Holmes's friend Owen Wister, desiring to ride to New York in the engineer's cab, went to Dewitt Cuyler for a pass. Wister must buy a ticket, Cuyler said genially. The halcyon day of free passes was done. "We have to be good now."

We have to be good now. . . . But if Theodore Roosevelt was out to bust the trusts, the corporations themselves were out to bust the labor unions and to outwit also, where they could, the new state laws regulating the hours of workmen. Ten-hour laws, eight-hour laws . . . Why, if the employers didn't look sharp, the courts would forget all about "freedom of contract"; the police power of the states would prevail over that sacred and conveniently misty phrase of the Fourteenth Amendment — "*due process of law*."

To Justice Holmes, combination on the one side was as lawful, within limits, as on the other. In the Northern Securities dissent he had upheld the side of capital — although he would have disliked to hear it called a "side." Now, a year later, he was to uphold the other — the right of a state to regulate the hours of labor. Holmes's dissent in the Lochner case was among his most significant utterances in Court. It heralded a long and noble list of such dissents, opinions which were to prove him, old though he was, far younger in spirit than his brethren, at once prophetic in vision and tough-minded in the law.

The fact that Holmes's most famous opinions were dissenting opinions by no means sets him down as a rebel or a no-sayer. Holmes always regretted the necessity of dissenting, believing that too many dissents detract from the prestige of the Court. But the blunt fact remained that in a period of vast and almost revolutionary social change, Holmes found himself on the Bench with a majority so conservative as to be not merely stubborn but blind. He had to voice his dissent — to remain silent would have been to shirk his duty.

Moreover it was not the number of his dissents that won for Holmes the title of the Great Dissenter. Some of his brethren dissented more often than he did.* It was the quality of Holmes's dis-

* See Table on page 456 giving number of Holmes's dissents in 1902–1932 in proportion to dissents of the other Justices.

sents that made them famous, it was what he said and how he said it. When a Justice writes a majority opinion, he is speaking for the Court. But when he dissents he has a chance to say what he thinks personally, and these individual expressions play a very significant part in the function of the Supreme Court. "A dissent in a court of last resort is an appeal to the brooding spirit of the law, to the intelligence of a future day, when a later decision may possibly correct the error into which the dissenting judge believes the court to have been betrayed." *

The Lochner dissent was most certainly such an appeal — and as certainly it became, years later, the majority opinion and therefore the law of the land. The Lochner case concerned moreover a conviction that Holmes held very deeply: the conviction that under the Constitution, the states have a right to make their own social experiments. When these experiments — these state laws — seem to conflict with federal authority, then let the case be decided not on the basis of whether the Supreme Court believes the law concerned to be a good law or a bad law. Let it be decided solely on the basis of whether the Constitution forbids it. "I strongly believe," Holmes said from the Bench, "that my agreement or disagreement [with a certain economic theory] has nothing to do with the right of the majority to embody their opinions in law."

Whether these theories, these economic experiments, resulted in disaster was not, Holmes thought, a judge's business. Just now, in 1905, the experiments tended all towards combination, collectivism. And whether the combination was of capital, as in the Northern Securities case, or of labor wishing to protect itself by state laws, as in the Lochner case — at all events let the experiments be made. Those men who, fearing experiment, desire to preserve the *status quo*, let those men — be they judges, capitalists, or laboring men — not hide behind the Sherman Act or the vague phrases of the *due process* clause.

The Lochner suit was a perfect case in point. New York State had passed a law prohibiting more than ten hours work per day in bakeries. A man named Lochner who owned a bakery in Utica broke the law twice and was fined for it. Lochner appealed on the grounds that the ten-hour law was class legislation, favoring the

* From *The Supreme Court of the United States*, by Charles Evans Hughes.

workers. It denied, said Lochner's counsel, "equal protection of the laws."

Justice Holmes, listening to the defendant's long harangue, summed up the case before Mr. Lochner's lawyer had been at it ten minutes. The Justices went into conference, voted five–four in favor of Lochner. Justice Peckham wrote the majority opinion, and on April 5, 1905, announced it in Court. The ten-hour law, he declared, was a "meddlesome interference"; the spread of such laws in the various states was deplorable. The men who passed this particular law had called it a health protective measure. But surely their real motive had not been the manufacture of healthy bread! Their motive had been to regulate the hours of labor. Which then should prevail, the police power of a state, or "freedom of contract"? In other words, should the individual be a slave to the state, or should he remain free, under the Constitution, to manage his factory as he pleased?

What Justice Peckham defended was not merely the right of one employer to work his bakers more than ten hours a day. He was defending a whole social system. He did not once use the words *laissez faire*. He did not need to. Obviously, *laissez faire* was the social system he favored — was indeed the only system he recognized. Revolutions had been fought to achieve it, Herbert Spencer had endorsed it. It had sufficed for a hundred years and more, under it our country had grown great and fat. Why endanger the system then, with these interfering laws? "Clean and wholesome bread," said Justice Peckham serenely, "does not depend on whether a baker works but ten hours per day or only sixty hours a week."

Almost anywhere else, Rufus Peckham could have spoken these words with little harm done. But the majority opinion of the Supreme Court becomes the law of the land. It creates a precedent that may sway future courts for decades. Justice Peckham, giving voice to the majority opinion in favor of Mr. Lochner who worked his bakers more than ten hours a day, was fixing the fate of workingmen for a generation to come.

Oliver Wendell Holmes was only three years younger than his esteemed colleague from New York. It was not youth, then, which told him that economic systems are far from indestructible. He had been brought up, like Peckham, under the most favorable circumstances which the social concept of *laissez faire* could create. Yet

Holmes sensed that the system was dead at heart. A giant industrial society was busy making its own new pattern.

When Justice Peckham had finished, Holmes rustled his papers, leaned forward, and began to read his dissent. The first line of it gave the gist of what he was going to say: —

> This case is decided upon an economic theory which a large part of the country does not entertain. . . .
>
> It is settled by various decisions of this Court that State constitutions and State laws may regulate life in many ways which we as legislators might think . . . injudicious . . .
>
> The liberty of the citizen to do as he likes so long as he does not interfere with the liberty of others to do the same, which has been a shibboleth for some well-known writers, is interfered with by the school laws, by the Post Office, by every State or municipal institution which takes his money for purposes thought desirable, whether he likes it or not. The Fourteenth Amendment does not enact Mr. Herbert Spencer's *Social Statics*.
>
> The other day we sustained the Massachusetts vaccination law . . . The decision sustaining an eight-hour law for miners is still recent. . . . Some of these laws embody convictions or prejudices which judges are likely to share. Some may not. But a constitution is not intended to embody a particular economic theory, whether of paternalism and the organic relation of the citizen to the State or of *laissez faire*. It is made for people of fundamentally differing views, and the accident of our finding certain opinions natural and familiar or novel and even shocking ought not to conclude our judgment upon the question whether statutes embodying them conflict with the Constitution of the United States.

These were fighting words, and to that portion of the nation which understood them, they were words of hope. On the Court there was no other man equipped to say them. That Holmes himself hated to dissent, that he by no means desired to be known as fighter, reformer, or dissenter, did not matter one whit to the people who read his words. As a matter of fact he had said earlier that Supreme Court Justices must be careful not to let the Constitution become the mere partisan of their own set of ethical or economic opinions. But he had not said it so well, and the cases where he expressed it had not been so striking.

"*The people have a right to make their own mistakes.*" A man poles apart from Holmes had spoken these words a decade earlier: William Jennings Bryan, demagogue and inspired rabble rouser who was far closer to the people than Holmes was when he gave the Lochner dissent in 1905. Yet in different ways and from different spheres the two had said the same thing. But the conviction that breathes from the Lochner dissent is neither the oratory of the demagogue nor the hot fury of the reformer — of a Brandeis, angry because laboring men are being exploited. It is rather the cold clear anger of the intellectual who believes that freedom means, above all, the right to experiment.

This was Holmes's stand. He had been on the Supreme Court for three years. In the past thirteen months he had given voice to two important dissents, one on the side of capital, one on the side of labor. The people did not think of him, so far, as one of their great Justices, their great men. It would be a long time indeed before the people became really aware of Justice Oliver Wendell Holmes.

But he had taken his stand. It was calm, it was consistent. It stemmed from intellectual conviction. And it was a stand the nation could count on him to sustain for twenty-six years, until at the age of ninety he would leave the Court forever.

CHAPTER THIRTY-FOUR

The Justice is seventy. Holmes's
Annuals. He makes a prophecy.

MARCH, 1911 . . . Taft was President. With vast reluctance, Theodore Roosevelt had torn himself from the White House, refusing a third term — fifty-two years old, "fit as a bull moose," and longing to finish the work he had begun. Before he left he sent the Fleet around the world, a huge gesture, hitherto unheard of and in this case highly symbolic. Manifest Destiny was achieved, the U.S.A. was a world power. Over Porto Rico, Guam, the Philippines, Alaska, Hawaii, the flag flew. Since 1900 the Monroe Doctrine had taken on new significance; sixteen battleships went out to advertise the fact. The Great White Fleet, putting into Yokohama, Hamburg, Southampton, Cherbourg, bands playing, guns bristling, the U.S. flag at the masthead.

The national boundaries were drawn, it was time for America to keep house. There was a new word in the U.S.A.: *conservation.* T.R. had set the machinery in motion. Save the forests, save the game, fish, the wild life of the prairies and Western mountains.

Power bubbled up from below; everywhere, the people found their spokesmen. Jacob Riis in New York, Jane Addams in Chicago, fought the slums. Harvey Wiley had talked the nation into the Pure Food and Drug Act. The Meat Inspection Act went through, the Narcotics Act, the Employers' Liability Act, the Income Tax Amendment. States that wanted it had prohibition. The American Federation of Labor had nearly one million eight hundred thousand members; other unions combined had over two million.[1] The spirit touched also those in high places. Andrew Carnegie put forty million dollars into free libraries. Rockefeller, just beginning to set his philanthropic pace, gave a million dollars to fight hookworm, twenty million to fight cancer, forty million for education.

And the wind still blew against monopoly.

March 8, 1911 . . . Oliver Wendell Holmes is seventy. "Give my love to Lady Pollock," he writes. "Tell her the old man swept round the last post to the home stretch going strong."

On the Supreme Court are four new Justices: Lurton, Van Devanter, Hughes, Lamar. White of Louisiana has moved up to the seat under the red canopy. Holmes says he doesn't care who is Chief Justice; he himself is too old to be appointed, he likes White and trusts him. He likes Charles Evans Hughes, too, red-bearded Baptist from New York, a good fellow, "with doubts that open vistas through the wall of a non-conformist conscience."

But the nation watched a trifle anxiously. Would Taft's new Justices be in line with the times? Oklahoma, new to statehood, swamped the Court with legislation. Cases piled up.

To Holmes, his brethren seemed possessed of a very demon of long-windedness. They took from two weeks to six months to write an opinion he could turn off between Saturday and Monday. Washington knew him as the only Justice who could sum up a case while the lawyer was still arguing — no mean intellectual feat. But the lawyers themselves, if they lost a case, protested loudly: this haste on the part of Justice Holmes must mean "inadequate consideration." They petitioned for rehearings; Holmes, they complained, should deliver longer opinions with the citations written out, not just signified by number. "May God twist my tripes," roared Oliver Wendell Holmes, "if I string out the obvious for the delectation of fools!"

As a matter of fact, Holmes was the only Justice of the nine to be seen in the Court library reading the Year Books. He loved them, paged them over like a story. But this did not mean, he said, that he was going to spoil a good argument by stopping for three pages of quotations any jackass of a Graduate School Magazine editor could look up for himself. "Such humbugs prevail!" he wrote Pollock. "If a man keeps a case six months it is supposed to be decided upon 'great consideration.' It seems to me that intensity is the only thing. A day's impact is better than a month of dead pull."

Each Justice was entitled to a secretary, paid by the government. Holmes had a new one every year, sent down by John Gray * from the Harvard Law School. They arrived in September, the pick of the graduating class. Filled with zeal they sat down at the big desk beyond the open double doors from Holmes's study, expecting to read important briefs for the Justice, to examine motion papers, petitions for certiorari.† It did not take a day to discover that the Justice did not need a secretary. He wrote out his opinions, looked up his citations, read every petition for certiorari — he called them "petes for cert." The young men, recovering from this shock, made their own job — which was to learn from the Justice whatever he chose to teach about life, law, philosophy, and the nature of man. And the measure of their success was the measure of their capacity. "*The ferment of genius in its creative moments is quickly imparted. If a man is great, he makes others believe in greatness. . . .*"

The young men were like sons to Holmes. "Lad," he called them. "Sonny — Young Feller — Idiot Boy." He showed them his written opinions, talked to them about the cases. Sometimes he lent one of them to another Justice; none of his brethren had secretaries beyond the stenographer class, and it was good to have someone who could be trusted with details of cases while they were pending.

The program left much spare time, during which the young men made themselves extremely useful, paying the family bills, balancing the checkbooks, cutting coupons at the bank, and leaving the Justice's calling card at a score of official doors. There were in the end thirty of them.[2] "Holmes's Annuals," they were called. They became, later on, Attorney Generals of the United States, Chairmen of the Board of U.S. Steel, Presidents of New York Life Insurance, Presidents of Federal Banks, professors at Harvard and professors elsewhere. But when they arrived in Washington, autumn after autumn, they were young, eager, and some of them were shy. Mrs. Holmes took charge immediately, saw that they met everyone, showed them Washington from the Monument to Great Falls, and took them to parties at the White House.

---

* Later sent by E. R. Thayer and Felix Frankfurter.
† Lawyers call these petitions for "surshurairee." They are applications to the Supreme Court to review the action of a lower federal or state court.

The household was settled now on I* Street, not far from Lafayette Square, in a comfortable, four-story brick house. The Holmes family had become old inhabitants of Washington. How far away seemed that other life, that long, cramped Northern winter! Here, spring came early. Fanny, strewing suet in the yard, called out that she had seen a bluebird, a scarlet tanager. There were trees one never saw in New England, the pagoda tree, the polonia with its purple blossoms. Even the housekeeping was different, with grouse plentiful in the markets, railbirds, blackbirds, and pigeons. Instead of Yankee bargaining one heard the soft, slow voices of the colored people. Fanny liked them, repeated their sayings to her husband and one day announced that she had engaged a colored houseboy. Annie and Mary would have to learn to like him, she said.

Yet Washington would never be home, really. New England was home. Granite rocks and barberry bushes, the sparse steep pastures of the Berkshire Hills. Beacon Street in February, with the blackened snow piled in the gutters and an east wind sweeping down from the Narrows. New England was in their bones, it was the tradition of their house and the visitor felt it the moment he entered the front door. To the left of a narrow hallway the white staircase rose, mahogany-railed; there was a gleam of dark furniture. Chippendale from the Jacksons, Queen Anne tables from the Olivers, and comfortable, ugly tufted rockers from 296 Beacon Street. Holmes's study was on the second floor, books went up to the ceiling all round. Sun from the south window flowed past Grandfather Jackson's high desk in the corner and over the mantel Holmes's sword hung, the colors of the Twentieth Regiment drooping from its hilt. On the big desk where he worked were his father's inkstand and a conch shell reminiscent of the pearly nautilus that had lain so long on Dr. Holmes's table. *Build thee more stately mansions, O my soul, As the swift seasons roll.*[3]

Yet there was in this quite elderly household an extraordinary air of life and movement. Young people came in often — to tea and dinner; young men from the embassies brought their best girls. At night Holmes's secretaries, passing very late, would see lights blazing from cellar to attic. "You may call on us any time up to two a.m.," Mrs. Holmes told her friends.

* Washingtonians call this Eye Street.

Toward his work also, Justice Holmes had the attitude of a young man — a young man's eagerness, a young man's stage fright if a big case came his way. Each Saturday afternoon when his messenger brought the portfolio from Court — "There is no such thing as a hard case," Holmes told himself, but the formula did not work until he actually took pen in hand. "I am frightened weekly," he confessed to Pollock. "But always when you walk up to the lion and lay hold the hide comes off and the same old donkey of a question of law is underneath."

The *New York Sun* seized upon an opinion he wrote in a New Jersey water-rate case. "Is this," the paper demanded, "the son of Oliver Wendell Holmes? This writing is as obscure as Emerson's Brahma. Is this the way they talk at Harvard?"

Holmes was mightily depressed. His brethren had complained that brevity too often obscured his meaning. Maybe they were right. Holmes took his next opinion to his secretary, swore at him when he could not understand it. "I write for the expert," Holmes said stiffly. "What you are looking for is contained in that one word. Here! You can find it in the dictionary." He stalked to his desk. The secretary returned the manuscript. Yes, that word did mean a whole sentence — but . . .

"Oh God damn it!" Holmes said. "If you don't understand it, there will be some other fool who won't." And he wrote in the extra sentence.

In May, 1911, Chief Justice White delivered the majority decision in two huge anti-trust cases: Standard Oil and American Tobacco. Once more the Courtroom was crowded to suffocation, once more John G. Johnson had summoned all his eloquence. But Standard Oil and American Tobacco went down before the hailstorm of their own recorded sins.

The country acclaimed it as a total victory. Big business knew better, this was only a technical defeat. In his decision, White had ruled out Standard Oil as an *unreasonable* combination or monopoly in restraint of trade. Unreasonable . . . The word, read into the Sherman Act, was a loophole for the future. The trusts seized upon it, looking forward to a rule of reason with a careful sliding scale.

Justice Harlan dissented angrily; it was he who had written the opinion dissolving Northern Securities and he wanted dissolution with no pink ribbons attached. But Holmes concurred in White's opinion. He still considered the Sherman Act "a humbug, based on ignorance and incompetence," and he was by no means convinced that it expressed the will of the majority. Were the people's howls over individually owned wealth really proportionate to their sufferings from the same? The men of fortune howled in their turn over any attempt at combined power on the part of workingmen. Justice Harlan wanted every moneyed combine scattered to the winds of heaven. Justice McKenna wanted the same for every labor union. It seemed to Holmes that Justice White had done as well as he could under the circumstances.

"There is a very important truth to be extracted from the popular discontent," Holmes told his friends of the Harvard Law School at a dinner in New York. "We must . . . try to see what we can learn from hatred and distrust and whether behind them there may not be some germ of inarticulate truth."

Holmes had not wanted to make this speech and he had come with reluctance to New York; he did not approve of Supreme Court Justices mounting the rostrum to give off their private views. All the way up in the train, he had thought about what he was to say. People invented nostrums, panaceas, cure-alls for the public ill. Holmes could not believe in any of them. *Socialism!* How men had feared it, twenty years ago. Judges everywhere translated their fears into doctrines that had no proper place in the Constitution or the common law. Yet making a law doesn't quiet a man's fears . . . Holmes took out an envelope, scribbled on the back of it. "For most of the things that properly can be called evils in the present state of the law I think the main remedy is for us to grow more civilized."

That night in New York, standing in the crowded, smoky dining room, his knuckles resting on the cloth, Holmes looked slowly round at his old friends in the law.

How many eras, how many patterns of thought he had seen pass! February, 1913 . . . In eighteen months the world would be plunged in war. Standing now at the end of an era, at the end of a way of life, Holmes could not know how prophetic his words would be. His voice was slow, there was a rhythm to it as always when he was deeply moved: —

. . . As I grow older I grow calm. If I feel what are perhaps an old man's apprehensions, that competition from new races will cut deeper than working men's disputes and will test whether we can hang together and can fight; if I fear that we are running through the world's resources at a pace we cannot keep; I do not lose my hopes.

I do not pin my dreams for the future to my country or even to my race. I think it probable that civilization somehow will last as long as I care to look ahead — perhaps with smaller numbers, but perhaps also bred to greatness and splendor by science. I think it not improbable that man, like the grub that prepares a chamber for the winged thing it never has seen but is to be — that man may have cosmic destinies that he does not understand. And so beyond the vision of battling races and an impoverished earth I catch a dreaming glimpse of peace.

The other day my dream was pictured to my mind. It was evening. I was walking homeward on Pennsylvania Avenue near the Treasury, and as I looked beyond Sherman's Statue to the west the sky was aflame with scarlet and crimson from the setting sun. But, like the note of downfall in Wagner's opera, below the sky line there came from little globes the pallid discord of the electric lights.

And I thought to myself the Götterdämmerung will end, and from those globes clustered like evil eggs will come the new masters of the sky. It is like the time in which we live. But then I remembered the faith that I partly have expressed, faith in a universe not measured by our fears, a universe that has thought and more than thought inside of it, and as I gazed, after the sunset and above the electric lights there shone the stars.

CHAPTER THIRTY-FIVE

*World War. The U. S. v. Child
Labor. War's aftermath. Holmes
defends the Bill of Rights.*

EUROPE was at war . . . Louvain in ruins. Rheims Cathedral shelled . . . America read the reports, looked at the pictures in the Sunday rotogravures. *Berlin accuses France of atrocities. England has cut the German cable to America.*

The United States was horrified, incredulous. Each side called the other wicked. Kitchener's soldiers sang "It's a long way to Tipperary" — America could understand that far better than she could understand the implications of *Der Tag*. Was it possible Germany had wanted this war?

President Wilson urged neutrality. Neutrality was our duty and he would make every effort towards mediation. The nation responded. *Let's keep out of it.* Thank God Columbus discovered America. Thank God for a cool-headed President and five thousand miles of ocean. The *Lusitania* was sunk in May, 1915. Three days later Woodrow Wilson told a stunned, bewildered nation there was such a thing as being too proud to fight. The nation preferred to ignore the fact that he was referring to Mexico.

Stay in America! the posters said. Citizens, keep off the high seas! Keep out of trouble! Wilson sent a note of protest to Germany. It was too strongly worded, Bryan said. Why couldn't the President protest against the English blockade while he was about it? Bryan resigned as Secretary of State, toured the country talking peace. Henry Ford launched his Peace Ship: if Europe desired a mediator he would be glad to oblige. Three weeks later he was home again. "I didn't get much peace," he said. "But I learned that Russia is going to be a great market for tractors."

By January, 1916, Bethlehem Steel had jumped to 479. On soapboxes in Herald Square, men shouted that war was made by Wall Street. Woodrow Wilson shifted his tune, tried to lead a reluctant nation in a new chorus: "Prepare! No man can be sure of the morrow."

From the beginning, Holmes's attitude did not change. He hated war. Three years of soldiering had not left him with an old man's bagful of tales concerning the glories of the field, the camaraderie of camp and barracks. "War is an organized bore," he had said when he was in the middle of it. But he had lived through many wars and could not believe, he said, that this one was the end of all things. Because moralists and philosophers declared that war was wicked and foolish, was that any reason to think it was due to disappear? "As long as man dwells upon the globe his destiny is battle and he has to take the chances of war." Years ago Holmes had said this, and had been called jingo by the press. "I loathe war," he wrote Pollock.[1] "But I do think that man at present is a predatory animal. . . . Between two groups that want to make inconsistent kinds of world I see no remedy except force."

At the French Embassy, the British Embassy, Jusserand and Spring-Rice talked less of war than of the enemy, of strategy, diplomacy, propaganda. But there was a new group of young men in Washington who talked far differently, who passionately desired this to be the last war of all wars, yet who were passionately critical of America. Felix Frankfurter, Francis Hackett, Walter Lippmann, Herbert Croly, Philip Littell.[2] They came and went — Frankfurter was already teaching at the Harvard Law School — but when they were in town they were to be found in bachelor quarters on Nineteenth Street. They were the fastest talkers, the quickest thinkers, Holmes had met in many a year. They used a new word — *internationalism*. They wrote books, brought them round to I Street hot off the press, with titles like *Drift and Mastery*, *Progressive Democracy*. They were starting a weekly, the *New Republic*. Holmes had subscribed to it "with hope," he said.

Holmes teased them a little about their come-outers' intensity.

"You young men seem to think that if you sit on the world long enough you will hatch something out. But you're wrong." The House of Truth, he called their quarters, and the name caught on in Washington. They were such very earnest thinkers! Surely he himself had not been like that, back in the days when with Peirce and James and Wright he had settled the affairs of the cosmos? "These young men," Holmes wrote to Pollock, "are so damned solemn. . . . At times I think the men in the trenches are the gayest people left. I was rather gay in the army when certainly I was unhappy enough. *Que sçay je?*"

Returning from Court in the afternoon, Holmes would find the young men at his house, talking about the war, arguing passionately. "What is it?" he would ask quickly. "Tell me, I'll take the opposite side." Everything they said he challenged, everything was put to the bitter test of proof, and when occasionally they worsted him, Holmes was delighted. He had not forgotten that period when the young made a fashion of indifference. *Fin de siècle* . . . how he had despised it!

Some, less tough-minded, fled the old man's "cynicism." Holmes let them go. *The capacity to want something fiercely and want it all the time* — this was the quality he sought, and those who lacked it feared him.

In January, President Wilson named Louis Brandeis to the Supreme Court. It was totally unexpected and it pushed the war temporarily off the front page. From coast to coast, newspapers took sides. Businessmen met in organized protest, declaring Brandeis was a socialist, a labor sympathizer — next door to an anarchist. For years he had been known as the People's Lawyer. How, Business demanded, could a man with such a record possess judicial detachment? Any oppressed minority could command his services for nothing; the fact that he usually won the case made him only the more dangerous. Boston said the President might as well have nominated Gompers, and why hadn't he asked the advice of Senator Lodge? President Lowell of Harvard headed a committee of fifty-five protesting citizens.

A Senate investigation was started, it lasted five months. Forty-three witnesses were heard, thirteen hundred pages of testimony taken. Throughout the battle, Holmes kept his mouth discreetly shut. No one knew better than he that the Court needed a Brandeis —

a judge who knew economics, a master of statistics, with a mind rapier sharp. Holmes divided lawyers into kitchen knives, razors, and stings. Brandeis, he said, was a sting.

Brandeis was a sting. Yet behind the sting was something more powerful than venom, something of illumination — an extraordinary faith in the future. All these young men had it — Frankfurter, Lippmann, Morris Cohen, Harold Laski the Englishman.

The Senate voted forty-seven to twenty-two in favor of Brandeis. The country forgot him; Wilson was campaigning for a second term. "He kept us out of war," the people said, and voted for him. In January, 1917, Wilson addressed the Senate, pleading for a speedy peace settlement. Let America use its prestige not only to make peace but to set up a super-state, a world union of all nations.

For answer, Germany announced unrestricted submarine warfare. "All sea traffic will be stopped with every available weapon and without further notice."

American soldiers began sailing for France late in 1917. Ten thousand a day, the troops embarked in the spring. Boys from Kansas, Pittsburgh, Cheyenne, who had never seen salt water, cheered and sang from the decks, waving lusty farewell.

The Yanks were coming, were on their way.

American mothers read picture postcards with foreign stamps, strange foreign names scrawled in a familiar, joking hand . . . Amiens, Ypres. . . . It was not necessary to pronounce the words. It was enough to know one's son might die there.

By July the first million had landed in France, by October the second million would arrive. It was the largest overseas movement of troops in history. To accomplish it America spent effort and money beyond her wildest dreams, built miles of barracks overnight, built ship towns, steel-making towns, moved whole populations across the country. Engineers, business executives, traveled to Washington to talk to Barney Baruch.

Oliver Wendell Holmes, walking from Court in the late afternoon, watched men and women pour from the great new office buildings. The wide familiar streets, the familiar quiet shops, were suddenly peopled with strangers. But within an ancient, shabby chamber of the Capitol, the business of the Supreme Court moved forward as usual. It was the concern of nine men to make it move, war or no war. Fighting abroad must not interfere with the administration of justice at home.

Justice! Holmes told his brethren he hated the word. When a man began to talk about justice, for one reason or another he was refusing to think in legal terms — in terms of the evidence and the law. Right now, in the very middle of the war — June 1918 — a case had come up that outraged every conception of justice. By a five–four vote the Supreme Court declared the Child Labor Law unconstitutional.

The Child Labor Law itself was only two years old. Fifteen years of struggle had been required to get it through Congress. Almost immediately a farmer named Dagenhart, desiring to keep his young sons in a North Carolina cotton mill, brought suit. Mill owners all over the country backed him, making it a test case. Sitting in Court, Holmes listened, cold with contempt, to the old Lochner argument over again . . . *Abuse of the police power, invasion of States' rights.* . . . If Congress can thus regulate matters, said Justice Day in the majority opinion, "our system of government will be practically destroyed."

It was flagrant, outrageous. Even crusty old Justice McKenna dissented. So did Clarke and so of course did Brandeis.

Holmes wrote the dissent, which was brief and wholly undramatic. . . . "If there is any matter upon which civilized countries have agreed . . . it is the evil of premature and excessive child labor. . . ."

Afterward in the robing room, Holmes and Brandeis eyed each other. It was too late for talk, the thing was done. . . . But walking toward I Street in the late June afternoon, Holmes went over the whole thing in his mind, wondered if he could not have expressed himself better, more forcibly. Moral conceptions don't belong in a court of law. Yet by the Lord, if judges were going to talk cant about freedom of the individual, this was certainly one case where all the powers of the United States should have been employed to uphold real freedom and individualism under the Constitution.

God only knew for how many years this decision would hold. Tomorrow a nation that was up to its ears in war and grief would take time from war and grief to read this new outrage in the newspapers.

July saw American soldiers battling on the Marne; the assault on the German lines had started. September . . . October . . . the Yanks drove forward at St.-Mihiel. The Meuse–Argonne offensive was only a fraction of a much larger plan of war — but it started the Germans on their last retreat. The Allies — which for America meant the Yanks — were headed for German soil.

And Germany knew it. On November 10, dispatches from Berlin said the city was in control of the revolutionists; the Kaiser had fled to Holland. On November 11 the Armistice was signed. President Wilson sailed for Europe, the United States got ready for peace. This had been the war to end wars and we had won it. We were the greatest nation on earth. Woodrow Wilson was over there saving the world for democracy.

At Versailles, Wilson signed the Peace Treaty, sailed home to what he thought was victory for an ideal. He found, instead, defeat and heartbreak. In six months a nation can change its heart: America no longer desired to save the world for democracy. America desired to save its skin. The U.S. screamed for Business As Usual — Give us the old days back again!

Germany was no longer the enemy. Far to the eastward a new bogy loomed: *Bolshevism, communism!* To America the words were synonymous with terror. Let a man open his mouth against "capitalism" and he was called Bolshevist, alien anarchist, and hunted down. The sport of Red-baiting had begun. For the next ten years the chase would lead again and again to the old Courtroom in the Capitol building, to seven Justices who hunted with the pack and two who dissented.

The 1920's were to be for America fat years, intolerant years. Oliver Wendell Holmes could stand the sight of his country suffering and heroic better than the sight of it sleek and intolerant. Where now were the virtues of 1918, of 1863 and 1776? "The prevailing notion of free speech," Holmes wrote to Pollock, "seems to be that you may say what you choose if you don't shock *me*. . . . The whole collectivist tendency seems to be toward underrating or forgetting the safeguards in bills of rights that had to be fought for in their day and that still are worth fighting for. I have had to deal with cases that made my blood boil and yet seemed to create no feeling in the public or even in most of my brethren."

Holmes wrote this letter just before the Abrams case. Abrams, a Russian-born American, had protested against the sending of American troops into Russia after the Revolution of 1917. It was a crime, said Abrams, for workers of America to fight a workers' republic in Russia. He and his friends, meeting in a basement room in New York, put their protest into print. "Our reply to this barbaric intervention has to be a general strike! It is absurd to call us pro-German. We hate and despise German militarism more than do you hypocritical tyrants. Awake! Awake! you workers of the world." Signed, "Revolutionists."

There was much more of the same. Let the workers remember that Capitalism was their real enemy . . . Let solidarity live! . . . Abrams and his friends went up on the roof and scattered their leaflets. The Department of Justice picked them up; a week later the pack was in full cry.

Privately, Holmes considered the leaflets "drool, a creed of immaturity"; the whole thing should have been ignored. Under the Espionage Act a man was punished only if he threatened the United States with *immediate* danger. Only seven months earlier, Holmes had written the majority opinion that sent Eugene Debs to jail[3] — but that had been a different matter altogether. Frohwerk, Schenck, and Debs had actually tried to obstruct recruiting. Abrams had scattered his leaflets in the middle of the war, but he had not tried to hamper the war effort. He had merely differed with United States policy concerning intervention in Russia. "Congress," Holmes said in Court, "certainly cannot forbid all effort to change the mind of the country."

Seven Justices thought differently. Outside the Courtroom waited a nation that feared and loathed every word that Abrams had spoken. Seven Justices listened to the nation. In the majority opinion, Justice Clarke referred not to "the defendants" but to the "defendant alien anarchists." There was no need for spectators to hear further.

Oliver Wendell Holmes waited. This was not a trial but a travesty of a trial; these men were being condemned not for what they did but for what they believed. Justice Clarke finished and the Courtroom was silent. Holmes began to read . . .

. . . Sentences of twenty years' imprisonment have been imposed for the publishing of two leaflets that I believe the defendants had as much right to publish as the Government has to publish the Constitution of the United States now vainly invoked by them.

Even if I am technically wrong and enough can be squeezed from these poor and puny anonymities to turn the color of legal litmus paper . . . the most nominal punishment seems to me all that possibly could be inflicted, unless the defendants are to be made to suffer not for what the indictment alleges but for the creed that they avow. . . .

. . . When men have realized that time has upset many fighting faiths, they may come to believe even more than they believe the very foundations of their own conduct that the ultimate good desired is better reached by free trade in ideas — that the best test of truth is the power of the thought to get itself accepted in the competition of the market, and that truth is the only ground upon which their wishes safely can be carried out. That, at any rate, is the theory of our Constitution. It is an experiment, as all life is an experiment. . . . While that experiment is part of our system I think we should be eternally vigilant against attempts to check the expression of opinions that we loathe and believe to be fraught with death. . . .

. . . I regret that I cannot put into more impressive words my belief that in their conviction upon this indictment the defendants were deprived of their rights under the Constitution of the United States.

Justice Holmes need have had no regrets. His words were impressive enough. Behind them lay the weight of his whole life, his days as they had been lived since the beginning. Shouts of the mob, fighting by torchlight around Boston Courthouse to free a runaway slave. Bells tolling through the frosty morning, a boy in his nightshirt by a bedroom window, his heart full to bursting with shame and rebellion because a black man walked manacled through the street.

Behind the Abrams dissent were all the *Annals of America* . . . Grandfather Abiel, a gentle scholar who would have died for his religion . . . Dr. Holmes, battling puerperal fever in hospital wards and on public forums. "*I am too much in earnest for either humility or vanity, but I do entreat those who hold the keys of life and death to listen to me for this once.*" Behind the Abrams dissent were all the sights and sounds of a man's youth . . . Granite rocks of New England . . . the yellow-paneled courtroom after the Bar examination, with Peleg Chandler standing near . . . "*I, Oliver Wendell Holmes, do hereby swear*" . . . Uncle John, sitting by the window in his little Cambridge house, waving a cigar and saying something very earnestly . . . What was he saying?

It did not matter. Nothing was remembered, nothing forgotten. Sitting in the United States Supreme Court on a November afternoon, Justice Holmes raised his head, laid aside his glasses. "I regret that I cannot put into more impressive words my belief . . ."

CHAPTER THIRTY-SIX

"The Great Dissenter."

MARCH, 1921 . . . Oliver Wendell Holmes watched with curiosity the approach of his eightieth birthday. He felt well, filled with vigor. How could a man tell if his mental powers were diminishing? When he was a boy and the dentist pulled a second tooth, he had been confident he would grow another if he needed it. Experience had discouraged this prophecy. But William James, when they were in their twenties, used to say a man's health should be measured not by how he felt but by how much work he got done in a day. Surely this applied to old age as well?

"I used to think that the main-spring was broken by 80," Holmes wrote to Pollock, "although my father kept on writing. I hope I was wrong for I am keeping on in the same way. I like it and want to produce as long as I can."

Well, he could look forward to what had impressed his childhood as most wonderful — to being carried in civic processions as a survivor. . . . Obviously, Fanny would do something to celebrate his eightieth birthday. That morning, Holmes went to Court. He had a dissent to give under the Fourteenth Amendment; Stone and Brandeis also were dissenting. Newspapers noted that Justice Holmes moved to his seat with a firm step, his shoulders back, and gave his opinion eagerly.

In the afternoon he walked home. Brandeis went with him. It was a fine day, spring was in the air. Brandeis was gloomy. Was the Court never going to recognize which way the world was moving? Brandeis, Holmes said jovially, was suffering from the pessimism of youth. When he reached eighty he would begin to see you couldn't reform a world by legislation but only by making men more civilized.

Brandeis laughed — he was sixty-four. At his door Holmes turned . . . "Well, Brandeis, at least we gave our brethren pain." He went in, called Fanny. There was no sign of a birthday party. The cook was sick, Mrs. Holmes said. They would have to go round to the Arlington for supper. Wendell must put on a white tie; they would try to make a celebration of it — although Prohibition would prevent drinking his health in public.

Grumbling, Holmes went upstairs and struggled into his dress suit. Grumbling he came down, roared at the houseboy. "Child of hell! Black son of Satan, where are my cigars?"

Grinning, Jones pointed to the drawing room. Holmes walked in. Before the fireplace stood Fanny in her best gray satin. Her white hair swept grimly to its topknot, carrying her eyebrows with it. At eighty-one, she seemed somehow smaller, thin almost to transparency. But as he looked at her, an enormous pride filled Holmes. This woman, so frail and old, with her ridiculous net guimpes under her *décolletage*, her spectacles, the prim violets at her bosom — this woman still had fire enough for ten. Behind myriad fine wrinkles her eyes were deep and bright.

The dining-room doors flung open. In a blaze of light — white damask, silver, flowers — stood a whole crowd of young men. Holmes saw in amazement that it was his secretaries, at least a dozen of them. Fanny had got them here from all over the country . . . Derby, Fish, Irving Olds, Francis Biddle, Clarke, George Harrison. . . .

"We came up through the cellar!" someone shouted. "Mrs. Holmes made us hide in the coalbin nearly an hour."

Holmes stood motionless in the doorway. He drew a long breath. "I knew that she-devil was up to something." He moved forward, greeted the company, then walked over and picked up a long-stemmed glass at his place. "What are these for?"

"Champagne," Fanny said.

"Close the shutters." Holmes grinned. "I wish my daddy could see me now. He always said I'd die a drunkard."

Eighty years. . . . Where, Holmes asked himself as the days passed, were the dreary prophecies concerning old age? April came, and the Holmeses drove out to see the spring. Down by the Tidal Basin the cherry blossoms were a cloud of glory. Holmes wrote to his friends about it. At Great Falls, wild white water tumbled in the glen, the dogwood flashed against a dark forest border. And in one's own back yard the magnolia put out great gleaming flowers. "The divine polonia" — Holmes called it — leaned purple blossoms across the garden wall.

These things did not change, these wonders were not dimmed. It was among one's friends that time made ravages. John Gray was gone, William James, Bowditch, Hallowell, Shattuck, Magnitzky. Who was left but Fanny to call him by his first name? Not only the friends of his youth but the friends of his middle years were dead or dying — Dicey and Maitland in London, Bryce and Leslie Stephen. Pollock was almost his oldest friend. . . . What had his father said? *Changing one's whole suit of friends leaves moments when a man feels naked, and shivers.* . . . Odd, how close one's father came as one grew older. . . .

And of the Justices who had been on the Bench when Holmes came, only two remained, McKenna and Chief Justice White. In the spring of 1921, White died. McKenna was the senior. Holmes knew he was too old to be appointed, yet knew also that if he were younger the place would be his. "I *really* don't care," he wrote to Pollock.

It was true; Holmes had never been motivated by ambition for office. If at the end he could tell himself that in the law somehow, somewhere, he had touched the superlative, he would die content. No office, no title, could give him that.

The President appointed Taft. The Justices liked him. Taft was good-humored, laughed readily. "Not quite rapid enough," Holmes reported, "but keeps things moving pleasantly." The Chief Justice himself, however, varied widely from year to year in his estimate of Holmes. In the beginning, association with Holmes was "a delight"; he was "the most brilliant and learned member of the Court . . . a well of pure common law."

But the trouble was, Holmes was too apt to be on the wrong side. Taft was a property man. So was Holmes. But Holmes read the Fourteenth Amendment the way a radical would read it — the way Brandeis read it. Holmes and Brandeis, from Taft's point of view, made more trouble than the whole Court put together.

It began in December, 1921, with the case of *Truax* v. *Corrigan*, when the Court upheld an injunction against pickets in Arizona.

Holmes dissented. The Court, Holmes said, had applied to the words of the Fourteenth Amendment a *delusive exactness.* "Delusive exactness is a source of fallacy throughout the law. By calling a business 'property' you make it seem like land. There is nothing that I more deprecate than the use of the Fourteenth Amendment . . . to prevent the making of social experiments that an important part of the community desires . . . though the experiments may seem futile or even noxious to me and to those whose judgment I most respect."

It was not surprising that Taft, soon afterward, remarked that Holmes was too old to be on the Bench. He ought to retire. It was true Holmes had not, Taft continued, lost his mental acumen, and his power of rapid work was still marvelous. But surely his age made him a little more subordinate to Brandeis — the two were always together. Holmes gave more attention to his dissents than to the opinions he wrote for the Court, Taft said gloomily. And his majority opinions themselves were "very short and not very helpful."

The nation thought otherwise. It was now, in his eighties, that the nation became aware of Justice Holmes. People liked his brief opinions and most of all they liked his dissents. "The Great Dissenter," they called him. Holmes was annoyed. How could he help dissenting when the Court rendered such decisions? He did not want to undermine his brethren or the prestige of the Bench. But Taft and McKenna were forever meddling with his written opinions. Only the other day Taft had objected when Holmes used the phrase "to stop ratholes." Holmes complained bitterly to Pollock. The boys, he said, cut the genitals out of his decisions. Were dullness, long-windedness, forever to be the proof of sound scholarship?

The older he got, the more Holmes admired economy of expression. He would like, he said, to write a first book of the law, keeping to hard fact and using no images. The trouble was, men twisted words, made fancy tools of them. *Delusive exactness* — it was the curse of legal thinking. Men should think *things*, not words. Long ago, Charles Peirce had taught him that — Peirce the black-browed, the magnificent.

"A word," Holmes said — and said it in Court — "is not a crystal, transparent and unchanged; it is the skin of a living thought and may vary greatly in color and content according to the circumstances and the time in which it is used." .

To Holmes it was extraordinary that so elementary a formula needed affirmation. Old age, it would seem, reduced a man to the ultimate simplicities; at eighty a man had neither time nor spirit for these complicated self-deceptions — he was too near the abyss. Was there perhaps actual qualitative difference in the mode of thinking of the young? Holmes watched his secretaries and their friends. Just now, in the 1920's, intellectual youth flaunted a bright and brittle cynicism. Patriotism they called an empty superstition, a dangerous delusion.

Holmes listened and was not alarmed. The boys, he said, were merely experimenting in negation.

But in truth it went deeper than this. Not only the young but all America was experimenting in negation; this was the famous "lost generation" of postwar days. Woodrow Wilson was dying and with him the Covenant of the League of Nations. America drew into herself. Harding's administration was not a spectacle to inspire the nation. In the spring of 1923 a case under the Minimum Wage Board brought from Holmes another roaring dissent. *Adkins* v. *Children's Hospital:* once more Holmes threw himself against the old Lochner argument that twisted "due process of law" to a meaning convenient to employers.

Was the battle never to end? Men actually believed the enemy lay outside themselves and could be scourged to obediency. New laws, new systems of laws, a new President, another political party. . . .

Harding died and a Vice-President from Vermont took his place. A year later, Coolidge ran for office in his own right. Alfred Emmanuel Smith threatened to run against him; on Southern hillsides the fiery crosses blazed . . . *To hell with the Pope!* . . . A hundred years ago, Abiel Holmes had seen that slogan scrawled on charred and ruined convent walls just east of Cambridge.

A century had not changed men's hearts, Abiel's grandson reflected now. Negro-baiting, Red-baiting, assumed the virtues of a crusade. The State of New York convicted Benjamin Gitlow of "advocating criminal anarchy." Gitlow had written a pamphlet called *The Left Wing Manifesto.* His counsel said the state had proved no definite act of criminal anarchy and that a man could not be punished for abstract doctrine or academic discussion.

But Justice Sanford, speaking for a majority of the Court, read aloud from Gitlow's pamphlet: "The Communist International

calls the proletariat of the world to the final struggle!" This, Sanford declared, was no philosophic abstraction but the language of
direct incitement. There was peril in a single revolutionary spark;
Gitlow's conviction was sustained.

Justice Holmes waited his turn . . . *"Mr. Justice Brandeis and I
are of the opinion that this judgment should be reversed. . . . Every
idea is an incitement.* The only difference between the expression
of an opinion and an incitement . . . is the speaker's enthusiasm for
the result. Eloquence may set fire to reason. If in the long run the
beliefs expressed in proletarian dictatorship are destined to be accepted by the dominant forces of the community, the only meaning
of free speech is that they should be given their chance and have
their way."

Benjamin Gitlow and Abrams in New York . . . the *Toledo
News-Bee* versus the United States . . . the *Milwaukee Leader*
versus Postmaster Burleson. . . . Freedom of speech and the Bill
of Rights. Freedom of the press, of the mails. . . . *"Mr. Brandeis
and I are of the opinion judgment should be reversed. . . ."*

Chief Justice Taft was harassed. Holmes, he said, was a poor
constitutional lawyer, lacking the experience in affairs of government that would keep him straight on constitutional questions.

How Brandeis would have laughed at this, and John Gray too
could he have heard it. Gray had once said that constitutional law
was not law at all but politics.[1] To Brandeis, Holmes's lifelong remoteness from both politics and government contributed not a little
to his ability to interpret the Constitution.

That spring, 1928, Holmes was eighty-seven and proud of it.
If he could live until November he would be the oldest Justice on
record, beating even Taney. In magazines and law reviews, legal
scholars wrote articles about him. Roscoe Pound from Harvard,
Wigmore from Northwestern University. Frankfurter had just got
one out in the *Harvard Law Review* — his third on the subject:
"Mr. Justice Holmes and the Constitution." It seemed indecent to
pick up such things and read them — as though one were peering
illicitly from the coffin, eavesdropping at the minister's eulogy.

Regularly each year, the newspapers announced that Holmes was
planning to retire. It annoyed him vastly. He remembered old Chief
Justice Fuller, shouting that he was not to be paragraphed out of
his place. But the papers did not say they wanted Holmes to go.

They said the High Court could ill spare a man so much younger than his brethren in mind and spirit. "His opinions have such freshness, his mind is so penetrating and in tune with the age and his general view of life has such tang and piquancy that we hope he will stay right where he is as long as his powers permit."

As long as his powers permit. . . . Holmes was a little scared about this. How could he tell? The work was hard and unremitting. Even Hughes, who had been Governor of New York and a Presidential candidate, said no job of his life had ever taken the gimp out of him like the Justiceship. In 1927, Holmes had produced more opinions than any other of the Justices . . . but were the opinions clear, and forcible? Well, he would soon know; there was nothing merciful about public opinion.

Late in the spring of 1928 a famous wire-tapping case came up. *Olmstead* v. *the United States.* Four Seattle rum runners had been convicted on evidence obtained by tapping the telephone wires to their homes and offices.

They lost their case. Chief Justice Taft said there had been no violation of the Fourth and Fifth Amendments — no searching, no seizure, no entry; the only thing employed was the sense of hearing.

Holmes dissented. Courts were apt to err by sticking too closely to the words of a law. Wire-tapping was "dirty business." . . . "I think it less an evil that some criminals should escape than that the Government should play an ignoble part. . . ."

The old gentleman, Taft called Holmes now. Strange, how the old gentleman's words struck home to the nation, how deeply they had begun to bite! Even men who would not have dreamed of reading a legal opinion had become somehow aware of him. One day when Holmes was eighty-seven a newspaperman, seeking copy, decided to walk round Capitol Square and ask passers-by if they had heard of Justice Holmes.

A mechanic in overalls was sitting on a bench reading the sports page. The reporter strolled up. "Holmes?" the mechanic said. "Oh, sure! He's the young judge on the Supreme Court that's always disagreeing with the old guys."

CHAPTER THIRTY-SEVEN

*Fanny Dixwell Holmes. "Tell him
I loved him." Philosophy in a hard
hour.*

FANNY HOLMES was eighty-eight. For some time it had been
obvious that she was failing. No one dared tell her, dared hint that
she looked badly, help her up the long stairs or out of her blue
chair by the sitting-room fire. Fanny Holmes had always been impatient of illness; the last time she had been sick, even with severe
pain it had been hard to keep her in bed. She had joked, hung a bunch
of violets outside the window upside down, announcing that it was
absent treatment by Christian Science and would cure her.

Now, at eighty-eight, her back was straight as ever, her eye as
bright. But the faithful Mary, helping her mistress dress in the morn-
ings, heard her sigh, saw her close her eyes, lean her head against the
chair. At breakfast, going round the table, Mary noted that Mrs.
Holmes did not touch her food. "You will die if you don't eat,"
Mary said, standing before her mistress, speaking bluntly in her
Irish voice, her blue eyes wide with distress. "Nonsense!" Mrs.
Holmes said briskly. "It is my business to stay alive."

Moving slowly from the dining room, Fanny Holmes went to the
glass-enclosed porch to feed her birds. She was very fussy about
the housekeeping. The white fur rugs in their bedroom must be
shaken every week. Often, in the evenings, Holmes watched her
run her hand along the mahogany strip at the sofa back, then look

at her fingers. How well he knew this gesture! Smiling, he shook his head.

More than ever, Fanny seemed glad when June came and they could go to Beverly Farms, to the brown house beside the pines, to her rose garden, the tall delphinium by the gate. Preparing to leave Washington, she walked round her house, looked at the furniture, stopped before her needlepoint pictures. The apple orchard, the bay at Eagle Point. "I want my pictures destroyed some day," she told Mary. "It's dreary for people to feel they must cherish the works of departed aunts."

Beverly Farms was glad to see the Holmeses come. At the Public Library Miss Larcum had saved a whole pile of new detective stories for the Judge. The crossing keeper hobbled forward, inviting Holmes to stay for a chat. O'Brien the policeman brought his guitar round, sat on the steps and sang Irish songs. "The Judge comes each year," the older people said in the town, "and brings us such comfort."

But this summer they noticed the change in Mrs. Holmes. What would the Judge do without her? The two had been together fifty-six years. Reminiscently the town talked it over. At the livery stable, Larcum told about a summer not long ago when he had driven Mrs. Holmes to the depot to meet the Judge. The horse started running and didn't stop till they got to Pride's Crossing. Mrs. Holmes hadn't acted scared. She just leaned out and called, waving her parasol. "Larcum! If you kill me, tell him I loved him."

The stories were endless. Mary Donnellan said the Judge was very fussy about his books. One time in Washington some old volume was lost and the Judge made an uproar, cussing at his secretary, at Jones and everybody that came near. All through it Mrs. Holmes hadn't said a word, just looked at him in that sharp way she had.

But when the Judge came back from Court the book was in its place on the shelf. An American flag stuck out above it and underneath Mrs. Holmes had hung a sign, neatly printed: "*I am a very old man. I have had many troubles, most of which never happened.*" Mary said the Judge laughed until he cried.

Late in September, Beverly Farms bade good-bye to the Holmeses. The leaves were already turning on the maples when Larcum drove them to the station. "Be sure to bed down my roses," Mrs. Holmes told him, "before the frost comes."

But when they got home to Washington, Fanny did not seem refreshed by her summer. In the evenings, rising from her chair she swayed, reaching for the chairback. "It was the journey," she said. "I am a little tired. I shall be all right as soon as we are settled."

But as the weeks passed her fatigue did not leave her but rather increased as the cold came on, and the brief Washington snows. She spent more and more time upstairs in her sitting room. Her friends called, the Misses Tiffy and Thwing, bearing flowers, little gifts. In the late afternoon Fanny dressed and went downstairs. Holmes, coming in, would find her dozing in her chair and when he spoke she started, rousing herself with difficulty. If it was a wife's business to outlive her husband, then for Fanny Holmes it was the hardest bit of business she had ever undertaken. Her days, her hours, had become a perpetual struggle to stay awake, to keep alive, to remember.

All the small anniversaries, the rituals and ceremonies of half a century of married life, she observed now with a rigid, almost desperate care. On Washington's Birthday the red and black hatchet lay as always by Holmes's place at the table, and in March the shamrock. As April Fool's Day approached, Fanny consulted the secretary as to what they should do to the Judge. . . . No no, she said . . . She had used the unlightable-matches trick years ago; the Judge had spent half an hour vainly striking box after box she had planted in his desk drawer. . . . And the false ink spots made of blotting paper — the Judge had let out a roar when he came to the study after breakfast and saw his beautifully written opinion with a huge ink spot on the top page. . . . And the celluloid roaches in the flour barrel — that had been perhaps the most successful of all. . . .

A few days before the turn of the month, at the hour when Mrs. Holmes usually dressed for dinner, Mary Donnellan went into the room — and found her mistress lying on the bed, breathing heavily, her face distorted. She had fallen, managed somehow to reach the bed. She had not called out. "It's nothing," she said. "Mary, tell the Judge it is nothing."

The doctor came. Mrs. Holmes had broken her hip. He spoke gravely. They would put it in a cast, do all they could. But the bone would never knit, the patient was too old.

The days passed. The house was filled with nurses carrying trays, visits from the doctor. The windows were open to the garden; apple blossoms blew their soft breath in the bedroom and from the porch below a mockingbird called. The figure on the bed moved. "Mary! Where is Mary? Has she fed my birds?"

Wendell Holmes, sitting by the window, got up, went downstairs. Standing on the porch he reached clumsily into the cage. A man's hand was too big for this door. . . . One time — how many years ago — Fanny had let a new bird loose and he had flown at the starling and killed it. Fanny had shut the murderer in a cage by himself, hung crepe on the wire door. . . . Looking out to the garden, Holmes saw the magnolia was beginning to bloom. He would ask the nurse if Fanny's bed could be moved so she could see it. . . .

Friends came; their questions were kind, solicitous. But to Holmes, answering them, no future could seem as menacing as this terrible present. The doctors said that Fanny did not suffer. She had no actual illness, no fever. But sitting by the bedroom window in the evenings, the late afternoons, Holmes saw her face drawn as though with suffering. Her head turned toward him slowly. "I am tired, Wendell," she said. "That's all — I am very tired. Perhaps you had better go away now, and I will take a little nap."

One afternoon late, Walter Howe, the young lawyer from next door, rang the bell. "I won't come in," he told the colored man. "I just wanted to ask — "

"Please come in, sir," Jones said. "I know the Judge would like to see you. He is lonely."

Holmes came down the long stairs. He had on his velvet smoking jacket. "Come in, Walter," he said. "Fanny is asleep. . . . She is asleep. She was very tired." He paused. "We don't think she will wake up, ever."

He led the way to his study, took out a little etching. "I made that myself when I was eighteen." He was silent, then spoke slowly, as though rehearsing a lesson learned with pain, yet learned thoroughly, hour by hour. "When you are eighty-nine, you can't *really* expect to live much longer."

That evening — it was the last day of April, 1929 — Mary brought Mrs. Holmes's supper tray as usual. She found her mistress dozing, the Judge in his chair by the window. It had been a warm, bright day, in the growing dusk the garden was still, a thrush spoke from the branches of the apple tree. Gently, Mary roused her mistress, propped her on the pillows and turned to the tray.

Before she could turn back — without a sigh, without sound or complaint — Fanny Holmes leaned her head against the pillows and died.

Holmes did not want a funeral. When Taft came to the house, Holmes met his questions stiffly. Fanny would not want a funeral. She hated all that kind of thing.

Taft had been very fond of Fanny Holmes; he had known her years ago in Beverly Farms. Like her, he was a Unitarian. He left the house, consulted with Hughes. The two returned, told Holmes gently it would not do. This was the wife of a Supreme Court Justice; the country would be shocked, would misunderstand.

Holmes yielded and Taft took charge, making arrangements for a simple service at home. It was Taft also who secured a plot in the soldiers' burying ground at Arlington. Holmes had always wanted to be buried there, but he had been too shy to ask the Secretary of War for this favor. Now he and Fanny would lie there together.

Fanny's body was taken to Arlington, but the service at home was delayed some two weeks. There was no one in the house now but the servants and John Lockwood, Holmes's secretary. In those weeks, alone with the Judge, young Lockwood saw philosophy tested in a hard hour. Often, Holmes had talked of life and death, saying gravely that life was action, the use of one's powers. And now, with half his life snatched from him — and there was no possible doubt that this woman had been half his life — the Judge went serenely on. The routine did not break, the work was done hour by hour. It was like the routine of a soldier, inexorable, accomplished moment by moment in the face of death itself. Simply, the Judge was living out his philosophy.

A case had come up in Court concerning freedom of speech. *The United States* v. *Schwimmer*. Holmes knew which way the majority would vote — and with every drop of his blood he disagreed. Sitting at his desk he examined the briefs and the evidence. . . . Rosika Schwimmer had been denied citizenship. She was a pacifist . . . fifty years old. She had testified that in case of war she would not bear arms. . . .

Holmes pushed aside the papers, reached for his pen.

. . . If there is any principle of the Constitution that more imperatively calls for attachment than any other it is the principle of free thought — not free thought for those who agree with us but freedom for the thought that we hate. . . . I would suggest that the Quakers have done their share to make the country what it is. . . . I had not supposed hitherto that we regretted our inability to expel them because they believe more than some of us do in the teachings of the Sermon on the Mount.

It was the last week of May[1] before the Court rendered decision. Holmes read his dissent. When it was over he drove to Arlington, across the Potomac and up the winding hill to Fanny's grave. Above on the hilltop, the columns of Lee's mansion showed through the trees, the flag waved. Far below the river moved, broad and shining.

Holmes got out of the car. Buckley, the colored driver, got out too and followed across the grass. Standing a little aside, Buckley watched his master — as he would watch again and again for six long years when they came to this place.

The ritual would be always the same. Walking to the stone, Holmes laid his flower on it — a rose, a poppy, a spray of honeysuckle — then stood silently. Silently still, his hand touching the stone, he moved round it with a little patting motion of the fingers. Then he turned, and walked downhill through the trees.

CHAPTER THIRTY-EIGHT

*Holmes's last dissent. He resigns from
the Court. A nation's greeting.*

WHEN Court opened for the autumn term, Chief Justice
Taft looked at his brethren with an anxious eye. Old age, it seemed,
had in no way modified Holmes's wrong-headedness; he still read
the Fourteenth Amendment the way Brandeis read it, and he was
almost a fanatic on the subject of free speech. There were, luckily,
five to steady the boat: Van Devanter, McReynolds, Sutherland,
Butler, and Sanford. But "Brandeis," Taft remarked, that December of 1929, "is hopeless, as Holmes is, as Stone is."

By all the laws of nature, Holmes should retire. As the New Year
approached, newspapermen came round with the usual question.
Taft read Holmes's reply and was not comforted. "I shall not resign or retire," Holmes had said stoutly, "until the Almighty Himself requests it."

But the Almighty saw fit to request — and suddenly — a quite
different retirement. On Holmes's eighty-ninth birthday, March 8,
1930, Taft himself died, aged seventy-three.

The President appointed Hughes Chief Justice. Coming back to
Court after fourteen years, Hughes watched Justice Holmes a trifle
apprehensively. Was a man of eighty-nine capable of a full day's
work in this most exacting job? Lately, Holmes's legs had become
very weak. On that first day, Hughes noted how Brandeis helped
him to his seat.

The first lawyer stood up. Holmes took out his notebook, unlocked it, slipped the key in his pocket and began to write. The Chief
Justice smiled; he had forgotten this old trick of Holmes's. At the

lunch hour he asked to see the notebook. . . . Holmes had not missed a detail. It was a perfect synopsis.

But after lunch when the Justices were in their places and the lawyer had talked for ten minutes, Holmes put his fingers to his forehead and went off to sleep. Hughes reached out cautiously, poked him in the leg. Holmes sat up. "Jesus Christ!" he said loudly, and the Courtroom stirred. Later that afternoon, McReynolds interrupted a lawyer who was young and obviously inexperienced. Holmes took his hand from his forehead and leaned forward. "I wouldn't answer that question if I were you," he said clearly to the young man, and went back to sleep.

In May, Holmes got ready a dissent that would sum up what he had tried to say so often concerning the rights of the states to make their own economic experiments. This was a tax case — the third in rapid succession where a man's heirs balked at paying a transfer tax on bonds moved across the state line. In all three cases McReynolds, speaking for the Court, said it was a violation of the Fourteenth Amendment for a man to be taxed in two states on transferred securities, and in all three cases Holmes dissented.

Preparing his dissent in the last case — *Baldwin* v. *Missouri* — Holmes talked about it to his secretary. Of course it was disagreeable for a bond owner to be taxed in two places at once, and he would say so in Court. But why did men make such an infernal fuss over these things? With taxes a man buys civilization — by no means a bad bargain.

If Missouri wanted to levy this particular kind of tax, Holmes saw nothing in the Constitution to prevent it. In nullifying these state taxes the Court, it seemed to him, acted on their own economic theories — and then called upon the Constitution as a sanction. Holmes had already stated his views briefly in the first two cases.[1] But there was more to say and he intended to say it: —

"I have not yet adequately expressed," he began on that day of May 26, "the more than anxiety that I feel at the ever increasing scope given to the Fourteenth Amendment in cutting down what I believe to be the constitutional rights of the States. As the decisions now stand, I see hardly any limit but the sky to the invalidating of those rights if they happen to strike a majority of this Court as for any reason undesirable. . . ."

No limit but the sky. The phrase caught the nation's ear. The *New*

Republic said no graver words had been spoken on the Supreme
Court since Justice Curtis read his dissent in the Dred Scott case.
The *Baltimore Sun* said Holmes had given an "inside spanking" to a
Court that was far too concerned with property rights. The *Chicago
Daily News*, the *New York World*, the *Milwaukee Journal*, ap-
plauded this judicial prod in the ribs of a property-conscious Bench.
Holmes's picture was printed, showing him walking to work on his
eighty-ninth birthday. "Alert Justice Holmes," the caption read.

Holmes saw it. *Alert* — that was how he felt himself; it was good
to know he was not deceived. The phrase was more reassuring somehow than any compliment to his intellectual powers or that "legal
acumen" the papers loved to talk about. . . . Standing before the
hall mirror on a fine afternoon late in May, Holmes looked at his
reflection. His light gray suit fitted him nicely, the Legion button
looked well on it too. He put on his gray fedora with the wide
black band and stepped back . . . This was a better effect than
that portrait his secretaries had commissioned last summer for the
Law School. Charles Hopkinson had painted it — full length in
judicial robes, crowned with white hair and mustache. "That isn't
me," Holmes had said when it was finished, "but it's a damn good
thing for people to think it is."

Holmes's ninetieth birthday — March 8, 1931 — fell on a Sunday.
The newspapers greeted him warmly. "He is one of us, and few
people can say that of such a man. He is part of all our past. It is
hard to think of a future that he will not share."

Sitting in his library, Holmes read his birthday messages. From
England came notice that he had been made a member of the Honorable Society of Lincoln's Inn — the first time the Benchers had
elected anyone outside the British Empire. The *Harvard Law Review* for that month was dedicated to him. The Lord High Chancellor and the Attorney-General of Great Britain had written in
it; so had Pollock, Chief Justice Hughes, and Roscoe Pound. Frankfurter came down from Harvard, in his hand a new book entitled
Mr. Justice Holmes, filled with articles about him by such men as
Cardozo, John Dewey, Professor Wigmore, Walter Lippmann,
Judge Learned Hand. Frankfurter himself had an article in it.
Holmes turned the pages slowly as Frankfurter, beaming with
pleasure, stood before him.

Holmes looked up, trying to joke it all away, but could not, and wept a little instead at the tone of affection that lay so plainly beneath these public greetings. . . . Strange not to hear Fanny's voice, breaking in. "*Wendell! Your hair needs cutting*. . . . *Wendell, did you know the* New York Journal *thinks you are 'the laboring man's hope'?*" . . . So many to praise — but none, not one, to cut through with the sharp familiar voice that alone dares bring a man back to earth, back to the battle where he belongs while his powers endure. . . . "*Wendell — I see by the* Transcript *that if you keep on you may be almost as famous as your father, some day*."

That Sunday evening there was a microphone on Holmes's desk. At half-past ten, the President of the Bar Association and Dean Clark of the Yale Law School would speak from New York, Chief Justice Hughes from Washington. Holmes was to answer them briefly. The day before, the Associated Press had said the Justice would probably not use all his five minutes; he didn't like speeches and publicity. "But let everyone listen; this man is one of the few who make literature out of law."

Up in Cambridge, five hundred people gathered in Langdell Hall. There were speeches about Holmes, and reminiscences, until at last the room was silent, all faces turned to the microphone. The familiar voice came through, speaking slowly — a little tired but clear and articulate, rhythmic as always: —

In this symposium my part is only to sit in silence. To express one's feelings as the end draws near is too intimate a task.

But I may mention one thought that comes to me as a listener-in. The riders in a race do not stop short when they reach the goal. There is a little finishing canter before coming to a standstill. There is time to hear the kind voices of friends and to say to one's self: "The work is done." But just as one says that, the answer comes: "The race is over, but the work never is done while the power to work remains." The canter that brings you to a standstill need not be only coming to rest. It cannot be while you still live. For to live is to function. That is all there is in living.

And so I end with a line from a Latin poet who uttered the message more than fifteen hundred years ago: —
'   "Death plucks my ear and says, Live — I am coming."

Next day — Monday — the nation noted with pride that Justice Holmes was at his place on the Bench and delivered a majority opinion. All that spring he did not miss a day. To watch him was a miracle. "Justice Holmes," the papers said, "makes of old age a pleasure, something to look forward to."

But the people near him, the household, knew that his strength was very limited now — that he tired quickly and could no longer work at night. Next autumn, after the summer at Beverly, a great change was noticeable. Holmes was bent nearly double. In the afternoons after Court, Brandeis came round to go driving with him. They walked down the steps and across the pavement to the car, Brandeis on one side, Buckley on the other. "Straighten up there, Judge!" Buckley would say imploringly. "You don't want to walk all bowed over like that." Together the two men tried to pull him straight. "It's not so easy as you think," Holmes said, cursing jovially.

On the morning of January 11, 1932, Holmes had a majority opinion to deliver — a case under the Prohibition Act: *James Dunn* v. *the United States*. In the robing room, Arthur Thomas, the tall, gray-haired Negro who had been Holmes's messenger for so long, helped him on with the heavy silk gown. The Justices entered the Courtroom, climbed the dais. Brandeis was not in Court that day. Chief Justice Hughes, holding tightly to Holmes's arm, felt him lean heavily, stagger a little.

When his time came, Holmes leaned forward, picked up the papers in *Dunn* v. *the United States*. Spectators noticed how well he looked; the cheeks were pink against the white hair and mustache. But when he began to read, Holmes's voice faltered, thickened. He shook his head impatiently and went on. But what he said was barely audible beyond the front row of benches.

At the noon recess, Holmes left the Courtroom with the other Justices, ate his box lunch and returned to the Bench. When Court rose at four-thirty, he got his hat and coat, walked over to the Clerk's desk. "I won't be down tomorrow," he said.

That night, Holmes wrote his resignation to the President . . . *The time has come and I bow to the inevitable. I have nothing but kindness to remember from you and from my brethren. My last word should be one of grateful thanks.*

It was Brandeis who missed him most. Next day at noon the Justices wrote to Holmes and sent the note around by messenger. Holmes sent back his reply: —

My Dear Brethren:

You must let me call you so once more. Your more than kind, your generous, letter, touches me to the bottom of my heart. The long and intimate association with men who so command my respect and admiration could not but fix my affection as well. For such little time as may be left for me I shall treasure it as adding gold to the sunset.

Affectionately yours,
OLIVER WENDELL HOLMES.

Holmes's resignation left a solid conservative majority on the Bench. At such a time this was more than a misfortune, it was a disaster. The choice was in Hoover's hands — and in January, 1932, three years of depression had wiped out the nation's confidence in its President's ability to do anything right, let alone choose a liberal justice. The Senate had turned down Hoover's last appointee to the Court — Judge Parker of North Carolina; with protest they had accepted Hughes as Chief Justice.

What if Hoover put in Calvin Coolidge? His name was on the list. Or John W. Davis, or Rugg of Massachusetts? Republican insurgents like Senator Norris, Democratic Senators from Arkansas, Montana, Texas, issued statements that were half praise for the departed, half angry warning for the future. Holmes, of course, was a Republican. The actual party affiliations of the new Justice wouldn't matter; the history of the Supreme Court proved that. What mattered desperately was whether Hoover's appointee was going to vote down every reform Congress put through. In this worst financial panic of history, the nation turned to the government for relief, asked control over prices, credit, commerce. The demand, carrying more power and more desperation than any such popular demand before, bore almost the aspect of revolution.

The nation, in short, asked protection against a system that had let disaster come upon it. Newspapers ran angry editorials: —

Government is at stake! The resignation of that noble old justice, Holmes, destroys a liberal majority of one. Let the U. S. Senate put Hoover's choice of that liberal majority of one under a microscope — and fight to the last ditch for a new justice having the views — if not the legal acumen — of an Oliver Wendell Holmes!

Holmes read the reports, heard all over the nation the alarums sound — and was not afraid. Ninety years of living does not encourage a man to panic. People talked of revolution. An ugly word, a terrible word. Holmes had heard it before. Seventy years ago he had seen the country come through a revolution — they called it a Civil War. He had prophesied that not internal disputes but competition from new races would test whether our government "could hang together and could fight." He still believed it. There were plenty of things wrong with the United States Government and while free speech endured there would be, fortunately, plenty of people to stand up and shout about it. But Holmes believed the United States Government was strong and would endure. He had said so more than once.

As for his own immediate successor on the Court, he hoped it would be Cardozo. Not only was Cardozo's legal philosophy close to his own; the man's sensitiveness of perception, his generosity of view, were extraordinary. But it was not Holmes's business to make known his choice. He was out of it. He had resigned, retired.

Silence, resignation. To sit in one's library in the morning and read eulogies of oneself, receive admiring visitors. . . . Was there any praise, were there any crowns in heaven or earth to take the place of the work a man loved and had relinquished? In all his life, Holmes had never been without a job. At night the papers on his desk, the Year Book with the marker at the page — these had been for him the bridge between night and morning. The very act of waking each day had been exciting, with the battle waiting. *"Bugler, blow the charge! I am ready. . . ."*

And now the bugler blew his charge no more. The battle was over, the challenger was still. Holmes felt tired, exhausted. When he tried to write his friends about his resignation, it was hard even to hold the pen.

Anxiously the household watched him. For the past ten years Dr. Adams,[2] the family physician, had said the Judge would die if he stopped work. Holmes, indeed, had said it himself. Now the prophecy seemed in danger of fulfillment.

But it was not fulfilled. For Holmes, fate had not reserved this particular defeat — to die of heartbreak because he was no longer useful. Three years of life remained, and they were not to be unhappy years. Once more Holmes rallied, once more his spirit re-asserted itself.

It was to Pollock he gave testimony. It was "wonderful and incredible to have no duties"; he could not have believed how much he would like it. There was so much to learn! His secretary read aloud by the hour while Holmes played solitaire or sat listening. Often he seemed to doze, but if the secretary stopped reading, Holmes sat forward instantly. "What?" he would say. "What, Sonny?" And he would begin instantly to discuss the book. Just before they went to Beverly Farms, Holmes wrote to Pollock that he must surely be getting cultivated — his secretary calculated they had read 4,500,000 words! Spengler and John Dewey, Salter and Belloc and McDougall and C. E. Broad — "sweetened," Holmes said, by rereading all of Sherlock Holmes. He couldn't agree with Parrington and Beard that the American Constitution represented a triumph of the money power over democratic individualism. Belittling arguments always have a force of their own. "But you and I," Holmes added to Pollock, "believe that high-mindedness is not impossible to man."

Frankfurter came, one day, with the manuscript of a book about Brandeis, a companion volume to the one he had got out about Holmes. Would the Judge write an introduction? Very gladly, Holmes said. He had known Brandeis — how long? Why, it was half a century! Ever since the '70s when Brandeis emerged from the Law School to be Sam Warren's partner on State Street. . . . "In moments of discouragement that we all pass through," Holmes wrote, "Brandeis always has had the happy word that lifts one's heart. It came from knowledge, experience, courage and the high way in which he has always taken life. Whenever he left my house I was likely to say to my wife, 'There goes a really good man.'"

Beverly that summer was beautiful. Fanny's rose garden bloomed riotously and his own patch of wild flowers seemed lovelier than ever. Old friends came out from Boston, bringing their grandchildren. Holmes enjoyed these young people. There was a singular and striking beauty now to Holmes's face, a quality almost luminous. Sitting on the porch he discussed life with Betsy Warder, aged sixteen. "I won't refrain from talking about anything because you're too young," Holmes told her, "if you won't because I'm too old."

In the fall when he returned to Washington, Frankfurter sent down a new secretary as usual. It would do the young men good, he said, to be with Holmes even if he was no longer on the Court. Holmes protested, but he was very glad to have a man in the house to talk to. The secretary, arriving in October, watched the Judge with amazement, particularly at breakfast. Why, the old man attacked his breakfast like a cavalry officer in the field! Porridge — a heaping plateful with thick cream, lots of sugar. Fruit, broiled fish, muffins, marmalade, coffee. After breakfast the Judge announced he was going to loaf all day. "Ninety-two has outlived duty," he said with what seemed a vast satisfaction. Half an hour later he was calling for the secretary to read to him. "Let's have a little self-improvement, Sonny."

Beyond all other traits, this perpetual thirst to learn surprised both young and old. Franklin D. Roosevelt, a few days after his inauguration in 1933, came round to call. He found Holmes in his library, reading Plato. The question rose irresistibly. "Why do you read Plato, Mr. Justice?"

"To improve my mind, Mr. President," Holmes replied.

It was true. *The rule of joy and the law of duty seem to me all one.* Years ago, Holmes had said it, and time had not disproved it. To the beholder there was something enormously reassuring in this spectacle of a man so old and so wise, who still desired to learn.

The morning the President called, Frankfurter was there, and Harold Laski. Three days earlier — March 5 — Roosevelt had closed the banks, laid an embargo on gold and called a special session of Congress for March ninth. March ninth was tomorrow. Tomorrow the President, standing before Congress, would present his plan for the national emergency.

Rising when his visit was ended, Roosevelt paused at the door, turned earnestly to Holmes and addressed him as the greatest living American. "You have lived through half our country's history; you have seen its great men. This is a dark hour. Justice Holmes, what is your advice to me?"

Holmes looked at him. "You are in a war, Mr. President," he said. "I was in a war, too. And in a war there is only one rule: *Form your battalions and fight.*" [3]

CHAPTER THIRTY-NINE

Death of Oliver Wendell Holmes.
A soldier's burial. The great affirmer.

THE seasons rolled by . . . Spring and summer. . . . Beverly, with Fanny's delphinium still blue and tall by the gate. Washington again, with the Justices coming round to call. Brandeis and Cardozo, Stone with a new etching for Holmes to pass upon. Frankfurter, bounding up the long stairs to the library, his arms full of new books, talk bubbling on his tongue. More than ever, the country was impatient with the Supreme Court. The papers were full of it; except for Stone, Brandeis, and Cardozo the Court didn't have an idea which way the world was turning.

Roosevelt's National Recovery Act was under bitterest attack. Obviously, the Court was going to vote it out of existence. They did. Reporters rang the bell at I Street. "There is nothing to howl about," Holmes told them. "There have always been changes in the interpretation laid on the Constitution, and there always will be."

One day — it was the twenty-third of February, 1935 — Holmes came down the steps in the early afternoon with his secretary and got in the car to go for a drive. It was a bitter day, windy, with a threat of snow. Next morning Holmes had a cold. "You shouldn't have let him go out," Mary Donnellan told the secretary. "Mrs. Holmes wouldn't have let him, on such a day." The household gathered round reproachfully. "Why don't you call the doctor, Mr. Rowe? Mrs. Holmes would have called the doctor."

The Judge went to bed, sneezing, and the sneeze turned to a cough, to something worse. Holmes was ninety-three, and he had pneumonia. By the first of March, the city knew that he was mortally ill.

Holmes knew it too, and was not dismayed. "Why should I fear death?" he had remarked to his secretary a few weeks earlier. "I have seen him often. When he comes he will seem like an old friend." Holmes had loved life. . . . "If the good Lord should tell me I had only five minutes to live, I would say to Him, 'All right, Lord, but I'm sorry you can't make it ten.'" He had loved life and he had believed in it . . . "*If I were dying my last words would be: Have faith and pursue the unknown end.*"

Now he was dying — and he said nothing half so dramatic. He lay quietly, joking with the nurses. What was the use of all this trouble — coaxing an old man to eat, giving him stimulants? "Lot of damn nonsense," Holmes grumbled, moving his long legs under the covers. Life was — what had he called it, in that speech at Harvard? "Life is action and passion." People said death was a rest from labors. It wasn't a rest — it was an obliteration, a passing of bone into dust, of one set of chemicals into another set of chemicals. And that was right too. Very right and proper.

He had had his share. Six years ago, half of life had died, with Fanny. But even half of life had been good. *To have done what lay in you to do, to say that you have lived, and be ready for the end* . . . Oliver Wendell Holmes waited quietly in his bed.

March 2, 3, 4 . . . Across the street in an office building, newspapers held the death watch. Was the Justice going to live until his ninety-fourth birthday? Photographers hung round the front door, taking pictures of Chief Justice Hughes, of Brandeis and Mrs. Roosevelt. Taxi drivers, cruising by, called out to the policeman stationed at the door. "How is he? How is the Judge?"

In his long white iron bed, Holmes breathed heavily now, his eyes closed. In the next room, the doctors consulted and beyond that in the secretary's study a group of men sat. Mark Howe and Tom Corcoran and Rowe. Frankfurter, John Palfrey, Edward Jackson Holmes, down from Boston.

On the fifth of March, late in the afternoon, newspapermen saw an ambulance stop outside the door. An oxygen tent was carried in. Holmes, opening his eyes, watched the huge, unwieldy contraption wheeled to the bed, saw them lift the tent above his face. He made a movement. "Lot of damn foolery," he said clearly.

People were kind; they went to enormous trouble to give an old man a few more breaths. . . . His father hadn't died this way, boxed under a tent with a glass window. His father had died sitting in the library at home. The book had fallen from his hand. . . . How red the sky had been, above the Charles River! . . . *"What is it for me, Wendell — King's Chapel? Very well, that is all I want to know."*

Very well . . . very well. . . . *It is well.* . . . There was something his mother used to read to him and Ned and Amelia, on Sundays, from the Bible . . . "And they asked, 'Is it well with thee? Is it well with the child?' And she answered, *'It is well.'* " . . .

At two in the morning the doctors knew the end was near. They took the oxygen tubes away. Holmes lay with his eyes closed, breathing quietly. Outside, in the March garden, wet branches creaked and from the alley came the sound of wheels. As the doctors watched, Holmes died, taking his departure so quietly it was hard to tell when he was gone.

Mark Howe, the signs of grief plain on his face, went downstairs, opened the front door. From across the street a dozen newsmen rushed at him, notebooks in hand. They listened, then raced for the telephone. Justice Oliver Wendell Holmes was dead.

The funeral was held at All Souls Church — the old, white-pillared building that stands at the head of Sixteenth and Harvard Streets. A wet wind blew across the square. People stood on the curb, watching the Justices at the church steps. The bell tolled. . . . That was Brandeis, they said, going up the steps; the Justices were to be pallbearers. Those six men waiting beside them had been Holmes's secretaries. The service wouldn't be long; this was a Unitarian Church. Afterward the army would carry the Judge to Arlington.

"And Moses chose from among the people able men, such as feared God, men of truth, hating unjust gains, and set them over the people to judge them at all seasons. . . ."

The minister's voice was slow. . . . Outside, mounted policemen turned traffic away from the church. . . . "At the grave of a hero — " the minister was reading from Holmes's own words now — "at the grave of a hero we end, not with sorrow at the inevitable loss, but with the contagion of his courage; and with a kind of desperate joy we go back to the fight."

The President and Justices waited beside Holmes's grave. The procession came in sight, winding down the hill past Lee's house. Soldiers lifted the coffin, covered with the American flag, bore it across wet turf. Eight infantrymen raised their rifles and fired . . . a volley for each wound. . . .

Ball's Bluff . . . Antietam . . . Fredericksburg.

A soldier, standing a little apart, raised his bugle and blew taps.

OLIVER WENDELL HOLMES
CAPTAIN AND BREVET COLONEL
20th Massachusetts Volunteer Infantry, Civil War
JUSTICE SUPREME COURT OF THE UNITED STATES
March 1841   *March 1935*

From the floor of Congress, from the White House, from the Inns of Court in London, scholars and statesmen gave tribute, and for a few days the people mourned.[1] But Holmes's real fame was to come slowly; the growth of his influence was to be as measured, as deep and sure, as the forces that had shaped him. Time, events, history itself, would prove his dissents. One by one they became law . . . *Hammer* v. *Dagenhart.* Child labor can be regulated by Congress. . . . *Lochner* v. *New York.* The liberty of the citizen to do as he pleases does not mean he can force other men to work twelve hours a day. . . . *Coppage* v. *Kansas.* . . . *Truax* v. *Corrigan,* and in Massachusetts, *Vegelahn* v. *Guntner* and *Plant* v. *Woods.* "I think the strike a lawful instrument in the universal struggle for life."

Free speech, like truth itself, cannot be achieved by statute. But the Bill of Rights was still worth fighting for. *Abrams* v. *the United States.* . . . *Gitlow* v. *the People of New York.* . . . *United States* v. *Rosika Schwimmer.* . . . "Free thought — not free thought for those who agree with us but freedom for the thought that we hate."

There was indeed a great contagion in this courage — a courage not born with Holmes but handed down with all the accumulated force, the deep spiritual persuasion, of the generations behind him. Abiel Holmes and Abiel's father, Captain David. Great-grandmother Hewet, teaching herself to read Vergil in a log cabin. Sally Wendell and Sally's father the Judge. Abiel's eldest son, small and light-minded but as fierce, when his heart was roused, as any patriot of them all. . . . "Ay, tear her tattered ensign down!" . . . "I am too much in earnest for either humility or vanity, but I do entreat those who hold the keys of life and death to listen. . . ."

Men called the doctor's son the Great Dissenter. The title was misleading. *To want something fiercely and want it all the time —* this is not dissent but affirmation. The things Holmes wanted were great things, never to be realized. How can man realize the infinite? *Have faith and pursue the unknown end.*

"*Whether a man accepts from Fortune her spade and will look downward and dig, or from Aspiration her axe and cord, and will scale the ice, the one and only success which it is his to command is to bring to his work a mighty heart.*"

Notes

CHAPTER ONE

1. Like most of my quotations from the *Annals*, this is taken from the second edition (1829) rather than the first (1805).

2. I found only two witnesses for the color of Sally Wendell's eyes, and these witnesses conflict. One is Dr. Holmes's great-niece, Dorothy Quincy Upham Vaughan, who told me: "When I was a little girl, Dr. Holmes took me between his knees and looked at me and said, 'Child, you have my mother's eyes.'" Dorothy Vaughan's eyes are a bright chestnut brown. . . . The other witness is Dr. Holmes himself, in the character of The Professor at the Breakfast-Table. (See *Holmes of the Breakfast-Table*, by M. A. DeW. Howe.) "There!" says the Professor, peering at his portrait. "That is just the look my father used to have. . . . The mother's eyebrow and grayish-blue eye, those I knew I had." . . . But is the doctor, here, referring to himself or to an imaginary Professor? I preferred to take the great-niece's testimony and call Sally's eyes brown.

CHAPTER TWO

1. Louisa Storrow married Stephen Higginson and became the mother of Thomas Wentworth Higginson, who appears many times in this story.

CHAPTER THREE

1. Additional authors who speak of Holmes as "Oliver" are William Sloane Kennedy (*Oliver Wendell Holmes*, Boston, 1883), and Walter Jerrold (*Oliver Wendell Holmes*, London, 1893).

2. The Paddock elms stood until 1874, when over Dr. Holmes's vigorous protest to the city fathers, they were cut down to widen Tremont Street.

3. Judge Wendell, ninth child of a ninth child, was born on March 3, 1733, and died January 15, 1818.

CHAPTER FIVE

1. Abiel Holmes's friend, William Ellery Channing, said this. One of the most brilliant and admirable men New England produced in the early nineteenth century, Channing has as yet no adequate biography.

2. He ultimately grew to be five feet five inches tall.

CHAPTER SEVEN

1. On the marriage certificate in King's Chapel there is a penciled note in Dr. Holmes's handwriting — "Call me Wendell." The doctor much disliked his first name.

2. This was the ancestor whose portrait inspired Dr. Holmes's famous verses called "Dorothy Q."

> O Damsel Dorothy! Dorothy Q.!
> Strange is the gift that I owe to you;
> Such a gift as never a king
> Save to daughter or son might bring, —
> All my tenure of heart and hand,
> All my title to house and land;
> Mother and sister and child and wife
> And joy and sorrow and death and life!

CHAPTER NINE

1. John Q. Adams was buried in Quincy. I refer here to the official ceremony in Faneuil Hall, when Mayor Quincy, in the name of the city, received the body from the Congressional committee that had brought it from Washington.

2. Thomas Wentworth Higginson, 1823–1911, was called "Wentworth" by his friends and "T. W." by the part of Beacon Street that thought him a crank and a come-outer. To posterity he is an extremely attractive figure, generous, impulsive, and brave. Abolitionist, Free-Soiler, Unitarian minister, Higginson was in the forefront of such movements as the Worcester Disunion Convention of 1857. Yet like other Abolition disunionists he fought for the North as soon as war actually came. Colonel of the first regiment of freed slaves, his letters in wartime are superb reading.

3. During Wendell Holmes's boyhood, in 1849, the Webster-Parkman murder shook Boston to its foundations. I cannot forbear

to give the outlines of the affair. Parkman and Webster were highly respected citizens of Boston — old friends, of course, of Dr. Holmes's. Webster, a professor at the Medical School, owed Parkman money, and Parkman kept reminding him of it. On the afternoon of November 23, Parkman came to Webster's classroom and found Webster alone. Right overhead, Dr. Holmes was giving his one o'clock lecture. When Parkman asked for his money, Webster hit him with a heavy stick of wood from his botanical collection, cut him up with his anatomical saw, stuffed part of the body down the lecture-room toilet, part in the brick vaults in the basement, and burned the rest in the laboratory stove. At the trial, Webster pleaded not guilty. But the janitor, suspicious, fished in the stove and brought up a piece of charred jawbone. As anatomists, Dr. Holmes and his colleague, Jeffries Wyman, were called to the witness stand. So were the Doctors Keep, who had made the murdered man a dental plate, and Morton the famous dentist-anesthetist. Keep said he recognized his patient's teeth; Morton said it was impossible. Jeffries Wyman made some beautiful colored drawings of the jawbone — they can be seen today in the Anatomical Building. These, more than anything else, convinced the jury. Webster was convicted, confessed, and was hanged. The *Boston Medical Journal* then printed a long controversy about the value of scientific witnesses as experts, to which Dr. Holmes could not forbear contributing anonymously. The article, signed "A Medical Witness," is instantly recognizable, murder or no murder, by the inevitable Holmesian light touch.

CHAPTER ELEVEN

1. The official notice says — Morning prayers at 6.45 "as long as the light permits."

CHAPTER THIRTEEN

1. Norwood Penrose Hallowell, from Philadelphia, was the son of Morris L. Hallowell and the brother of Edward Needles Hallowell. He joined the Massachusetts Twentieth with Wendell and later became Colonel of the Fifty-fifth.

2. Thomas Rodman Robeson, Harvard, '61.

3. Henry Livermore Abbott, Harvard, '60, died after the Battle of the Wilderness, May 6, 1864.

4. Thomas Greely Stevenson, born 1836. Later made a Brigadier General. He was killed in May, 1864.

5. Boston newspapers showed great interest in the Harvard enlistments. The *Post* for April 25, 1861, notes that Captain Stevenson is a member of Porcellian, and that Josiah Porter, class of '52, "was the first graduate of Harvard College called into active service." The Fourth Battalion, Home Guard, was Boston's pet. On Sunday, May 5, when Stevenson was made a Major and the boys cheered until they could not speak, the *Post* hoped solicitously they would not contract lung disease.

6. At Commencement that year the bookstore sold "views." There was a view of the new college racing shell, a view of Stoughton Hall and so on. Included were pictures of only three men, listed exactly as follows: —

> Molineaux — Sitting
> Molineaux — Standing
> Rarey, Horse Tamer
> Dr. Holmes

7. Robert Gould Shaw was a distinguished soldier, and greatly beloved in Boston. As Colonel of the Fifty-fourth Regiment, Massachusetts Volunteers — colored troops — Shaw was killed leading his regiment at Fort Wagner, S. C. The Confederates buried him in a trench with his men. On Boston Common opposite the State House is a bas-relief of Shaw by Saint-Gaudens.

CHAPTER FOURTEEN

1. James Jackson Lowell, Harvard, '58, was killed at Glendale in 1862.

2. William Lowell Putnam enlisted with James Lowell when the two were students at the Harvard Law School at the beginning of the war. Putnam died after Ball's Bluff as described, October 22, 1861.

3. William Francis Bartlett. Like Shaw, Bartlett was very well liked in Boston. He lost a leg at Yorktown in April, '62. He ended the war a Brigadier General.

4. Edward Needles Hallowell, older brother of Norwood, became a lieutenant in the Fifty-fourth Massachusetts (colored) under Shaw. He was brevetted Brigadier General at the end of the war.

CHAPTER FIFTEEN

1. Captain John C. Putnam lost an arm at Ball's Bluff.

2. Edward Everett Hale to his brother Charles. These quotations

are from four different letters, all written between July 31 and August 15. I have not given the quotations in their exact order.

CHAPTER SIXTEEN

1. Gray's letter was dated November 30th. The December *Atlantic* must have been issued early, that month.

CHAPTER EIGHTEEN

1. The Book of Entries gives Holmes's registration as September 5.

2. The ceremony took place at eleven in the morning. The veterans were commanded by Captain Magnitzky. Colonel Palfrey was there, and William Raymond Lee, now a Brigadier General. Newspaper accounts ended in a plea for enlistments, with the current rallying-cry, "Fill up the ranks."

3. It was Mr. Edwards.

4. From Pollock's essay on *Modern Theatres of Sovereignty and Legislation* (1890). Pollock does his worst blasting in footnotes. It is in a footnote that he says Austin's manner "is so repulsive to me that I never can feel sure of being quite just to his matter." A footnote to *The Beginnings of Political Science* says, after praising the Athenians, "To me the Spartans have always appeared the most odious impostors . . . they produced in the whole course of their wars only two officers who are known to have been gentlemen, Brasidas and Callicratidas." Pollock, it is obvious, was not troubled by any romantic notions of social democracy.

5. For instance, the *Boston Post* paused in the middle of heart-rending eyewitness accounts of Ball's Bluff for a long poem called "Baby's Shoes." It began

> Oh, those little, those little blue shoes,
> Whose sight makes such fond tears start . . .

CHAPTER TWENTY

1. My authority for this story is Henry Cabot Lodge (*Early Memories*). Lodge visited the Russell Sturgises in London shortly after Holmes had dined there with General Hamley and made the famous remark. Lodge describes Hamley as a notorious American hater. Holmes himself, writing the story to Pollock sixty years later, says the man was Kinglake, author of the monumental history of

the Crimean War. I think Holmes said it to both of them. It was a favorite question of British military men; Holmes told Pollock he had expected it. And Wendell Holmes, like his father, believed a good remark was worth making twice.

2. Dr. J. Monroe Thorington, President of the American Alpine Club, writes me that Holmes's climbing record "was not a great one, but he was one of the last links with the Golden Age of Mountaineering in the Alps. His ascents with Leslie Stephen (President of the Club) include Balmhorn, Mönchjoch and Mönch, Tschingel Pass and Col du Géant. The Club, to which Holmes was elected in 1866, was a great influence in the lives of young University men. Stephen was known as one of the fastest climbers in the fraternity. Hence, for a young man to be invited to climb with him was a signal distinction."

CHAPTER TWENTY-ONE

1. The Sewing Circles were, up to about 1916 when the Junior League was firmly established, important in well-bred Boston feminine lives. Tradition says they were started by John Adams's daughter Abigail "to sew for the poor." They met on Wednesdays from eleven to one and had lunch. They were fun, and they were as hard to get into as Porcellian. Girls were invited the year they emerged from school into society. Foreigners (persons not born in Boston and environs) were frowned upon. Wedding presents and first-baby presents from one's Sewing Circle were cherished; membership was a badge and an identification.

2. Bishop Lawrence (1850–1942) gave me my best scenes of the household both on Charles and on Beacon Streets. "Pitter patter all the time in that library," the Bishop said. " 'Melia Holmes (Wendell's sister) was the only person in Boston who could out-talk Phillips Brooks. Wendell had a romantic quality the others lacked. People felt it as soon as they saw him, even when he was only a boy."

3. Peleg Whitman Chandler, 1816–1889.

4. James Bradley Thayer, 1831–1902, left Chandler's office in 1873 to be Royall Professor of Law at Harvard. Later he held the Weld professorship. His son, Ezra Ripley Thayer, was from 1910 to 1915 Dean of the Law School.

5. Asaph Churchill, A.B. Harvard, 1831.

6. Charles Whiting Huntington. Biographies of Massachusetts lawyers abound in stories about these Bar examinations. (See the autobiography of Charles Francis Adams, son of the Ambassador.)

Back in Judge Story's day candidates were sometimes grilled for hours. But between 1850 and 1876 (Justice Horace Gray stabilized the rules in '76) the whole thing depended on the fancy of the examiner.

CHAPTER TWENTY-THREE

1. Richard Henry Dana, Jr., 1815–1882, author of *Two Years before the Mast* (1840). Dana, after a radical, Abolitionist youth, became uncompromisingly conservative in everything. He lectured at Harvard on international law for a few years, was Overseer from 1865 to 1877, and from first to last was a terrific social snob.

2. Francis Edward Parker, class of 1841, was Overseer from 1868 to '79 and from 1880 to '86.

3. The Metaphysical Club flourished in the early '70s. During the rest of the chapter I have not kept to strictest chronology. The last quotation, from Mrs. James, was dated 1873.

4. John Chipman Gray, 1839–1915, Wendell Holmes's old friend, taught at the Law School from 1869 to 1913. Lawyers call his *Nature and Sources of the Law* the wittiest book on jurisprudence in the language.

5. Henry Parkman, A.B. Harvard, 1870, LL.B. 1873.

6. Joseph B. Warner, A.B. 1869, LL.B. 1873. A brilliant student.

CHAPTER TWENTY-FOUR

1. The *Autocrat* was published in book form in 1858, *The Professor* in '59, and *The Poet* in '72. They all appeared first in the *Atlantic Monthly*.

2. This letter is quoted from an article in the *Maryland Historical Magazine* for June, 1938, by Mrs. Howard Kennedy's daughter, Anna Howell Kennedy Findlay.

3. Christopher Palles, 1831–1920, was Lord Chief Baron of the Irish Court of Exchequer from 1874 to 1916.

4. Once more I cannot forbear a word about a famous Boston event that lack of space forced me to omit. . . . On November 9, 1872, Dr. Holmes heard the fire bells. From his Beacon Street windows he saw a column of light down by Boylston and Tremont Streets. He and Wendell went out together. It was the beginning of the great fire that raged for two days, destroying millions of dollars' worth of property. Writing Motley, the doctor quotes Wendell's remark to the effect that huge buildings crumbled and came down without a sound, as if they had fallen on feather beds.

5. William Adams Munroe, Harvard, 1864, was described to me by Justice Brandeis, who knew him, as a "good enough run-of-the-mill lawyer." I might add that Brandeis's characterization of Holmes himself as a practising lawyer did not go much higher.

6. In 1941, before the Holmeses' house at 296 Beacon Street was dismantled, I visited it and had tea in Dr. Holmes's library, by courtesy of Mr. and Mrs. Edward Jackson Holmes. Stepping in the front door, I was instantly back in the nineties. Over the banister hung the portrait of Abiel Holmes, handsome with brown eyes and flowing curly hair. Upstairs in the library the books, the statuettes, the carpet and fringed lampshades, the *Spy* cartoon on the wall, breathed of the doctor. Mr. Edward Holmes crossed the room and opened a door. On its inner side hung a small mirror, level with my chest (I am not tall). Dr. Holmes had hung that mirror. It was just the right height for him to brush his hair.

CHAPTER TWENTY-FIVE

1. From Sir Frederick Pollock the elder, *Remembrances*, under date of June 19, 1874. Quoted from Sir John Pollock's review of the *Holmes–Pollock Letters, Quarterly Review* for July, 1941.

2. James Barr Ames, 1846–1910. One of the most brilliant men who ever taught at the Harvard Law School. When appointed Assistant Professor in 1874, he was the first teacher who had not practised law, and the Overseers were skeptical. He was Dean of the Law School from 1895 until 1910.

3. In 1880, the word *pragmatism* had not appeared in print. But William James in 1898, speaking at the University of California (Philosophical Conceptions and Practical Results), referred to "the principle of practicalism, or pragmatism, as he [C. S. Peirce] called it, when I first heard him enunciate it at Cambridge in the early '70s." Peirce, in his *Popular Science* articles of November, 1877, and January, 1878, does not use the word *pragmatism*. But he makes the idea very clear. "The *final* upshot of thinking is the exercise of volition. . . . The whole function of thought is to produce habits of action. . . . I only desire to point out how impossible it is that we should have an idea in our minds which relates to anything but conceived sensible effects of things." In 1899, Justice Holmes used the phrase, since widely quoted, "*We must think things, not words.*" It is interesting to see where he got it. Peirce, in the 1878 article, speaks of mistaking a mere difference in grammatical construction for the distinction between the ideas expressed. "In this pedantic

age, when the general mob of writers *attend so much more to ideas than to things,* this error is common enough." (The italics are mine.)

CHAPTER TWENTY-SIX

1. I have been unable to ascertain the month of Holmes's Lowell Lectures. Mrs. Harriette Smith in *The History of the Lowell Institute* says merely that he was the third lecturer in the autumn of 1880.

CHAPTER TWENTY-EIGHT

1. See *Some Table Talk of Mr. Justice Holmes and "the Mrs.,"* by Richard Walden Hale, privately printed, 1935. Holmes is speaking: —

"I argued a case before the Supreme Judicial Court of Massachusetts in a gray cutaway coat. (Yes. You are right. It had split tails and buttons behind.)

"Judge Horace Gray sent me word afterwards:

"'Colonel Holmes ought not to do that. It shows a lack of respect for the Court.'

"But I think the gray coat was reasonable enough when properly cut. On the other hand, I remember that when Taft was Chief Justice we had a westerner. When we took a second look at his shirt front there was no waistcoat. Taft would not stand that. I think Taft was right."

CHAPTER THIRTY

1. According to custom, Harvard had offered President Cleveland an honorary degree. He refused, saying he was not scholar enough for such a distinction. This was in November, 1886, at Harvard's 250th anniversary.

2. Some Bostonians say it was old Isaac Barnes who made this remark. I prefer to think it was John Holmes. I got the story from Chief Justice Hughes, who had it direct from Justice Holmes.

CHAPTER THIRTY-THREE

1. It is not within the scope of this book to criticize Holmes's legal opinions or to give any hint at interpretation or prophecy from the point of view of the student of constitutional history. I have tried to write the cases as a journalist would write them, sitting in the courtroom, giving the primary facts, then something of the case's impact upon the country at the moment. To this, as biographer,

I add something of Holmes's own feelings and the feelings of persons concerned in our story, such as Theodore Roosevelt.

Possibly my objectivity is misleading in that it makes Holmes seem too good to be true — perfect in all decisions, all theories and ideas. I myself by no means agree with all his decisions any more than I agree with all his philosophies. In the Northern Securities case my sympathies lie, in fact, with Justice Harlan. But my sympathies and the reasons for them can be of no possible interest to the reader. I append them in this one case simply because it may clear up a misapprehension concerning Justice Holmes. I have tried to present the facts surrounding these cases in a form simple and readable. Let the reader make his own judgment as to the right or wrong of Holmes's decisions.

CHAPTER THIRTY-FOUR

1. The exact figures as of 1911 are: American Federation of Labor — 1,761,833 members. All other labor unions in the U. S. combined — 2,282,000.

The figures for Rockefeller are conservative. When he died in 1937, he had given upwards of five hundred million dollars.

2. See list of secretaries in Appendix A.

3. Dr. Holmes said there were times when a man wrote better than he knew how, and that such had been the case when he wrote "The Chambered Nautilus."

CHAPTER THIRTY-FIVE

1. The long and loyal friendship between Holmes and Pollock is to many people something of a puzzle. Pollock was a superb scholar. He was also dry, reserved, and could be rude even to his best friends. The description oftenest given me was that Pollock was an old curmudgeon. The stories are endless . . . How, at a dinner party given him by an old friend on one of his visits to America, Pollock never spoke a word all evening, much to his hostess's embarrassment. Long afterward he said — surprised at being asked — that he had been saving his voice for a lecture next day. The last time Pollock visited Holmes was in 1930, when he was eighty-five and Holmes was eighty-nine. It is rather touching that Pollock was a trifle jealous of the fine state of Holmes's health. "How is his appetite," Pollock would ask. "Isn't it failing a little?" And when he saw Holmes putting away dish after dish he cautioned

him. Was it wise, at the Justice's age, to eat so recklessly? "What," roared Holmes down the table, "is a mere ninety between friends!"

But Holmes loved him, and Pollock loved Holmes. "One of the greatest abiding happinesses of my life is your friendship," Holmes wrote Pollock in 1921.

2. The following notes are for purposes of identification as of 1914. The later history of these men does not concern this book.

Francis Hackett, born in Ireland in 1883, came to America in 1901. He became an editorial writer with the *Chicago Evening Post* and in 1914 was made associate editor of the *New Republic*.

Herbert Croly, born in New York in 1869, was graduated from Harvard in 1890. He wrote *Marcus Alonzo Hanna* in 1912, *Progressive Democracy* in 1914, and that same year became editor of the *New Republic*.

Philip Littell was born in Brookline, Massachusetts, in 1868. Graduated from Harvard in 1890, he became associate editor of the *New Republic* in 1914.

3. Holmes's opinion in the Debs case has been widely criticized, more so perhaps than any of his opinions. Again, such discussion is not within the plan of this book.

CHAPTER THIRTY-SIX

1. See Felix Frankfurter, *Mr. Justice Holmes and the Constitution. Harvard Law Review* for December, 1927.

CHAPTER THIRTY-SEVEN

1. Decision rendered May 27th.

CHAPTER THIRTY-EIGHT

1. *Farmers Loan and Trust Co.* v. *Minnesota.*
   Safe Deposit and Trust Co. v. *Virginia.*

2. During the last years, Dr. Claytor was the family physician. I have been unable to find out just when he began his attendance.

3. This story has been told many times. I include it because it is a recognized part of Holmes's history. But I don't like it. It is out of character. It smacks of the grandiose, and I suspect the witnesses of blowing it up because they loved the Justice. . . . *"Don't call me Hero!"* Holmes said. . . .

CHAPTER THIRTY-NINE

1. There was much interest in Holmes's will. He left the bulk of his fortune, $250,000, to the United States Government. Rich people called it a foolish gesture — what good would that little bit do the government? But the plain people liked it and said so. The Justice was giving his money back where he got it.

Material and Sources

I. A WORD ABOUT METHOD

THIS book is a picture and a translation, an attempt to bring Justice Holmes out of legal terms into human terms. All my search for material and all my selection of material were based on this conception.

The statements and conversations of the main characters came from published records, records in manuscript or the word-of-mouth testimony of people who knew the Holmes family. I have never distorted these statements or changed their meaning, although in quoted material I have occasionally shifted the sentence sequence. But I have often embellished them, deliberately and with purpose. In a portrait, authenticity is not achieved by names and dates, but needs something further. When it seemed especially necessary to engage the reader's attention for something Justice Holmes was going to say — or the doctor, or Uncle John or Fanny Dixwell — I invented the chairs in which they sat, the window out of which they looked as they spoke. For instance, when Wendell Holmes was ten, I had him lean against a tree and suck a blade of grass while his Uncle John told a story about Caesar Augustus. But I knew the tree was there, beside the Gambrel-roofed House, because I had seen a picture of it, and I knew that Uncle John had told that story not once but many times.

Since I began work on this book, early in 1940, two important books on Justice Holmes have appeared: Francis Biddle's *Mr. Justice Holmes* (1942) and Max Lerner's edition of the speeches, legal opinions, etc., called *The Mind and Faith of Justice Holmes* (1943). To Mr. Biddle's book I am indebted for verifications of character traits and anecdotes which I had already incorporated in my text, and for two new items: Dr. Holmes's remark about his son's neck being too thin for a public lecturer, and the fact of Wendell Holmes's visit to Emerson in 1864. Mr. Biddle left out of his book something he once said about Holmes which is so good I cannot resist including it here: "Holmes was skeptical of everything except life itself."

While I was at work, not only books but frequent articles appeared, containing anecdotes that had long since become part of my text. This seemed to me no reason for deleting them. After all, the stories were old when I found them; they are anybody's property. I had been at pains to trace my stories as close as possible to source; I often disagreed with other versions as they appeared. But writers' quarrels make tedious reading. I omit therefore all controversy about points of fact and confine this brief statement of bibliography to a broad outline of my principal sources.

Because my book covers three generations, it was impossible to stop long over any one period of time. I was forced to omit or pass quickly over many persons closely concerned with Justice Holmes's life. Count Kaneko, for instance, about whom I discarded many carefully assembled data; Morris Cohen, Laski, and others who were important to Holmes's later life. I am reassured in the certainty that these omissions will be remedied by the official biographer, Mark DeWolfe Howe, when his book on Justice Holmes appears. Other series of letters can be hoped for, notably the correspondence with Frankfurter and Laski.

Not only persons had to be omitted, but ideas — which was more serious because Holmes was a man to whom ideas were beyond all else interesting. But to deal adequately with the flood of new ideas that pushed upward in America in the late nineteenth and early twentieth century would need a volume. The impact of Dewey's post-pragmatic philosophy which so much interested Holmes, and the application of pragmatism to a theory of jurisprudence propounded by Pound, Cardozo, Frankfurter, Aronson — all this is not even touched upon. My book is a narrative, not a discussion.

Concerning the Washington period: In eight brief chapters I was able to do no more than sketch a background, touch upon the high points of Holmes's dissents and representative opinions from the Court. The danger of this treatment is its tendency toward dramatization where drama does not belong. I have avoided therefore all Courtroom scenes except one, in the Northern Securities case, where, as Holmes intimated in his dissent, public opinion, pushing into the Courtroom, shared with legality the honors in determining the issue. If Holmes's dissents and opinions emerge as dramatic in the highest degree, it is due to no stage setting of mine but to the extraordinary impact of Holmes's words. He himself said the purpose of art was to touch the hair trigger of an emotion.

The best bibliography of Justice Holmes is found in Max Lerner's book, before-mentioned. For Dr. Holmes, the bibliography by G. B. Ives, Boston, 1907. For Abiel Holmes the principal sources are listed here. My own complete bibliography for the three generations is too general to be of use to the student. To list the works of Parkman, Fiske, Bancroft, Bryce, Rhodes, the Adamses, Morison, Schlesinger, Parrington, Gabriel, the Beards, Slosson, Allan Nevins, and so on, would be like making up a bibliography of Bibles. I confine my list therefore to books that gave me actual detail.

A large part of my material came from people, not books. For the reader's convenience there follows a flat list of the persons who contributed most. This list, however, gives no hint of the time and trouble some of these people took in behalf of my book. Beginning with Justice Holmes's literary executor and friend, John Gorham Palfrey, all but two of the many persons approached during three years of work talked freely to me about the Holmes family. I take this opportunity to thank them deeply for the confidence they showed in me and also for their patience in answering questions which at the time may have seemed trivial or downright unnecessary. The big things are easy to find. It is the lesser names, the lesser dates and sounds and colors, that are difficult to track down through the years.

II. PERSONS INTERVIEWED

The persons listed below are in no way responsible for the use I made of their material.

Literary executors, estate of Justice Holmes: Mr. John G. Palfrey, Justice Felix Frankfurter. *Relatives of the Holmes family:* Mr. and Mrs. Edward Jackson Holmes, Mrs. Lloyd Brown, Dorothy Quincy Upham Vaughan (Mrs. T. Wayland Vaughan). *Friends of Justice*

Holmes: the late Justice Louis D. Brandeis, Mrs. Felix Frankfurter, Chief Justice and Mrs. Charles Evans Hughes, Chief Justice Harlan B. Stone, the late Bishop William A. Lawrence, the late Mr. A. Lawrence Lowell, the late Mr. Richard W. Hale, Mrs. Richard W. Hale, Mrs. John G. Palfrey, Mr. and Mrs. Arthur Hill, Mr. Robert S. Barlow, Mr. and Mrs. Walter B. Howe, Mrs. Charles P. Curtis, Mr. Charles P. Curtis, Jr., Mrs. Russell Codman. *Others who talked to me about the Justice and his family:* Miss Katharine P. Loring, Mrs. Nicholas Longworth, Miss Sallie Fairchild, Mrs. Charles B. Perkins, Mrs. Frederick Winslow, Mr. Roland Gray (son of John Chipman Gray), Mr. George R. Farnum, Mr. Lee Friedman, Mrs. Rosika Schwimmer.

Mr. and Mrs. Gifford Pinchot gave me interesting material about Charles Peirce, their neighbor in Milford, Pennsylvania.

Supreme Court messengers and clerks who worked for Holmes in Boston and Washington: James J. Doherty, the late James F. McCarthy, the late Arthur Thomas. *Holmes's coachman,* Charles Buckley. *Holmes's secretaries:* Augustin Derby, Leland B. Duer, Irving S. Olds, Francis Biddle, Stanley Clarke, Harvey H. Bundy, Chauncey Belknap, W. Barton Leach, Thomas G. Corcoran, John E. Lockwood, Alger Hiss.

III. BOOKS AND OTHER SOURCES

PART I

ABIEL AND HIS SON OLIVER. 1800–1841

1. 1800–1820. Abiel Holmes and His Times

Material about Abiel Holmes came largely from the source library assembled by Dr. Raymond Calkins in the First Congregational Church in Cambridge. Records of the First Parish are here, in Abiel's handwriting, covering the whole period of his ministry. (*Records of the First Church, from 1632–1830,* edited by Stephen Paschall Sharples, were published in Boston in 1906.) Abiel's sermons, with his marginal notes, are in the First Congregational Church, and there are pictures of the old parsonage where Abiel lived before 1807 and of the First Meeting-house. (Abiel was pastor of the Fourth Meeting-house.) The Harvard College Library has autograph letters of Abiel Holmes. Abiel's poems are published in a slim volume called *A Family Tablet* (Boston, 1796). The first edition of his *The American Annals* was published in Boston in 1805, the second (*Annals of America*) in 1829. His *Life of Ezra Stiles* was published in Boston in 1798, his *History of Cambridge, Massachusetts* in 1801 (Mass. Hist. Soc. Col., v. 7).

The quotations from Abiel's diary are from *Life and Letters of Oliver Wendell Holmes*, by John Torrey Morse, Jr. (Boston, 1896, 2 v.). Also from the same, facts about Abiel's ancestors and brothers. Facts lacking in Morse I found in *Holmes of the Breakfast-Table*, by Mark Antony DeWolfe Howe (New York, 1939). *Cheerful Yesterdays*, by Thomas Wentworth Higginson (Boston, 1898), has material about Abiel. The story about Abiel's writing on the frosted pane came from T. W. Higginson's speech at the Holmes Breakfast in December 1879, recorded in the *Atlantic Monthly* for February 1880.

Wendells, Olivers, and Jacksons can be found in the standard encyclopedias: *Appleton's*, the *Dictionary of American Biography*, the *Columbia Encyclopedia, Notable Americans*. Some of the material about Sally Wendell I got from Morse's life of Dr. Holmes, some from Dr. Holmes's letters, some from newspaper notices after Dr. Holmes's death when his friends wrote about his early life and the character of his mother. Samuel Adams Drake in his *Old Landmarks and Historic Personages of Boston* (Boston, 1900) mentions the mansions of Jacob Wendell and his son Judge Oliver Wendell. Dr. James Jackson's delightful *Letters to a Young Physician* (Boston, 1855) I first found in Justice Holmes's own library, now housed in the Library of Congress.

The Gambrel-roofed House is listed in the Recorder's Office in the Boston State House, with the price paid by Judge Wendell in 1807. Pictures of it, inside and out, are at the Boston Athenaeum. The furniture and silver I saw in part at 296 Beacon Street (since dismantled), part at Georgetown, Maryland, at the house of Mr. and Mrs. Thomas Wayland Vaughan.

Material was taken from the following books: —

The Controversy between the First Parish in Cambridge and the Rev. Dr. Holmes, Their Late Pastor. Published by the Parish Committee, 1829.

Services at the Celebration of the 250th Anniversary of the Organization of the First Church in Cambridge. Cambridge, 1886.

Sketches of Some Historic Churches of Greater Boston. (Privately printed.) Boston, 1918.

McKenzie, Alexander, *History of the First Church in Cambridge.*
Cambridge, 1873.

Much of my background for New England Federalism came from
volumes 1, 2, 8, and 9 of Henry Adams's *History of the United States*
(New York, 1889–1891, 9 v.). Also his *Documents Relating to
New England Federalism. 1800–1815* (Boston, 1905). I used James
Truslow Adams's *The Adams Family* (Boston, 1930), his *The Epic
of America* (Boston, 1932), and *The March of Democracy* (New
York, 1932–1933, 2 v.). Henry Cabot Lodge's biography of his
grandfather, who was president of the Hartford Convention of
1814, is at the same time documented and delightfully biased:
The Life and Letters of George Cabot (Boston, 1877). It not only
makes no excuse for the Convention, but persuades the reader that
the venture was undertaken from the noblest of motives. For this
period and a little later, William Ellery Channing's *Works* were
invaluable. I used the 1875 edition of the American Unitarian
Association.

2. *1809–1841. Boyhood and Early Manhood of Dr. Holmes*

For Dr. Holmes's boyhood I had an inexhaustible mine in his
own works. The doctor's autobiography runs through everything
he wrote, even the novels and medical essays. A background for
Commencement scenes in old Cambridge came from John Holmes's
own incomparable account in the *Letters of John Holmes to James
Russell Lowell and Others*, edited by William Roscoe Thayer
(Boston, 1917). James Russell Lowell's *Literary Essays* were used
(Boston, 1892–1893). Also *Old Cambridge*, by Thomas Wentworth
Higginson (New York, 1899). From *The Flowering of New Eng-
land*, by Van Wyck Brooks (New York, 1936), I learned of
Mrs. Bell's saying "Kick a tree for me."

The works of Mark Antony DeWolfe Howe are a rich source
for nineteenth-century Boston. I referred often to his *Boston, the
Place and Its People* (New York, 1903). From Howe's *Memories
of a Hostess* (Boston, 1922) came the episode about Samuel F. Smith
and "My country, 'tis of thee."

I made use of: —

Ellis, George Edward, *Memoir of Charles Wentworth Upham.*
Cambridge, 1877.
Higginson, Thomas Wentworth, *Contemporaries.* Boston, 1899.
Howells, William Dean, *Literary Friends and Acquaintances.* New
York, 1900.

Material for Dr. Holmes's college years came mostly from his own books. Josiah Quincy's *History of Harvard University* (Boston, 1860, 2 v.) was a valuable source. The Anatomy Building at the Harvard Medical School has Dr. Frederic T. Lewis's collection of Holmesiana — the doctor's microscope, reports, photographs. Also much interesting material about Holmes's colleague, Jeffries Wyman. The Boston Medical Library on the Fenway has volumes of newspaper clippings about Dr. Holmes. Here can be seen the shell that inspired Dr. Holmes to write "The Chambered Nautilus." From *The Early Years of the Saturday Club*, by Edward Waldo Emerson (Boston, 1918), came details about Dr. Holmes as a medical lecturer, also the story about Agassiz as founder of the Museum of Comparative Zoology.

PART II

OLIVER WENDELL HOLMES, JUNIOR. 1841–1861

1. *1841–1857. Boyhood*

The Justice's boyhood was far more difficult to trace than his father's. The butcher-boy story came from Charles Pelham Curtis, Jr., to whom the Justice told it. Dixwell's School came from contemporary memoirs, notably *A Late Harvest*, by Charles William Eliot (Boston, 1924), *Early Memories*, by Henry Cabot Lodge (New York, 1913), and *Only Glimpses, Nothing More*, by Mrs. George Wigglesworth, born Dixwell (privately printed). This last gave me much material on Fanny Dixwell herself. Bishop Lawrence told me about Dixwell's School, where he was a student in 1865. He remembered well the day when Dicky let the boys out to celebrate the fall of Richmond. *Old Boston Boys and the Games they Played*, by James D'Wolf Lovett (Boston, 1906), gave me the best account of Braman's Baths and the filling-in of Beacon Street along the Back Bay. Also helpful were *Charles W. Eliot*, by Henry James (Boston, 1930, 2 v.), *Fourscore, An Autobiography*, by Robert Grant (Boston, 1934), and *Autobiography of Seventy Years*, by George Frisbie Hoar (New York, 1903, 2 v.). Miss Katherine Peabody Loring of Pride's Crossing, born 1849, and Mr. A. Lawrence Lowell, born 1856, gave me invaluable color and stories. So did Mrs. Frederick Winslow and Mr. and Mrs. Edward Jackson Holmes.

2. *1857–1861. College Years of O. W. H., Jr.*

Holmes's classmates reconstruct themselves in the records of the class of '61 (Harvard College Library). Charging Books tell which volumes he took out of the college library. Rank Books and

Faculty Books give his marks and the misdemeanors of his class-mates. Undergraduate scrapbooks tell what the class ate and drank at its suppers and such items as the price of a beaver hat for Com-mencement. Other details came from Benjamin William Crownin-shield's *A Private Journal, 1856–1858*, edited by Francis B. Crownin-shield (Cambridge, 1941). Again, Henry James's life of Charles W. Eliot (v. 1) was useful. *Harvard and its Surroundings*, by Moses King (Cambridge, 1878), and *Harvard College, by an Oxonian*, by George Birkbeck Hill (New York, 1894), with their maps of the Yard and the Square, the frank pride of their writers in their subject, gave a feeling of contemporaneousness.

Best of all were guidebooks, sure key to contemporary scenes. The 1860 and 1865 editions of Midgeley's *Guide to Boston and Suburbs* told such things as how the depot looked in 1863 when the New York train pulled in. *Our First Men* (Boston, 1846) lists 1500 Boston men with their capital, stating not without malice which ancestor made the original pile and whether he came by it honestly. *Boston Events*, by Edward Hartwell Savage (Boston, 1884), lists without comment events around the Common from the day when the last Quaker was hanged up to the 1870's when a "flying machine" was exhibited.

Material was also used from: —

Fiechter, Frederick C., "The Preparation of an American Aristo-crat." *New England Quarterly*, March 1933.

Gibson, Rosamond Warren, *Recollections of My Life.* (Privately printed.) Boston, 1939.

Lawrence, Bishop William, *Memories of a Happy Life.* Boston, 1926.

PART III

THE SOLDIER. 1861–1864

Boston contemporary newspapers told the story of every battle in which Massachusetts troops took part. I read the *Transcript, Herald, Post, Advertiser, Liberator,* and *Commonwealth* (weekly). For the war records of Holmes's friends I went to the *Harvard Memorial Biographies*, edited by Thomas Wentworth Higginson (Cambridge, 1866, 2 v.), and *The Twentieth Regiment of Massa-chusetts Volunteer Infantry*, by George Arthur Bruce (Boston, 1906). At the Arlington Street Armory, Mr. Clark, Recorder, and Mr. J. Harris Aubin, Treasurer of the Massachusetts Commandery,

Loyal Legion, showed me uniforms of the Massachusetts regiments and verified Holmes's war record which I had obtained from the State House. At the Armory I saw an album containing photographs of nearly all Holmes's friends and fellow officers of the Twentieth Regiment, taken at headquarters and in the field: Hallowell, Bowditch, Bartlett, Whittier, etc.

Other war sources were: —

Adams, Charles Francis, *Richard Henry Dana*. Boston, 1891. 2 v.

—— *Autobiography*. *1835–1915*. Boston, 1916.

Adams, Henry, *The Great Secession Winter of 1860–1861*. Mass. Hist. Soc. Proc., v. 43, 1910.

—— *The Letters of Henry Adams*. Edited by Chauncey Worthington Ford. Boston, 1930–1938. 2 v.

Butler, Benjamin Franklin, *Autobiography*. (Butler's Book.) Boston, 1892.

Chandler, Peleg Whitman, *Memoir and Reminiscence of Governor Andrew*. Mass. Hist. Soc. Proc., v. 18, 1880–1881.

Gray and Ropes. *War Letters of John Chipman Gray and John Codman Ropes*. Boston, 1927.

Hale, Edward Everett, *Life and Letters*. Boston, 1917.

Higginson, Thomas Wentworth. *Letters and Journals of Thomas Wentworth Higginson*. Edited by Mary Thacher Higginson. Boston, 1921.

Lee, Colonel Henry, *The Militia of the United States*. Boston, 1864.

Leech, Margaret, *Reveille in Washington*. New York, 1941.

Morison, Samuel Eliot, *The Oxford History of the United States*. London, 1929. 2 v.

Palfrey, Francis Winthrop, *The Antietam and Fredericksburg*. (Campaigns of the Civil War, no. 5.) New York, 1882.

Sandburg, Carl, *Abraham Lincoln. The War Years*. New York, 1939, 4 v.

Ballou's Dollar Monthly Magazine and *Gleason's Pictorial*, published in Boston in the 1850's and '60's, gave me the Water Jubilee, the Railroad Jubilee, events around the Common, theaters, and gossip. Accounts of Commencement at Harvard, 1861, came from newspapers as well as college records. Boston papers liked to describe in detail every procession and oration that had to do with Harvard.

The Glendale incidents, the picketing at night, Holmes's irritation because Boston thought of battles as being fought on Beacon Street in kid gloves, can all be found in Holmes's own *Speeches* (Boston,

1891 and 1913). Holmes told a secretary how he had thought a soldier should die to slow music, and other war stories such as the incident at Antietam where he hit the Irishman with the flat of his sword. Holmes said he had always been ashamed of this. Mr. Edward Jackson Holmes gave me the items about the wall clock and General Leduc. The rest about Antietam came from Norwood Penrose Hallowell's *Reminiscences* (privately printed), from an article in the *Maryland Historical Magazine* for June 1938 by Anna Howell Kennedy Findlay, called "Where the Captain was Found," from Dr. Holmes's own "My Hunt after the Captain," and from an article in the *Atlantic Monthly* for May 1935 by Mrs. Carolyn Kellogg Cushing, called "The Gallant Captain and the Little Girl." Holmes told Harold Laski about ordering President Lincoln off the parapet at Fort Stevens. I took it from Laski's "Memories of a Great American" in the *Listener* (British Broadcasting Corporation) for March 13, 1941. From the same source came Dr. Holmes's highly significant remark apropos of Wendell's decision to go to the Law School: "What's the use of that? A lawyer can't be a great man."

PART IV

THE LAWYER. 1866–1882

For old days at the Law School I used the *History of the Harvard Law School,* by Charles Warren (New York, 1908, 3 v.) and the *Centennial History of the Harvard Law School, 1817–1917* (Harvard Law School Association, 1918).

Material was taken from the following articles: —

Batchelder, Samuel Francis, "Old Times at the Law School." *Atlantic Monthly,* November 1902.

Shriver, Harry Clair, "Oliver Wendell Holmes: Lawyer." *American Bar Association Journal,* February 1938.

Vanderbilt, Arthur T., "University Legal Education and the American Bar." *American Bar Association Journal,* February 1938.

Material about the bar examination came from *Attorneys and Their Admission to the Bar in Massachusetts,* by Hollis Russell Bailey (Boston, 1908), from records at the Boston Courthouse, and from conversations with Richard Walden Hale of Boston. Justice Brandeis told me about Shattuck's office, down to details such as where each partner sat and how Magnitzky looked at his desk in the receiving hall. Material about Shattuck came partly from Holmes's own speeches, notably the speech at Shattuck's death in 1897. Information about Charles Sanders Peirce was given me by the Gifford Pinchots, who lived near him in Milford, Pennsylvania.

Material was used from: —

Peirce, Charles Santiago Sanders, *Collected Papers*. Edited by Charles Hartshorne and Paul Weiss. Cambridge, 1931. 6 v.

James, William, *The Letters of William James*. Edited by Henry James. Boston, 1920.

Perry, Ralph Barton, *The Thought and Character of William James*. Boston, 1935. 2 v.

Patterson, Edwin W., "Pragmatism as a Philosophy of Law." From *The Philosopher of the Common Man. Essays in honor of John Dewey to celebrate his eightieth birthday*. New York, 1940.

Peirce, Charles Santiago Sanders, *Collected Papers*. Edited by Charles Hartshorne and Paul Weiss. Cambridge, 1931. 6 v.

—— *Chance, Love, and Logic*. Edited by Morris R. Cohen. New York, 1923.

Weiss, Paul, "The Essence of Peirce's System." *Journal of Philosophy*, May 9, 1940.

Holmes's record as a professor at the Law School came from Charles Warren's *History of the Harvard Law School*, mentioned above; from the *Holmes-Pollock Letters*, edited by Mark DeWolfe Howe (Cambridge, 1941, 2 v.); from the *Harvard University Catalogue* for 1882–1883; from *Annual Reports* of the President and Treasurer of Harvard College, etc. J. Harris Aubin, who heard Holmes's Lowell Lectures, was witness for the reaction of the audience. Holmes's own *Speeches* (Boston, 1913) and his *Collected Legal Papers*, edited by Harold J. Laski (New York, 1920), have numerous references to his experience in teaching and his ideas as to how a law school should function. Holmes's *The Common Law* (Boston, 1881) and his edition of Kent's *Commentaries* (Boston, 1873, 4 v.) were used. Also Silas Bent's biography, *Justice Oliver Wendell Holmes* (New York, 1932). Constantly used were Felix Frankfurter's "The Early Writings of O. W. Holmes, Jr.," from the *Harvard Law Review* for March 1931, and Harry Clair Shriver's book, *Justice Oliver Wendell Holmes, His Book Notices and Uncollected Letters and Papers* (New York, 1936). Also Shriver's *The Judicial Opinions of Oliver Wendell Holmes* (Buffalo, 1940).

Articles that were especially helpful for this period were: —

Aronson, Moses J., from the *Journal of Social Philosophy:*
"The Promise of Social Philosophy," January 1938.

"Cardozo's Doctrine of Sociological Jurisprudence," October 1938.

"The Juristic Thought of Mr. Justice Frankfurter," January 1940.

"Roscoe Pound and the Resurgence of Juristic Idealism," October 1940.

—— "The Swan Song of Legal Realism." *Texas Law Review*, November 1941.

—— "Tendencies in American Jurisprudence." *University of Toronto Law Journal*, 1941, v. IV, no. 1.

Farnum, George Rossiter, from *The Lawyer:*
"Holmes, the Mystic Philosopher," December 1937.
"Holmes, the Solitary Scholar," June 1938.
"Holmes, the Soldier-Philosopher," February 1939.

Fisch, M. H., "Justice Holmes, the Prediction of Theory Law, and Pragmatism." *Journal of Philosophy*, February 12, 1942.

Hill, Arthur Dehon, "Oliver Wendell Holmes." *Harvard Graduates Magazine*, March 1931.

More general books about the period were: —

Chapman, John Jay, *Memories and Milestones*. New York, 1915.

Howe, Mark Antony DeWolfe, *John Jay Chapman and his Letters*. Boston, 1937.

—— *Portrait of an Independent. Moorfield Storey*. Boston, 1932.

—— *Barrett Wendell and His Letters*. Boston, 1924.

Mill, John Stuart, *Autobiography*. New York, 1873.

Rae, John, *Life of Adam Smith*. New York, 1895.

Spencer, Herbert, *An Autobiography*. New York, 1904.

Wright, Chauncey, *Letters*. Edited by James Bradley Thayer. (Privately printed.) Cambridge, 1878.

PART V

JUDGE IN MASSACHUSETTS. 1882–1902

Again, Holmes's *Speeches* and *Collected Legal Papers* were much used; also Shriver's edition of the Massachusetts opinions called *The Judicial Opinions of Oliver Wendell Holmes*, previously mentioned. Also the *Holmes-Pollock Letters* and *Mr. Justice Miller and the Supreme Court*, by Charles Fairman (Cambridge, 1939); and Dorsey Richardson's *The Constitutional Doctrines of Justice Holmes* (Johns Hopkins Studies in History and Political Science, no. 3, 1920). Justice Brandeis and Arthur Dehon Hill gave me interesting comments concerning Boston's attitude toward Holmes during this period. So did various of Holmes's secretaries, to whom he told stories such as the anecdote about the Wigglesworth boys' being warned about their radical uncle. Material about Brandeis was found in *Brandeis and the Modern State*, by Alpheus Thomas Mason (Washington, D. C., 1936); in Brandeis's own book, *Other People's Money* (New York, 1933); in "Resolutions adopted by a Meeting of the Supreme Court of the U. S. on December, 1942," by Judge Calvin Magruder, U. S. Circuit Court of Appeals, Boston, Massachusetts; in letters and conversations of Brandeis's nephew, Louis B. Wehle of New York.

The *Boston Post, Transcript, Advertiser,* and *Herald* gave contemporaneous local events. The description of Wendell Holmes receiving his Yale degree came from the *New Haven Daily Palladium* for July 1, 1886, through the courtesy of Carl A. Lohmann, Secretary of Yale University.

Scenes about Dr. Holmes's household during this period came from Dr. Holmes's own books, from Bishop William Lawrence of Massachusetts, from Mr. A. Lawrence Lowell and other Bostonians, and from contemporary memoirs such as Sir Leslie Stephen's essay on Dr. Holmes in his *Studies of a Biographer* (v. 2. London, 1898, 4 v.). I found material also in *The Letters of John Fiske*, edited by Ethel Fiske (New York, 1940). Mark Antony DeWolfe Howe's *Holmes of the Breakfast-Table* described Dr. Holmes's examination of William James in anatomy and quoted the report from the *New York Tribune* about Dr. Holmes's asking if his funeral was to be at King's Chapel. The Fido story is from A. Lawrence Lowell. In *Our Own Hundred Days in Europe* (Boston, 1887) Dr. Holmes tells about going abroad for his Oxford degree. The description of his eightieth birthday came from Reginald Fitz's article, "The Holmes Stamps," in the *Harvard Medical Alumni Bulletin* for June, 1942.

More general books from which material was used are: —

Blaine, James Gillespie, *Twenty Years of Congress. 1861–1881.* Norwich, Conn., 1884–1886.

Croly, Herbert David, *Marcus Alonzo Hanna, His Life and Works.* New York, 1919.

Gabriel, Ralph Henry, *The Course of American Democratic Thought.* New York, 1940.

Platt, Thomas Collier, *Autobiography.* Edited by L. J. Long. New York, 1910.

Rhodes, James Ford, *The McKinley and Roosevelt Administrations, 1895–1905.* New York, 1922.

Roosevelt, Theodore, *An Autobiography*. New York, 1913.
Schlesinger, Arthur Meier, *New Viewpoints in American History*. New York, 1922.
— and Fox, D. R., eds. *A History of American Life:*
Nevins, Allan, *The Emergence of Modern America, 1865–1878*. New York, 1927, v. 8.
Tarbell, Ida Minerva, *The Nationalizing of Business, 1878–1898*. New York, 1936, v. 9.
Schlesinger, Arthur Meier, *The Rise of the City, 1878–1898*. New York, 1933, v. 10.
Faulkner, Harold Underwood, *The Quest for Social Justice, 1898–1914*. New York, 1931, v. 11.
Slosson, Preston William, *The Great Crusade and After. 1914–1928*. New York, 1930, v. 12.
Sullivan, Mark, *The Turn of the Century* (v. 1 of *Our Times*). New York, 1926.

PART VI

WASHINGTON. 1902–1935

After 1902, when Holmes was on the U. S. Supreme Court, material is readily available in histories, newspapers, and periodicals. Scores of people are alive who knew Justice Holmes in Washington. I am particularly indebted to the late Justice Brandeis, whose estimate of Holmes was more intimate and original than any I found. He emphasized Holmes's remoteness from political life. Far from making his horizon narrower, this, Brandeis said, had somehow given Holmes a broader vision. "Holmes had a quality the rest of us lacked," he said.

I am greatly indebted to Thomas Corcoran, Holmes's secretary in the winter of 1926–1927. Mr. Corcoran has the kind of memory biographers long to meet and seldom do — warm, articulate, with a touch of Irish in it. Holmes's character contained baffling paradoxes: faith and skepticism, gentleness and a hardness that could turn friends away. Corcoran did not resolve these riddles, but he was the first, after Brandeis, to give me a clue.

Brief conversations with Felix Frankfurter were a challenge. There are questions that have no answer, and Justice Frankfurter knows how to ask them. But sometimes the quest itself is worth ten answers. I am grateful to Justice Frankfurter for setting me on that quest.

James Doherty, clerk in the Massachusetts Supreme Court, came to Washington with Holmes on December 5, 1902. He remembers the scene as if it were yesterday — the arrival in the station, the opening of the house on Lafayette Square. Charles Buckley, Holmes's coachman, drove with me to the grave at Arlington. He gave me details of the household routine. Arthur Thomas, the tall old Negro who served so long in the Supreme Court, said to me, "I've served many gentlemen, but never one like him. I was powerful fond of Judge Holmes, and I think he liked me, too." Until Thomas died in 1943, he wrote every Memorial Day a piece about Holmes for the *Washington Star.* He showed me the clippings, saying he was sorry he had not an education, so he could write finer things about the Judge. "I call these my tributes," he said.

The following books and articles by or about Justice Holmes were used: —

Biddle, Francis, *Mr. Justice Holmes.* New York, 1942.

Boorstin, D. J., "The Elusiveness of Justice Holmes." *New England Quarterly,* September 1941.

Derby, Augustin, "Recollections of Mr. Justice Holmes." *New York University Law Quarterly,* March 1929.

Frankfurter, Felix, "The Constitutional Opinions of Justice Holmes," *Harvard Law Review,* April 1916.

—— "Mr. Justice Holmes and the Constitution," *Harvard Law Review,* December 1927.

—— ed. *Mr. Justice Holmes.* New York, 1931.

—— *Mr. Justice Holmes and the Supreme Court.* Cambridge, 1938.

Gabriel, Ralph Henry, "The Philosophy of Mr. Justice Holmes." From *The Course of American Democratic Thought.*

Hamilton, W., "On Dating Mr. Justice Holmes." *University of Chicago Law Review,* December 1941.

Holmes, Oliver Wendell, *Dissenting Opinions of Mr. Justice Holmes.* Edited by Alfred Lief. New York, 1929.

—— *Representative Opinions of Mr. Justice Holmes.* Edited by Alfred Lief. New York, 1931.

—— *Justice Oliver Wendell Holmes, his Book Notices and Uncollected Letters and Papers.* Previously mentioned.

Lerner, Max, "Justice Holmes: Flowering and Defeat." From *Ideas are Weapons.* New York, 1939.

—— ed. *The Mind and Faith of Justice Holmes.* Boston, 1943.

Also used were: —

Adams, Henry, *The Education of Henry Adams, An Autobiography.* Boston, 1918.

Adams, (Mrs.) Marian Hooper, *The Letters of Mrs. Henry Adams*. Edited by Ward Theron. Boston, 1936.

Adams, Samuel Hopkins, *Incredible Era. The Life and Times of Warren Gamaliel Harding*. Boston, 1939.

Bacon, Gaspar Griswold, *The Constitution of the United States*. Cambridge, 1928.

Beard, Charles Austin, *The Supreme Court and the Constitution*. New York, 1912.

— *The Myth of Rugged American Individualism*. (Pamphlet.) New York, 1932.

— and Beard, (Mrs.) Mary Ritter, *The Rise of American Civilization*. New York, 1927–1942. 4 v.

Beard, (Mrs.) Mary Ritter, *The American Labor Movement*. New York, 1920.

Benson, Godfrey Rathbone, 1st Baron Charnwood, *Theodore Roosevelt*. Boston, 1923.

Bishop, Joseph Bucklin, *Theodore Roosevelt and his time, shown in his own letters*. New York, 1920. 2 v.

Bowers, Claude Gernade, *Beveridge and the Progressive Era*. Boston, 1932.

Cardozo, Benjamin Nathan, *Law and Literature*. New York, 1931.

— *The Nature of the Judicial Process*. (William Storrs Lecture Series.) New Haven, 1922.

Coolidge, Calvin, *Autobiography*. New York, 1929.

Dewey, John, *The Influence of Darwin on Philosophy and Other Essays in Contemporary Thought*. New York, 1910.

— *Experience and Nature*. Chicago, 1925.

— *Art as Experience*. New York, 1934.

Ernst, Morris Leopold, *The Ultimate Power*. New York, 1937.

Frankfurter, Felix, *The Public and its Government*. New Haven, 1930.

— ed. *Mr. Justice Brandeis*. New Haven, 1932.

— *Law and Politics; Occasional Papers. 1913–1928*. Edited by Archibald MacLeish and E. F. Pritchard, Jr. New York, 1939.

— and Landis, James McCauley, *The Business of the Supreme Court*. New York, 1927.

Hellman, George Sidney, *Benjamin N. Cardozo, American Judge*. New York, 1940.

Hughes, Charles Evans, *The Supreme Court of the United States*. New York, 1928.

Jackson, Robert Houghwout, *The Struggle for Judicial Supremacy*. New York, 1941.

Laski, Harold Joseph, *The Danger of Being a Gentleman*. London, 1939.

Longworth, Alice Roosevelt, *Crowded Hours. Reminiscences*. New York, 1933.

Maitland, Frederic William, and Montague, Francis Charles. *Sketch of Legal History*. Edited by Charles F. Colby. New York, 1915.

Pearson, Drew, and Allen, Robert Sharon, *The Nine Old Men*. Garden City, 1936.

Pollock, Sir Frederick, *Sovereignty and Legislation*. London, 1890.

Pollock, Sir John, "The Pollock-Holmes Correspondence." *Quarterly Review*, July 1941.

Pound, Roscoe, *An Introduction to the Philosophy of Law*. (William Storrs Lecture Series.) New Haven, 1922.

Pringle, Henry Fowler, *The Life and Times of William Howard Taft*. New York, 1939, 2 v.

Stephen, Sir Leslie, *English Thought in the 18th Century*. New York, 3rd rev. ed., 1920.

Sullivan, Mark, *Our Times*. New York, 1926–1935. 6 v.

Thayer, William Roscoe, *Theodore Roosevelt, An Intimate Biography*. Boston, 1919.

Warren, Charles, *The Supreme Court in United States History*. Boston, 1922. 3 v.

White, William Allen, *Woodrow Wilson, The Man, his Times and his Task*. Boston, 1939.

—— *A Puritan in Babylon, The Story of Calvin Coolidge*. New York, 1938.

Winkelman, Barnie Frank, *John G. Johnson, Lawyer and Art Collector*. Philadelphia, 1922.

Wister, Owen, *Roosevelt, The Story of a Friendship*. New York, 1930.

IV. FURTHER ACKNOWLEDGMENTS

Thanks are due to the Harvard University Press for the use of quotations from the *Holmes-Pollock Letters*, edited by Mark DeWolfe Howe; to Mr. Henry James and Little, Brown and Company for quotations from *The Letters of William James* and to Professor Ralph Barton Perry and Little, Brown and Company for quotations from *The Thought and Character of William James* (both are Atlantic Monthly Press books); to Mr. M. A. DeWolfe Howe and the Oxford University Press for quotations from *Holmes of the Breakfast-Table;* to Houghton Mifflin Company for quotations from the *Life and Letters of Oliver Wendell Holmes*, by John T. Morse, Jr., and from Dr. Holmes's own *Works* in the edition of 1892; to the estate of Mary Thacher Higginson and Houghton Mifflin Company for excerpts from *Letters and Journals of Thomas Wentworth Higginson*.

Acknowledgment is due also to the following publishers for the use of excerpts from the books listed: Central Book Company, *Justice Oliver Wendell Holmes. His Book Notices and Uncollected Letters and Papers*, edited by Harry C. Shriver; Columbia University Press, *The Supreme Court of the United States* by Charles Evans Hughes; Dennis Book Company, *Judicial Opinions of Oliver Wendell Holmes*, edited by Harry C. Shriver; Harcourt, Brace and Company, *Collected Legal Papers of Oliver Wendell Holmes*, edited by Harold J. Laski; Houghton Mifflin Company, *War Letters of John Chipman Gray and John Codman Ropes*, and *The Early Years of the Saturday Club*, by Edward Waldo Emerson; Little, Brown and Company, *The Common Law*, by Oliver Wendell Holmes, Jr., and also his *Speeches*, and *The Epic of America*, by James Truslow Adams (an Atlantic Monthly Press Book); Charles Scribner's Sons, *Selections from the Correspondence of Theodore Roosevelt and Henry Cabot Lodge* and *Early Memories*, by Henry Cabot Lodge; The Vanguard Press, *The Dissenting Opinions of Mr. Justice Holmes* and *The Representative Opinions of Mr. Justice Holmes*, arranged by Alfred Lief; Yale University Press, *Mr. Justice Brandeis*, edited by Felix Frankfurter.

I wish here to thank also the many people who sent me their letters from Justice Holmes: Thomas Barbour, Robert S. Barlow, Sallie Fairchild, Rosika Schwimmer, T. Wayland Vaughan, George Wharton Pepper, Henry S. Drinker, and others. Grateful acknowledgment is due for civilities shown me at the Boston Athenaeum, the Biddle Law Library in Philadelphia, the Haverford College Library, the Congressional Library, the Boston Medical Library, the Arlington Street Armory, the Harvard College Library — and all the other record rooms and archives whose custodians showed me courtesy. Thanks are also due to the following for the use of pictures: Professor Frederic T. Lewis of the Harvard Medical School for the photograph of Dr. Holmes; Houghton Mifflin Company for the etching of the Gambrel-roofed House in Cambridge; Mrs. Edward Jackson Holmes and Mr. M. A. DeWolfe Howe for the photograph of the Holmes children; Mrs. Lloyd T. Brown for the photograph of Fanny Dixwell; Harvard University for the photograph of Oliver

Wendell Holmes, Jr., at the time of his graduation from college, which was reproduced from a photograph that appeared in the *Harvard Class Book* of 1861; the Boston Athenaeum for the photograph of Oliver Wendell Holmes, Jr., in Civil War uniform; Dr. and Mrs. Thomas Barbour for the photograph of Justice Holmes about 1890; and Miss Sally Tate for her etching of Justice Holmes.

APPENDICES

APPENDICES

Secretaries to Justice Holmes

* Charles K. Poe	1905–1906
Augustin Derby	1906–1907
Howard Stockton	1907–1908
Erland F. Fish	1908–1909
Leland B. Duer	1909–1910
Irving S. Olds	1910–1911
Francis Biddle	1911–1912
Stanley Clarke	1912–1913
George L. Harrison	1913–1914
Harvey H. Bundy	1914–1915
Chauncey Belknap	1915–1916
Shelton Hale	1916–1917
Vaughn Miller	1917–1918
Lloyd H. Landau	1918–1919
Stanley Morrison	1919–1920
Day Kimball	1920–1921
Lawrence Curtis	1921–1922
Robert M. Benjamin	1922–1923
James M. Nicely	1923–1924
W. Barton Leach	1924–1925
Charles Denby	1925–1926
Thomas G. Corcoran	1926–1927
Wm. Anderson Sutherland . . .	1927–1928
John E. Lockwood	1928–1929
Alger Hiss	1929–1930
Robert W. Wales	1930–1931
H. Chapman Rose	1931–1932
Donald Hiss	1932–1933
Mark DeW. Howe	1933–1934
James H. Rowe	1934–1935

* Graduate of George Washington College and Law School in Washington, D. C. All others are graduates of Harvard Law School.

Comparison, Number of Holmes's Dissents with Those of Other Justices

Oct. Term	Total Cases	Dissents of Others	Holmes's Dissents With Opinion	Without Opinion	Total
1902	144	70	0	1	1
1903	211	97	1	3	4
1904	197	91	3	1	4
1905	172	92	1	4	5
1906	207	71	2	1	3
1907	176	49	3	2	5
1908	184	45	3	1	4
1909	178	45	4	6	10
1910	170	29	2	4	6
1911	236	25	3	0	3
1912	291	42	1	5	6
1913	293	42	0	4	4
1914	273	63	2	2	4
1915	244	39	0	2	2
1916	214	97	2	7	9
1917	217	61	3	3	6
1918	233	62	0	4	4
1919	180	108	5	8	13
1920	222	76	2	4	6
1921	176	75	5	3	8
1922	221	24	4	2	6
1923	213	37	0	4	4
1924	233	39	1	0	1
1925	212	28	3	0	3
1926	199	59	3	6	9
1927	175	55	10	6	16
1928	129	38	2	5	7
1929	136	21	4	6	10
1930	168	43	0	5	5
1931	46	10	1	4	5

Total decisions — 5950
Dissents by other Justices — 1633
* Dissents by Holmes — 173

* Prepared by Marie Macri under the direction of Professor Augustin Derby.

The reason there were fewer decisions in the 1902 and 1931 terms was that Holmes began and ended in the midst of a term.

Add to Holmes's dissents two opinions labeled by the reporter "Doubting opinions," making his total 175. Total cases in which he sat in which opinions were given, 5950. This does not include *Per curiam* cases in which all members of the Court agreed and the opinion was written under the name of no Justice; it does not include applications to the Court as for writ of certiorari where no opinion is rendered usually and when rendered is *Per curiam*.

In these 5950 cases, dissents by Justices other than Holmes were 1633, by Holmes 173. Dividing the total dissents, 1806, by the number of Justices, it appears that proportionally Holmes dissented less than the others.

INDEX